THE JAPANESE IN LATIN AMERICA

T0385763

THE ASIAN AMERICAN EXPERIENCE

Series Editor
Roger Daniels, University of Cincinnati

*A list of books in the series
appears at the end of this book.*

THE JAPANESE IN LATIN AMERICA

DANIEL M. MASTERSON
WITH SAYAKA FUNADA-CLASSEN

University of Illinois Press
Urbana, Chicago, and Springfield

Library of Congress Cataloging-in-Publication Data
Masterson, Daniel M.
The Japanese in Latin America / Daniel M. Masterson
with Sayaka Funada-Classen.
p.   cm. — (The Asian American experience)
Includes bibliographical references and index.
ISBN 978-0-252-02869-4 (cloth : alk. paper)
ISBN 978-0-252-07144-7 (paper : alk. paper)
1. Japanese—Latin America—History. 2. Immigrants—Latin
America—History. 3. Latin America—History—20th century.
I. Funada-Classen, Sayaka. II. Title. III. Series.
F1419.J3.M38   2004
980'.04956—dc21   2003002147

CONTENTS

FOREWORD

Roger Daniels

When I conceived this series more than a decade ago, it was my hope that it would attract scholarship from a number of disciplines and eventually include works that would give it a truly hemispheric scope. Previous books in this series concerned Canada, and now, in a work of broad temporal and geographic sweep, Daniel Masterson examines and analyzes the Japanese presence in Latin America, the broadest diaspora of a people of Asian origin in the hemisphere. While members of the many other Asian ethnic groups in the New World are more numerous in the United States than in all the other nations of the hemisphere combined, there are more persons of Japanese ethnic origin in just one South American nation, Brazil, than in all fifty United States, about 1.5 million as opposed to 900,000. And while the United States has had senators, representatives, governors, and one federal cabinet member of Japanese ethnicity, only Peru in the hemisphere has had such a person as head of state, albeit unhappily in the final analysis.

The major historical literature in English about the Japanese of Latin America is thin and quite uneven. The earliest books were produced during World War II and show it. Substantial modern historical scholarship begins with two postwar scholars: James Tigner, who was the first to write about Japanese, largely Okinawans, throughout Latin America, and the late C. Harvey Gardiner, who published important monographs on Peru in 1973 and 1981. There have been a number of lesser books, a clutch of articles, and a recent encyclopedic anthology.

Masterson, who teaches Latin American history at the United States Naval Academy, and his Japan-based associate, Sayaka Funada-Classen, have made extensive use of archival research, fieldwork in many nations, and the literature in several Western languages and Japanese. While most of their emphasis is on Brazil and Peru, which have the longest history of a significant

Japanese presence as well as the largest populations, the accounts of the smaller groups of Nikkei—Japanese people—in many other countries will be equally valuable. Above all, it is the variety of the Japanese Latin American experience that this work uncovers that makes it fascinating reading for those interested in comparative ethnicity.

The result is an impressive synthesis, which, one expects, will not only last for a long time but will also inspire further monographic studies that will, in time, modify it. But for this generation of scholars and perhaps the next, *The Japanese in Latin America* will be the one essential book on its subject.

PREFACE

The original idea for this work was more modest than the present volume before you. Initially, I intended to examine the diplomatic and domestic policies of the Latin American governments toward Japan just prior to and during World War II. As I began research on the Latin American governments' policies toward their Japanese residents, I became increasingly convinced of the need for a broader study that could offer a comparative view of the region's Japanese communities and their cultural evolution from the early years of settlement around the beginning of the twentieth century. Relying heavily on the pioneering work of C. Harvey Gardiner, James L. Tigner, Amelia Morimoto, Iyo Kunimoto, and Takashi Maeyama, I greatly expanded the scope of my research with the intention of completing a study that would examine all but the smallest Japanese communities from their formative years to the end of the twentieth century. As a Latin American specialist with no formal training in Japanese history, I felt I was venturing onto uncertain ground. Even after reading as widely as possible in pertinent studies in Japanese history, it was clear to me that research in Japanese language materials and archives was necessary for the study to be as complete as possible. In order to fill this need, I asked Sayaka Funada-Classen to join this venture, and she has been a vital contributor to the project ever since.

With Funada-Classen's valuable assistance, I conducted field research in Argentina, Brazil, Chile, Mexico, Paraguay, and Peru, as well as in archives and repositories in the United States and Japan. Primary emphasis was placed on consulting records in national archives, such as the Archivo General de la Nación in Mexico City, as well as in Japanese cultural and immigration centers, such as the Imin Shiryokan (Immigration Archive) in Tokyo, the Centro de Estudos Nipo-Brasileiro (Center of Japanese Brazilian Studies) in São Paulo, and the Centro Cultural Peruano-Japonés (Peruvian Japanese

Cultural Center) in Lima. Documents from national and private archives in Argentina, Chile, Mexico, and Paraguay are also a key component of this study. Interviews were conducted in the United States, Latin America, and Japan. Augmenting these personal interviews were recorded and transcribed conversations with former Japanese Latin American internees during World War II, made available by the San Francisco–based Japanese Peruvian Oral History Project and the Seabrook Educational and Cultural Center in New Jersey. My speaking tour in Japan in October 1998 was quite valuable in clarifying my views on the status of the Japanese Latin Americans who had returned to Japan in search of better economic opportunities.

Although this book is the only study in English that treats the Japanese in Latin America as a whole throughout the last century, it is not intended to be an exhaustive study. There are areas of the Japanese experience that warrant more complete analysis. Among these are the dynamics of the internal leadership of Japanese immigrant organizations, which were so fundamentally important in retaining cultural solidarity within the Japanese immigrant community. Also in need of further scholarship is the relationship of the Japanese community to the existing political leadership in Latin America. It is often assumed that the Japanese and their leaders sought to stay out of politics and refrained from close contact with local and national political leaders. While this was clearly the case in Peru until the Fujimori phenomenon, it was not characteristic of the leaders of the Japanese community in Mexico before World War II or in Argentina during the Perón administration. Yet another path of further inquiry is the process of what Jeffrey Lesser has called negotiating national identities.[1] For second- through fifth-generation Japanese in Latin America, ethnic and cultural identities have been in flux as the gradual loss of Japanese language skills and the acquisition of the dominant cultural traits of their Latin American homeland became significant. The question remains, however, to what degree did cultural adaptation occur among the later generations of Nikkei in Latin America? Very much related to this issue is how the Japanese in Latin America perceived themselves as the twentieth century unfolded. Without question, World War II was a critical turning point in determining cultural identity, association with traditions of the homeland, and the imagined future of the Nikkei in Latin America. This study addresses these questions, but much more research needs to be done to clarify these complex issues. The main avenue of inquiry for the study of cultural adaptation in this book was an analysis of the comprehensive census data for the Nikkei populations of Peru and Brazil. Further work needs to be done, especially in regard to the Latin American nations with smaller Japanese populations. What also must be taken into account is the impact of the mass migrations of Japanese Latin Americans to Japan beginning in 1988.

A book such as this one requires the early clarification of a number of important terms. For this purpose, the reader is referred to the glossary. Still, something more needs to be said about the terminology used in this study. There is no clear agreement on the exact definition of the term *Nikkei*. In a general sense, it refers to the Japanese overseas. The Japanese government legally recognizes that people are of "Japanese heritage" if their lineage can be traced back three generations. At the Eleventh Panamerican Nikkei Conference held in New York City in July 2001, a group of scholars arrived at a working definition of *Nikkei* that defined it as an individual "who was has one or more ancestors from Japan and/or anyone who self-defines as a Nikkei." These scholars also concluded that there were a number of elements common to the Nikkei experience in the Americas, including "the Japanese language and values, emotional orientations and a corporate view stressing cooperation, mutual aid, and the needs of the large group as a whole."[2] This study adopts a stricter definition of *Nikkei*. It assumes that the vast majority of the Issei, the first generation who immigrated to Latin America before World War II, did not intend to stay. Respecting this dominant viewpoint, this study will refer to these immigrants before World War II as Japanese (to include Okinawans). When the trauma of World War II made the return of the Issei generation with their children to Japan almost universally impossible, they and their children became, however reluctantly for the Issei, the true Nikkei. They will be referred to as such in the discussion of the post–World War II era. A further refinement of this terminology is the term *Nikkei-jin,* which will be used to refer to the second, third, and fourth generations (Nisei, Sansei, and Yonsei, respectively) when these generations are the dominant element in the discussion.

The Japanese were late arrivals in Latin America, arriving mainly after the waves of immigrants from Southern Europe and the Middle East. Like their European counterparts, the Japanese were both victims and benefactors of the modernization process promoted by the rise of world capitalism. The reforms of the Meiji era (1868–1912) in Japan, along with an increasing tax burden, made it progressively more difficult for young Japanese to stay on the land. Migration to the Americas seemed to offer temporary relief from their economic troubles, especially in view of the many opportunities originally available in Hawaii, Canada, and the United States. When the Japanese were barred from these immigrant venues during the first decade of the twentieth century, they turned to the emerging nations of Latin America, more out of necessity than of choice, in an effort to better their lives and those of their families in Japan. In 1899 they first settled in Peru, where harsh conditions in the sugarcane fields drove many immigrants to the cities. There they quickly established themselves as small-scale but successful urban merchants. This pattern of flight from the countryside to more stable economic opportunities in the cities would be repeated elsewhere in Latin America, most notably in Mexico. Beginning in 1908, immigration to Brazil would involve the most concentrated efforts at colonization of the Japanese in Latin America. Brazil's willingness to accept Japanese immigrants as coffee workers and *colonos* (colonists), and the availability of large tracts of land, soon made that nation the largest receiver of Japanese immigrants in the Western Hemisphere.

All the while the Japanese were migrating and settling in Latin America, the Issei (first-generation immigrants) held firmly to the notion that the experience was temporary and that someday they would return to Japan. This concept of Dekasegi, or temporary immigration, is one of the major themes of this study. It is not unique to the Japanese immigrants, of course, as many European immigrants to North and South America returned to their homelands after immigrating to the Americas. What is different about the Japanese is that very few first-generation immigrants were able to return to their homeland. Return rates for Japanese immigrants throughout Latin America generally averaged less than 10 percent.

While few Japanese immigrants abandoned their dream of returning to Japan before the trauma of World War II, they made determined efforts to maintain their cultural traditions in the often alien setting of their adopted Latin American homelands. From the firm foundation of a solid work ethic and an intense solidarity with their fellow immigrants, the Issei pioneers, mostly male in every country except Brazil, created the Japanese family in Latin America, as their North American counterparts had done, by means of the Yobiyose, or "called immigrant" system, which brought young Japanese "picture brides" from Japan to marry the Issei settlers. Once families were established, the Japanese, in the words of one prominent Japanese Peruvian, set out to create "organically constituted immigrant communal groups" or "nations within nations."[3] This perception of the need to remain apart from the adopted societies in which they had settled led the Japanese to establish a complex array of fraternal associations, language schools, and other organizations that bound them closely together. Their attempt to create tightly knit communities in Latin America, even while they retained the faint hope of reestablishing their lives in Japan, is another key element of this study. The tension these two conflicting aims created among the Issei in Latin America was at times nearly unbearable. Those Issei who could afford to made every effort to have their children educated in Japan. Others who could not sent their children to Japanese language schools, in an effort to have them retain the basic components of their cultural heritage. The efforts of the Issei in this regard were generally quite successful. Indeed, within the remote Japanese *colonias* in the interior of Brazil, the Japanese immigrants were building "nations within nations." In these communities, only Japanese was spoken, and awareness of mainstream Brazilian culture was very limited.

Inevitably, Japanese communities, set apart from mainstream societies in Latin America, encountered distrust and hostility. This study examines closely the anti-Japanese sentiment present from the very beginning of the immigrants' presence in Latin America. The Depression of the 1930s and the perceived affluence of the Japanese in Latin America, coupled with Japan's rise to world power status, sharpened already prevailing anti-Japanese sentiment. The U.S. government exploited this sentiment to accomplish its diplomatic and military objectives. The culmination of anti-Japanese feeling was the forced deportation of more than two thousand Issei and Nisei (second-generation immigrants) from Latin America to the United States during World War II. This unfortunate episode is now becoming the focus of an increasing body of scholarship, motivated in some measure by the ongoing attempt of the deportees and their descendants to gain redress from the U.S. government.

The future of the Japanese presence in Latin America is uncertain. The uneven economies of Brazil, Peru, Paraguay, and other Latin American nations have prompted a substantial exodus of third-, fourth-, and fifth-generation Japanese Latin Americans to Japan. This process of return migration has now been ongoing for more than a decade, and it appears that the relocation of a substantial number of Japanese Latin Americans to the home of their ancestors may well be permanent. Bereft of many of the best of their young people, the Japanese communities in Latin America are clearly facing a crisis. This problem is beginning to be researched, but it will require far more extensive scholarship. To date, most of the concern has been paid to the situation of the immigrants in Japan. Such scholarly attention is indeed necessary. What also must be examined, however, are the conditions in the Japanese communities of Latin America that are being progressively depopulated as they lose so much of the vitality of their youth and future leadership.

ACKNOWLEDGMENTS

Many individuals aided me in a number of ways in the completion of this book. Sayaka Funada-Classen, as previously mentioned, joined the project early on. She completed very important research in Japanese sources, did fieldwork in Brazil, and contributed to the discussions on the Japanese of that country. She also offered critical interpretations of Japanese cultural traditions that helped frame key elements of this study. John F. Bratzel was involved in the very early phase of this project and made valuable research contributions, particularly on the discussion of the Japanese in Argentina. Roger Daniels became interested in this project a number of years ago, offering important research assistance in the intervening years. I owe a great deal to him for his help. Before his passing, C. Harvey Gardiner, one of the pioneers on the topic of Japanese immigration to Latin America, kindly read early versions of the manuscript and offered a valuable overview of the subject. Sam Baily and Thomas Holloway, both noted historians of Latin American immigration, have offered suggestions for improving the project. Thomas Leonard, who has studied the Germans in Central America, made some valuable suggestions for research leads at the Franklin Roosevelt Presidential Library in the mid-1990s, and we have been sharing information on immigration and the question of enemy aliens ever since. David Block, the Latin American bibliographer at Cornell University Libraries, contributed significantly to the success of my research at Cornell. Leon Walters, fellow track coach and an authority on modern Okinawa, helped me a great deal by granting me access to his library on Okinawan history and culture. The Marshals—Phil, Dot, and Ralph—helped Sayaka and me in many ways.

Amelia Morimoto, a leading authority on the Japanese Peruvians, helped greatly by granting me access to the key records, particularly the Japanese community's two self-censuses of 1966 and 1989, which enabled me to gain insights into many aspects of the social evolution of the Japanese in Peru. The late Mary Fukumoto, who wrote the most complete history of the Japanese Peruvians to date, gave me important suggestions during an interview in the early days of my research. The personnel of the Jinnai Center, the Japanese cultural center in Lima, were always gracious and helpful during my research visits. My longtime friend and colleague, Jorge Ortíz Sotelo, helped me in numerous ways, as he has in the past. In particular, he introduced me to the late Felix Denegri, who graciously allowed me to use his extensive private library for background research into immigration issues in Peru. I am grateful to the staff of Temple University in Tokyo, and Professor Sachiko Takita at Yokohama City University, for allowing me to share my views on Japanese immigration and the impact of recent migration of Japanese Latin Americans to Japan. Also very helpful during my visit was Professor Miyuki Enari of Mie Prefectural University, who arranged a lively and rewarding discussion with the faculty and students of her institution that helped clarify key issues regarding the Japanese from Latin America now residing in Japan. I am also grateful to Professor Masako Iino for arranging for my participation in a seminar at Imin Kenkyu-kai (Association for Immigration Studies) at Sofia University in Tokyo. Professor Nabuku Adachi also clarified key issues for this study.

The saga of the Japanese Peruvians interned in the United States is an ongoing story as the redress movement continues to seek a measure of justice. A central figure in that movement who has been enormously helpful for my research on the Japanese Peruvians is Grace Shimizu, head of the Japanese Peruvian Oral History Project based in San Francisco. Teresa Masatani and the staff of the Seabrook Educational and Cultural Center in New Jersey have also contributed important information to this work. The records and recorded interviews available at the Seabrook Center are very valuable for any serious student of the Japanese Peruvians in the United States. Susan Ogawa helped organize interviews with Japanese Peruvians residing in Chicago that were quite valuable in helping me form early impressions of the experiences of these former internees.

Colleagues in the Naval Academy's history department whose contributions were particularly helpful are Maochun Yu, who read much of the manuscript and offered key suggestion on Japanese historiography, and David Appleby, who was a consistent sounding board for my ideas and read the majority of the early drafts for clarity of expression. A formal Naval Academy faculty member, Kenneth J. Hagan, made early efforts to secure a publisher for this book. The staff of the Nimitz Library, especially Flo Todd of interlibrary loan and Barbara Manvel, were unfailingly supportive of my many requests for books and articles. Connie Grigor, the history department secretary, was helpful to me in more ways that I can say, always ready to give assistance with typing, duplication, or other forms of support. Thanks also go to Cathy Higgins for technical help. The filmmakers Casey Peek and Irum Sheik were very helpful in acquiring photographs. Cindy Eckard brought her considerable editing skills to one important component of this book. For listening on many occasions to my ruminations about this book and for offering encouragement when my enthusiasm for the project would wane, I thank my friend Colleen Bentz.

The staffs of a number of libraries and archives not previously mentioned were instrumental in furthering this project: The United States National Archives in Washington, D.C.; the Archives of the Army War College in Carlisle, Pennsylvania; the Library of Congress; the Archivo General de la Nación and the Archivo de las Relaciones Exteriores in Mexico City; the Archivo General de la Nación in Santiago, Chile; the Archivo General de la Nación in Buenos Aires, Argentina; and the Domingo Rivarola private archive in Asunción, Paraguay. Assisting Sayaka Funada-Classen in Brazil were the staffs of the Centro de Estudos Nipo-Brasileiro and the Museo Histórico Municipia in Bastos. Funada-Classen's research in Japan was aided by the personnel of the Kokkai Toshokan (Congress Library) in Tokyo, Japan International Cooperation Agency (JICA) in Tokyo, and the Foreign Studies Library of Kobe City University.

I am grateful to the following agencies for their financial assistance during the course of this project: the Naval Academy Research Council, for a number of summer and travel grants; the Franklin and Eleanor Roosevelt Foundation, for funding research at the FDR library; and Cornell University, for providing two summer research grants to work at the university's libraries.

This marathon project took more than a decade to complete and involved research in eight different countries on three continents. As a result, I was often gone when it would have been better to stay at home. For their patience and support, I thank my family. To Erin, who helped with manuscript formatting, thanks for a job well done! To Katie, who understood the best, thanks again. To Andy, I hope we will make it to the Savanna cliffs before the next book. And to my wife, Debby, I owe a great deal for always being there.

THE JAPANESE IN LATIN AMERICA

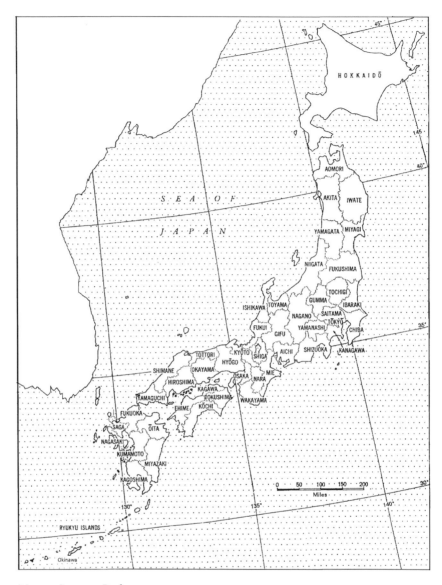

Map 1. Japanese Prefectures

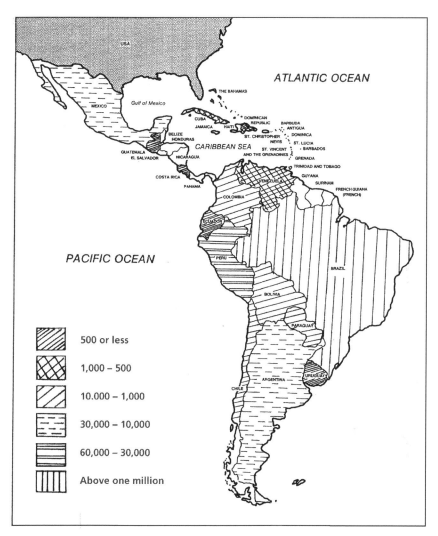

Map 2. Estimated Populations of People of Japanese Ancestry in Latin America by Country, 1998. Data from Gaimusho Ryoji Iiju-bu, *Waga kokumin no kaigai hatten: Iiju hyakunen no ayumi* (Tokyo: Ministry of Foreign Affairs, 1971), 137–47, and *The Encyclopedia of Japanese Descendents in the Americas: An Illustrated History of the Nikkei*, ed. Akemi Kikumura-Yano (Walnut Creek, Calif.: Altimira Press, 2002), 29. These estimates do not take into account still uncertain numbers of younger Japanese from Latin America who have migrated to Japan since 1990.

BEFORE LATIN AMERICA: THE EARLY JAPANESE IMMIGRANT EXPERIENCE IN HAWAII, CANADA, AND THE UNITED STATES

The Japanese Emigrants are not to be driven, but led with the silken thread of kindness.
—Hawaiian Immigration Commission, 1885

As the twenty-first century began, Mario Makudo, a Japanese Brazilian living in the Japanese city of Oizumimachi, was successfully beginning a new life in his forebears' homeland as the marketing director for a Portuguese language newspaper. Still, Makudo did not feel welcome. Upon his arrival, Japanese fellow workers told him "to go back to Brazil."[1] Makudo, like the first Japanese immigrants in Brazil and other Latin American nations, became a part of, but apart from, the society of his adopted homeland. Mirroring the patterns of the Japanese in Latin America during the first decades of the twentieth century, Japanese immigrants from Brazil and Peru in recent decades have formed their own networks in Japan as a means of retaining their familiar cultural traits. Their ethnicity could not shield them from the suspicion and resentment of native Japanese, who regard their speech and mannerisms as "foreign" despite their common ancestry.

Thus, little more than a century after the first Japanese arrived in Latin America, many of their third-, fourth-, and fifth-generation descendants are leaving the Japanese communities their forebears worked so hard to establish for the same reasons their ancestors left Japan. The Japanese in Latin America overcame many obstacles to build new lives in societies far different from their own, but again, the immigrants often felt apart from their new homes. Perhaps that is why later generations of Japanese Latin Americans sought new opportunities in Japan when new immigration laws opened the doors for them in the late 1980s.

From its beginnings, the Japanese experience in Latin America was influenced greatly by the earlier immigrant experience in Hawaii and North America. It was only after immigration to the United States and Canada was severely limited that the Japanese turned to the Latin American nations in significant numbers to seek opportunities to better their futures. The Japanese were the last of the large immigrant groups to arrive in Latin America, following in the aftermath of the immigrant waves from Southern Europe and the Middle East. This proved advantageous in many respects because the larger Latin American nations such as Argentina, Brazil, Peru, and Mexico were beginning to modernize. Diverse economic opportunities were thus available to the Japanese immigrants as the twentieth century unfolded. On the other hand, these nations were becoming increasingly nationalistic, and the presence of new immigrants with decidedly different customs and appearances frequently led to profound discrimination and hostility.

Despite rapid modernization during the Meiji era, the early immigrants retained most of their traditional Japanese values and an emotional attachment to their homeland. The vast majority saw themselves as temporary visitors who would return to Japan after a relatively brief but economically productive residency in Latin America. These attitudes were not peculiar to the first-generation Japanese immigrants to the Americas. In their studies of transatlantic migration to the United States, Canada, Argentina, and Brazil, both Walter Nugent and John Bodnar note that these four main "receiver" nations experienced high return rates of immigrants to their native homelands.[2] Indeed, Nugent suggests that European immigration to the Americas was, in reality, an extension of the historic pattern of internal European labor migration. He notes that "land seeking migration," implying permanent resettlement, may well have been exceptional in the long history of transatlantic movements, even though it occurred in all four New World receiving societies.[3] Bodnar emphasizes the role of emerging capitalism in Europe and the United States as a key component of immigration during the four decades before World War I.

Nugent's and Bodnar's work reveal some important patterns of European immigration to the United States that are useful points of reference for understanding Japanese immigration to the Americas. Capitalism and particularly the emergence of external market forces first drove European artisans, craftsmen, and small independent farmers to immigrate before their economic status declined severely. Subsequently, people of lesser means but with sufficient financial ability to immigrate followed. The latter immigrants, more often individuals rather than entire families, were more likely to return to their native lands. Bodnar, like many contemporary historians of immigration, rejects the traditional "flight from poverty" thesis, arguing that immigrants were highly pragmatic individuals primarily concerned with "insuring familial and household survival."[4]

Clearly, European immigrants were adjusting to the demands of world capitalism once it became a compelling force in their lives after 1800. Migration to the Americas, whether it was permanent or temporary, was often a carefully chosen option in confronting economic modernization. That fewer numbers of Europeans immigrated during periods of economic stagnation in the United States and Latin America confirms their pragmatism. Significant return rates also affirm strong attachments to the social relationships and traditions of their rapidly changing homelands. What, then, can be said about the motivations and aspirations of the Japanese as they followed their European predecessors in search of new options in the Americas?

The foundation of Japanese society before the Meiji era was the agricultural village. Densely populated and compact, with a strong corporate character, Japanese villages gained substantial autonomy after the Samurai (warrior) class was removed to castle towns during the early years of the Tokugawa era (1600–1867). Only as urban centers grew did the traditional societal bonds of hierarchy, loyalty, and obligation begin to undergo change. This change, according to Thomas C. Smith, occurred within relatively narrow limits, leaving small farm units, family organization of production, and heavy reliance on hand labor largely intact.[5]

The key to the gradual transformation of village life in the countryside was the growth of commercial farming and agricultural wage labor, which increased significantly during the Tokugawa Shogunate. Thus, although traditional in nearly all other respects, much of the Japanese peasantry was "unwittingly" preparing for factory employment for two centuries before the Meiji era by adapting to monetary incentives in the countryside. As Smith argues, "Working for wages taught [the peasant] that it was possible . . . to make his way alone."[6] Significantly, many of the architects of the Meiji modernization after 1868 were products of the Japanese countryside. Ambitious and resourceful but confronted with limited opportunities in the village, these individuals were not content with strictly conforming to the old ways. This adaptability in the context of an otherwise formalized societal structure aided Japan's first immigrants as they made the difficult adjustments to a new life in the Americas.

During the early years of the Meiji era, the alliance of lower Samurai and merchants that forged the regime's remarkable reforms soon realized that the modernizing nation must retain the primary values of premodern Japan in order to maintain social stability. Recent scholarship seems to indicate that pre-Meiji Japanese values allowed for more change and individual initiative than was previously believed. As Eiko Ikegami convincingly argues in her recent study, those pre-Meiji values included an evolving concept of honor among the Samurai class that became "an idiom . . . for self expression, a source of inspiration, or a legitimization of a choice or decision."[7] Ikegami rejects the image of a historical Japanese culture that prized "harmony and consensus above all other values."[8] Her interpretation suggests that the courage and initiative of the early Meiji leaders was grounded in values shaped during the Tokugawa era.

Since the early immigrants found limited opportunities to acquire large and contiguous plots of land in the Americas, they did not replicate the social structure of the traditional Japanese village except in some early *colonias* of southern Brazil. What was retained from the social climate of village life was an appreciation for the benefits of hierarchy and what Chie Nakane refers to as the "one set" principle of organization. Broadly interpreted, this principle means that "'every group in Japan tends to include an almost identical variety of selection of elements so that it does not require the services of other groups.'"[9] This meant that every agricultural village was self-supporting, with little need for outside specialists or assistance from other villages other than occasional agricultural wage labor. Japanese society for hundreds of years before the Meiji era was thus developing in such a way as to encourage group self-sufficiency for the assurance of survival. This trait would be of enormous significance to the immigrants as they created new lives in the often hostile societies of the Americas.

Because Japanese society stressed group autonomy and discouraged horizontal cooperation among similar societal entities, a fully integrated society was not possible. This allowed for the evolution of a central political administration that assumed authority in a vertical fashion down through the "competing clusters" of autonomous groups that would not cooperate to challenge the state administration.[10] This social reality allowed for the development of the feudal order of the Tokugawa Shogunate and, ironically, the reforms of the Meiji era. How these values influenced the attitudes of Japanese immigrants is effectively examined by Christopher Reichl in his work on Japanese immigrants in Brazil. Noting that the basic social unit of rural Japan is the Ie (household), which is marked by "an unbroken set of vertical kinship ties to ancestors and descendants," Reichl suggests that immigration clearly altered but did not completely disrupt this social unit. Immigrant sons at least retained the form of their social obligation by sending cash remittances back to their households, once they established themselves overseas.[11]

The Japanese peasantry, while experiencing far greater personal freedom as a result of the destruction of the feudal order, nevertheless struggled with significantly greater economic and social burdens imposed by the Meiji government. In reality, the peasantry was paying for the cost of modernizing Japan by a newly configured land tax. By 1872, Japanese peasants were given the freedom to own their land, raise any crop they desired, and buy and sell land. But landownership did not necessarily mean security. Approximately 40 percent of farm families in the 1870s owned less than 1.1 acre of land.[12] Moreover, a large portion of peasant farmers were tenants, not landowners. Higher land taxes were passed on by landlords, who required nearly half of a peasant's yearly crop in rent payments. Indeed, in the mid-1880s, 10 percent of all independent farmers lost their lands because they could not pay their increased taxes. In 1895 alone, 108,000 farms went into bankruptcy and 400,000 peasants lost their means of making a living.[13]

The efforts to modernize Japan based upon Western ideas added yet another obligation to the Japanese peasants' growing list of responsibilities during the Meiji era: the compulsory education of their children. Private educators such as Yukichi Fukuzawa argued, "We must take advantage of the moment to bring in more of Western civilization and revolutionize our people's ideas from the roots."[14] Toward this end, the Meiji leaders, seeking to eliminate illiteracy to hasten the adoption of Western thought, passed the Education Ordinance of 1872. Stating that there shall be "No community with an illiterate family, nor a family with an illiterate person," this ordinance established a national school system based upon French and American models. A significant portion of the cost of educating the nation's children for the compulsory minimum of four years fell upon the tax-paying peasant class. Unquestionably, the economic and social policies of the Meiji governments before 1890 led to the ruin of thousands of peasant families. Shojiro Goto, a wealthy Meiji businessman writing in 1888, decried the condition of his country's rural population. "'Our people [the peasantry] are unable to support the burden of taxation. They have been falling into an even deeper poverty and they have now reached the point where they cannot maintain life.'"[15] Japanese peasants responded to their increasing hardships during the early Meiji era in three primary ways: violent resistance, the "Popular Rights Movement," and temporary immigration.

As noted, internal migration served as a partial "safety valve" for the Japanese rural masses as the Japanese countryside began modernizing after 1750. The massive rural dislocations of the early Meiji era, however, soon forced the beginnings of the Japanese overseas diaspora that would continue, with the interruption of World War II, for nearly an entire century. Fewer than a thousand Japanese ventured overseas in the period 1868 to 1880, with most signing on as sugar workers in the cane fields of Hawaii. During the course of the next two decades, Japanese immigration substantially increased and was almost exclusively directed toward Hawaii, the United States, and Canada, until it was restricted by the Gentlemen's Agreement, a series of accords between Japan and the United States in 1907–8. More than 137,000 Japanese journeyed to North America before 1900, while only slightly more than 1,300 began a trend of limited immigration to Southeast Asia.

In Hawaii the collapse of the whaling industry and the emergence of sugarcane production after 1850 created a sharp demand for contract labor to harvest the newly planted cane fields.[16] Reduced by disease from an estimated 1 million before the arrival of Westerners to only 85,000 in 1850, Hawaii's indigenous population could not meet the increasing demand for sugar workers.[17] The passage of the Masters and Servants Act of 1850 permitted the Hawaiian growers to hire contract laborers wherever they could be found to meet their universal demand for cheap, reliable, and obedient workers.[18] Mirroring the labor circumstances of Latin American plantation owners in the nineteenth century, the growers in Hawaii first turned to Chinese, Filipino, and European labor before looking to Japan for most of their sugarcane cutters. As in many other areas of the world before 1880, Chinese contract labor in Hawaii supplied much of the semiservile labor the sugar growers wanted so badly. By 1884 the Chinese population in the Hawaiian Islands stood at nearly 18,000. Many growers by the early 1880s regarded the Chinese male laborers as "troublesome elements in a multiracial society" and looked upon the Japanese as a "counterweight" to the earlier Asian immigrants. The Japanese would work for lower wages and tended to have a more disciplined lifestyle than the earlier immigrants because they came as entire families instead of unmarried males.[19]

Japanese immigrants striving to achieve the Meiji value of *risshin shusse* (making one's way in the world) found their greatest opportunities in the United States before 1908. As was true in Brazil from the 1920s onward, available land and abundant opportunities in agriculture and urban commerce awaited those Issei—the first-generation immigrants—who were able to make the successful transition from their initial immigrant lives as poor students, railroad workers, agricultural laborers, and fishermen. Attractive opportunities in the United States materialized because of the booming economies of the western states and the limitation of Chinese immigration after the Chinese Exclusion Act of 1882. As they did in Hawaii, Canada, and Latin

America, Chinese male laborers preceded the first Japanese immigrants by more than three decades. Their population aging and still finding themselves largely outside the mainstream of American life, the Chinese nevertheless endured. Significantly, the pattern of denial of citizenship and exclusion applied initially to the Chinese after 1882 would establish the precedent for similar treatment of the Japanese during the ensuing four decades.

Despite the dominant sojourner attitude among Japanese immigrants and an increasingly virulent anti-Japanese movement, the roots of the Japanese immigrant family were set down in the United States before 1908. Discouraged but not defeated by exclusionist immigration and land ownership laws thereafter, the Issei looked to their children for the fulfillment of dreams that could no longer be fully realized. Laura Kessler's study tells the compelling story of how the family of Masuo Yasui, an immigrant from the prefecture of Okayama, built a stable and prosperous life in the community of Hood River, Oregon, until their displacement during World War II.[20] Beginning his new life in Hood River in 1908, Yasui was not typical of the many Japanese immigrants who were determined to be temporary visitors. Having settled in a town where anti-Japanese sentiment was initially minimal, he prepared well for success in America. Attending school, learning English, and carefully saving for a life as a merchant capitalist in Hood River, Yasui was one of the last Issei to begin life in America with such ambitions. Yasui and thousands of other Japanese immigrants to Hawaii and North America held on to their hopes and withstood the racism that made the experience of the Issei in these lands such a continual challenge. The patterns of their early lives far away from Japan would be remarkably similar to the experience of other Japanese immigrants who tried to better themselves in the even more distant lands of Latin America.[21] Let us now turn to the early experience of these immigrants.

THE LATIN AMERICAN PIONEERS

I have lived in Mexico for fifty-four and one half years. My wife
and I are thinking of leaving the [Chrysanthemum] business to our
children and moving to Japan, to retire in our original hometown.
—Antonio Kisaburo Yamani, a Mexican Issei, 1981

In many ways, the early Japanese immigrant experience in Latin America
until 1908 mirrored that of the Japanese in Hawaii and North America.
During the first decade of the Japanese presence in Latin America, the overwhelming majority of immigrants still migrated to North America. Between
1899 and 1908, 155,772 Japanese immigrants arrived in Canada and the
United States. The same era saw 18,203 Japanese sojourners seeking better
opportunities in five Latin American nations, nearly double the 10,197 who
traveled to the third main area of the overseas diaspora, Southeast Asia.[1]
Mexico and Peru attracted the great majority of the Latin American immigrants, but the pattern of migration to other South American nations also
was established before the second decade of the twentieth century as well.
Brazil did not receive its first major group of immigrants until 1908 because
it fulfilled its labor needs with African slaves and Italian immigrant labor
before 1908. Shortly after 1908, however, Brazil would become the leading Japanese immigrant society in the Western Hemisphere.

As in Hawaii, Canada, and the United States, the first immigrants to Latin
America were overwhelmingly male contract laborers who sought to better themselves financially and then return to Japan. These immigrants were
largely from the same prefectures in southwestern Japan and the Ryukyu
Islands (especially Okinawa) as their Hawaiian and North American counterparts. Swelling the ranks of the immigrants during the late Meiji era were
the continually hard-pressed peasantry and young Japanese males fleeing
military service. Conversely, veterans of Japan's wars with China and Rus-

sia, who had great difficulty reintegrating themselves into Japanese society, frequently chose to emigrate.

Japan's military buildup accelerated during the decade following the Sino-Japanese War of 1904–5. The army's divisions were increased from seven to thirteen, and total naval tonnage rose more than twofold. Much of these increased military expenditures were financed by yet another rise in the land tax, from 2.5 to 3.3 percent in the late 1890s.[2] The militarization of Japan was a reflection of the Meiji leader's goal of *fukoku kyohei*, the enrichment of the nation-state and strengthening of the military. This nationalistic goal, however, frequently conflicted with the short-term well-being of the Japanese people. The continuing hardships of the Japanese, as their nation modernized, are in some measure reflected in the steady flow of immigrants to Latin America during the last decade and a half of the Meiji era.

Unfortunately, the underdeveloped economies of Latin America did not offer the diversity of economic opportunities initially open to the Japanese immigrants who traveled to North America. Moreover, many of these early contract laborers confronted very harsh working conditions in the sugar haciendas and coal mines of Mexico and in the sugar plantations of coastal Peru. As we shall see, however, the work ethic and business skills of the Japanese in Latin America allowed them to compete very favorably within the less competitive economic environments of Mexico and South America. Above all, it must be remembered that Japanese immigration to Latin America occurred in large measure because the doors to more attractive wages and long-term opportunities in Canada and the United States were steadily closing after 1900. This chapter will discuss the initial phase of Japanese immigration to Latin America until 1908. The analysis will be made in the context of an overview of previous Chinese and European immigration patterns, the abolition of African slavery in Peru and Brazil, and the economic foundations of Japanese immigrant labor in the main receiver nations.

The Japanese who struggled to improve their lives in Latin America during the early years of the twentieth century added another important cultural dimension to the region's already rich and complex racial mosaic. As slaves, contract laborers, or free immigrants before the Japanese arrived, Africans, Europeans, Middle Eastern Arabs and Jews, Indians, and Chinese helped build Latin American societies with their labor. But given the challenges of the terrain, climate, and social structures of Latin American societies, their efforts were rarely sufficient. A captive, or cheap and servile, labor force was always in demand. Four centuries of Latin American development did not diminish the demand for obedient workers with strong backs. Coercive tribute or labor systems such as *encomienda* (tribute), *repartimiento* (draft labor), debt peonage, and slavery during the colonial and early independence eras created a legacy of economic and social control by Latin American landed elites that would cause many hardships for the first Japanese immigrants.[3]

The need for European and Asian immigrant labor was, in significant measure, created by the end of African slavery. Moreover, prevailing Social Darwinist beliefs prompted negative attitudes toward free black labor and especially the social integration of Afro-Latinos. These attitudes created opportunities for the Chinese, Europeans, and finally Japanese but not on terms that were initially substantially favorable to them. The Japanese did, however, have a distinct advantage over their Chinese predecessors; the Meiji government's increasing international prestige after 1899 did not leave them as helpless as the unfortunate Chinese coolies before them.

Japanese Modernization and Immigration to Latin America

The Meiji era inaugurated Japanese expansionism and the quest for world power status. Latin America's response to the Japanese must be viewed in this context, since Tokyo did not want its prestige undermined by the poor treatment or exclusion of its immigrants. In order to prevent this, Tokyo wanted to negotiate equitable treaties with the Latin American nations that would also provide guidelines for immigration policy. Such agreements were reached while formal diplomatic discussions were being negotiated with Argentina, Brazil, Chile, Ecuador, Mexico, and Peru before World War I. These understandings gave Japanese immigrants the right to enter and settle with their families in these Latin American nations at a time when they were no longer welcome in the United States and Canada.[4]

The negotiation of these treaties often proved to be a formidable task, given the lack of diplomatic contact between Japan and Latin America for more than two centuries during the Tokugawa Shogunate. The earliest contacts between them evolved from the famous Manila-Acapulco galleon trade begun in the mid-sixteenth century. Activity between Japan and the Philippines grew quickly, and by 1606, there were about 18,000 Japanese colonists in Manila and nearby Dilão. Japanese sailors were crewmen on some of the Spanish galleons traversing the Pacific and were most likely the first Japanese to reach the Americas. The profits earned by Chinese merchants in the silk trade with Spanish America established a trade network between the Orient and the west coasts of New Spain and Peru that eventually drew the interest of Ieyasu, the powerful shogun who ruled Japan during the late sixteenth and early seventeenth centuries.[5]

Hoping to forge an opening with the rigidly mercantile Spanish Ameri-

can empire, Ieyasu negotiated with the acting viceroy of the Spanish Philippines and in August 1610 permitted 23 Japanese tradesmen to accompany
the administrator on a voyage to New Spain. These tradesmen, along with
the 80 Japanese seamen who manned the vessel carrying the acting viceroy
to New Spain, were the first recorded Japanese to set foot in the Americas.
After a five-month visit, they returned to Japan with Spanish wine, cloth,
and velvet. This initial contact produced limited results, but the Japanese
persisted to pursue the possibility of a trade agreement. In 1613, Masamune
Date, a *daimyo* (lord) of Sendai, organized a mission to Spain and Rome.
Led by Tsunenaga Hasekura and including 180 Samurai and merchants, this
delegation also did not succeed in reaching a trade accord. The members of
the Tsunenaga group eventually returned to Nagasaki in 1620, but it is
possible that some of the delegation was left behind to permanently reside
in New Spain.[6]

Ieyasu's desire for extensive trade with Spanish America was never realized because Spain demanded significant political concessions and was never
truly willing to open its colonial American ports to outside commerce. Upon
Ieyasu's death in 1624, his grandson Iemitsu became shogun. Angered by
the growing influence of foreigners on Japanese soil, he expelled all but the
Dutch and closed Japan to the rest of the world by prohibiting his subjects
from leaving Japan upon pain of death. Although there would be isolated
incidents of storm-tossed Japanese seamen landing on Mexican soil in the
interim, it would be nearly 250 years before Japan and Latin America would
again be in formal contact.

A mutiny by Chinese coolies aboard the Peruvian ship *Maria Luz* sailing
in Japanese waters in 1872 finally led to formal diplomatic discussions between the new Meiji regime and a Latin American nation. After Japanese
authorities investigated the terrible conditions on the *Maria Luz*, the Peruvian government resolved to establish formal commercial ties with Japan.
Peru sent an envoy, Captain Aurelio García y García, in 1873 to secure a
treaty similar to those granted to European nations by Tokyo. García y
García succeeded in negotiating a ten-point agreement that granted most
favored nation status to Peru. This "unequal" treaty, signed only five years
after the beginning of the Meiji era, was reflective of Japan's relatively weak
international status. Peru's economy was only beginning to emerge from the
era when guano harvesting was its chief industry, and it offered few advantages for modernizing Japan.[7]

Moreover, the next two decades would prove to be the most turbulent in
modern Peruvian history as it suffered a disastrous defeat by Chile in the

War of the Pacific (1879–83) and a civil war in 1895. These unstable conditions very likely explain the failure of the first joint Japanese-Peruvian commercial venture, a silver mining enterprise sponsored by Japan's former foreign minister, Korekiyo Takahashi, in 1889. The Japan-Peru Mining Company sent seventeen Japanese technicians, miners, and mechanics to Peru in that year to begin Japan's first major commercial initiative in Latin America, but apparently the volatile political climate led to the rapid abandonment of the project.[8] Over the ensuing decade, Japanese-Peruvian relations continued to languish while Japan grew stronger and Peru struggled to maintain domestic order.

The renewal of Japanese contact with Mexico in the 1870s was facilitated by the mission of Mexican astronomer Francisco Díaz Covarrubias in 1874. Visiting Japan and China to observe the transit of Venus, Díaz Covarrubias wrote a detailed report on the cultures of both nations and advocated the establishment of diplomatic relations with Tokyo. Significantly, the astronomer turned diplomat also encouraged the Mexican government to solicit Japanese immigration.[9] During the course of the next fourteen years, the governments of Porfirio Díaz and Manuel González worked to establish formal commercial ties as one component of their effort to modernize the Mexican economy. The leaders of the Meiji government resisted these efforts because they feared that signing another diplomatic agreement with a Latin American nation, even if it were an equal treaty, still would hamper their efforts to favorably revise the unequal treaties signed with the leading Western powers during the last years of the Tokugawa Shogunate.[10] When these multilateral efforts to revise the unequal treaties failed by 1888, Japan changed its tactic and sought to negotiate with each of the Western powers individually. Now a new and equal treaty with Mexico was seen as a possible precedent for other such treaties that Japan hoped might be signed with the Western powers in the immediate future. After extended negotiations that centered primarily on the rights of extraterritoriality for Mexicans on Japanese soil, a treaty of amity and commerce between Mexico and Japan was officially ratified in July 1889. This represented the first equal diplomatic agreement between Japan and a Latin American nation. Ultimately, however, it did not provide the diplomatic leverage for Japan's relations with the leading powers that Tokyo had hoped it would.[11]

This bargaining power would come only with Japan's growing economic and military status. In fact, the Mexican press recognized that the 1889 treaty offered significant commercial advantages to Mexico even while minimizing the potential for mutual immigration. On this point, the Mexico City newspaper *El Tiempo* haughtily editorialized, "Our race does not emigrate except to Paris in order to spend its millions."[12] Nevertheless, modern Japanese-Mexican relations began with the 1889 treaty. Even though commercial contact between these two nations was never significant during the administration of Mexican president Porfirio Díaz (1876–1911), known as the Porfiriato, the foundations of Japanese immigration to Latin America were created with this treaty and the similar diplomatic agreement with Peru in 1873.

As was the case in Canada and the United States, Japanese immigration companies were instrumental in facilitating the flow of the first Japanese to Mexico and Peru. These companies were formed in response to the demand for Japanese laborers not only in Hawaii and the Western Hemisphere but also from labor contractors in New Caledonia, Australia, Fiji, and the Philippines. The formation of these companies was further encouraged by the increased availability of potential immigrants from the dislocation of many former peasant conscripts at the end of the Sino-Japanese War of 1895. The first private immigration company was established in 1891, and by 1908 fifty more such enterprises joined the profitable business of recruiting and shipping Japanese overseas.[13] During the early years, most of the operations of Japanese immigration companies were centered on Hawaii and North America. But after 1899, many of these same companies were forced to redirect much of their business to Mexico, Peru, and, beginning in 1908, Brazil. The most prominent of these privately owned companies included the Toyo Imin Gaisha (Oriental Immigration Company), the Tairiku Shokumin Gaisha (Continental Immigration Company), the Morioka Imin Gaisha (Morioka Immigration Company), the Kokoku Shokumin Kabushikigaisha (Kokoku Colonization Company), the Takemura Yoemon Gaisha (Takemura Colonization and Bonding Company), and the Meiji Shokumin Gaisha (Meiji Immigration Company).[14] As we shall see, the Japanese government encouraged the merger of these companies during World War I and began to subsidize their operations in an effort to advance overseas immigration. The actions of these companies and the Japanese government's policy regarding immigration in general was regulated by the Imin Hogoho (Immigrant Protection Ordinance) proclaimed by the imperial government in April 1894. Modified on three separate occasions over the course of the next thirteen years, the ordinance emphasized Tokyo's control over labor contracts, demanded security deposits for immigration companies to assure the return of immigrants, and regulated the recruitment and shipping practices of the companies.[15]

The First Asians in Spanish America

Japanese immigrants went first to Mexico and Peru in the late 1890s because these nations had demands for cheap manual labor that were not being met by the native population and, particularly in the case of Peru, no longer by the Chinese. The political leaders of Mexico and Peru from the mid-nineteenth century onward sought to meet some of their labor needs through European immigration. These efforts failed for a number of reasons. During the two decades after the war with the United States, Mexican leaders sought European immigrants as the nation's population grew slowly and the marginally productive lands of the north and west remained sparsely populated. But the protracted political turmoil caused by the War of Reform (1858–61) and the French Intervention (1862–67) turned most potential European settlers away from Mexico. A national image of religious intolerance and the poor administration of immigration policy also undermined Mexico's efforts to attract European immigrants before the Porfiriato. Indeed, in 1876, Mexico's foreign-born residents numbered only 25,000 out of a total population of nearly 9 million.[16]

The negative image of Mexico among potential European immigrants prevailed throughout the Porfiriato despite the efforts of its intellectual elite, known as the *científicos,* to foster an image of a positivist-oriented, stable, and modernizing nation. Reflective of the inability of Mexican leaders during the Porfiriato to attract substantive European immigration was the failure of a project begun in 1881 to settle Italian immigrants in six separate colonies in the states of Veracruz, Puebla, San Luis Potosí, and the Federal District. More than 2,600 Italian immigrants entered Mexico during the first year of the colonization program, but within two years their numbers were reduced to 1,050 colonists. By 1908 only 217 Italian settlers remained on the originally settled lands. Undermining this colonization effort were financial problems, poor relations with neighboring settlements, and a lack of adequate roads and communications that made it difficult for the colonists to market their agricultural products. The difficulties of the Italian colonists drew the attention of the Italian-American press in New York. In September 1884, *Il Progresso Italio-Americano* accused the Mexican government of being "disloyal" and "despicable" in its dealings with the Italian colonists.[17] Small colonies of Mormons were established in northern Mexico in the aftermath of the failed Italian experiment, but they were not sufficiently successful to foster any significant immigration from North America.[18] During the last decade of the nineteenth century, Mexican business and government leaders, like their counterparts in the western sectors of Canada and the United States, were thus compelled to look first to Chinese and ultimately to Japanese immigrants to fulfill their growing labor requirements.

The Chinese first began arriving in Mexico in 1876 and settled primarily in the north and west. Overwhelmingly composed of males, the Chinese immigrant stream to Mexico increased dramatically after the United States passed the Chinese Exclusion Act of 1882. Finding work in a wide variety of occupations as laborers, miners, merchants, shopkeepers, and artisans, the Chinese settled primarily in the northwest region bordering the Pacific and in the state of Sonora, south of Arizona.[19] The comparatively late arrival of the Chinese in Mexico is explained by the unstable political climate and undeveloped state of plantation agriculture. With the majority arriving after the end of the coolie trade, Mexico's Chinese were not brutalized by the inhumanity of the contract labor system that tormented their compatriots in Cuba and Peru. By 1910, 13,203 Chinese had immigrated to Mexico. Only 80 of them were women. As in the rest of the Western Hemisphere, these demographics assured that the Chinese family would not be established by the first generation of immigrants in Mexico. Extended bachelorhood and mixed marriages with Mexican mestizas thus became the norm for the Chinese Mexicans.

More than a third of Mexico's first Chinese immigrants established themselves in the northern state of Sonora, where expanding economic opportunities associated with the Díaz regime's promotion of foreign investment in the borderlands were achieving success. A significant majority of the Chinese in Sonora and the rest of Mexico soon opened small businesses; some worked as truck farmers and miners, others made their livelihood as cooks, launderers, bakers, shoemakers, and day laborers. At the end of the Porfiriato, Sonora's Chinese represented the largest foreign colony in the state. Still, the Chinese population numbered less than 2 percent of Sonora's 265,383 inhabitants.[20] Their prominent role in Sonora's commercial sector, however, made the Chinese very vulnerable to the virulent xenophobia erupting in Mexico during the Mexican Revolution. As we shall see, Sonora's Chinese would be particularly victimized by the extreme nationalism of the revolution. Elsewhere in Mexico, the Chinese by 1910 had settled in every state except Tlaxcala. Nevertheless, they never fulfilled Mexico's demand for cheap labor as hoped. This was the role Mexican *hacendados* (owners of large estates) and mine owners envisioned for the Japanese.[21]

Mexico's willingness to eventually solicit Japanese immigration must be viewed from at least three different perspectives. Unquestionably, the demand for cheap manual labor was a decisive motivation to Mexico as it was throughout the Americas. Secondly, Japan's rapid rise as an Asiatic power after 1895 enhanced the image of the Japanese people in the minds of positivist-oriented leaders of Mexico. Finally, Mexican leaders seemed not to be bound entirely by the rigid concepts of race prevailing in this era of Social Darwinism. Martin Stabb has argued, for example, that the roots of the liberal racial policy *indigenismo* (Indian identity), so prominent in Mexico in the 1920s, in fact can be identified in the writings of such influential late-nineteenth-century social writers as Ignacio Ramírez and Justo Sierra. Stabb concludes, "If one were to compare the race-thinking of the Mexicans with the literature of what might be called the 'classic' school of nineteenth century European racism . . . it would be perfectly clear that Mexican thought remained relatively uncontaminated by these doctrines."[22] It may be noted in passing that the virus of "classical racism" had by contrast made considerable headway in the late nineteenth century and early twentieth century in other parts of Spanish America. In his analysis of the prevailing ideas of Porfirian Mexico, William Raat maintains that Mexico's intellectual leaders and policy makers were motivated principally by notions of "secular progress and material development" founded on a "kind of reforming Darwinism." He, too, argues that Mexico's leaders were not racists but cautions that they viewed the Indians as "second class citizens" who must be integrated into Mexico's social mainstream to be "saved."[23]

Because the number of Japanese immigrants in Mexico was never large, it is difficult to judge how relatively "tolerant" Mexicans were toward their Japanese racial minority. Before 1908, the number of Japanese immigrants in Mexico never exceeded 15 percent of the foreign-born population, which was only approximately 115,000 of the nation's 15 million people.[24] It is important to consider, however, that Japan's leaders during the late Meiji era viewed Mexico as a racially tolerant nation. Mexico was portrayed in Japan as a "land of hope" with "vast lands, temperate climate and friendliness toward the Japanese."[25] For example, Bunzo Hasiguchi, an agricultural specialist and Tokyo's first representative to speak directly with Porfirio Díaz about Japanese settling in Mexico, was impressed with the president's "very positive and friendly attitude toward the Japanese immigration policy."[26] Subsequently, Japan's diplomats and military leaders stressed what they viewed as the ancient ancestral ties between the Japanese and Mexican peoples on a number of important occasions during the first two decades of immigration.[27] These attitudes sharply contrasted with those commonly held in Peru and other nations with sizable Indian populations, like Mexico. In other Latin American nations, there was little affinity between the Japanese and native peoples.

Peru's demand for Japanese immigrant labor was driven by the expansion of commercial agriculture, particularly sugar and cotton, following the abolition of African slavery in 1854 and the termination of Chinese coolie labor two decades later.[28] Peru's protracted war for independence (1810–24), Great Britain's closure of the nation's external slave trade, and the natural decline in the slave population reduced the number of bondsmen from 40,377 in 1792 to 25,505 when slavery was abolished in 1854.[29] Only six years after African slavery was ended, the need for plantation labor was so pronounced that Peru's Agricultural Society requested that the government help sponsor the colonization of African free laborers to alleviate the shortage of agricultural workers.[30] This effort was, of course, futile, but the importation of Chinese contract laborers had been encouraged by government subsidies approved as early as 1839. Substantial compensation to owners for liberating their slaves was also granted in 1854.[31] Prompted by these incentives and the continuing need for inexpensive servile labor, Peru imported 100,000 Chinese male immigrants during the years of the coolie trade (1847–74).

Mirroring the working conditions in Cuba, where 125,000 coolies labored with African slaves in the sugarcane fields, Peru's Chinese immigrants before 1874 were really "wage slaves." Viewed by Peruvian sugar planters as "better than slaves and without the problems," coolies were contracted in China with a cash advance and a promise of a wage of five pesos per month. Food, clothing, and the cash advance were deducted from the coolies' wages, however, frequently reducing them to the status of wage slaves at the mercy of a Peruvian overseer's accounting methods. Studies by Watt Stewart and Michael J. Gonzalez depict a grim fate for most of Peru's first Asians.[32]

Peru's guano-based economy of the mid-nineteenth century was supported by Chinese coolie labor. Thousands of Chinese during the 1860s toiled in unspeakable conditions in the guano beds of the coastal Peru and the Chincha Islands. A British observer described the misery of the Chinese workers: "'No hell has ever been conceived of by the Hebrew, the Irish, the Italian or even the Scotch mind for appeasing the anger or satisfying the vengeance of their awful gods that can be equaled by the fierceness of the heat, the horror of the stink, and the damnation of those compelled to work there, to a deposit of Peruvian guano being shoveled into ships.'"[33] As might be expected, disease and suicide claimed the lives of many coolie laborers in the guano beds. During the 1870s, life was less harsh for the 5,000 Chinese employed on the railway construction gangs of the American entrepreneur Henry Meiggs. Ultimately, many coolies fled the coastal sugar plantations to seek the relatively high wages and better working conditions of the Meiggs venture.[34]

Since Peruvian sugar planters were unsuccessful in employing Indian or free African labor on their coastal plantations, they were continually seeking ways to bind Chinese laborers to the cane fields well beyond the end of the coolie trade in 1874. As Gonzalez has demonstrated, patterns of coercion similar to those being used against Chinese workers in the sugarcane fields of Cuba were implemented.[35] Confinement to the plantation, floggings, imprisonment, and even murder characterized the treatment of Chinese coolies in Peru. Fully twenty years after the coolie trade was abolished, Peru's *chinos libres* (free Chinese) were deprived of their freedom by debt peonage and the often autonomous "law of the plantation." The frequently desperate Chinese resisted in many ways, including flight and rebellion. With all of its injustices, Chinese coolie labor provided the transition from slave to coercive contract labor and "saved" Peru's sugar plantations in the process. Sadly, the social climate confronting Peru's aging Chinese immigrants never substantially improved after the 1880s. Replicating the same attitudes of workers in the western United States, the free Chinese who survived the cane fields were often hated by Peru's laboring classes, who resented their suppression of wages and their success in urban commerce. Alone in a society that often regarded them with suspicion and contempt, the Chinese were deprived of the protection of the Chinese government, weak as it was, or the social cohesion enjoyed by the Japanese immigrant culture that soon developed in Peru. Still, some of Peru's free Chinese would become landowners or proprietors of large businesses. Most, however, would leave the land and establish new lives in Peru's coastal cites as small shop owners, restaurateurs, and artisans. This pattern of flight from the sugar estates to the stores and shops of Lima and other Peruvian cities would be emulated by the first generation of Japanese immigrants.

Like Mexico, Peru was unable to attract large-scale European immigration before 1890 largely because of the political and economic dislocations caused by the War of the Pacific. Years of slow economic recovery following the Treaty of Ancón (1883), which ended the war, were not sufficient to avert continuing political unrest, which culminated in the 1895 civil war. Additionally, very restrictive landholding patterns and the consolidation of both coastal commercial plantations and hacienda holdings in the *sierra* (mountainous regions) discouraged the large-scale immigration of poor Europeans seeking land.[36] Despite these problems, some of the relatively few European immigrants venturing to Peru after 1850 did well.

During the 1860s and early 1870s, political leaders such as Pedro Galvez and Manuel Pardo tried to promote European immigration as a solution to the dwindling labor supply on Peru's coastal plantations. In 1872, for example, the Pardo government formed the Sociedad de Inmigración Europa (European Immigration Society) for this purpose. During the brief three-year existence of the poorly funded society, 3,000 immigrants arrived in Peru, the majority of whom were Italians. By the end of the 1870s, the Italians were the largest European colony in Peru, numbering more than 7,000. Small groups of British, French, Spanish, and German settlers, each totaling less than 4,000, migrated to Peru as well.

Growing slowly during the years before 1908, when it reached its peak of 13,000, the Italian community mainly settled in Lima. Far fewer new arrivals from Italy worked as agricultural laborers than the Peruvian government originally had hoped. Conditions on the sugar plantations were simply too harsh and the pay too low to attract even the poorest Italian immigrants, who worked instead as street vendors or porters. Those with more financial resources usually made their livelihoods by operating small shops, restaurants, and pensions. Better-educated northern Italians soon became the elite of the community, and this relatively small group, generally numbering no more than 200, became very prosperous and politically influential. The Banco Italiano, Banco Popular, and Banco del Peru y Londres, three of Peru's leading financial institutions in the twentieth century, were founded primarily by Italian investors. Additionally, by 1908, Italian entrepreneurs dominated the textile trade and the food processing and beverage industries.[37] Some Italians such as the Larco family in sugar production, and some Germans, most notably the Gildermeister family in sugar, fishing, mining, and oil, joined the ranks of Peru's foremost families.

Before the early 1890s, these individual successes still did not generate the desired influx of European immigrants. Accordingly, an effort was made by the Peruvian government during the early 1890s to especially encourage greater German and Italian immigration with the passage of the Law of Immigration and Colonization in October 1893.[38] Specifically calling for immigrants of the "white race," this legislation never achieved for Peruvian sugar planters what Brazilian coffee growers were able to do between 1890 and 1908, that is, to draw upon European immigrants to meet their labor needs. This can be explained by Peru's lack of arable land, its unstable political environment, and its rigid social structure.

Peruvian sugar growers tried unsuccessfully to bind Chinese laborers to their plantations long after the end of contract coolie labor in 1874. The expansion of sugar production in the 1890s and a later boom in cotton agriculture beginning in 1905 thus created an acute labor shortage in Peru. From 1890 to 1910, cotton and sugar consistently accounted for at least a third of the value all Peruvian exports. Peru's output of sugar alone grew more than 60 percent during this same period. When British textile mills adapted to Peru's long-standing staple, *aspero* (rugged) cotton, after 1900, this crop gradually began to supplant sugar in the heavily capitalized coastal estates.[39] New cotton lands were opened through irrigation of scrub and desert land, primarily in northern and central Peru during the first three decades of the twentieth century. As we shall see, cotton was a crop that a minority of Peru's Issei adapted to quite well as they made the gradual transition from contract laborers to tenant farmers and eventually prominent landholders in Peru's central coastal valleys. Although agriculture did not become the calling of most Japanese Peruvians, it was of central importance to the first Japanese immigrants in Brazil.

It was coffee, and not sugar, that was the economic foundation of the initial Japanese immigrant experience in Brazil. By the time of the arrival of the first Issei in Brazil in 1908, fundamental changes were occurring in that country's agricultural and labor systems that altered the outlook of the *fazendeiro* (planter) class in Latin America's largest nation. A clear appreciation of the origins of Japanese immigration to Brazil requires some understanding of African slavery before its abolition in that country in 1888. Furthermore, it will help to examine the broad outlines of earlier European immigration, particularly Italian contract labor during the last decade of the nineteenth century, in the state of São Paulo—that dynamic region of southern Brazil to which Japanese immigration was overwhelmingly directed.

Brazilian Labor in Bondage

The modern nation of Brazil was founded largely upon the labor of the 3.5 million African slaves in bondage from 1550 to 1888. Sudanese, Bantus, Guineans, Wolofs, Mandingos, Songhais, Mossis, Hausas, and Kamite Peuls labored mainly in the sugarcane fields of Paraiba, Pernambuco, and Bahia. Others toiled in the diamond and gold mines of Minas Gerais and ultimately in the *fazendas* (coffee plantations) of southern Brazil.[40] Brazil's political stability during the long rule of the nation's constitutional monarch, Emperor Dom Pedro II (1850–89), rested firmly on the support of the planter class, which was experiencing a shift from sugar to coffee production. The majority of Brazil's slaves were gradually transferred to the newly planted coffee fields of Rio de Janeiro, Paraná, and São Paulo before 1870. Even while Great Britain opposed the Brazilian slave trade, it reached its peak when as many as 55,000 Africans per year entered Brazil as late as 1845–50.[41]

The end of the African slave trade in Brazil in 1853 did not, of course, necessarily mean the rapid demise of the institution. But with African slavery outlawed everywhere in the Western Hemisphere except Cuba and Brazil by 1870, it was inevitable that opposition to the institution would emerge even in Latin America's largest slave society. The abolitionist movement thus gained strength with the 1885 law freeing bondsmen who lived to the age of sixty and the manumission of slaves by individual provincial governments in northern and central Brazil. During the fifteen years after 1873, more than 200,000 of Brazil's slaves were manumitted.[42] By 1887, slaves were abandoning São Paulo's coffee plantations by the hundreds, and in early 1888, São Paulo's planters freed 40,000 slaves, or one-third of the state's bondsmen. On 13 March 1888, the São Paulo provincial assembly requested that the Brazilian government abolish slavery, and exactly two months later Princess Regent Isabel signed the *lei aurea,* the "golden law" that ended more than three and one-half centuries of African bondage in Brazil.[43]

In the aftermath of the abolition of slavery, the subsequent fall of the monarchy in 1889, and the creation of the Old Republic (1889–1930), São Paulo's *libertos* (freed slaves) quickly became marginalized members of a society that was undergoing vast social and economic changes. São Paulo's planters soon decided to turn their backs on the freed slaves and begin a program of subsidized European immigration. São Paulo's elites hoped that European immigration would provide a capable yet servile labor force to augment and eventually fully replace the freed slaves, whom they regarded with what has been called the *ideologia de vadiagem,* the belief that people of color were innately lazy and irresponsible.[44] With this decidedly racist view firmly fixed in their minds, São Paulo's planter class further hoped that European immigration would lead to the "whitening" of their society over the course of future generations. Thomas Skidmore, in a valuable analysis of this concept of whitening, notes that, unlike attitudes regarding race mixture in the United States, influential Brazilian intellectuals such as Gilberto Freyre regarded racial miscegenation in a positive light. It must be understood, however, that the Brazilian constitution of 1890, by banning further African and Asian immigration to Brazil, reflected the dominant view of the Brazilian elites that miscegenation was their only means to achieve a future society where people of color would be a distinct minority.[45]

The first non-Iberian immigrants to settle in Brazil were small colonies of Germans who began new lives away from the coffee fields beginning in the 1820s in Paraná, Santa Catarina, and Rio Grande do Sul in Brazil's southern region. In 1874, colonists from Italy's Po Valley settled north of the Germans in Rio Grande do Sul.[46] Despite these colonization efforts, total immigration to Brazil in the years between 1820 and the early 1870s never exceeded a few thousand per year. Chinese immigration, which augmented slave labor in Cuba and Peru, was viewed favorably by some Brazilian leaders, but no serious attempt was ever made to bring coolie labor to the sugar and coffee plantations. When the institution of slavery began to weaken in the 1870s, 218,000 immigrants entered Brazil. The following decade saw that number more than double to 530,000. Once slavery was abolished, immigration to Brazil peaked during the last ten years of the nineteenth century at 1,144,000. The end of Italian contract labor in 1902 brought about a decline in the number of immigrants in the period 1901–10 to 695,000, just as Japanese immigration was beginning.[47] In order to understand immigration to São Paulo in a broader perspective, it would be useful to consider that for the period 1827 to 1939, 2,439,490 immigrants disembarked at the port of Santos for a new life in Brazil. Of this total, 38.8 percent were Italians, 17.4 percent Portuguese, 15.8 percent Spaniards, and 7.7 percent Japanese. German, Austrians, Poles, and other Eastern European peoples entered São Paulo in significant numbers during this era. While Japanese immigration totals are substantially lower than those of the European immigrants, this migration of Japanese before World War II takes on greater significance when one considers that it occurred well after the mass migrations of the pre–World War I era. Moreover, the immigrants, primarily from Japan's agricultural rural districts, arrived while São Paulo was making the rapid transition from a coffee-based economy to that of the leading industrial region of a modernizing Brazil.[48]

The cornerstone of the São Paulo planters' subsidized immigrant labor program was the private but state-financed Sociedade Promotora de Imigração (Society for the Promotion of Immigration), formed in 1884. Italian immigrant families, particularly Lombards, Venetians, Piedmontese, and Ligurians, quickly became the focus of São Paulo's subsidized immigration program. Eventually, Venetians became the dominant Italian immigrant group. By 1887, São Paulo's state government funded the society at a rate of 75 milreis (approximately $40) for each immigrant above the age of twelve, and about half as much for those under twelve. This funding financed the travel costs of half a million immigrants from Italy to the São Paulo coffee plantations at a cost of 42 million milreis, or $14 million in subsidies.[49] The program was initially a great success. Between 1887 and 1898, Brazilian records list 804,598 Italian immigrants entering São Paulo. This accounted for more than two-thirds of all Italian immigration to Brazil from 1820 to 1908.[50] The relatively lighter work in the coffee fields, which could make use of the labor of women and children, often called for immigrant families to tend a few thousand coffee trees and harvest the berries, lending itself to family work units far better than the heavy fieldwork in the sugarcane fields of northern Brazil, where male slaves made up the main body of the work force. Moreover, São Paulo's planters were well aware that the male heads of immigrant families were inclined to be far more reliable workers than single males. These *colonos* (colonists), as they became known, were provided with rudimentary housing and frequently were allowed to cultivate small garden plots in the planters' fields to supplement their meager wages. Thus these immigrants were both tenant sharecroppers and wage laborers who were compelled to buy high-priced supplies at the plantation store.

While not as harrowing as plantation labor in the sugarcane fields of Peru, which European immigrants to that nation universally avoided, low-paid labor on the coffee plantations of São Paulo was still never as attractive to European immigrants as were other opportunities in Argentina and the United States. This fact, and the planters' continuing slave-master mentality, seems to explain why Brazil, with its vast lands and relatively small population, never attracted even larger numbers of immigrants than it did before World War I. Thomas Holloway presents evidence that land acquisition by even the poorly paid colonists was not uncommon. By 1934, Italians were the second most important landholding group in São Paulo, accounting for 11.1 percent of the units and farming more than 5.7 million acres.[51] On the other hand, the repatriation rates of Italians and other immigrants as reflected in records of steerage departures from the port of Santos from 1882 to 1908 indicate that many of these colonists were sojourners. During this quarter century, departures account for 46.5 percent of total immigration figures.[52] Because these Italian immigrants to São Paulo surely benefited from the stability of family units, these return rates are surprisingly high. Clearly, life on the coffee plantation was one of isolation and limited opportunities for many immigrants. Robert Foerster, in his pioneering study of Italian immigration, concluded that for most of the colonists in São Paulo, their lives were marked by "broken hopes and vanished dreams."[53]

Without São Paulo's immigrant subsidy program, the level of immigration would have clearly been much lower after the end of slavery. Still, colonists ultimately replaced African slave labor and, as Holloway demonstrates, provided a transition labor force for the São Paulo planters. Warren Dean's study concurs, and in his estimate, immigration "saved" the coffee plantations and "energized" them with the inflow of labor.[54] Thus, when the Italian government, responding to reports of mistreatment of the colonists on the plantations by its consulate in Brazil, ended further subsidized immigration with the "Prinetti decree" of March 1902, São Paulo planters were again compelled to search for a labor source to augment the dwindling supply of nonsubsidized European immigrant labor. Aware that Japanese immigrants were meeting the labor needs of planters in Hawaii, the United States, Mexico, and Peru, Brazil's planters welcomed this labor source beginning in 1908.

Although their labor needs were becoming acute after 1890, Mexico, Peru, Brazil, and the other Latin American nations were not able to compete successfully with the attractive economic opportunities offered by Canada and the United States before 1908. As a consequence, Japanese immigration to Latin America was relatively minimal before the nations north of the Rio Grande imposed entry restrictions. As noted earlier, between 1899 and 1908, 18,203 Japanese immigrants entered Latin America. Mexico received 10,958 of them and Peru 6,315. Brazil's first contingent of 781 Japanese arrived at São Paulo's port of Santos aboard the vessel *Kazatu-maru* in 1908, marking the beginning of the world's foremost Japanese immigrant experience. Additionally, a small group of 126 Japanese arrived in Chile in 1903, while Cuba and Argentina recorded their first few arrivals in 1907. Transmigration of small numbers of Japanese contract laborers from Peru to Bolivia before 1908 initiated the Japanese presence in that Andean nation.[55]

After a failed attempt at Japanese colonization in Mexico, contract immigration for plantation labor, coal mining, and railroad construction characterized the first phase of the Japanese immigrant presence in Mexico and Peru. It should also be remembered that Mexico initially appealed to many Japanese immigrants who planned to transmigrate to the United States to seek greater economic opportunity.

Mexico and the First Issei

The first organized Japanese immigration to Latin America involved the so-called Enomoto Imin (Enomoto's immigrants), who arrived in the southern Mexican state of Chiapas in May 1897. Organized by the former Japanese Minister of Foreign Relations and ardent proponent of immigration, Takeaki Enomoto, this group of settlers was not typical of the later contract laborers who arrived in Mexico and Peru as sojourners during the following decade. Enomoto envisioned "outposts" of Japanese immigrants who would permanently settle throughout the world and thereby facilitate Japanese commercial and political expansion. During the early 1890s, Enomoto sent agents to Mexico, the Philippines, Malaya, New Hebrides, and Fiji to determine the possibilities of establishing permanent settlements in these nations.[56] Encouraged by the cooperation of the Díaz regime in Mexico, Enomoto's enterprise eventually purchased 160,550 acres in Escuintla, department of Soconusco, in the southern state of Chiapas in 1896, for the purpose of establishing a permanent agricultural colony of Japanese immigrants. Mexico required a payment of one and one-half pesos per hectare (2.47 acres) of largely uncleared and undeveloped farmland. The Escuintla holding was to be developed by the Japanese colonists exclusively but was only one of twenty such colonization projects commissioned by the Mexican government in 1897.[57]

The first group of thirty-four young Japanese men was recruited with an emphasis on agricultural skills and higher education. An agricultural specialist, Toraji Kusakado, led the group's effort to clear the land in preparation for the planting of coffee trees. From the very beginning, the Enomoto Imin met with insurmountable problems. A poorly-timed planting schedule, disease, and a breakdown in the group's financial support doomed the effort after less than six months. The Mekishiko Iju Kumiai (Mexican Immigration Cooperative), the Japanese agency that administered the funding for the project, was not willing to risk further losses and quickly suspended funding. Nevertheless, only nine of the original Enomoto Imin chose to return to Japan. After a new sponsor and financing were obtained, those that remained were joined by more agricultural specialists, who attempted to diversify the operation by planting sugarcane and rubber trees, in addition to coffee. The same problems coupled with the remote location of the Escuintla colony led to the demise of the second cooperative effort as well.[58]

The circumstance of the ill-fated Escuintla colony is instructive because it predates the patterns of settlement of later Japanese immigrants in Brazil, Paraguay, and Bolivia who successfully founded self-sufficient agricultural colonies in remote regions in these nations. These later colonization efforts, however, were subsidized by the Japanese government with far larger core groups of settlers. From another perspective, the fate of the Escuintla settlers is useful to know because it demonstrates the adaptability of early Issei in Mexico and throughout Latin America. The stranded survivors of the failed colony who remained in Mexico farmed small plots of land, took jobs from local commercial enterprises, and combined their capital to open small cooperative businesses of their own. Some of the original colonists formed a Japanese-Mexican Cooperative society, which later purchased land to be developed by the society. By 1908, there was an established community of fifty Japanese in Escuintla, a quarter of whom had married Mexican women and were raising twenty-one Japanese Mexican children. Reflecting the higher education levels of Escuintla settlers was the construction of a community school and the contracting of teachers from Japan to educate their children.[59]

The Escuintla colonization project did not mark the end of cooperative efforts by the Japanese and Mexican governments to promote colonization projects. In 1897, a contract was signed to establish a colony of 100 Japanese, European, and Mexican settlers in the state of Sinaloa, but the project never materialized. Clearly, the Escuintla colony and the other reported projects were anomalies in the course of Japanese immigration to Mexico and did not reflect the dominant trend of Japanese migration of the period before 1908. Contract immigration to Mexico and Peru would be far more representative of the trend in that period.

Labor contract immigration to Mexico can be seen as a reflection of the failure of the Díaz regime to successfully promote the colonization of immigrants on the marginal lands of northern Mexico. It is also an indication of the reluctance of Mexico's *hacendado* class to remain exclusively dependent upon native labor for fear of losing their workers to higher paying neighboring agricultural enterprises or to U.S. farming operations. This vision of Mexico's future, however, fell victim to the more pressing problem of *falta de brazos,* or lack of hands on the land, and Japanese contract labor was seen as one possible solution to this problem.

The expansion of the Mexican mining industry, funded in significant measure by foreign capital during the Porfiriato, also required large numbers of foreign workers. The Mexican Mine Law of 4 June 1892 opened the way for foreign investment by emphasizing the "facility to acquire, liberty to exploit, and the security to retain" newly acquired mining properties.[60] By the outbreak of the Mexican Revolution in 1910, U.S. interests owned 75 percent of all the dividend-paying mining operations in Mexico.[61] The Guggenheim family's interests in Mexican mining, for example, were greatly facilitated by this law, and by the first years of the twentieth century they dominated the Mexican smelting industry. The mining and processing of coal, silver, lead, zinc, and copper saw expansion rates between 50 and 1,000 percent in these industries during the period 1890 to 1908, largely through expanded operations made possible by foreign investment. Japanese labor was solicited for initial coal mining operations in the state of Coahuila, which were funded by individual American entrepreneurs such as William Ludlow, whose Mexican Coal and Coke Company's success prompted other enterprises to begin operations in the region. French financial interests backed the El Boleo copper mines near Santa Rosalia in Baja California, which also initially sought contract labor from Japan. Japanese laborers in large numbers were brought in to supply the labor force for these coal and copper mining operations that were begun in remote locations where native labor was not easily available. In some cases, they replaced or augmented Yaqui Indian laborers, who were some of the most severely exploited workers in all of Mexico. Once again, it should be noted that this demand for cheap labor mirrored the labor situation in Canada and the United States during this same period, and consequently it drew the attention of the newly formed Japanese immigration companies.[62]

Japanese companies administered the immigration of 8,706 Japanese contract laborers to Mexico between 1901 and 1907.[63] This represented the vast majority of the approximately 11,000 Japanese who migrated to Mexico during that time span. These immigrants were employed in the coffee, hemp, and sugar plantations, railroad and road construction, and the mineral mines of northern Mexico.[64] The two main immigration companies doing business during this era in Mexico were the Kunimoto Imin Gaisha (Kunimoto Immigration Company), which sent 1,242 contract laborers to the coal mines in Esperanzas and Fuente in Coahuila; and the Toyo Imin Gaisha, which contracted 3,048 immigrants to labor in the El Boleo copper mines and the coal mines of Esperanzas and transported 4,416 Japanese to work on coffee, sugar, and hemp plantations, the Central Railroad in Colima, and the Black Mountain gold mine at Magdalena, in the state of Sonora.[65]

Working conditions for the contract laborers were rarely favorable for Japanese immigrants. Typical of the contract terms for Japanese plantation laborers were those written by the Toyo Imin Gaisha for the workers on the Oaxaquenia sugar plantation, an agricultural enterprise in the state of Veracruz encompassing more than 40,500 acres. Travel expenses from Japan to Mexico were paid for by the immigrants, but the immigration company often loaned them a portion of the boat fare. The Toyo Imin Gaisha paid the travel expenses of the contract workers from the port of entry to the plantation. The contract term was for four years, calling for a six-day work week of ten hours a day. Work was generally not required on Sundays and holidays. Men were paid slightly more than 50 cents per day, while the few women who migrated earned only 30 cents. The workers were given free health care, but this was often far from adequate, considering the unsanitary and disease-ridden conditions of many of the work sites in Mexico. The Oaxaquenia plantation had a company store where workers could buy groceries and other daily needs. After the initial influx of immigrants reached the Oaxaquenia and the distressing working conditions became known, the length of the contract was reduced to two years, but the work-week hours remained the same.[66]

The greatest difficulty Japanese contract workers faced in the plantations, railroad lines, and mines of Mexico was disease. Unsanitary and strenuous working conditions, poor nutrition, and the harsh tropical climate all combined to result in numerous cases of beriberi, typhoid, and malaria. In the early years of contract labor on the Oaxaquenia plantation, two or three workers died daily, and on at least one occasion it was reported that sixteen succumbed to disease in one day. By 1906, these conditions led 1,000 Japanese contract workers on the plantation to go on strike demanding better working conditions. The strike was put down by government troops, and ninety Japanese laborers were jailed and eventually expelled from the plantation. A number of these strikers appealed to the Japanese legation in Mexico City, and after an investigation, working conditions on the plantation were reported to have been slightly improved.[67] As was the case in Hawaii and Peru, flight from harsh working conditions on the plantations of Mexico was common among Japanese contract laborers. The runaway problem was so serious on the Oaxaquenia plantation that the company eventually offered a reward of 500 pesos for the return of those laborers fleeing the cane fields.

Working conditions on Mexico's new rail lines were better than those in the plantations and the mines, but health conditions were still poor. Japanese workers serving on the Central Railroad's construction crews near Colima received little direct care; the thirty camps along the line were served by only one "hospital," with one Dutch doctor and his Japanese assistant.[68] Despite the slightly better working conditions on the railroad construction gangs, flight from this form of contract labor was also frequent. For instance, Mizuno Zenichi, an immigrant contract worker from Hiroshima who arrived in Mexico in 1908 to work on a Central Railroad construction crew, fled his contract obligations after only two months with a group of thirty other laborers. Zenichi eventually found work as a paymaster in the service of a general in the Mexican Revolution. In another instance, Ken Tochihara from Kumamoto, who arrived in 1907 to work on the rail lines, abandoned his construction crew to seek better wages in the United States.[69] His flight to the United States was typical of the pattern of many Japanese immigrant contract workers in Mexico. Railroad workers, cane cutters, and particularly coal miners in the northern state of Coahuila commonly left their work sites after only a short time to transmigrate illegally to the United States. In 1905, thirty Okinawan contract workers fled the Esperanzas coal mine. Led by Isoichiro Kanashiro, Tokiko Hamamoto, and Kamado Ota, they were aided by fellow Japanese or Okinawans in Chihuahua, El Paso, and finally Los Angeles. After enduring much hardship during the six-month journey from the mines of northern Mexico, this immigrant group eventually found work picking strawberries at the Toro Peak farm near Los Angeles for wages of $1.35 per day. Significantly, these Okinawans were originally attracted to the United States after stopping briefly in San Francisco on their way to Mexico. Clearly, the dark prospects of contract work in the coal mines of Mexico contrasted sharply with their vision of the working life in the United States.[70] In some cases, Japanese workers tried to better their conditions through collective action rather than flight, as the workers did on the Oaxaquenia plantation in 1906. Japanese coal miners in the Esperanzas fields also refused to work during a 1902 walkout, and in 1904 the 500 Japanese contract laborers at the El Boleo copper mine withheld their labor in a dispute over the implementation of the original contract terms. Eventually, 450 of these immigrant laborers at the El Boleo mine were repatriated to Japan. Given the problems with working conditions in Mexico, it is not surprising that many Japanese workers took great risks to flee to the United States.[71]

Notwithstanding the poor working conditions in Mexico, daily wages of up to $3 per day (equal to 6 Mexican pesos or 6 Japanese yen) were the principal attraction drawing Japanese contract laborers from Mexico to the United States. As we have seen, Japanese laborers were earning an average of only half a yen per day, and the plantation or mine worker's wage in Mexico was often less than half of what could be earned in the United States. As Michael Meyer and William Sherman have noted, the desperate poverty of the laboring class and peons of Mexico during the last years of the Porfiriato was reflected in the declining purchasing power of their meager wages. As the cost of living rose in Mexico and wages remained stable or declined, comparable workers in the United States had nearly twelve times the purchasing power of their Mexican (and Japanese) counterparts south of the border.[72] Because of the limitations imposed by the Gentlemen's Agreement, many Japanese immigrants went to Mexico with the intention of continuing their migration to the United States. Indeed, recruiters for the Toyo Imin Gaisha openly promised, "'If you go to Mexico, you can enter the United States even on the following day.'"[73] Transmigration to the United States via Mexico by Japanese who had originally immigrated to Peru also occurred before 1908. The number of Japanese contract workers who illegally abandoned their contract obligations in Mexico for the better wages in the United States is, of course, impossible to accurately determine.

Nevertheless, the frequency of this occurrence is suggested by the estimate offered by the minister to the Japanese legation in Mexico City in a 1908 report. Minister Yoshida reported, "'Immigrants who have run away from contract so far number over 5,000 and most of these seem to have entered the United States.'"[74] This figure approaches nearly half of the 10,956 Japanese who entered Mexico from 1901 to 1907. The transmigration of Japanese contract laborers, of course, foreshadows the massive illegal cross-border migration of Mexico's rural poor in the post–World War II era. But given the already intense anti-Japanese sentiment in the United States during the first decade of the twentieth century, it is not surprising that the American government adopted strong measures to curtail the influx of illegal Japanese immigrants from Mexico at the same time it was limiting legal immigration from Japan.

✿   ✿   ✿

One component of the Gentlemen's Agreement of 1907–8 was the commitment of the Japanese government to limit immigration to territories adjacent to the United States. The levels of Japanese immigration to Mexico during the last two years before the Japanese government imposed its restrictions were the highest in the history of sojourner migration to that Latin American nation. In 1906, 5,068 Japanese entered Mexico, and in 1907, 3,822 more arrived.[75] Many of these immigrants appeared to have been seeking the fleeting opportunity to enter the closing door of opportunity in the United States, because by 1910 the number of Japanese residing in Mexico was declared by the national census to be only 2,623. The location of the Japanese in Mexico as reflected in this census seems to confirm the pattern of transmigration to the United States. While the largest concentration of Japanese (664) was in heavily populated Mexico City, three northern states—Sonora, Coahuila, and Chihuahua—listed 1,145 Japanese residents, nearly half of the total for all of Mexico. The Japanese in these three northern states were very likely working in the mining industries as contract laborers, and death from disease may have been a partial factor in reducing the number of them residing in Mexico. But if one considers that only 167 female Japanese immigrants were recorded as residing in Mexico by the 1910 census, it appears that few Japanese were seeking to establish families in Mexico during the first decade of substantive immigration. Clearly, transmigration to the United States was the primary goal of many Japanese immigrants to Mexico.[76]

By 1907, an immigrant assistance network was established at Ciudad Juárez–El Paso on the border to aid newly arrived Japanese in Mexico to enter the United States. Termed by the U.S. State Department the "Japanese Bureau" and the "Japanese Benevolent Association," these organizations reportedly operated offices and lodging facilities for cross-border escapees from contract labor in Mexico.[77] Indeed, Koichi Sugimura, Japan's minister plenipotentiary in Mexico, in a report published in the *Japan Times* of Tokyo in 1907, wrote, "'The possibility of better pay has led many [Japanese immigrants] in Mexico to secretly cross the northern border to the United States.'"[78]

Responding to the influx of Japanese from their southern neighbor, the U.S. government sought to stem the flow, and the Japanese government complied. In 1908, no Japanese reportedly entered Mexico, and over the course of the next decade, only slightly more than 200 legal immigrants arrived in Mexico. The decision to halt immigration to Mexico was made by Tokyo even while the demand for Japanese labor was high. The Mexican Revolution that began in 1910 also prevented significant further immigration before 1920. The termination of substantive Japanese immigration to Mexico ended what some observers felt was the possibility of that nation becoming the leading recipient of Japanese immigrants in Latin America in the twentieth century. After 1908, however, diplomatic pressure by Washington on Japan served to sharply limit further Japanese immigration to Mexico. This initiative by Washington was enormously influential in shifting the focus of future Japanese immigrants from North to South America. Peru and especially Brazil would become the leading Japanese immigrant nations of Latin America as a result of these developments.

Hope and Harsh Reality in Peru

Unlike what happened in Mexico, no serious attempt was made to colonize Japanese immigrants in Peru. A Japanese from the United States and a graduate of the University of California at Berkeley, Ikaturo Aoyagi, did, however, conduct unsuccessful negotiations with a representative of the Peruvian government's immigration service in 1893 to initiate a colonization project. The Peruvian representative and Aoyagi spoke about the possibility of settling Japanese immigrants on land near the junction of the Perene and Ucayali rivers to cultivate coffee. Like the earlier Japan-Peru Mining Company venture, this colonization scheme appears to have been a casualty of Peru's uncertain political climate, because this potentially successful project was never pursued after the Peruvian government's initially positive talks.

Mirroring the early immigrant experience in Hawaii, Peru's first Japanese came as sugarcane harvesters on the rapidly expanding plantations of the coast. The Andean country's relatively constant coastal climate meant that there was no seasonality to the sugar-growing cycle. Multiple crops assured that the demand for sugarcane workers was consistent throughout the year with relatively little need for temporary workers.[79] African slave labor from the late seventeenth century until abolition in 1854 provided the primary labor force for coastal sugar plantations. Additionally, after 1890, sugar production was becoming concentrated in a relatively few very large holdings, particularly in the Chicama Valley and the Santa Catalina Valley on the north coast near La Libertad. Here the Gildermeister and Chopitea families and the New York–based W. R. Grace Shipping and Merchant house soon dominated north coast sugar production. In the Cañete Valley, south of Lima, the Santa Barbara plantation, consolidated from a number of smaller operations by the Scottish immigrant Henry Swayne, sought Japanese immigrants to satisfy its need for cane workers. Sugar production continued to expand in Peru until World War I, but as the industry became more heavily capitalized, the number of sugarcane workers did not significantly expand nor did real wages increase.[80] Thus, the sugar industry never offered any meaningful opportunities for early Japanese immigrants to make the transition from laborers to entrepreneurs in that enterprise. This was not the case with cotton production, as will be discussed in a subsequent chapter.

Two individuals, one Japanese and the other Peruvian, were primarily responsible for initiating Japanese immigration to Peru under the contract labor system in 1899. Teikichi Tanaka, an official of the Morioka Company, and Augusto B. Leguía, a prominent sugar planter and future president of Peru, began negotiations to bring Japanese workers to Peru after Tanaka's earlier efforts to promote his company's interests in Brazil in 1898 met with little success. Subsequent negotiations between the Japanese and Peruvian governments led to the issuance of a decree by President Nicolás Piérola that permitted Japanese contract labor under an initial four-year agreement. This decree stipulated that the recruits were to be primarily experienced male agricultural workers between twenty and forty-five years of age who would work ten hours a day in the cane fields or twelve hours in the sugar mill. Specific issues such as wages, travel expenses, housing, medical facilities, and deductions for the return fare to Japan were stipulated in the contract. The wage rate was established at 25 yen per month (approximately $12). Housing and beds were provided by the employers, and since the cost of food was estimated to be about 10 yen per month, these workers could hope for as much as 15 yen per month to be remitted back to Japan or saved for their return to the homeland.[81] Rarely, however, were these terms strictly adhered to by Peruvian sugar planters during the first year of Japanese contract labor.[82]

The Japan Mail Line vessel *Sakura-maru* arrived at Peru's main port of Callao in April 1899 with the first 790 Japanese contract workers destined for the cane fields. The majority of these first immigrants were poor farmers or laborers from Niigata (372), Yamaguchi (187), and Hiroshima (176) prefectures, maintaining the pattern of earlier Japanese immigration to Hawaii, Canada, and the United States.[83] These 790 workers were then deposited at sugar plantations along the coast near Ancón, Chancay, Salaverry, Supe, Pacasmayo, Eten, and Cerro Azul. The largest single contingent of 226 immigrants began work at the British-owned Casablanca plantation, with which Augusto Leguía was associated.[84] From the very start of their arrival in Peru, that nation's first Japanese had to deal with the legacy of a plantation labor system that had depended almost exclusively on African slave or Chinese coolie labor before the arrival of the first contract laborers. Peruvian sugar planters were not prepared to deal with workers who demanded adherence to labor agreements and who readily sought the assistance of their home government to help them redress their grievances.

Suffering a similar fate as the Japanese contract laborers in Mexico, the initial group of contract laborers in Peru was devastated by malaria, typhoid, yellow fever, and dysentery. Violations of the terms of the original labor contracts also drove many of the contract laborers to flee the plantations. As many as 143 of the original 790 Japanese reportedly died during their first year in Peru from disease, the majority from malaria.[85] Language difficulties, misunderstandings over work assignments, and disagreements over the obligation to purchase supplies at plantation stores were the main points of contention between the immigrants and the sugar plantation managers. Conditions were particularly grim for Japanese laborers on the Hacienda San Nicolás on Peru's central coast during their first months in the cane fields. In late April 1899, the administrator of San Nicolás brought in ten soldiers from the subprefecture's garrison to intimidate the Japanese workers after they refused to work in protest against perceived violations of their contract terms. The administrator complained that the "lack of respect" and "insolence" demonstrated by the immigrants led him to call for military assistance in having his contract enforced. The attitudes of the immigrants struggling under similar circumstances on the Cayaltí hacienda were intensely angry. Their complaints were expressed in a memorandum by the Morioka Company's immigration agent in Peru, Teikichi Tanaka, who lamented the barriers to his attempt to settle the dispute at Cayaltí: "'The plantation is a country unto itself into which the national law does not enter; the owner a potentate; and punishment a matter of course. Even life and death are at the will of the plantation.'"[86]

Conditions at the Casablanca plantation on the Cañete plain near Lima were equally bad. Owned by the British Sugar Company and managed by Augusto Leguía, Casablanca housed the immigrant laborers in run-down sugar mills without any partitions. Within two months, only 30 of the original 226 Japanese workers were well enough to work after many fell ill with malaria. During the months of May and June 1899, 40 Japanese workers at Casablanca died. The remainder found it very difficult to buy enough food with their meager wages. Eventually, many of the original workers requested that the Morioka Company's agent arrange for their return to Japan.[87] When Tanaka did not accomplish this, Monzaburo Ishii, a contract laborer at Casablanca, wrote a letter to the governor of his home prefecture, Niigata. Writing on behalf of ninety-one of his fellow laborers at Casablanca, Ishii asked the governor for his help in returning home. Protesting that the Casablanca managers refused to pay the original contract rate of 25 yen per month and then forced the workers to do underpaid piecework, Ishii insisted, "'We cannot continue working under these circumstances.'"[88]

Within less than six months of their arrival in Peru, 321 Japanese contract laborers left their plantations and traveled to the port of Callao to await passage back to Japan. A lack of available shipping and the inability to pay for their return passage kept most of them in Peru. Most troubling of all, Peru's first Japanese immigrants were met with hostility and were the subject of physical attacks and of false and destructive rumors. Although the wages paid to Japanese contract laborers were often not what had been promised in the original contracts, they were higher than those paid to native Peruvian laborers, and this undoubtedly contributed to the climate of resentment against the first Japanese. These hard feelings provided fertile ground for the creation of distorted images of Japanese immigrants. One rumor circulated at the Hacienda San Nicolás held that the Morioka Company had actually brought 800 Japanese soldiers in the guise of agricultural laborers to Peru. Japan's recent defeat of China and the inclusion of some former soldiers among the ranks of Japan's new immigrants may have sparked this rumor. In another instance, contract workers who had abandoned their plantations and were living in temporary housing in Lima provided by the Morioka Company were attacked by *Limenos* in an incident marked by the stabbing of one Japanese immigrant.[89] On the other hand, the language barrier also led to incidents where Japanese workers, feeling they were being dishonored, attacked native laborers in retaliation. These violent incidents and rumors were harbingers of future violence and only the first of many such false reports over the course of the next forty years that would periodically raise tensions between the sojourners and native Peruvians to a high level.[90]

The Japanese government responded to these incidents of violence and mistreatment of contract laborers by sending Ryoji Noda, chancellor of the Japanese legation in Mexico, to Peru to investigate conditions among the immigrants. An effective negotiator who was fluent in Spanish, Noda was attached to the Honorary Japanese Consulate in Lima. He would go on to have a long career in the Japanese foreign service in Latin America, finishing his tenure in Brazil in 1935. After reviewing the distressing situation in Peru, Noda wrote to his home office in September 1900, concluding, "'If all the workers were sent home today, it would be beneficial not only for them but also for the [Morioka] Company.'"[91] Lack of funding and available shipping prevented Noda's recommendation from being realized, but his mere presence in Peru served to calm the immigrants' fears. Noda's skills as an intermediary probably assured the continuation of the Japanese contract labor system in Peru. By the end of 1900, the Morioka Company had replaced the ineffective Tanaka with a new administrator in Peru, and Noda had secured agreements to stabilize wages at approximately 20 yen per month.[92]

Largely due to Noda's efforts and despite the hardships and poor work record of the first contingent of Japanese immigrant laborers, Peruvian sugar planters remained convinced that Japanese immigrant labor was essential. A preference for foreign labor by Peruvian planters and the sizable initial investment by the Morioka Company largely explain the persistence of both parties. Working conditions for the small number of Japanese who remained under contract in Peru did improve. This was also very likely due to Noda's efforts and the Japanese government's insistence that the terms of the Immigrant Protection Ordinance be adhered to by the Peruvian government. Undoubtedly, little information regarding the unfortunate fate of the first Japanese contract workers reached Japan because of the poor communications between the two countries, so very likely it was not commonly known in Japan, which may have helped further recruiting efforts.

Recruiting in seven Japanese prefectures and having the greatest success in Fukuoka, Hiroshima, and Kumamoto, the Morioka Company succeeded in bringing the second group of 1,070 workers to Peru in July 1903. This contingent was unique in the early history of Japanese immigration to Peru in that it included 108 women, who were mainly the wives of male contract laborers, and 184 "free laborers." The small number of free laborers was a harbinger of future immigration trends in Peru after November 1923, when all contract labor would end. The immigrants of 1903 were still primarily destined for the sugarcane fields of haciendas such as Casablanca, Estrella, Tuman, San Jacinto, and El Agustino along Peru's central and south coast. More of the 1903 contingent than the 1899 group fulfilled their four-year contracts, largely because of improved working conditions and the greater social stability of this group made possible by the presence of the wives of nearly 20 percent of the laborers.[93] Still, labor conditions continued to be a very troublesome problem as Peruvian sugar planters began shifting from wage labor to the *tarea*, or piecework, system. Under the *tarea*, pay scales were differentiated by the nature of the work, with cane cutting and related work such as leaf cutting, ditch digging, and cultivation ranging from 45 to 70 sen (23 to 35 cents) per piece. Few Japanese laborers could complete more than one piece per day. With their food costing as much as 40 sen per day, many sojourners were unable to save or even subsist under the *tarea* system.[94] Thus, this system was strongly resisted by most immigrants even while it was increasingly favored by the sugar planters.

Substantial numbers of these early immigrants left the cane fields to work as laborers in Lima or to begin establishing small businesses. In some cases, this transition began quite modestly, as cane cutters first turned to tenant farming. On the Santa Barbara plantation on the Cañete plain, for example, a group of Japanese sugar workers established "a small community patterned after the village system in Japan."[95] The workers pooled a sum of approximately 500 yen ($250) to rent small plots of land and established offices in the village "for the general welfare" of the tenant farmers.[96] With the ownership of land not easily attainable, these former peasants did what the Chinese and their fellow compatriots did before them: they began totally new lives in urban settings as small business owners. For many, this was the only option open to them. Thus, most of Peru's first Issei migrated to the shops and cafés of the Lima-Callao metropolitan area to begin building more stable lives outside of agriculture.

Some of the most successful initial Japanese businesses were barbershops. The first Japanese-owned barbershop opened in Lima in April 1904, only nine months after the arrival of the second group of Japanese in Peru. By 1908, an additional thirty-four Japanese immigrants were cutting hair, not sugarcane, in their privately owned shops in Lima. Presaging the tendency of Japanese immigrants in Peru and elsewhere in Latin America to organize, these immigrant barbers formed the Japanese Barbers Association of Lima in 1907.

During the six years following the arrival of the second group in 1903, seven additional shiploads of Japanese totaling 4,330 immigrants arrived in Peru, to bring the total to 6,065 by October 1909. The Meiji Immigration Company administered the transportation and negotiation of contracts of 1,004 of these immigrants, the majority of whom planned to work in the forests near Tambopata, adjacent to the Bolivian border. Contracted to work for the Inca Rubber Company, only 100 of these workers were eventually employed as rubber gatherers, owing to competition from better-established Peruvian and Bolivia companies in the area. Consequently, when two shiploads carrying 754 immigrants organized by the Meiji Immigration Company arrived in Peru in 1908, these Japanese discovered to their despair that the Inca Rubber Company refused to offer them work. Eventually, they were scattered over seven different locations in coastal Peru. The Meiji Company was forced to suspend operations because of this serious violation of Japan's Immigrant Protection Ordinance.[97] Despite their bad fortune with the Inca Rubber Company, many of the original immigrant rubber gatherers in the Tambopata forests did quite well. During their two years working near Tambopata, they remitted 38,000 yen to their families in Japan. One of the rubber gatherers, Senryu Kinoshita, wrote to the Lima consulate in June 1907, reporting favorably on working conditions and claiming, "'The work is easier than in the coastal areas, we can relax and smoke at times.'" Kinoshita reported a substantial wage of 2 yen 50 sen per day, which was more than double the pay of Japanese sugar workers on the coastal plantations. The rubber worker's food costs were estimated at 70 sen per day, thus allowing them to acquire substantial savings and to send large remittances to their families. Moreover, these rubber workers frequently were allowed to plant their own garden plots, further reducing their food costs.[98]

The demise of the Meiji Immigration Company and the end of the rubber boom very likely explain why more Japanese did not choose to seek better wages in Peru's eastern rubber forests. Thus, the remainder of the 4,330 Japanese immigrants who were brought in by the Morioka Company through 1909 continued to be placed on sugar haciendas on the coast. The Morioka Company brought the first contingent of 36 immigrants from the Ryukyu Islands in November 1906 to work in the sugarcane fields on the haciendas at San Nicolás, Paramonga, Cañete, and Huachipa. Primarily from the main island of Okinawa, these Ryukyuans would become an increasingly larger component of Japanese immigration to Peru and the other South American nations over the course of the ensuing three decades. Migrating from the overpopulated Ryukyus and their insufficient arable land, these immigrants would constitute one-third of all Japanese in Peru by 1941. As will be discussed at greater length in chapter 3, these Ryukyuans, or Okinawans as they were commonly called (depending upon the time period and Japanese government policy) did not achieve full cultural acceptance by the Naichi-jin (mainland Japanese) in the immigrant community in Peru. The Ryukyuans, however, have always considered themselves culturally Japanese.[99]

Only 230, or less than 4 percent, of these first immigrants who arrived in Peru before 1909 were women, and all but 184 were contract laborers.[100] In sharp contrast to the early immigrant experience in Mexico, by 1909 approximately 80 percent of the original immigrants were still living in Peru.

Of the more than 6,000 immigrants to Peru during these years, 481 had died and 414 had returned to Japan. Only 242 had transmigrated to other Latin American countries, mainly to Bolivia, and a small number to Mexico. It seems clear that most of these original Japanese in Peru stayed in that country not out of choice but out of necessity. Wage scales were so low that they prevented most from saving a sufficient amount to return to Japan. As already noted, shipping was also generally not available. The Japanese commonly expressed their discontent with contract labor by migrating to the Lima-Callao and Arequipa urban centers. By 1910, nearly one in five Japanese immigrants in Peru were living in Lima-Callao. They were employed as barbers, restaurant operators, small traders, grocers, carpenters, waiters, masons, fishermen, and common laborers.[101]

Two of the most remarkable examples of success among this group of Issei pioneers were the careers of Shintaro Tominaga and Ikumatsu Okada. Tominaga was a carpenter who arrived among the first immigrants on the *Sakura-maru*. In 1903, with money saved from his contract labor work, Tominaga opened a small carpenter shop in Lima's La Victoria district directly on the newly opened railroad line to Chorrillos. Within six years, Tominaga built a furniture factory specializing in products manufactured from Chilean pine and Nicaraguan woods. With his growing profits, the carpenter/entrepreneur purchased a hectare of land on the recently constructed Iquitos Avenue in Lima, where he built a second factory in 1916 producing rubber products. Bolstered by high prices during World War I, Tominaga began manufacturing rubber tires in 1917, and within two years his factory was employing more than 100 persons. His personal fortune only twenty years after arriving in Peru was estimated to be more than 100,000 British pounds sterling.[102] By the early 1920s, Tominaga had diversified his business holdings even more by becoming involved in smelting and construction. His construction enterprise became so respected that he won the contract to build Peru's presidential palace. Working primarily with skilled Japanese carpenters and masons, the company completed the palace on time, and Tominaga received a letter of commendation from President Augusto Leguía, who had retained his long-term interest in Japanese immigrants. By the time of his death in a construction site accident in the late 1920s, Tominaga was one of the most respected members of the Japanese community in Peru.[103]

Ikumatsu Okada was one of the relatively few early immigrants to remain in agriculture. Soon after arriving in Peru in 1903, Okada, who quickly learned Spanish, rose from a contract laborer to become the administrator of a hacienda in the Huaral district, north of Lima. Working with other Japanese immigrants, he cleared new land for cotton cultivation, constructed or repaired new irrigation canals, and rebuilt the hacienda's main house. In 1912, he purchased the hacienda and became the largest Japanese landowner in Peru, only nine years after arriving in Callao to cut sugarcane. Okada would go on to become one of the leading cotton producers in the Chancay Valley, where cotton cultivation would be dominated by Japanese immigrants before World War II.[104]

With the exception of those Issei who prospered in cotton production in the Chancay, Rimac, and Pachacamac river valleys after the early 1920s, these first immigrants established a pattern of leaving agriculture for urban commerce that later Japanese immigrants to Peru would emulate. As we have seen, small groups of Japanese immigrants also transmigrated to Mexico and Bolivia, establishing a trend that would see later Japanese immigrants in Peru migrate to Paraguay and Argentina as well. Ultimately, Japanese immigration to these South American nations could not compare with the tens of thousands of their compatriots who immigrated to Brazil, beginning with the arrival of 781 sojourners from 168 households in 1908.

✿ ✿ ✿

Japanese immigration to Brazil differed from that to Spanish America in that it was heavily subsidized and accompanied by significant capital investment by both Brazilian and Japanese interests. These considerations, the demand for Japanese labor on the coffee plantations, and the availability of land for the creation of Japanese colonies in the states of São Paulo and Paraná largely explain the ultimate success of the Japanese immigration experiment in Brazil after 1908. In sum, with opportunities in North America closed to most Japanese, and with harsh working conditions and limited economic opportunities prevailing in Peru, Brazil offered the most hope for the Issei pioneers in Latin America. As discussed earlier, African slavery and subsidized European labor delayed the arrival of Brazil's first Japanese immigrants. Nevertheless, efforts to bring the Japanese to Brazil began as early as the mid-1890s.

A New Future in the Tropics: The Japanese Enter Brazil

The Prado Jordão Trading Company made the first attempt to bring Japanese to Brazil in 1894, but the lack of formal commercial relations between these two nations led to the failure of this venture. The Japanese government, however, remained actively interested in pursuing immigration to Brazil and soon assigned Tadashi Nemoto to further explore the possibility. Nemoto filed a very favorable report concluding that Brazil was a "'suitable place'" for Japanese immigrants and specifically praising the opportunities in São Paulo State: "'The state of São Paulo is the best place for the permanent residence of the immigrants. They can construct many towns in this vast land, increase their income, own property, educate their children, and live comfortably.'" Nemoto's enthusiastic support clearly helped Brazil and Japan conclude their first commercial treaty in Paris in 1895. Two years later, the Prado Jordão Trading Company and Japan's Toyo Imin Gaisha signed an agreement to transport 2,000 Japanese contract workers to São Paulo. A significant drop in coffee prices forced the cancellation of this agreement as the sojourners were assembling in the port of Kobe to board the transport ship *Tosa-maru* for Brazil.[105]

Over the course of the next decade, further attempts to initiate Japanese immigration were thwarted primarily by continually low coffee prices that averaged less than half the $2.84 per ten-kilogram bag paid on the world market in 1895.[106] Moreover, before 1905, Japanese diplomats, operating from their Brazilian legation established in 1897, advised against Japanese immigration, based on their perception of poor treatment of Italian immigrant labor in São Paulo State.[107] There were subsequent attempts by Brazilian landholders in the states of São Paulo and Paraná to sell large tracts of land for the purpose of establishing agricultural colonies, but these efforts were not successful. What finally stimulated more concerted efforts to bring Japanese immigrants to Brazil was the imminent curtailment of Japanese immigration to the United States and Canada, the economic depression that occurred in Japan after the Russo-Japanese War, and a coffee valorization agreement in Brazil that stabilized the price of that nation's main export crop. Thus, by 1905, discussions among the Brazilian president, São Paulo state government officials, and Fukashi Sugimura of the Japanese legation and the decision by the São Paulo government to allow the settlement of Russian immigrants on state-owned land created renewed interest in Japanese immigration.

Sugimura, the former director of the Bureau of Commerce in the Japanese Foreign Ministry, was very interested in promoting increased trade between Japan and Brazil. He was convinced that Japanese immigration and the establishment of regular shipping routes between the two countries would accomplish this objective.[108] Allowing his enthusiasm to cloud his judgment, Sugimura wrote optimistic and naive reports praising Brazil's lack of racial prejudice and the opportunities for Japanese immigrants to achieve immediate success in Brazil. Saburo Kumabe, a retired lawyer and judge from Hiroshima, was among twenty Issei pioneers who ventured to Brazil on their own before 1908. Captivated by Sugimura's reports on Brazil, Kumabe abandoned his profession and immigrated to São Paulo with his family and two other adventurers. Unable to make a living initially in agriculture, Kumabe and his family rolled cigarettes in their apartment in São Paulo City before raising enough money to buy a tract of wasteland near the town of Macae. Clearing the land with the help of local laborers, the Kumabe family eventually established a highly productive rice farm. Kumabe's hard work and persistence would presage the efforts of later Issei who would turn marginal lands into thriving agricultural holdings in São Paulo. Sadly, Kumabe also confronted the harsh reality of many immigrants to Brazil. He failed to secure firm title to his land and was eventually swindled out of his hard-earned efforts.[109] The lack of properly surveyed and registered land proved to be a consistent impediment to immigrant land purchases in Brazil and was clearly a factor in reducing overall immigration to Brazil in the early twentieth century.[110]

An agreement to finally initiate large-scale Japanese immigration to Brazil was reached on 6 November 1907, when Ryo Mizuno, president of the Toyo Imin Gaisha, and Brazilian president Jorge Tibirica signed a contract to bring 3,000 Japanese immigrants to São Paulo. These immigrants were to be "agriculturalists fit for farming" and were to consist of families of three to ten members each. They were to be paid on a piecework basis at a rate of 450 to 500 reis ($.25 to $.50) for every fifty liters of picked coffee beans and the equivalent of $1.09 to $1.37 per day for occasional labor.[111] The first shipload of immigrants was originally contracted to include 1,000 Japanese, but only 781, of whom 190 were females, were eventually signed on to the agreement. This first contingent traveled to Brazil aboard the *Kazatu-maru* in May 1908.

Before leaving the port of Kobe, these Brazilian-bound Japanese and Okinawan immigrants were addressed by a representative of the Japanese government, who warned them that they should "not disgrace Japan" and that if they did not succeed they should not return to Japan, even in death. Among the immigrants was a carpenter from Kumamoto who was naively convinced that he would return "with a suitcase full of money." Another young couple's expectations were equally unrealistic but typical of the sojourner mentality. They hoped to put away 10,000 yen for their return, upon which they planned to immediately visit the temple at Kyoto to pray with the man's mother.[112]

As noted earlier, the immigrants brought by the *Kazatu-maru* differed in a fundamental way from previous sojourners in the Western Hemisphere. Significant components of this contingent were families, not the single male laborers of past migrations to Hawaii, North America, and Peru. São Paulo's immigration officials were thus following the same practice with the Japanese as they had with the earlier Italian immigrants. Indeed, a family of ten was among the *Kazatu-maru* group, and many young couples actually married or arranged temporary liaisons in order to travel to Brazil to better their lives. The Brazilian government supplied a 100-yen subsidy for each adult immigrant, but the cost of passage to Brazil was 160 yen. Each family needed at least 300 to 400 yen to make the voyage, forcing many to sell some of their family's land or dwellings to raise the necessary funds. The labor contracts for the *Kazatu-maru* group obligated them to a minimum of six months' labor at the equivalent of more than 30 yen per month. In contrast, a police officer in Japan earned only 12 yen for the same period. The immigrants were hired to harvest coffee and to weed around the coffee trees on the six plantations in the Mojiana region of São Paulo State.

Nearly half of the first Japanese immigrants were Okinawans, reflecting the growing numbers of Ryukyu Islanders who were migrating to Latin America after 1905. Despite having the opportunity of being able to rent or purchase land upon the completion of their contracts, few of the initial sojourners intended to stay. "To work, earn, and return" was their primary goal, but this simple objective was denied them from the very beginning of their work on the plantations of São Paulo.[113] The immigrants immediately confronted the same problems that Japanese contract workers had faced when they arrived in Peru in 1899. Despite being employed by six of the most "reputable" plantations in São Paulo, they found that most of the plantation owners refused to pay the wages stated in the contract and also compelled them to purchase their food and supplies at inflated prices in the plantation stores.[114] The immigrants' situation was particularly bad on the Dumont plantation, the largest in São Paulo State. Japanese workers there complained bitterly that they could not earn more than half their anticipated pay, given the low crop yields and poor working conditions. Their housing was also deplorable; they were expected to sleep on straw fouled with cow dung. Eventually, all of the 210 immigrants assigned to the Dumont plantation deserted their contract.[115] Nearly all of the immigrants refused to tolerate the unhealthy working conditions and poor housing they were forced to endure on the plantations. Although the Italian government had cancelled its contract labor agreement with São Paulo's planters in 1902 because of their unfair treatment of Italian immigrant laborers, the planters still would not adjust to legitimate wage labor demands on their coffee lands, where their will remained the same as the law. Of the original 781 in the *Kazatu-maru* contingent, 400, mostly Okinawans, fled the plantations before their six-month contract was concluded. More than 200 of the immigrant refugees found work on other plantations offering better wages and working conditions. Others drifted to São Paulo City or to

Argentina, where 120 eventually settled. The most fortunate found work on two of the Northeast Railroad's construction sites at the port of Santos or as stevedores on the docks, where some were able to earn quite high wages.[116] Not all the blame for the failure of the *Kazatu-maru* enterprise can be laid at the feet of São Paulo's plantation owners. According to Junnosuke Kato, the interpreter on the Dumont plantation, fewer than 15 percent of the immigrants were farmers. He characterized the remainder as "'policemen, prison guards, school dropouts, small businessmen, fishermen, coal miners, railroad workers, school teachers, civil service employees, pettifoggers, itinerant performers, gamblers, sailors, barmaids, country *geishas,* and disguised prostitutes.'"[117]

If Kato's report reflects the highly pluralistic nature of Brazil's first contract immigrants, then it helps explain why their adjustment to the harsh and demanding conditions on the plantations proved so initially overwhelming. A letter written by an Okinawan immigrant to his father in December 1908 underscores the desperation of some of these first Brazilian Issei. After fleeing the Floresta plantation because the low yields of the coffee trees made it impossible to earn a decent daily wage, Kameichi Kakazu, his wife, and three cousins lived in the hills for a few weeks and were then forced to separate. Even when his wife found work as a maid in Itu and he began to pick coffee on another plantation, he appealed desperately to his father to "take care of his debt" for the shipping fare so he and his wife could return home. Kakazu complained bitterly to his father: "'Japanese immigrants in Brazil have all dispersed. Many women had to separate from their husbands. . . . It is unbelievably difficult to make a fortune in Brazil. Moreover the price of commodities is ridiculously high. We are in real trouble.'"[118]

The *Kazatu-maru* immigrants were thus victims of the same problems as the Enomoto Imin in Mexico and the sugar workers in Peru. They confronted their own unrealistic expectations, their lack of preparation for harsh working conditions, and their inability to deal with the often unscrupulous employment practices of plantation owners. Nearly all these early Issei were forced to strike out to survive on their own. Most did so with imagination and resolve, even in such nations as Chile and Bolivia, which saw very few Japanese arrive before 1908.

Only Chile, among the other Latin American nations, recorded any legal Japanese immigration before 1909. This analysis of the first Japanese immigration to Latin America will conclude with a discussion of the first Japanese settlers in Bolivia and the 126 Japanese who immigrated to Chile in 1903. An overview of general immigration trends in Argentina, Bolivia, and Paraguay will be presented in chapter 3, when substantive Japanese immigration to these nations is discussed.

Japanese Immigrants Enter the Andes, Bolivia, and Chile

Japanese immigration to Bolivia was primarily a post–World War II phenomenon. Only 202 legal Japanese immigrants entered Bolivia through 1941. Many more, of course, crossed the border from Peru, generally by way of Puerto Maldonado and Tambopata, to seek work in northeastern Bolivia. The first contingent of Japanese to arrive in Bolivia were refugees from Peru's sugar plantations. Ninety-one of the Japanese contracted by the Morioka Immigration Company eventually found other work as rubber gatherers in the lower Beni River region of eastern Bolivia in 1900.[119] Little is known of these 91 pioneers except that they reported much harsher working conditions than the rubber gatherers who labored in the Tambopata area after 1907. The Bolivian census of 1900 did list 79 Japanese residing in the nation. Most of these immigrants from Peru seem to have worked as rubber gatherers for two to three years, saved most of their earnings, and then moved to small villages in the immediate vicinity. Eventually, the majority of them married Bolivian women and settled in Riberalta, where Bolivia's first Japanese immigrant association, with 66 members, was established in 1915.[120] It is not surprising that the first immigrants soon abandoned rubber gathering. Bolivian rubber operations in this region were dominated since the early 1890s by the Suarez brothers' enterprise headquartered at Cachuela Esperanza, in the department of Santa Cruz. Reports of working conditions on the Suarez operations are instructive for determining the status of laborers in the industry. The Suarez brothers' workers were frequently bound by contracts that were no more than thinly veiled forms of debt peonage. One clause of the typical worker's contract stated, "'I pledge my person and my goods, those that I have now and those of which I may become possessed, renouncing domicile and all other privileges that the Law affords of my own free will.'"[121] This eastern frontier region, which had only been open to economic development in the late nineteenth century, was exceedingly remote. Consequently, reports of slavery and brutalization of rubber workers in the region could not be confirmed by formal investigations. Conflict between Brazil and Bolivia over the Acre region to the north, which was eventually settled in Brazil's favor in 1903, further complicated the regulation of conditions among Bolivian rubber workers.

The Japanese government's demand for close supervision of its immigrant laborers and the relatively high wages required by prospective Japanese rubber gatherers prevented contract labor from being introduced into the Beni region before the rubber boom collapsed during World War I.[122] A few hundred Japanese drifted independently into the region from Peru, finding work with the American Rubber Company, the Suarez brothers' enterprise, and four other Bolivian- and European-owned rubber companies.[123] As we shall see in chapter 4, with the demise of the rubber industry after 1915 there was no longer a need for substantial Japanese labor in Bolivia. Tin mining, the nation's major industry, was well supplied with Indian and mestizo labor. Japanese immigration would be insubstantial during the period 1908 to 1938, but the foundation of the Japanese community in Bolivia would still be established during these years.

The first Japanese in Chile were 126 immigrants hired to work in the mining industry in 1903. Approximately 20 additional Japanese drifted covertly across the border from Peru between 1900 and 1903. This small core represented the main group of Japanese to arrive in Chile before the 1980s. Some of these Japanese may have been attracted by economic opportunities associated with the 1906 Japanese-Chilean Exposition held in Santiago. The first Issei in Chile tended to be widely dispersed and generally worked for themselves as barbers, hatters, merchants, bakers, and cobblers. These were occupations requiring little overhead, previous experience, or knowledge of Spanish.[124] Among the 20 immigrants who transmigrated from Peru was Heisuke Senda, who became known as "the father of Japanese immigrants in Chile." Senda soon prospered after opening his own export-import business. With his own funds, Senda eventually financed the travel of 20 families "called" from his home prefecture of Ishikawa, thus earning his illustrious title among his fellow Japanese in Chile. Senda's efforts appear to be extraordinary, because by 1941, 519 Japanese had legally immigrated to Chile. Interviews conducted by James Tigner in the early 1950s with Chilean Issei point to a "lack of opportunities" for immigrants as the principal reason that the Japanese presence never became more substantial.[125]

The economics and culture of the agricultural and mining sectors explain why immigrant contract labor was never in great demand in Chile. Characterizing Chilean agriculture before World War I, Brian Loveman concludes, "Chilean agriculture, based upon the large haciendas, could not provide year-round employment to the growing number of rootless rural laborers."[126] Chilean *inquilinos,* or rural laborers, were service tenants who often were required to augment the labor force of the *hacendados,* particularly at harvest times. Without a flourishing plantation agriculture, such as sugar or coffee, Chilean agriculture retained its labor self-sufficiency based on the *inquilino* system until the agrarian reforms of the 1960s. There simply was never a need for Japanese or other immigrant labor so long as the poverty-ridden rural laborers existed. By 1907, only 1 percent of the Chilean rural labor force, 5 percent of its skilled tradesmen, and 3.8 percent of its industrial workers were foreign born.[127] The same situation prevailed in the mining industry that dominated Chile's twentieth-century economy. At times after 1890, Chile was actually exporting laborers to Argentina and Peru.

In a broader perspective, total Chilean immigration during the period 1889–1914, the era of world mass migrations, was only 55,572, by far the lowest of the Southern Cone nations. Given Chile's generally expanding economy after its victory in the War of the Pacific in 1883, these very low immigration totals require explanation. Carl Solberg argues that the native-born Chilean middle class particularly opposed immigration because it deeply resented the commercial success attained by the small number of European, Syrian, and Chinese immigrants before 1914. *La Lei* (The Law), a Chilean newspaper with a middle-class readership, proclaimed in a June 1907 editorial, "'Immigration, by snatching small commerce away from the natives, is taking from them one of the steps of the social ladder, thus interrupting the social climb anyone who wants to better his economic and social condition must take.'"[128] As was the case throughout the Americas, the small group of less than 2,000 Chinese who operated 456 businesses in the nitrate provinces of Tarapacá and Antofagasta were characterized in racist terms as "'pirates, who gain all they possess through robbery.'"[129] The middle-class Radical Party in the early twentieth century employed the immigration issue in nationalist terms, and similar political parties throughout the Americas after World War I tried to transform anti-immigrant attitudes into one component of militant patriotism. Middle-class opposition, however, does not completely explain the lack of substantive immigration to Chile. Labor conditions in mining, Chile's leading source of revenues, were also critical.

Nitrate mining in Chile's northern territories employed as many as 40,000 workers through 1908 and would continue a general trend of expansion until a disastrous decline during the Great Depression of the 1930s. But major declines in world prices on seven occasions between 1896 and 1930 threw thousands of nitrate workers out of their jobs and made the labor picture uncertain. The Chilean copper industry was heavily mechanized by such U.S. companies as American Smelting, Kennecott, and Braden during the first decades of the twentieth century. The industry never required a large immigrant labor force, as was the case in the early years of the mining industry in the western United States. Chilean miners, despite violent government repression, formed some of the most militant labor unions in Latin America prior to World War II. This militancy created another additional impediment to manning the mines with immigrant labor.

The first Japanese immigrants to Chile, like their counterparts in Mexico,

Peru, Brazil, and Bolivia, arrived after earlier immigrants had begun to significantly reconfigure the landholding patterns, labor forces, and commercial sectors of Latin American nations. Since most Japanese originally saw themselves as sojourners, it is understandable, given the harsh conditions of contract labor, that most immigrants soon abandoned the plantations and the mines for more independent and profitable lives in urban commerce. Some Japanese immigrants, however, following the pattern of the Italian colonists in Brazil, would begin acquiring marginal or cheaply priced frontier lands. Most of all, the first Japanese immigrants mirrored their predecessors in Hawaii, Canada, and the United States. When it became clear that many could not soon return to their home villages with their hard-earned savings to begin a better life in Japan, they began to establish the schools, fraternal groups, and economic associations that would enhance cultural solidarity in the new nations that most would not soon accept as their permanent homelands. Over the course of the next thirty years, the majority of Japan's immigrants would go to Latin America, where they would build the cultural and economic foundations for permanent settlement.

ISSEI AND NISEI IN MEXICO, PERU, AND BRAZIL, 1908–37

In time, I came to see that the Japanese in Peru shared unique attitudes that could not be found in Japan. I was deeply impressed with the strong bond that linked the immigrants—they interacted with a closeness and intimacy that was even stronger than brothers and sisters in Japan.

—Seiichi Higashide, a Japanese Peruvian from Hokkaido, 1993

Immigrants to Settlers

Within a generation of their arrival in Latin America, the Issei successfully made the transition from sojourners to settlers. Driven from the plantations and mines of Latin America by harsh conditions and poor wages, very few Issei saved the hypothetical 960 yen ($480) that would enable them to return to Japan dressed in "golden brocade," as they had naively dreamed when they left their homeland.[1] Forced to forfeit their dreams of a triumphant return to Japan, the Issei adjusted to their new homelands. They were aided by their strong work ethic, fertile imaginations, and solidarity with their immigrant compatriots. This was the era when the Japanese Latin American family was created. Predominantly male, the majority of the first Issei who arrived before 1908 chose not to intermarry with the native population. Instead, they married "picture brides" from Japan or younger Nisei women. Indeed, with the nearly universal failure of contract immigration before 1920, this became the era of the Yobiyose, or "called" immigrant. Joining the "picture brides" were the relatives and friends of the pioneer Issei who journeyed to Latin America before World War I. Most importantly, the first Japanese immigrants created, in the words of one prominent Peruvian Issei, the "organically constituted" immigrant communal group. As they did in North America, the Issei of Latin America formed Japanese "nations within nations." Communal solidarity made life far easier for the Japanese immigrants trying to create new lives in Latin America. But on the other hand, the exclusivity of their communities clearly worsened anti-Japanese sentiments throughout the region. With the rise of Japanese militarism, the immigrant communities became increasingly vulnerable to intimidation and violence. Still, Japan's rapid rise to dominance in Asia fostered fierce pride among the immigrant communities in Latin America that in some cases reached fanatical proportions both during and after World War II. Pride in their homeland, which often surpassed their feelings for their new homes in Latin America, served to impede their cultural adaptation. Moreover, increasing threats to the security of the Japanese communities after 1930 further reinforced cultural solidarity during the years immediately prior to World War II.

Throughout the three decades following 1908, Japanese either transmigrated or immigrated directly to twelve Latin American nations. In addition to Mexico, Peru, and Brazil, which continued to be the main receiver nations, more than 5,000 Japanese immigrated to Argentina. Small communities of less than 700 immigrants were created in Cuba, Colombia, and Panama. The Japanese populations of Chile and Bolivia received only a few hundred new immigrants directly from Japan but also benefited from transmigration from Peru and Brazil. The first Japanese community in Paraguay was established with 150 immigrants at the pilot colony of La Colmena, southeast of Asunción, in 1936. A handful of independent-minded immigrants ventured to Uruguay and Venezuela, where no Japanese sojourners had previously immigrated.[2]

Most of the immigrants maintained the Dekasegi (temporary immigrant) mentality, hoping to return to Japan after their stay in Latin America. The reality was quite different. Repatriation rates are most reliably known for the Japanese Brazilians during the period 1908–33, and they are quite revealing. More than 93 percent of Japanese immigrants to Brazil during this era did not return to Japan. This extremely high rate of permanent settlement contrasts with that for immigrants from Spain (51.05 percent), Germany (24.49 percent), Portugal (42.0 percent), Turkey (53.22 percent), and Italy (12.82 percent).[3] The reasons for this high retention rate are complex and will be discussed in greater detail later in this chapter. It appears that Japanese repatriation was also quite low in the rest of Latin America as well. If Japanese immigrants were unhappy with their initial situation, they usually migrated to urban areas, transmigrated to another Latin American nation, or, in rare instances, illegally entered the United States or Canada.

Looking at Japanese immigration during this era from a broader perspective, it is useful to note that more Japanese immigrated to Latin America than to any other region of the world, and during the so-called Brazilian immigration (1909–31), more of them immigrated to that nation than to any other. Only with the Japanese military occupation of Manchuria in 1931 and the restrictive immigration law of 1934 did Japanese immigrants shift the direction of their hopes to Asia rather than Latin America. More than one of every five immigrants were attracted to the newly established *colonias* and other economic opportunities in the states of São Paulo and Paraná in Brazil. Nearly 4 percent of all Japanese immigrants, impressed by the success of the Peruvian Issei in urban commerce and cotton agriculture, entered the Japanese communities in that Andean nation. This pattern, of course, was determined by the further restriction of Japanese immigration to the United States and Canada during the early 1920s. Immigration that would have clearly gone to North America thereafter was diverted either to Latin America, Southeast Asia, or Manchuria.[4]

Social and Economic Conditions in Japan

The era from the initiation of the Gentlemen's Agreement in 1907–8 to the outbreak of the Sino-Japanese War in 1937 saw more Japanese immigrate than in any other similar period in Japan's history. Yet the total of nearly 475,000 immigrants, when viewed against the total population of Japan, was far less than the great European migrations to the Western Hemisphere from 1870 to 1914. The Japanese immigrants could not compare in numbers with their counterparts from Great Britain, Ireland, Italy, Portugal, or Spain who immigrated to the Western Hemisphere.[5] Still a traditional society in many ways as late as the 1930s, Japanese culture exerted a powerful hold on its people, making it very difficult for them to leave their homeland. Commenting on the strength of tradition near the end of the Meiji era, Kakuzo Okakura concluded that Japan had become "accustomed to accepting the new without sacrificing the old. . . . the adoption of western methods has not so greatly affected the national life as is generally supposed. One who looks beneath the surface of things can see, in spite of her modern garb, that the Heart of Old Japan is still beating strongly."[6] Another careful observer as late as 1940 saw traditional Japan reflected in the endurance of "'the ideal of feudal loyalty, the patriarchal system, the attitude towards women, [and] the exaltation of martial values.'"[7] These traditional values remained more firmly rooted in the countryside, and the majority of the population remained on the land until World War II.

After the death of the Emperor Meiji in 1912, the next three decades witnessed the continuing economic and political modernization of the nation. But the Japanese people also endured sharply increased militarism. Moreover, these changes occurred without a substantive improvement in the standard of living of most Japanese. The rural population and the emerging labor sector never truly benefited from Japanese economic growth before 1937. Most Japanese did not eat much better nor did their life expectancy improve. As late as 1930, nearly one in every five Japanese families was earning less than 200 yen ($100) per year. Industrial workers' wages did increase significantly, but much of this increase was counteracted by inflation that proved to be a continuing problem before the Great Depression. For example, the most widespread rioting in modern Japanese history occurred during the summer of 1918 following a sharp rise in the price of rice, a result of the inflation induced by World War I. More than 700,000 desperate Japanese rioted for fifty-five days in protest in hundreds of municipalities throughout Japan.[8] Increases in the price of rice affected urban dwellers very hard, but those in agriculture fared even worse. In 1917, more than half of all cultivated land in Japan was under tenancy. These renters, many of whom had formerly owned the fields in which they now toiled, paid an average of between 51 and 55 percent of their crop in rent.[9] Natural disasters, such as the terribly destructive Kanto earthquake of 1923, intensified these problems and stimulated large-scale immigration.

Labor began to organize during these years but never unionized more than 8 percent of the workforce.[10] Still, the increasing discontent of Japanese workers was reflected in the increase in strikes even before the Depression. During the period 1925–30, for example, the number of strikes rose from 270 to 760. Even more significant was the duration of these strikes. In 1930, 937,312 labor days were lost through strikes, in contrast to only 2,108 days five years earlier.[11] Japanese workers were unquestionably becoming more militant in the face of difficult economic conditions. At the same time, significant material benefits were still not being obtained. Criminal activity also increased sharply during the late 1920s, perhaps in response to economic hardship and the urbanization of Japanese society. The government, in response to popular pressure, did institute universal male suffrage in March 1925, giving the vote to men over the age of twenty-five who were not impoverished.[12] In the view of Harry D. Smith, however, these democratic reforms did not lead to democracy. Smith argues that the rapid pace of change involving modern economic development, higher levels of education, and, particularly, rising economic expectations "was often unsettling, even terrifying."[13] This anxiety, when coupled with the economic fears prompted by the Great Depression, provided a climate for the nationalism and militaristic antiliberalism of the 1930s.

✿ ✿ ✿

The reasons for the rise of Japanese militarism in the 1930s that so adversely affected the lives of Japanese immigrants in Latin America are still being debated. It is certainly not possible to address the roots of militarism at length in this study. Nevertheless, it is useful to present some recent interpretations to place post-1930 Japanese domestic affairs in a proper perspective. Junichiro Kisaka is convinced that the policies of "Rich Country, Strong Military" and "Increase Production, Promote Industry" that were consistently maintained between the two world wars suppressed the domestic market by keeping the workers and rural population in poverty.[14] Overseas economic expansion either by military means or by immigration thus became imperative if economic growth were to continue. The bureaucratic foundations of nationalism and militarism, according to Richard J. Smethurst, were created during the Meiji era with the formation of the Home, Education, and Army ministries. Traditional Japanese values were used by these agencies to define modern nationalism. Smethurst cites the military reforms of Major General Tanaka Giichi during the early Taisho era (1912–26) as fundamentally important in imbuing a military consciousness based on the "natural community" of the Japanese rural hamlet. Military reservists in these hamlets built the positive image of the military by such activities as harvesting the rice of active-duty servicemen's families, serving as volunteer firemen, and leading the community's youth activities, all while wearing the reservists' uniform. The military, in essence, sought to create "national villagers" or "hamlet soldiers" who retained the qualities of decorum, courage, and loyalty to the emperor and superiors.[15] These activities would certainly have been welcomed in the countryside, where the rural population faced a constant struggle for survival. What also must be kept in mind is that the Japanese army's occupation of Manchuria after 1931 created new opportunities for immigration at the very time that the Latin American nations were beginning to close their doors to Japanese immigrants.

This discussion is intended to provide an overview of the domestic conditions during Japan's most active period of immigration. Still, the decision to immigrate was often based upon a myriad of individual circumstances and aspirations. It will be helpful to discuss the experiences of the immigrants themselves to understand why they made the difficult decision to leave Japan for a very uncertain future.

Profiles of the Issei

Speaking in 1917 to a group of young Japanese women who had just completed a course in "Emigration Training" at an immigrant center in Yokohama and were about to embark for Hawaii and the Americas, their woman instructor offered this advice: "'You are going far away from home. You are going where everything will be strange to you. You must dress and act like the people around you so that they will not dislike you. If you are in trouble or in any difficulty, go to the nearest Japanese association. They will help you. Above all, do nothing to make Japan ashamed that she sent you to represent her.'"[16] Such was the dilemma of the Japanese immigrants; their government asked them to try and assimilate as much as possible to reduce the climate of racial prejudice, but in order to deal with their strange new environment, they were told to rely upon their associations and ethnic solidarity as a source of strength and security.

Toshio Katagiri wept when the ship carrying him to a new life in Mexico passed the last lighthouse on the Boso Peninsula, near the port of Yokohama, in March 1927. He feared that he "'might not set foot on Japanese soil again.'"[17] Only thirteen years and nine months old when he left Japan, Katagiri was from the village of Nanakubo in Nagano Prefecture, where his family struggled to survive by farming and silk raising. The sixth of eight children and the fourth son, this young Issei dreamed of emigrating from a very young age. Shortly after the Russo-Japanese War, one of Katagiri's uncles went to Mexico as a contract worker on a sugar plantation in the state of Sinaloa, only to die soon after from malaria. His uncle's fate did not discourage two other relatives from leaving for Mexico soon thereafter to work in a mine in the state of Sonora. Moving to Mexicali during the revolution, Katagiri's relatives began to prosper in cotton farming, and soon his sister left for Mexico to marry her cousin. Recalling his decision to leave Japan, Katagiri stressed the significance of the declining state of the silk industry and his lack of a prospect for a meaningful inheritance. The young immigrant at first wanted to travel to Brazil or Cuba, but his father insisted that he join his sister in Mexico and offered to pay his passage. Once in Mexico, he worked for thirty-six months in his sister and brother-in-law's soda pop factory, washing bottles for fourteen hours a day. After working for a short time as a laborer on a cotton plantation, Katagiri, still only nineteen, became an independent farmer raising the same crop.[18] The pattern of chain migration, relatively common in Japanese immigration to Latin America, is clear in these case studies.

Seiichi Higashide, the author of a compelling autobiography about his early life in Hokkaido and later as an immigrant to Peru, recalled that he felt that Japan held no promise for him. After moving to Tokyo and struggling to acquire an education to fulfill his life's dream to become an architect, Higashide decided to leave Japan. Explaining his decision in his autobiography, Higashide recalled: "After some time in Tokyo, I started dreaming of going abroad. I considered my prospects—even if I did become an outstanding architect, Japan did not hold great promise for my future. Without a single hopeful path for me, I could not endure the wretchedness of having to grope about in the darkness and uncertainty of those times in Japan. . . . I was physically and mentally exhausted by my hardships, to which I saw no end. . . . I began to pursue a dream of escaping from Japan."[19]

Higashide immigrated to Peru in April 1930. He began a new life in Peru because he had the impression that, "Aside from the United States, Peru had the next largest number of Japanese immigrants who had found success."[20] Twenty-one years old when he left Japan, Higashide was especially impressed with Shintaro Tominaga's "success story" in Peru.[21] Such accounts of fortunate immigrants in Latin America were published widely in Japan.[22] Higashide seems to represent well the restless generation of young Issei who immigrated to Latin America following the Meiji era. The grandson of a prominent village leader from Ishikawa Prefecture who was bankrupted and disgraced, he was determined not to live the burdened life of his well-educated father, who was forced to start a new life in Hokkaido after the family's financial collapse.

Many Japanese immigrants to Latin America were influenced by the published letters of Issei who had previously settled in the region. These accounts frequently were quite favorable and were used by immigration companies to recruit future clients. Nevertheless, stories such as that of Hiroshi Kato of Fukushima Prefecture, who migrated to a coffee plantation owned by an Issei in São Paulo State in Brazil, are instructive. Arriving in December 1932 in the midst of political unrest in São Paulo, Kato reported no troublesome incidents in the interior, where his coffee plantation was located. The young man claimed he was proud to be helping establish the Japanese culture in Brazil, but he also expressed relief that he had left behind the "'fidgety'" and "'meticulous'" life in "'small Japan.'" Kato claimed that the Japanese government fully subsidized his passage to Brazil and that Japanese immigrants on his colony had "'total control over everything.'" He finished his letter with the endorsement that "'those who are healthy, hard working and tolerant, should think about coming to Brazil.'"[23] A number of these letters of Japanese immigrants in Brazil expressed regret that they could not immigrate to the United States or Canada, where some of their relatives or fellow villagers had previously settled. Hiroshi and Taketaro Endo of Oka-yama Prefecture, who arrived in São Paulo in January 1932, lamented, "'We are refused by the U.S. and Canada, [and] Brazil with its vast undeveloped land and small population, is the best and only direction we Japanese can take.'"[24]

The Japanese monthly magazine *Chou Koron* (Public Discussion) as early as 1917 resorted to hyperbole to convince potential immigrants to direct their attention to Portuguese America. "'Brazil is an enormous country, 21 times bigger than Japan and can accommodate hundreds of millions more inhabitants than now,'" Marquis Okuma proclaimed in *Chou Koron*. Okuma elaborated even more enthusiastically: "'I am in favor of South America where the Japanese are welcomed, where the soil is rich, and where many of the customs of the people resemble ours. There is plenty of room for millions of Japanese in this part of the world.'"[25]

These anecdotal reports can be framed in the context of one careful study conducted in Wakayama Prefecture in 1937. Based on interviews with those Wakayama residents who were preparing to emigrate or who had repatri-ated from overseas, "stability of life after retirement" (in Japan) and "ob-taining a fortune at once" were the two most prevalent reasons given for leaving their homeland for Latin America. Of least importance to this study group was the "attraction of foreign countries." The Japanese wanted to emigrate and to return. The reality was that few would ever make their home again in Japan.[26]

Establishing Roots in Mexico

With its vast tracts of uninhabited and marginal land in the north and west, Mexico should have been an ideal home for Japanese immigrants whose skills in intensive agriculture had already been proven in the United States and Canada. The success of Japanese cotton farmers in the arid fields of Baja California Norte after 1925 offers additional evidence of Mexico's poten-tial. The number of Japanese in Mexico was limited, however, to less than 2,500 by 1937 for several reasons: Washington's pressure on the Mexican government to restrict Japanese immigration; the Mexican Revolution, which saw more than 1 million Mexicans die between 1910 and 1920; and further limits on immigration during the early years of the Great Depres-sion. Still, the relatively few Japanese immigrants who settled in Mexico during this era generally succeeded in establishing meaningful and produc-tive lives at a time of great turmoil in Mexico's modern history.

The Gentlemen's Agreement of 1907–8 was accompanied by a proclamation by President Theodore Roosevelt that refused entry to Japanese or Korean laborers, with or without skills, who were originally issued passports to Hawaii, Canada, or Mexico. After the onset of the Mexican Revolution in 1910, significant numbers of Japanese immigrants sought refuge in the United States. Strengthened by President William Howard Taft's proclamation in 1913 mandating the cooperation of the departments of Commerce and Labor in the enforcement of existing immigration laws, legal Japanese transmigration to the United States from Mexico effectively ended.[27] The passage of the highly restrictive alien land laws in California and other western states after World War I actually encouraged some Issei in the United States to seek better opportunities in Mexico. This would occur, however, only after the worst violence and disorder of the Mexican Revolution came to an end after a decade of tumult in 1920.

Of the more than 2,400 Japanese immigrants in Mexico at the beginning of the revolution in November 1910, the vast majority were highly mobile, unmarried male laborers working in the mines and fields of the Mexican states of Sonora and Coahuila. Their numbers declined by more than 10 percent during the course of the revolution, as mines were closed, haciendas were looted and burned, and foreign investors fled Mexico, further reducing the opportunities for employment for the often rootless Issei. For the few Issei who had managed to become landholders, life was very precarious. For instance, one Japanese farmer had his building set afire four times and was nearly hanged by marauding soldiers when he tried to prevent them from confiscating his cattle.[28] Because they were denied even temporary admittance to the United States, even with the status of refugees fleeing the violence of the revolution, northern Mexico's itinerant Issei suffered inordinately during the worst years of the violence. Some Japanese were even killed by mistake when Mexican revolutionaries confused them with the even more hated Chinese. Nevertheless, the Japanese were not specifically targeted for persecution by the revolutionaries as were the Sonoran Chinese. This seems to be explained by the low profile of Japanese immigrant laborers who had not yet entered the retail trades that produced such tension between native Mexican consumers and the highly efficient, small-scale Chinese shopkeepers.

As might be expected, Japanese immigrants also served as soldiers in the federal or revolutionary armies. Often enlisting because they had no other means of survival, Issei soldiers in Coahuila reportedly numbered nearly 20 percent of the state's Japanese population. The Japanese were welcomed into the armies of the revolution in some measure because of the favorable reputation gained by the Japanese military in the Russo-Japanese war. Some Issei were given the immediate rank of second lieutenant, with attractive pay scales. For example, Antonio K. Yamani, an Issei from Nuevo León, entered the army of the Constitutionalist forces of Venustiano Carranza and served as a captain in the Fifth Battalion of the First Division. It seems likely that some of the Japanese who were brought into the Mexican military were Japanese army veterans, but evidence of this is lacking. Ultimately, some Japanese rose to the rank of field-grade officers in the revolution, as battlefield promotions became commonplace when the fighting grew intense.[29]

The suffering of the dislocated Issei in Sonora and Coahuila finally brought the response of the Japanese government in 1914, when Tokyo sent Shotuko Baba, the secretary of the Japanese consulate in Chicago to northern Mexico to look after its nationals. Failing to gain temporary access to U.S. border towns for Issei refugees to escape the violence, Baba used his Spanish language skills to negotiate labor contracts for Japanese from Sonora and Coahuila to work on American-owned cotton plantations in Baja California. Originally working on plantations near the town of Calexico, Japanese laborers thrived in the relatively peaceful Baja. Working for wages of a dollar a day during the World War I cotton boom, Japanese immigrants soon sent for friends, relatives, and wives, and within a decade, Baja California Norte became the site of the largest and most cohesive Japanese colony in Mexico before World War II. Mirroring the success of Peruvian Issei in opening up new cotton lands in Huaraz, the Mexican Issei of Baja California would eventually dominate cotton agriculture in the region. Additionally, Issei who hired on as laborers on the few fishing boats operating out of Ensenada in Baja soon became the leaders of the burgeoning fishing industry in the region.[30]

With the rise to power in 1920 of the shrewd pragmatist of the Mexican Revolution, General Alvaro Obregón, Mexico began to rebuild after the violent decade, and the Japanese began the only decade of Yobiyose immigration in its history. As the Issei began to establish roots, primarily as small business owners, retail managers, and small farmers in the Baja, the Japanese immigrant family began to emerge. But except for Baja California Norte, where most of the Yobiyose immigration appears to have occurred, the first Japanese immigrants in Mexico intermarried with native Mexicans at a rate unprecedented in the rest of Latin America, the United States, or Canada. With the notable exception of Baja California Norte, this phenomenon is largely explained by the dispersed nature of the Issei throughout northern Mexico and by the low rate of new immigrant arrivals during the 1920s.

New Japanese arrivals averaged only slightly less than 200 per year during the 1920s, reaching a peak of 434 in 1930.[31] Despite the arrival of 350 Japanese female immigrants during the 1920s, male Issei in Mexico outnumbered their female counterparts by a four-to-one ratio at the end of the decade. In the midst of the Depression in 1932, the Mexican government prohibited the entry of foreign common laborers but welcomed those with special skills. This applied to the vast majority of Yobiyose immigrants. With this ban in effect, less than 300 Japanese immigrants were admitted to Mexico in the next five years, effectively ending Japanese immigration to Mexico until after World War II. These demographics virtually assured the Japanese immigrant community in Mexico could not resist assimilation, as nearly all other Japanese communities throughout Latin America were able to do before World War II.

A marriage survey conducted by a Japanese Mexican community newspaper in 1935 offers revealing evidence of the level of racial assimilation of the Issei in Mexico. Surveying 1,152 Japanese men, the newspaper reported that 265 claimed to have Japanese wives, while 354 were married to Mexican women. While nearly half of those surveyed claimed to be single, many of these were assumed to have married Mexican women but were unwilling to admit it because of the strong cultural preference for endogamy among the Japanese.[32] As noted by Yasutaro Taki and Chizuko Watanabe, the predominance of mixed marriages among Mexico's Issei ensured that the Nisei generation would be quite small and largely limited to the Japanese colony in Baja California Norte. Watanabe concluded: "The offspring of mixed [Japanese and Mexican] parentage tended to be Mexican culturally and were likely to marry Mexicans when grown up. When their Japanese progenitors died, they would have little chance to maintain ties with the Japanese community. . . . Mexicanization of the Japanese was well underway with the *Nisei*, the born citizens of Mexico."[33]

✿ ✿ ✿

The Japanese community in Baja California Norte was the largest and most cohesive group of Issei in Mexico before World War II. By the early 1930s, nearly twice as many Japanese were residing in Baja California Norte as in the states with the next largest concentrations of Issei, Sonora and metropolitan Mexico City. The more than 700 Japanese immigrants in the region were closely linked to the Japanese community in the Imperial Valley of California. Indeed, some of California's Issei lacking landholding rights in the United States maintained agricultural interests in Baja California. Working primarily as tenant farmers on the cotton lands leased to them by the American-owned Colorado River Company and the Jabonera del Pacifico, these Issei farmed two-thirds of the cotton lands in the immediate vicinity of Mexicali at the peak of cotton production in 1936. The scale of Japanese immigrant cotton production in the area was impressive. Japanese farmers cultivated nearly 18,000 acres of cotton fields for a total annual production of $450,000 in the mid-1930s.[34]

By the mid-1930s, Mexicali became virtually a Japanese enclave in Baja California Norte. More than 300 Japanese families lived in the immediate vicinity of Mexicali, accounting for an estimated 80 percent of the population of the area. The Issei in Mexicali operated restaurants, specialty stores, barbershops, and even brothels. Japanese was the primary language of the Issei in Mexicali, unlike in many other areas of Mexico. According to Taki, the Issei in the Mexicali region tended to avoid most contact with the Mexican population, and only a about a dozen were married to Mexican women. Taki concluded that the Mexicali Issei "formed an exclusive homogeneous ethnic community, with many of the characteristics of the traditional Japanese rural community."[35] But this pioneering venture would be of short duration. Acting on the Agrarian Reform Law of 4 April 1934, the reformist president Lázaro Cárdenas ordered the expropriation of most of the American-owned cotton lands. Mexican peasants were given primary rights to the cotton lands previously cultivated by the Issei. Many of the Japanese were compelled to begin new lives by clearing new lands or starting new businesses in other areas of Baja California Norte. Just as they were beginning to recover from the dislocation of the Cárdenas reforms, they confronted the even greater challenge of World War II relocation.[36]

Beyond the relatively familiar cultural confines of the homogeneous Japanese community of Baja California Norte, the Japanese in Mexico by the mid-1930s were establishing the same occupational patterns as their counterparts in the rest of Latin America. Overwhelmingly contract or temporary laborers when they first arrived in Mexico, the Issei by 1935 had moved on to find work in a variety of occupations. A survey of 937 Japanese family heads found that more than 25 percent of the group operated their own grocery stores, 10 percent were farmers, and more than 5 percent had established practices as pharmacists, dentists, or medical doctors. Significant numbers of this group appeared to be succeeding financially as barbers, carpenters/plasterers, drivers, ice cream vendors, and independent fishermen. Only 67 continued to work as wage laborers. The small core of medical practitioners would provide the occupational foundation for many more Japanese immigrants to enter the medical professions in Mexico during the ensuing decades. Thus, the pattern of rapid upward economic and social mobility so characteristic of the Japanese immigrants in the United States and Canada was being emulated by the Issei in Mexico, despite the relatively culturally amorphous nature of their community outside of Baja California Norte.[37] As elsewhere in North America, the success of a few Japanese immigrants was remarkable, given the cultural barriers they were forced to overcome.

Shin Tsuji, an Issei who settled in Tapatula in the southern state of Chiapas, began importing Japanese silk products and within a few years had opened department stores in Tapatula, in the city of Torreón, and in the large Mexican cities of Monterrey and Mexico City. Known as the "great merchant," Tsuji was joined in his great commercial success by, among others, Yuzabro Minakata of Guadalajara, who made a fortune in furniture sales and soap manufacturing; Sanshiro Matsumoto, who arrived in Mexico in 1910 as a gardener for the presidential palace and subsequently operated ten large nurseries throughout Mexico City; Arthur K. Ota, who transmigrated to Baja California Norte from the United States and became one of the most successful truck gardeners in the region; and Morita Takeshi, a highly successful independent fisherman in Ensenada before World War II, who, after being relocated during World War II to Mexico City, opened a paper factory in the Federal District.[38]

The overall success of Mexico's small Japanese immigrant community must be measured against the difficult challenges they faced in Depression-era Mexico. Still troubled by continuing episodes of violence and political instability until Lázaro Cárdenas was able to consolidate his corporatist state in the late 1930s, Mexico was further burdened with the repatriation of 400,000 Mexican and U.S. citizens of Mexican heritage between 1929 and 1937. They were deported from the United States, often without legal due process, in order to reduce the cost of relief there, and this repatriation program made the nation's labor sector far more competitive.[39] Most Japanese immigrants prospered by transcending wage labor to become self-employed in a wide array of economic endeavors. Their self-sufficiency and work ethic helped them weather the severe economic crisis of 1937 in Mexico. Nevertheless, the Japanese of Mexico did not confront the growing world military crisis after 1937 as a culturally unified community, as they did in the United States and most other Latin American nations. Rather, the children of many Mexican Issei who had married native Mexicans became quickly assimilated culturally and ethnically. The same process would not occur among other Japanese communities in Latin America until the Sansei or Yonsei, third or fourth generations.

From *Haciendas* to *Tiendas* in Peru

In contrast to Mexico's Japanese, Peru's sojourners were able to build a stable and homogeneous immigrant community even while anti-Japanese sentiment grew steadily stronger during the three decades after 1908. Unlike violent and unstable Mexico prior to the 1930s, Peru remained politically and economically stable until the Great Depression prompted the emergence of mass politics and economic hardship. This era was dominated by the long dictatorship of Augusto B. Leguía (1919–30). As we have seen, Leguía was one of the principal sponsors of Peru's first Issei plantation laborers, and his presidency witnessed the entry of slightly more than 1,000 immigrants per year. Despite the increasing attractiveness of Brazil for Japanese during this era, 29,455 sojourners chose instead to seek new opportunities in Peru. A majority of the immigrants were from the Ryukyu Islands, thus establishing an ethnically dualistic character to the Japanese immigrant community in Peru. Okinawans and the Naichi-jin (mainland Japanese) as groups tended to keep apart when possible in Peru. This did not seriously fragment the larger Japanese community. Still, Tigner notes in his comprehensive 1956 study, "Nowhere else in Latin America was the division between Okinawans and the *Naichi-jin* as pronounced as it was in Peru."[40] As will be discussed, there was considerable out-migration to Japan and other South American countries during the Depression, but the core of what today is Latin America's second largest Japanese community was established by hardworking Issei and Nisei in Peru before 1938.[41] The very success of the Japanese community before 1930, however, made the sojourners targets and often pawns in the intense struggles of the populist politics of the 1930s.

By the second decade of the twentieth century, the trend of Japanese immigrants leaving plantation agriculture for opportunities in urban commerce was becoming well established. Nevertheless, there were notable exceptions to this phenomenon, particularly in the production of Peru's most successful export crop, cotton. Changes in Peruvian coastal plantation agriculture between 1908 and 1930 hastened the demise of Japanese contract labor in the sugar industry. As we have seen, most Japanese soon fled the unfavorable conditions on the sugar estates for new opportunities in urban commerce. But increased demand for Peruvian cotton, prompted by World War I and the improving international economy of the early 1920s, opened new opportunities for some Issei in cotton production. Reflecting a long decline in world sugar prices, the amount of new coastal properties devoted to sugar production did not increase significantly. In contrast, new irrigation projects such as the "Pampas Imperial" initiative in the Cañete Valley, which when completed in 1923 opened 12,350 acres to cultivation, increased opportunities for even small cotton producers. Overall, new lands opened to cotton increased by more than 170,000 acres, most of this on marginal arid land that was not previously devoted to food production.[42]

By the mid-1930s, Japanese cotton production was prominent in the Lurín, Pachacamac, Rimac, and especially the Chancay valleys. The town of Huaral in the Chancay Valley served as the center of commercial activity for the Japanese colony in the region. Mirroring the circumstances of the Mexican Issei in Baja California Norte, Japanese immigrant tenant farmers in the Chancay Valley soon came to dominate cotton production in the vicinity of Huaral. Ikumatsu Okada, an Issei who arrived in Peru in 1903 as a contract laborer, was able to acquire a number of small parcels of land near Huaral and begin profitable cotton cultivation within the next two decades. Joining with other Japanese cotton growers in the valley, Okada helped form three Japanese cooperatives, the Peru Menka Kabushiki Gaisha, S. A., the J. Mechima, and the Sociedad Agrícola Retes, that facilitated the expansion of Japanese holdings in the valley. By the late 1930s, Japanese cotton producers were farming 19,432 acres, or 42 percent of all the cultivated land in the Chancay Valley.[43]

Led by Okada, who would become president of the Sociedad Central de Japonesa del Valle de Chancay, the Issei opened a Japanese school in 1924 and soon extended their interests to commercial activities in the valley. Japanese economic success beyond cotton production was also enhanced by the creation of associations such as the Sociedad Industrial de Japonesa and the Sociedad de Comerciantes de Japoneses.[44] By the end of the 1930s, nearly half of the 960 families and 5,800 Japanese residing in the Chancay Valley were active members of these associations.[45] As was true elsewhere in Latin America, the ability of Japanese immigrants to pool their resources and rationally integrate their economic activities within the broader Japanese community gave them a significant advantage over their native competitors. As can be imagined, this success even in the midst of the Depression generated animosity. Bitter denunciations of Japanese economic monopolies in the Chancay Valley appeared in the Lima press. One critic charged, "'No Peruvian can prosper as an artisan, merchant or professional; the Japanese reserve everything for their fellow nationals; the Peruvian is systematically excluded.'"[46] Another critic ominously warned, "'After the merchant comes the soldier.'"[47] The soldiers would indeed come during World War II to the Chancay Valley. But they would be Peruvian soldiers ordered to seize Japanese lands and deport the leaders of the Japanese community. Okada would lose all his holdings and be interned in the United States in 1942.

The intense anti-Japanese sentiment that grew steadily stronger in Peru both in the rural and urban sectors from the early 1920s onward in large measure can be explained by the poor economic performance of the nation's emerging middle class. Thorp and Bertram harshly characterize Peru's middle class before World War II as "unformed and inexperienced." Moreover, these economic historians view the Peruvian economy entering the 1930s as one plagued by a "moribund manufacturing sector" that was still dominated by the "traditional ruling class" and large foreign capital. The ruling elites stayed in power through an alliance with the military rulers, such as Luis M. Sánchez Cerro (1930–33) and Oscar Benavides (1933–39).[48] Armed with their intense work ethic and community solidarity, Japanese immigrants took advantage of the opportunities offered in a relatively noncompetitive business environment. But the Issei never "monopolized" entire sectors of Peru's urban economy, as was frequently alleged by their nativist opponents. Feeling weak and vulnerable during difficult economic times, Peru's middle- and working-class population accepted the myth of Japanese economic dominance. Sadly, the Issei of Peru were regarded in the same distorted way as were the Jews of other nations. The parallels between these highly successful ethnic minorities would become quite apparent during World War II.

Throughout the period 1910–20, the Japanese established a pattern of Lima-based commercial activity that would dominate the economic life of the nation's Issei and Nisei until World War II. At the same time, the growing Japanese community in Peru began organizing itself more diligently than any other ethnic group in the nation. The Japanese population of the Lima-Callao metropolitan area in 1910 was approximately 950, with barbers, restaurateurs, grocers, and small-scale vendors comprising a third of them. Following the pattern of the Nihonjin Doshi Shakai (Japanese Brotherhood Association) formed in 1909, within the next decade the Issei in these professions organized a Japanese Chamber of Commerce, the Lima Restaurant Association, the Household Goods Association, and the Central Market Association. Numerous other Japanese associations were created throughout Peru in the ensuing three decades to provide economic assistance, assure the perpetuation of traditional Japanese culture, and afford protection to the Japanese community against the threat of increasing anti-Japanese sentiment as times grew hard for most Peruvians.[49]

Seeking to coordinate the activities of these various associations, leaders of the Japanese community in October 1917 formed an umbrella organization called the Peru Chuo Nihonjinkai (Central Japanese Association of Peru). The original prospectus for the Central Japanese Association urged the creation of the organization to meet "'the urgent necessity of having a central organ among ourselves to protect our interests in this country, to promote the welfare of every component of our society, and to encourage the means of mutual help, and thus build up our social standing to aim earnestly to strengthen the ties of friendship between our country and

Peru.'"[50] Not mentioned in the prospectus was the desire of the Japanese community's leaders to prevent the proliferation of Japanese immigrant associations from dividing the community along local or economic lines. This could not be completely prevented because the large Okinawan community in Peru created its own fraternal organization that reflected their differences with the Naichi-jin.

It is useful to notice the use of the phrase "our country" in this prospectus. Clearly, the Central Japanese Association of Peru, like similar organizations in Canada and the United States, was established to serve as a liaison between the sojourners and their still-perceived homeland. This association quickly became a powerful force within the Japanese community. All "called" immigrants before 1924, for example, had to be first approved by the association before being submitted to the Japanese consul in Lima. Additionally, the Japanese immigrant seeking to call relatives to Peru was required to be a member in good standing of the association for two years prior to the calling process. A fee of 5 Peruvian soles ($1.15) was paid by the caller to the association for each immigrant brought to Peru. After 1924, when the Peruvian government adopted more restrictive measures regarding Japanese immigration, the Central Japanese Association required that all those seeking to call immigrants must have at least 8,000 soles in cash or property assets.[51]

The Central Japanese Association and similar local agencies outside of Lima assumed a predominate role in the education of Peru's Nisei during the years between the world wars. Japanese elementary schools were largely financed by fees collected by these associations, and the vast majority of the instructors in these schools were hired in Japan after being selected by the associations. These schools were patterned closely after those of Japan. The model for these immigrant schools in Peru was the elementary school in Lima founded by the Central Japanese Association in 1920. By the 1930s, this school enrolled more than 1,000 Nisei boys and girls who studied in both Spanish and Japanese. The curriculum was designed to prepare the students for secondary school in Japan, if possible. Indeed, at the outbreak of World War II, 3,500 Peruvian Nisei, or *kibei,* as they were known, were attending secondary school in Japan. Ultimately, the Japanese community opened 50 of these schools throughout Peru during the interwar years, and 26 were still operating at the end of the 1930s. Most of these were small, enrolling no more than 30 to 50 students.[52]

Seiichi Higashide offers particular insight into the operation of some of the smaller provincial schools outside of Lima. Hired as a teacher at the San Vicente Japanese Elementary School in Cañete two years after he arrived in

Peru in 1930, Higashide characterized most of the teachers in Japanese rural schools as young male "intellectuals" recently arrived from Japan and unable to find work because of a lack of a facility in Spanish. Concluding that many of these Issei were "instant teachers" without formal training, he recalled, "I too had been selected more for my youth and vitality than my educational background or technical training."[53] Higashide, one of only three teachers at San Vicente, was paid by the local Japanese community, which financed the school solely by "compulsory donations," even from single and elderly members of the Japanese community in Cañete. An energetic young immigrant, Higashide demonstrated his vitality by organizing a school baseball program and other sports and handicrafts for both boys and girls at the San Vicente School.[54]

The Japanese language press in Peru played an integral role in maintaining community solidarity as well as enhancing the cultural ties the sojourners maintained with Japan. The biweekly *Andeseu Jiho* (Andean Times), which first appeared in November 1913, was the first Japanese language newspaper published in South America.[55] By the early 1920s, a second newspaper, also based in Lima and called the *Nimpo Shimpo* (Japan-Peru News), was being circulated to more than 1,200 readers on a triweekly basis. Eventually, these two papers merged in 1929 to form the *Rima Nippo* (Lima Japanese News), which remained in publication until the day after the attack on Pearl Harbor, when it was ordered closed by the Peruvian government. The *Rima Nippo* had a circulation of 1,500 nationwide throughout the 1930s. This readership was maintained even when confronted with competition from the *Peru Jiho* (Peru Times), which opened in 1934 under the ownership of its founder, Kuninousuke Yamamoto, and maintained a circulation of 1,200 until it, too, was closed on 8 December 1941.[56]

By the late 1930s, *Peru Jiho* was also published in a Spanish edition, undoubtedly so that news of the Japanese community would be available to the growing Nisei population, but it is questionable how many of the second generation actually read this paper. A May 1939 edition of *Peru Jiho*, for example, included a regular feature entitled "Noticias de la Colonia y del Japón" (News from the Colony and Japan). An editorial commentary clearly emphasized the need to enhance the "reciprocal understanding" of the "customs, arts, ideals, and culture" of the peoples of Japan and Peru. Toward that end, this edition of *Peru Jiho* offered a column entitled "Suggested Readings in Japanese Culture" and another entitled "Japanese Traditions."[57]

The mainstay of *Peru Jiho* and the other Japanese language publications was, of course, local news of the Japanese community in Peru. This coverage emphasized the activities of the many active associations while keeping the sojourners informed of events in Japan and East Asia. Most importantly, the Japanese language press served the Issei, whose Spanish language skills were not always well developed, by keeping them informed of new laws and regulations issued by the Peruvian government that influenced their welfare. As C. Harvey Gardiner repeatedly emphasizes, the Japanese language schools and press "reinforced the separatism" of the Japanese community in Peru, while paradoxically they aided immeasurably in easing the settlement of Issei there. What, of course, was being created in Peru by the late 1930s was a "nation within a nation" that Higashide describes so well in his autobiography.[58]

Of all those who published attacks against the Japanese in Peru during the interwar years, Victor Guevara, the well-known Peruvian writer, most succinctly summarized the prevailing sentiments of the Peruvian public. Guevara concluded in 1939: "'They [the Japanese] are not susceptible to assimilation . . . in the national life like other foreigners since they preserve intact their racial and political personalities, with their own customs, morals, laws, intellectual culture, ideas, religion, language, patriotism for the fatherland, their own newspapers, holidays, clubs and schools where they are taught allegiance not to Peru, but to Imperial Japan.'"[59]

Seiichi Higashide's experiences as a late-arriving Issei in Peru during the 1930s offer valuable insights into the prevailing issues of the Japanese immigrant community during that troubled decade. Arriving in Lima with few funds in 1930, Higashide was assessed a huge customs fee when he failed to offer the agent a small bribe. Having been assessed nearly half of his meager funds before even officially entering Peru, the young Issei soon went to Cañete, where he sustained himself as a "working guest" in the homes of local Issei until he could find meaningful work. Trained as an architect and engineer in Japan, Higashide found few opportunities for his skills in Depression-ridden Peru, especially lacking the ability to speak Spanish. Struggling with bouts of malaria, possible deportation to Japan for avoidance of military service, and loneliness, Higashide was often able to withstand the pressures of his first months in Peru only because of the timely intercession of supportive Issei. Eventually, his hard work and imagination displayed during his stints as a laborer, carpenter, and school teacher in Cañete caught the attention of a local businessman who wanted to sell his properties and establish a new life in Manchuria. The businessman, who was the president of the parents' association of the San Vicente elementary school where Higashide taught, told the young immigrant, "'I was struck by your upbringing and personality, so I decided to transfer my businesses to you.'"[60] Higashide soon accepted the offer to purchase the luxury goods store, barbershop, and bar under a joint-ownership agreement with a fellow Issei of his own age. Once established as a reputable businessman, Higashide's thoughts turned to marriage and the troubling prospect of a Peruvian Issei finding a "suitable" wife in Peru.

Even by the mid-1930s, Japanese men outnumbered women by more than two-to-one in Peru's immigrant community. Very few Issei males could afford to return to Japan to choose a wife. Immigration restrictions by the late 1920s had also effectively ended the "picture bride" system in Peru as well. As confirmed by Higashide, strong cultural notions prevented male Issei from marrying local Peruvian women. According to Higashide, "The Japanese community in Peru was self-contained and tightly closed, so young Japanese of marriageable age had almost no opportunities to get acquainted with Peruvians." Moreover, as Higashide candidly recalled, "First generation immigrants harbored a strong sense of discrimination" against native Peruvians.[61] These cultural attitudes were so strongly held, Higashide noted, that a significant number of older Issei men chose never to marry after their arrival in Peru. One of these Issei was the principal of the San Vicente school where Higashide taught for eighteen months. The young Issei sadly recalled that this lonely immigrant, whose only pleasure seemed to come from playing cards, eventually ended his life with an overdose of sleeping pills.[62]

Higashide's marriage dilemma was eventually resolved when he met and married a young Nisei woman whose parents were impressed with his character and growing social stature in the immigrant community. His young wife soon accompanied Higashide to Ica, in southern Peru, where the couple began another successful business venture using their savings and capital from their former operations in Cañete. These young immigrants continued to prosper with their growing family until their deportation to the United States during World War II.

The population of the Japanese community in Peru reached its pre–World War peak in 1934, when the Issei population was calculated to be 20,385. The immigrant community was overwhelmingly centered in the Lima-Callao metropolitan area, where 17,725 Issei resided. No other department of Peru counted more than 800 Issei among its residents. The highly centralized nature of the Japanese community in the Peruvian capital reflected the degree to which the Issei turned to urban commercial enterprise for their livelihoods during the interwar years. The 1934 statistics list 1,899 family heads working in the agricultural sector, 451 in manufacturing, and 4,763 in commerce.[63] Clearly, the still lightly capitalized Japanese community was prospering but not dominating any national sector of the Peruvian economy. The "typical" Issei and their Nisei children were the proprietors and principal workers in the bazaars, barbershops, auto repair shops, and restaurants of

Lima. Unlike the Japanese in Mexico or Brazil, who did not migrate to the most populous cities before World War II, the Japanese Peruvians, by choosing to reside in Lima, effectively raised the "ethnic profile" of the Japanese immigrant in the minds of disgruntled Peruvians. As we shall see, this made the Japanese frequent targets of violence during the pre–World War II years.

After the Japanese community was victimized by violence and looting during the revolution of Lieutenant Colonel Luis M. Sánchez Cerro that toppled the autocrat Leguía in August 1930, the Japanese consul in Lima, Saburu Kurusu, sought to redirect future Japanese immigration to the interior in an apparent attempt to placate the Peruvian government and defuse growing anti-Japanese sentiment. (In December 1941, Kurusu would have the unfortunate duty of delivering Japan's note declaring a "diplomatic impasse" to U.S. government officials in Washington soon after the Pearl Harbor attack.)[64] Toward this end, the Peru Takushoku Kumiai (Peruvian Colonization Association) was established in March 1931 under the slogan "Go to the *montaña*" (referring to the eastern slopes of the Andes Mountains). Although small numbers of Issei had previously migrated to the Iquitos region on the upper reaches of the Amazon and had gathered in isolated groups in the Huallaga River valley, poor communications and roads that badly impeded the marketing of crops discouraged any significant new Japanese settlement outside Lima. Unlike in Brazil, where, as we shall see, Japanese colonization companies purchased large tracts of land for new settlement in the interior of São Paulo State, only one such venture was undertaken in Peru. The 2,450 acres purchased by the Peruvian Colonization Association in the remote Chanchamayo Valley on the eastern slope of the Andes eventually drew only sixteen Japanese families to the *montaña*.[65] Thus the Japanese community of Peru remained localized and vulnerable in Lima and Peru's coastal desert plain.

It is important to discuss here, however, the background to the 1936 Immigration Act that effectively ended substantive Japanese migration to Peru. As World War I drew to a close, the Peruvian Congress, undoubtedly following the lead of the United States and Canada, was considering the passage of an "anti-Asian" bill that would prevent what some legislators saw as the "ethnic degeneration" posed by the continued immigration of Chinese and Japanese.[66] The proposed measure was met with strong diplomatic resistance by the Japanese government and was never enacted. Still, during the rule of Augusto Leguía, who favored Japanese trade and better diplomatic relations, pressure continued to mount to curtail immigration. The 1924 Immigration Act in the United States was soon seen as a model for Peruvian "nationalists" to emulate. Thus, even while he was negotiating with Tokyo's representatives regarding a new commercial treaty in 1924, Leguía was also cynically conducting discussions with U.S. embassy officer Wallace Thompson regarding the exclusion issue. Leguía told Thompson that although the Japanese were unwelcome and unpopular in Peru, any attempt at "'Japanese exclusion without the support of the United States would have meant war.'"[67]

When Leguía was toppled by Sánchez Cerro in 1930, Kurusu was forced to deal with the attacks on the Japanese community by insisting that the Peruvian government allow them to form armed "vigilance committees." Tokyo's aggressive intervention served to quell anti-Japanese violence, but as noted by C. Harvey Gardiner, it undoubtedly lent false substance to the continuing rumors that the immigrants were well armed and bolstered by veterans of Japan's recent military campaign in Manchuria.[68] With Kurusu's departure in 1932 and the establishment of the six-year military dictatorship of General Oscar Benavides following Sánchez Cerro's assassination in April 1933, Tokyo's diplomatic leverage in Peru lessened substantially, in part because of the continuing Depression and increased Japanese militarism in Asia. During the ensuing three years, the Benavides regime enacted a constitution that required foreigners to renounce their dual citizenship but then later denied aliens the right to be naturalized. Moreover, legislation that required that 80 percent of workers in any business be Peruvians was soon implemented. Finally, the Treaty of Commerce and Amity that Japan had signed with the Leguía government was renounced. By the mid-1930s, the Japanese were the largest immigrant group entering Peru, so there was no question who the target of these measures were. But the total number of Japanese immigrants arriving on Peruvian soil as late as 1936 was only 593.[69] Furthermore, during most of the early 1930s, immigrants were increasingly leaving Peru, either to return to Japan or to transmigrate to another South American nation. Just as in the United States and Canada, the relatively small number of Japanese immigrants in the country did not matter. Issues of race, economic hardship, and cultural misunderstanding undermined logic and understanding.

Like the Immigration Act of 1924, Peru's legislation of 1936 definitively determined the future course of the Japanese there. The legislation was a direct response to Brazil's restrictive immigration quotas included in the constitution of 1934, enacted by the Getulio Vargas government, which would have reduced Japanese immigration to 2,848, slightly more than the number of Japanese who arrived in 1933.[70] Peru's anti-Japanese nationalists feared that with Brazil's doors closing to the Japanese, those bound for South America would be redirected to Peru. Peru's 1936 Immigration Act included specific components that were clearly directed against the Japanese. For example, immigration by "racial groups" was prohibited; foreign residents of Peru who returned home could only reenter under newly established limited quotas; and the 80 percent employment legislation passed earlier was extended to all occupations and professions.[71] Bolstered by increasing support from the United States as Japanese militarism increased, the Benavides government rejected Tokyo's protests to these restrictive measures, and Japanese-Peruvian relations continued to deteriorate. After more than four decades of being viewed as a land of potential, if temporary, opportunity, Peru permitted entry to only 116 Japanese in 1937. Because of limited economic opportunities, the scarcity of inexpensive arable land, and xenophobia, Peru never fulfilled the high expectations of Tokyo or its Japanese immigrants. However, great progress regarding these expectations occurred in Brazil.

Immigrants to *Paulistas*

More Japanese immigrants were drawn to Brazil than any other country except Manchuria during the three decades after 1908. Most settled in the southern states of São Paulo and Paraná. Boasting the most dynamic economy in Latin America, large tracts of affordable land in São Paulo State, favorable immigration legislation initiated by both Rio de Janeiro and Tokyo, and a continuing need for labor, Brazil witnessed the entry of 182,268 immigrants during this era, mostly through the port of Santos in São Paulo State. The immigrants arriving during this period comprised 75 percent of all Japanese arrivals in Latin America before World War II.[72] The Japanese thus became the final integral component of the nation's multiracial mosaic created by immigration after the abolition of slavery in 1888. Like their Japanese counterparts elsewhere in Latin America, these immigrants to Brazil before 1941 saw themselves as sojourners, unaware that they would probably never return permanently to Japan. Adding to the complexity of the sojourner mentality in Brazil was the continuing arrival of substantial numbers of new immigrants through 1937. The Brazilian Issei were thus divided between the Japanese pioneers who arrived before 1925 and the nearly 150,000 new immigrants who migrated to Brazil with the support of grants from the Japanese government thereafter (see table 1).

As with previous immigrants from Germany, Italy, Spain, Portugal, and the Middle East, the Japanese were attracted to Brazil's dynamic south. Led by its four southern states, Brazil changed from an overwhelmingly rural, agriculturally based nation reliant on coffee and rubber exports to a country rapidly building the foundations of industrial infrastructure that would

Table 1. Japanese Immigrants Entering the Port of Santos, Brazil, 1908–41

Year	Women Only	Men and Women
1908	180	797
1909	0	0
1910	391	906
1911	0	0
1912	833	2,844
1913	3,026	6,948
1914	1,397	3,497
1915	0	0
1916	6	13
1917	1,499	4,038
1918	2,458	5,903
1919	911	2,679
1920	289	982
1921	359	923
1922	247	528
1923	232	516
1924	2,786	4,985
1925	2,009	4,912
1926	3,387	7,639
1927	4,574	10,050
1928	5,155	10,812
1929	5,797	11,515
1930	5,293	12,600
1931	2,299	5,332
1932	4,887	15,887
1933	9,480	21,000
1934	7,062	21,702
1935	2,520	6,400
1936	2,523	5,373
1937	2,100	4,642
1938	835	2,552
1939	618	1,294
1940	712	1,556
1941	616	1,350
Subtotals	74,481	180,175
Immigrants to the colony of Iguape before 1920	689	1,744
Totals	75,170	181,919

Sources: Data from Gaimusho Ryoji Iiju-bu, *Waga kokumin no kaigai hatten: Iiju hyakunen no ayumi* (Tokyo: Ministry of Foreign Affairs, 1971), 143; and Sociedade Brasileira de Cultural Japonesa, *Uma epopéia moderna: 80 anos da imigração japonesa no Brasil* (São Paulo: Editora Hucitec, 1992), 138.

make it one of the ten leading economies of the world by the 1960s. The dynamic population growth of Brazil's south is revealed in the 1872 and 1920 censuses. The nation's population more than tripled to 30.6 million from 1872 to 1920. Most revealing, however, was the pattern of growth that saw the southern states of São Paulo, Paraná, Santa Catarina, and Rio Grande do Sul experience population increases of 418 to 548 percent. By 1920 nearly one in five southern Brazilians was foreign born, as compared with one in ten in 1872, and 3.1 million immigrants entered the nation during those years, with more than half of them choosing to live in São Paulo State.[73]

During roughly the same period, the focus of political power shifted from the *coroneis* (colonels), the rural bosses who dominated during the Old Republic (1889–1930), to the Estado Nôvo (New State), the highly centralized corporate dictatorship established by Getulio Vargas in 1937. For most of this era, however, coffee still ruled the economic life of southern Brazil. The states of Rio de Janeiro and São Paulo supplied the majority of Brazil's political leaders until Vargas, the former governor of Brazil's southernmost state, Rio Grande do Sul, rose to power after the 1930 revolution. São Paulo's coffee barons were primarily responsible for producing most of Brazil's coffee crop that never fell below a 60 percent share of the world's production throughout this era. The highly labor-intensive coffee industry thus remained dependent upon immigrant wage labor until the Depression. Brazil's reign as the second largest "receiver" nation of immigrants in South America was brought to an end with the termination of subsidized immigration in 1928 and the highly restrictive 1934 Immigration Act prompted by the Depression.

The emerging industrial sector provided significant new opportunities for immigrants. In 1907, Brazil counted less than 3,000 industrial establishments and only 136,000 employees. By the end of the 1930s there were more than 70,000 industrial firms employing 1.4 million workers.[74] The major cities of Rio de Janeiro and São Paulo led the way as the textile industry, food processing, and light manufacturing grew rapidly. The Issei who arrived in Brazil before 1934 remained overwhelmingly in agriculture, but Brazil's rapidly expanding industrial base would afford great opportunities for Nisei and Sansei in the post–World War II years.

The era of Brazil's 35,000 Japanese pioneers (1908–25) was characterized by the successful transition of most Issei from the status of *colono* wage laborers on one of the huge coffee plantations to that of a *sitiantes,* or small farm owners. This process took from two to five years and most often involved periods when the Issei worked as *meeiros* (sharecroppers) or *arrendatários* (lease farmers). After the successful precedent by the Japanese government to open an agricultural colony for immigrants near Iguape on São Paulo State's southern littoral before World War I, opportunities for Nikkei pioneers to prosper in rice farming, produce, and coffee growing increased significantly. Nearly 90 percent of all Japanese immigrants before 1925 migrated to São Paulo State, and unlike the ill-fated *Kazatu-maru* immigrants of 1908, most were experienced farmers from Japan's southern prefectures.

Perhaps because of their previous experience as independent farmers, the Japanese were very reluctant to remain as colonists on the coffee plantations for any longer than was necessary to make the transition to independent farming. The Japanese immigrant thus acquired a reputation among the planter elites as not a "reliable" long-term labor source. At various times before 1924, the São Paulo government sought to suspend the immigrant subsidies to the Japanese while continuing them for European newcomers to the state. Nabuya Tsuchida, in his study of the Japanese in Brazil, noted that the planters knew the Issei "loathed" their colonist status and wanted to advance more quickly. He also links the anti-Japanese sentiment of the planters to racism that became more focused after the California legislature enacted the Alien Land Law of May 1913.[75] As we shall see, some legislators in Rio de Janeiro were continually attempting to discourage or restrict Japanese immigration. They did not succeed until the Depression years because of the state's persistent labor needs and the growing acceptance of the Issei as the most disciplined and hardworking immigrant group in Brazil. In 1924, for example, federal congressman Francisco Chavez de Oliveira Botelho, commenting on Japanese rice farmers in the Registro colony in São Paulo, was effusive in his praise. "'How admirable their farming is! In our agricultural properties, swamps are scorned and considered as unusable areas; in Registro they are the most valuable lands. The Japanese till the swamps painstakingly, draining or irrigating them as the crop may require it.'"[76]

Despite their disdain for the wage labor of the *colono*, the Issei used their time spent in this capacity to supplement their income and build small savings by planting cash crops such as corn, beans, or other vegetables between the rows of coffee trees they tended. Additionally, planters frequently permitted them to plant rice in the lowland areas of their holdings that were not suitable for coffee production. Tsuchida notes that one Japanese colonist family of five in 1922 was able to realize a small savings of 1,119 milreis ($135), primarily from the sale of its cash crops. Since these crops were also consumed by the family, their yearly expenses were minimal. Thus the savings could be directed toward future leasing or purchasing of new land in undeveloped areas of São Paulo State.[77] Some early Japanese immigrant families undertook creative landholding arrangements with planters or other Issei families to realize enough savings to become fully independent land-owners. One example saw former Issei colonists settle on virgin land owned by a planter to plant coffee trees and their own cash crops without paying rent. They would then harvest the first coffee crop after five years, which they were permitted to keep and sell. The land would then be turned over to the plantation owner with its producing coffee trees. Sometimes the Issei would then purchase a plot of land with the savings from this arrangement and strike a similar deal with another Japanese immigrant family. Because their small savings often were exhausted with the initial land purchase, they would return to colonist wage labor to earn additional savings for their return to a producing coffee holding in four to five more years.[78]

Unlike the experience of the Japanese in Peru, Brazil's first Japanese im-migrants were able to stay on the land where they felt the most comfortable and prospered in a rural setting that offered far better opportunities in agri-culture than anywhere else in Latin America. Still, the lives of many of these pioneers were often filled with hardships. Perhaps most troubling was the uncertainty about where their real home was. Most Issei refused to acknowl-edge that they would very likely never return to Japan. They were thus re-luctant to seek permanence in their relationships with native Brazilians or even with fellow Issei. They were simply unwilling to build a new life in the land so far from their ancestral home. As in Peru and to a lesser extent Mexico, they tended to group themselves by their home prefectures in their evolving social settings and soon were referring to all non-Japanese in Bra-zil as *gajin* (foreigners). Their early lives in Brazil were marked by constant sacrifice and denial. They commonly had rudimentary furnishings in their dwellings and very little diversity in their diets. The poetry written by one of the immigrant pioneers reflects this sense of sacrifice: "It is sad to see those that hurry to succeed and are sipping rice porridge like water."[79]

If the life of the early Japanese colonists was hard, after World War I they frequently had the option of leaving the coffee plantations and settling on one of a growing number of immigrant colonies being established in fron-tier areas in São Paulo State. After 1920 this process was made increasingly possible because of the financial assistance offered by Tokyo-sponsored Japa-nese immigration companies. The scale of these independent Japanese colo-nies was unique to the Western Hemisphere. Significantly, they would estab-lish a pattern of colonization later to be emulated in Paraguay and Bolivia.

Similar *núcleos,* or immigrant colonies, had previously been established for small groups of Swiss, Italians, and Germans in São Paulo and Rio Grande do Sul between 1885 and 1911, with some success.[80] Thus, the state government of São Paulo felt reasonably comfortable with the arrangement when well-funded Japanese colonization corporations directed their venture capital to southern Brazil. Near the end of World War I, the Tokyo government, seeking to facilitate immigration to Brazil, amalgamated three smaller and financially insecure immigration companies into the Kaigai Kogyo Kabushiki Kaisha, or KKKK (Overseas Development Corporation), which was capitalized at nearly $5 million. After 1920, the KKKK became the only immigration company operating in Japan. Its function was to recruit and transport contract immigrants, extend loans to immigrants and colonists, and invest in colonization projects abroad.[81] During this period of Brazilian immigration (1920–34), the KKKK's operations focused almost exclusively on that South American nation. In 1927, the KKKK would open and operate an "Immigrant Training Center" in Kobe, where recruits would have free temporary lodging before leaving for Brazil. At the center in Kobe, short courses in Portuguese and Western customs were also taught to better prepare the sojourners for their experience abroad.[82] The most significant contribution the KKKK made to the Japanese immigration experience in Brazil, however, was its funding of the colonization effort in São Paulo.

The early success of the Iguape colony, located in the Ribeira de Iguape basin, 137 miles southwest of the port of Santos, encouraged the Japanese government to offer financial support to the Brazilian colonization initiatives during the 1920s. It must be understood, however, that the Iguape colony was unable to attract sufficient numbers of new recruits from Japan, and it thrived initially only because it was able to continually attract transient Issei from other parts of São Paulo, who took up rice and sugarcane farming on a large scale and moved on in three to four years to become farm owners. The Iguape colony offers stark evidence of the unwillingness of the early Japanese immigrants to commit fully to new lives in Brazil. Only three Japanese families initially joined the so-called vagabonds in this pioneering colony. Similar recruiting problems would mark the initial colonization efforts of the KKKK in Brazil until the late 1920s, when it became apparent to prospective immigrants that the new colonies were prospering enclaves of Japanese culture where savings could be more quickly earned than on the coffee plantations of São Paulo and Paraná States.[83]

By 1924, three separate colonies had been established in the Iguape Valley—Registro, Sete Barras, and Katsura. Facilitating communication and commerce between the colonies and the city of Iguape were 151 miles of roads constructed with the financial aid of the Japanese government. Additionally, four schools serving 318 Japanese and Brazilian students had been constructed and donated to the state of São Paulo. Eventually these colonies would have medical facilities, mills, and processing plants for the commercial crops raised by the colonists. As noted by Tsuchida, the establishment of these prototype colonies "served as a turning point, at which Japanese immigration to Brazil began to undergo a structural change from *colono* labor to independent farming."[84] During the years before 1934, additional Japanese immigrant colonies were established at Bastos, Lins, Bauru, Aracatuba, Tietê, Andradina, and Aliança in the state of São Paulo, and at Londrina and Tres Barras in the state of Paraná. All of these colonies were situated in frontier areas, where land was more readily available. These colonies served as the magnet for the massive migration of Japanese immigrants in the decade after 1924. They also assured that the Brazilian Japanese would remain rural based and largely independent of the rapidly urbanizing mainstream culture of southern Brazil.

The year 1924 was a watershed for Japanese immigration to Brazil. Responding to the dislocation caused by the great Kanto earthquake, difficult economic conditions, and the end of Japanese immigration to the United States, Tokyo placed great emphasis on immigration issues at the Imperial Congress for the Economy held from April to June 1924. Japanese officials were particularly concerned about the increasing anti-Japanese sentiment that was confronting their immigrants everywhere in the Western Hemisphere. Attempts by a small clique of anti-Japanese national legislators from Rio de Janeiro to emulate the restrictive immigration measures of the North American nations caused particular concern.[85] Brazil was perceived in Japan as the most "friendly" nation in the Americas for the Japanese, and thus possible measures to blunt anti-Japanese feeling in this critically important receiver nation were carefully reviewed at the Imperial Congress. It was hoped by the government leaders in Tokyo that Brazil would not only help alleviate Japan's growing labor problems through the "safety valve" of massive and permanent immigration but would also aid the depressed Japanese economy by the remittances of new immigrants to their home country. Tokyo also anticipated that Brazilian immigration might stimulate Japanese trade with Portuguese America and other South American nations and, in the process, aid Japan's shipping industry.[86]

Toward these ends, the delegates at the Imperial Congress concluded that the educational level and preparation of Japanese immigrating to other nations must be improved to reduce the potential for racial discrimination. Most importantly, however, the delegates concluded that the sojourner mentality was primarily responsible for the separateness and insularity of the Japanese immigrants in the Americas.[87] Seeking desperately to avoid repetition of the abject failure of Tokyo's immigration policy in the United

States, a new immigration policy termed "prosperous coexistence" was advocated in a resolution adopted by the Imperial Congress. "Prosperous coexistence" meant that Tokyo resolved to send both labor and capital to the host country and to encourage development in frontier areas for the mutual benefit of the pioneering immigrants and their new homeland. Even more significantly, naturalization of the Japanese was encouraged in an effort to undermine the sojourner mentality. This policy, of course, represented a sharp break with the imperial government's previous attitude toward immigration, which had always stressed continued loyalty to the Japanese nation and emperor by the Japanese in other lands. Despite this new imperial policy, few Issei in Brazil or elsewhere in Latin America would seek to become citizens of their adopted nations before World War II. The immediate impact upon Brazilian immigration policy was to discourage contract immigration and foster the growth of permanent Japanese colonies in São Paulo and Paraná.

Tokyo's decision to discourage sojourner immigration after 1925 had momentous implications for Brazil's Japanese. Most Issei were simply unwilling to even contemplate breaking their ties with their homeland, and thus Japan's new policy created increased tensions for immigrants. In separate studies, Takashi Maeyama and Christopher Reichl each examine the evolutionary stages of ethnicity of the Japanese Brazilians and how the Issei in that nation adapted to their new environment. Reichl notes that when Ie (household) ties were suspended or broken by immigration, they were frequently replaced in Brazil with fictive relationships created for both administrative and social purposes. The Brazilian authorities required that only families could migrate to Brazil, so many "false" families were created on the immigrant ships en route to the port of Santos. Reichl further elaborates: "Kin ties broken by immigration were replaced by fictive kin relations with those from the same prefecture . . . and those who worked together for the first years after immigration."[88] The numerous associations, youth groups, and fraternal societies that were quickly created in Brazil's colonies and elsewhere among Latin America's Japanese were, according to Maeyama, merely a logical attempt to replicate the egalitarian neighborhood relationships known in Japan as *kumi* (group).[89]

Holding even greater significance for the socialization of the Japanese Brazilians were their religious views. Maeyama and Reichl contend that once the immigrants left Japan their religious expression underwent a profound change in Brazil. Having broken the ties with the Ie, the Issei had little reason to actively practice their Shinto traditions, which were primarily based upon ancestor worship. The social construct of religious expression in Japan involved the household, the village, and the nation. In a tangible sense, all that was left for the new immigrants when they arrived in Brazil was the symbol of national unity, the emperor. As Reichl concludes, "When the Japanese communities in Brazil were formed, the relationship between each Japanese national and the emperor was the common thread that provided the basis for ethnic expression."[90] Emperor worship thus replaced ancestor worship and became the single most important mode of ethnic and religious behavior. As the Japanese nation grew in military strength and international prestige, this was naturally reflected in increased nationalism among the Issei in Brazil and elsewhere. As discreet as the Japanese Brazilians were in their manifestation of this nationalism and emperor worship, such forms of cultural expression still aroused suspicion in Brazil. Coupled with Japanese militarism in the early 1930s in Manchuria, these modes of cultural expression fueled the Japanese exclusion movement that resulted in the restrictive 1934 Immigration Act. Moreover, as we shall see, fear of intense Japanese nationalism was not completely unfounded. That nationalism was later to take the form of "victory" societies following World War II that refused to accept the reality of Japan's defeat in August 1945.

Japan policy's of encouraging Brazilian immigration by means of subsidies, underwriting of travel costs, colonizing projects, and the extension of loans to new immigrants proved to be very successful in the decade after 1924. During those ten years, 131,388 Japanese migrated to Brazil, with the peak year being 1934, when 21,702 immigrants arrived at the port of Santos.[91] These years of the "Brazilian immigration," as it was known in Japan, saw the creation and consolidation of new independent colonies in São Paulo and Paraná and less successful attempts to introduce the Japanese to the Brazilian Amazon region. Opening new lands in southern Brazil to rice, cotton, and produce farming, these pioneering Issei established the precedent of successful small farming in Brazil. The new immigrants also sought to continue the early success of Issei pioneers in coffee production. But the long-term investments required in coffee cultivation and, more importantly, the dramatic drop in coffee prices during the Great Depression, discouraged the Issei from favoring coffee production after 1928.

By 1937 the Japanese Brazilians had become the middle-class agriculturalists populating the virgin lands of the interior that had been the dream of Brazilian positivists since the late nineteenth century. Their success in helping fulfill the vision of Brazilian development, even while they remained a distinct racial minority isolated from the mainstream of national society, helped blunt the suspicion and racial prejudice that was inevitably directed toward them during the 1930s. Ironically, the very success of Tokyo's campaign to foster large-scale Brazilian immigration served to maintain the sojourner mentality. New immigrants brought renewed contacts with the homeland, potential Japanese brides for Issei bachelors, and fresh news of Japan's growing international power.

The vitality of the Issei family in Brazil also fostered the continuing of the sojourner mentality. Unlike what happened in Peru and certainly in Mexico, entire Japanese families immigrated to Brazil in comparatively large numbers, because the São Paulo planters felt that colonist families would create a more stable workforce on the coffee plantations. As a consequence, very few of the Issei were the single male immigrants under the age of twenty-five that were so common elsewhere. As has already been noted, some of these "families" were artificially constituted to conform to Brazil's immigration guidelines. Indeed, almost one in six Issei during the pre–World War II years were classified as *kosei-kazoku* (incorporated family members).[92] Adopted children composed the largest share of the *kosei-kazoku*, particularly among the early arrivals. Family heads prior to the 1930s tended to be under the age of thirty. But as the colonization program began in earnest after 1925, older, more "legitimate" family heads began to predominate. While still a distinct minority of the Issei, female immigrants constituted a larger share of the Japanese in Brazil than anywhere else in the Americas. For those Issei males who chose to marry late, for example, the gender ratio was most evenly balanced in the age range of twenty-five to forty years. The specter of aging Japanese males who could not find a suitable Issei marriage partner was generally not present in Brazil as it was in Peru and Mexico.

The centerpiece of Tokyo's immigration policy in Brazil after 1925 was the heavily subsidized colonization program in São Paulo and Paraná. As noted by Tsuchida, three types of colonies were created in Brazil. The most significant were the large *núcleos colonias*, which were well funded through private and public Japanese financing. Well equipped and maintained, these colonies attracted the majority of Japanese colonists, whether they were newly arrived from Japan or had migrated from other locations in southern Brazil. Particularly successful among these colonies was the Bastos in western São Paulo State. The second type of colony in southern Brazil was the smaller settlements founded by former colonists, primarily in the forested interior lands of São Paulo and Paraná. Finally, colonies established by private Japanese companies in the northern state of Amazonas, downriver from Manaus at Monte Alegre, Vila Amazonia, Maués, and Acará, represented the third type of colonial venture in Brazil.[93]

✿ ✿ ✿

The administrative agency for promoting Japanese settlement in Brazil was the Federation of Immigration Cooperative Societies established under a law passed by the Japanese Diet in March 1927. These societies were created in 44 of Japan's 47 prefectures by the mid-1930s. In order to facilitate the purchase of land for new colonists in Brazil, the Japanese government extended nearly $800,000 in loans to the federation during its first year of operation. The member societies provided more than $324,000 in grants to 5,264 colonists in the years between 1929 and 1934. Eventually, 541,112 acres of land were purchased in São Paulo and Paraná for colonization before immigration was sharply curtailed in 1934. The charter company established under Brazilian law to administer these colonies in Portuguese America was the Sociedade Colonizadora do Brasil Limitada (Brazilian Colonization Company). Known by the Issei in Brazil as BRATAC, for its Japanese name Burajiru Takushoku Kumiai, this agency would oversee the largest of the colonies in Brazil, including those at Bastos, Tietê, Aliança, and Tres Barras.[94] For purposes of brevity, this discussion will concentrate only on the colony at Bastos.

BRATAC supported the colonization initiative by acquiring real estate, constructing the infrastructure of roads and rail lines, and subsidizing related business activities in Bastos and the other colonies. At Bastos the colonization effort gave the new immigrants a distinct advantage over the earlier Japanese pioneers in Brazil and certainly those in the rest of Latin America. Colonists immigrating directly from Japan could purchase a sixty-acre plot in Bastos for $718, with payment deferred for the first four years. Full payment was then required within three years but with no interest accrued. To assure its initial investment, BRATAC required that each new colonist household arrive from Japan with $798 in transferable capital. This clearly discouraged large numbers of the poorest Japanese from immigrating, but because most of the transportation costs were subsidized, the Japanese of some reasonable means could be assured immediate landholding status in a culturally friendly setting. Former colonists who migrated to Bastos from other areas of São Paulo and Paraná were allowed to buy more land than the colonists from Japan, on the theory that they were more familiar with Brazilian agriculture. On the other hand, these former contract laborers were required to put a down payment on the land, purchase a share in BRATAC, and possess "sufficient" operating capital before beginning life in Bastos.[95]

Despite the liberal financial terms for settlement in Bastos for immigrants coming directly from Japan during the five years after 1929, this colony was primarily settled by former contract workers and not by newly arrived immigrants. By 1934, BRATAC had distributed nearly all of the original land to more than 700 Japanese households. Responding to the sharp fall in coffee prices, the Issei in Bastos diversified their agricultural base by engaging in highly profitable cotton, tobacco, and rice production, which was augmented by poultry, hog raising, and dairy farming. These activities were so successful that by 1938 Bastos boasted a population of 10,000, less than a decade after it was founded by BRATAC. Emulating the Japanese in Baja California Norte, some of the original Issei colonists in Bastos turned to commercial activities that largely sustained the needs of the colonies' inhabitants. Still, nearly 170 miles of roads built by BRATAC during the 1930s served to connect the colony to markets in eastern São Paulo State.[96]

Clearly, the Japanese government made a very concerted effort to establish a permanent Japanese presence in Brazil to facilitate further immigration in years to come. Bastos and the other colonies were designed to become "Japanese villages" in Brazil. Toward this end, BRATAC launched a campaign in the early 1930s, *Gozar a Terra,* or GAT. This "Love the land" initiative included the distribution of pamphlets to the colonists at Bastos with slogans such as "'Love the land, enjoy the work, be rooted for the children.'" These attitudes, the pamphlet claimed, would "'bring prosperity to the colony.'"[97] The constant theme in this antisojourner propaganda was the need to provide for the new Japanese family in Brazil, to make the long-term commitments to the land that successful agriculture required, and to live in peace and harmony with the Brazilian environment. It is difficult to determine the success of the GAT campaign because it coincided with the "nationalization" campaign begun by the Vargas regime in the mid-1930s. The Vargas government program sought to diminish ethnic solidarity in Brazil in favor of loyalty to the Brazilian nation. As will be subsequently discussed in more detail, the nationalization campaign alienated many Issei and further strengthened their longing for their homeland.

The views of one Issei colonist from Tietê reflect this sentiment. The father of two Nisei and a resident of Brazil for twenty-five years, he sadly lamented, in the midst of the nationalization campaign, "We did not come to Brazil to live permanently, but for attaining material. Japan is the country we love and returning home with success is what our heart desires. . . . It has been thirty years since our countrymen landed in this country. Since then 20,000, young and old, men and women have been sacrificed. It is not the way for us to leave our ancestors, leaving their cemeteries. . . . Our im-

migration will mean something only if our blood purifies the Brazilian im-
purity with our superior tradition."[98] In the end, this immigrant seemed
resigned to staying in Brazil and working for a better life for his children in
his reluctantly adopted homeland. As was the case everywhere in the Americas, the education of the Nisei was the key to this better life in the minds of
the Issei. For many of the more affluent Japanese, this meant schooling in
Japan as well as in Brazil. Thus dual cultural identities continued to be perpetuated until access to the culture of the Japanese homeland was cut off
by World War II.

THE SMALLER JAPANESE COMMUNITIES, 1908–38

> We are all Japanese. The Japanese race is not inferior to any of the European peoples. We are supported by the great Japanese Empire and have the protection of the Imperial family that has no equal in the world.
> —A Japanese diplomat addressing the Japanese immigrants of Trinidad, Bolivia, 1931

Patterns of Settlement

Japanese immigration to Latin American nations other than Mexico, Peru, and Brazil during the period 1908–38 was primarily a product of transmigration from these main receiver nations. It was also the result of attempts to establish core colonies in nations with limited economic opportunities. Before 1938, with the exception of Argentina, Bolivia, and Paraguay, these communities never drew significant numbers of Japanese immigrants. Thus the pattern of settlement of the Japanese in only six Latin American nations was firmly established as World War II approached.

The pattern of immigration and settlement of the Japanese in Argentina resembled that of Peru, with a significant majority locating in the capital city of Buenos Aires (see table 2). In Paraguay, a core colony was established southeast of Asunción at La Colmena. Modeled on the Brazilian *colonias*, La Colmena became the magnet colony for future Japanese settlement in Paraguay after World War II. Japanese settlement in Bolivia included transmigration from Peru, Brazil, and Chile and limited direct immigration from the Japanese main islands and Okinawa. The insubstantial immigration to these smaller receiver nations is easily explained. No Latin American nation other than Brazil before World War II offered the immigrants travel subsidies or easy access to affordable land. The Japanese simply settled in the nations with

Table 2. Growth of the Japanese Population by Province in Argentina

	1914			1947			1960		
	Male	Female	Total	Male	Female	Total	Male	Female	Total
Federal District	446	96	542	1,396	537	1,933	1,195	822	2,017
Buenos Aires	110	12	122	1,481	730	2,211	2,427	1,692	4,119
Córdoba	25	1	26	228	74	302	189	128	317
Santa Fe	115	4	119	206	49	255	192	117	309
La Pampa	1	1	2	2	0	2	0	0	0
Entre Rios	3	2	5	36	10	46	38	14	52
Corrientes	3	0	3	38	8	46	23	10	33
Misiones	0	0	0	83	46	129	230	172	402
Chaco	2	0	2	0	0	0	42	18	60
Formosa	2	0	2	2	0	2	3	1	4
Sgo. del Estero	0	0	0	38	9	47	14	2	16
Tucumán	25	1	26	48	17	65	33	11	44
Salta	18	0	18	42	4	46	43	12	55
Jujuy	96	26	122	15	4	19	8	2	10
Catamarca	0	1	1	5	1	6	8	4	12
La Rioja	0	0	0	2	1	3	1	0	1
San Juan	1	0	1	6	2	8	2	0	2
Mendoza	11	3	14	38	13	51	58	37	95
San Luis	0	0	0	5	0	5	6	0	6
Neuquén	0	0	0	4	2	6	5	1	6
Rio Negro	0	0	0	3	1	4	23	18	41
Chubut	2	0	2	0	0	0	4	1	5
Santa Cruz	0	0	0	2	1	3	0	0	0
T. del Fuego	0	0	0	0	0	0	0	0	0
C. Rivadavia	0	0	0	2	1	3	0	0	0
			1,007			5,192			7,606

Source: Data from *Nihonjin Aruzentin Iju-shi Hensan Iinkai* (Tokyo: Raten Amerika Kyokai, 1971), 265.

the best economic opportunities or where immigrant support networks already existed, such as Peru. Nevertheless, the experience of these smaller Japanese communities offers valuable insights into the pattern of adaptation by the Japanese of diverse Latin American social and economic settings.

The Japanese and the Argentines

The Japanese who settled in Argentina were but a small fraction of the many immigrants who arrived mainly from across the Atlantic beginning in the 1870s. Following the axiom of the Argentine positivist Juan Bautista Alberdí, "to govern is to populate," the nation's leaders sought to people the pampas with white European immigrants and thus to "civilize" the lands of the rootless gauchos in the same manner as the frontier was being opened in the western United States. Indeed, Argentina was second only to the United States as a haven for immigrants during the great migrations of the late nineteenth and early twentieth centuries.

According to Japanese immigrant lore, Kinzo Makino, a former sailor who arrived in Buenos Aires in 1886, was the first Japanese to become a permanent settler anywhere in South America. Makino traveled almost immediately to Córdoba, where he found work on the railroad construction gangs in the province. During the next two decades, however, only fourteen more Japanese immigrants, with only one woman among them, followed in Makino's footsteps.[1] Although legal immigration by the Japanese was negligible during these years, Argentina and Japan were interested in establishing better relations for commercial reasons. With negotiations primarily conducted by Toru Hoshi, a fervent advocate of Japanese colonization and Tokyo's minister in the United States, Argentina and Japan established formal diplomatic ties by signing the Treaty of Friendship, Commerce, and Navigation on 3 February 1898. The treaty opened the way for future Japanese immigration to Argentina, especially when North American nations began closing their doors after 1908.[2] One year after the treaty was signed, Argentina sent a naval frigate, the *Sarmiento,* on a good-will cruise of Japanese ports. While in Yokohama, the captain of the *Sarmiento* hired a thirteen-year-old Japanese cabin boy named C. Yoshio Shinya. The young man arrived in Buenos Aires in 1900 and began a new life in Argentina. Shinya would go on to become one of the leading intellectuals of the Japanese community, married an Englishwoman, took Argentine citizenship, and became a successful journalist and a cofounder of the newspaper *El Mundo.*[3]

✿ ✿ ✿

In April 1902, Japan established a diplomatic presence in Buenos Aires with Narinori Okoshi serving as Tokyo's representative, and the next year, Argentina sent Alfonso de Laferrère to represent its interests as consul in Yokohama.[4] Some of the Japanese who settled in Argentina before 1908 found work in the small Japanese craft stores in Buenos Aires that were opened after the commercial treaty of 1898 was signed.

As elsewhere in Latin America, 1908 was a watershed year in the settlement of the Japanese in Argentina. In that year the arrival of the initial contingent of Japanese immigrants to Brazil prompted the first significant influx of discontented colonists from the coffee plantations of São Paulo. By the following year, 160 Japanese had settled in Argentina, and some of these early immigrants moved on to the interior province of Jujuy, where by 1914 more than 200 were listed by the provincial government as workers in its sugarcane fields.[5] The largest concentrations of Japanese immigrants were drawn to the cities of Buenos Aires, Rosario, and Córdoba, where they tended to find work in small manufacturing plants and hotels and as gardeners or agricultural workers. Some were already beginning to become involved in the fresh-cut flower trade, which became a profitable enterprise for many Japanese settlers in the ensuing years. Until the first year of World War I, nearly all Japanese immigrants from Okinawa and the main islands arrived in Argentina after first immigrating overland and by ship to Peru or Brazil. In a real sense, they were refugees from the poor conditions on the sugar and coffee plantations of these two nations, and many of the Japanese pioneers in Argentina entered the country covertly. But there is little evidence that the Argentine authorities took action to expel these illegals.[6] Argentina assumed greater appeal for the immigrants because wages there were significantly better than those of Brazil or Peru and at least five to seven times those in Japan. For example, during the second decade of the twentieth century, a Japanese domestic servant in Buenos Aires could expect to earn 50 to 80 Argentine pesos per month, or about $20 to $32. A gardener earned approximately $20 to $40, and a worker in a small shoe factory about $60. Workers in Japanese factories were rarely able to earn more than $.50 per day, or approximately $13 a month, at this time.[7]

The first Japanese known to have "called" a fellow immigrant to Argentina was Magojiro Taira, an Okinawan, in 1914. Subsequently, a significant number of Japanese immigrants settling in Argentina before World War II were from the Ryukyu Islands. In order to be eligible to call, a Japanese in Argentina was required to be an "independent business operator." This generally meant that the caller had an independent income or owned certain business equipment, and it was not rigidly interpreted to mean the ownership of property or land. If employees wished to call, they had to be certified by their employer or have an associate or a friend guarantee financial responsibility for the new immigrant.[8]

World War I stimulated the flow of Japanese immigrants to Argentina, most of whom were Yobiyose immigrants, not the migrants from Brazil and Peru that had been arriving before the war began. In 1917 the Japanese company Osaka Shosen opened a commercial shipping line between Japan and Buenos Aires. The following year Tokyo opened a consulate in Buenos Aires to facilitate further trade and to deal with the growing number of Japanese nationals in the nation. By 1920, 1,958 Japanese immigrants had established residence in Argentina, of whom 387 were women.[9]

There was one abortive and one short-lived attempt to begin Japanese government-sponsored colonization programs in Argentina. The first was initiated as early as 1915 by the Japanese immigration promoter Seinosuke Tanaka of Kagoshima City. The original plan called for the settling of 50 to 130 immigrant families from Kagoshima on 6,200 acres of land in the Misiones province. Although there appeared to be substantial interest among the people of Kagoshima in this colonization scheme, the Ministry of Overseas Affairs in Japan rejected the project. The second and more ambitious project was founded by the Nichia Takushoku Gaisha (Colonial Society of the Argentine Japanese). The society sought to acquire 24,000 acres of virgin land near Las Palmas in the province of Chaco for cotton production and to raise one million yen in capital. Four hundred young Issei were originally recruited to form the core of the settlers in the new colony. It was hoped that the core group would be joined by other Japanese settlers in western Argentina. As will be recalled, this pattern of attracting new Japanese settlers to recently established colonies from other parts of the nation was very successful in Brazil. This was not the case in Argentina. Lacking the funding that the Brazilian colonization venture consistently attained, the Chaco venture floundered, and most of the original colonists migrated to better opportunities in Buenos Aires.[10]

As they did throughout Latin America, the Japanese in Argentina began to form fraternal associations as their numbers grew more substantial. On 31 October 1917, eighty leaders of the mainland Japanese community formed the Zai-a Nihonjinkai (Japanese Residents Association) at the Hotel Phoenix in Buenos Aires. Okinawans in Argentina formed their own association, the Okinawa Kenjin Kai, the following year. A number of *kenjin-kai,* or prefectural associations, were also created by 1920. By that year, the Sei-nen-kai, or Japanese youth association, was serving the young Japanese of Argentina.[11] Also serving the Japanese youth before World War II were five elementary schools in Buenos Aires and the surrounding districts of Burazco, Moron, Escobar, and San Miguel. As in the United States, these schools augmented the education provided in regular primary schools operated by the government and technically administered by the Argentine Ministry of Education. Students generally began attending these schools at the age of eight. Instruction in the Japanese language and culture was conducted for approximately six hours per week until the students reached the age of fourteen. Approximately 600 to 700 Japanese students attended these schools before World War II, which derived their financial support from an average 50-peso annual tuition paid by the parents. Unlike in Peru or Brazil, where the schools were constructed, maintained, and administered by the Japanese associations in those nations, the Argentine elementary schools were generally rented facilities and, more importantly, were not directly administered by the Japanese associations.[12] This was characteristic of the pattern of relatively low cultural autonomy marking the evolution of the Japanese community in Argentina.

From the beginning of their presence in Argentina, the Japanese, perhaps because of their relatively small numbers and the primarily urban setting of the community, were more prone to exogamous marriage. There were a number of reasons why mixed marriages were more common in Argentina than in Peru or Brazil. Most important was the lack of contract immigration and subsidies for those male Issei who wished to call picture brides from Japan. Forced to call their future wives at their own expense, smaller numbers of male immigrants did so. This was also true in Bolivia and Mexico, where contract immigration also did not exist. The urbanization of the Japanese Argentines and the fact that many transmigrated from Peru and Brazil suggests that these "above average and progressive" immigrants were more adaptable and more willing to culturally adopt Argentine society, which was predominately European in origin.[13]

Commenting on the social status and mobility of the Japanese immigrant in Argentina in 1956, James Tigner noted, "It is apparent that Japanese immigrants have the same degree of social mobility as the European, assuming that their education and circumstances are equal."[14] He further concluded that the acceptance of Japanese immigrants was facilitated by their willingness to adapt the Catholic religion. These Issei pioneers also rejected the racial exclusivity practiced by the Japanese of Peru and Brazil in the establishment of their social and recreational organizations. The admittance of native Argentines to these clubs, which were often some of the best managed in Argentina, was in sharp contrast to the exclusiveness that caused such resentment against the Japanese in Peru and to a lesser extent in Brazil.

Despite a greater tendency to adapt to the native population, the Japanese of Argentina still did not appear to completely reject the sojourner mentality so characteristic of their compatriots in other Latin American lands. This is evidenced by their very low rate of naturalization—generally less than 10 percent—before World War II. Although the Argentine government made citizenship relatively easy to acquire, only 1 percent of the Issei chose to make this definitive break with their homeland, as most of them were steadfast in their plans to return to Japan. Although not as low as those of the Japanese, the naturalization rates for Argentina's main immigrant groups, Italians and Spaniards, were far less than Argentine government leaders had hoped. Until the early twentieth century, many of these European immigrants were the *golindrinas,* or birds of passage, who wanted only seasonal agricultural labor rather than a permanent home in Argentina.

By the early 1930s, the patterns of economic activity of the Japanese Argentines were well established. Lacking sufficient capital and without the help of the Japanese government or subsidies that aided their compatriots in Brazil and Peru, relatively few Japanese had the funds to become independent agriculturalists. A survey of 2,550 Japanese Argentines completed in 1931 found only 162 Japanese farming their own land. Of these, a substantial number were floriculturists who raised their lovely products on very small plots of land in the immediate environs of Buenos Aires. This activity attracted increasing numbers of Japanese immigrants throughout the 1930s, when they began to make a good living selling carnations, chrysanthemums, gladiolas, and roses in the Plaza de San Martín in downtown Buenos Aires. Small plots of land and usually at least two greenhouses and perhaps a truck were enough to start a Japanese grower in the floricultural business after a general "apprenticeship" of two to four years as a helper of an established Japanese floriculturist. Overall, the survey showed that nearly 20 percent of the immigrants were supporting themselves as farm laborers, particularly in the sugar and cotton plantations of the western provinces. More than 400 Japanese were working in the emerging small manufacturing plants in the immediate vicinity of Buenos Aires. As might be expected, late-arriving immigrants who came with little capital or had few connections with existing economic support groups found work in easily accessible service jobs such as waiters, taxi drivers, and domestics. These accounted for the largest group, or 848 of those employed. Unlike their counterparts in Peru, the Japanese of Argentina did not immediately venture into small retailing or open their own small restaurants. Instead, laundries and dry cleaning establishments (*tintorerías*), which required little initial investment or skills, became the most popular form of independent economic activity. The Japanese dominated the dry-cleaning business in Buenos Aires before World War II, renting buildings with small shops and nearly always living with their families on the premises. Very few of the Issei pioneers were established in the professions or trades by 1931. The survey listed only seven physicians, six journalists, five artists or photographers, and twenty carpenters.[15]

By the late 1930s, more Argentine Issei, particularly the Okinawans, were beginning to acquire enough capital to begin small-scale truck gardening within a seven- to twenty-mile radius of Buenos Aires. Interviews conducted by Tigner with Naichi-jin and Okinawans in Buenos Aires are a valuable tool for evaluating their quality of life as they struggled to attain economic security in their newly adopted lands.

One such case study is quite revealing in its details of an immigrant's work ethic, self-sacrifice, determination, and support from fellow immigrant networks. Kicho Sukagawa, an Okinawan born into deep poverty in Motobu in 1896, was interviewed by Tigner in 1956. Sukagawa worked on a farm as a youth but was still able to complete an elementary school education. His driving ambition as a young man was to buy a farm, but he realized, given the economic opportunities in Okinawa, that would never happen unless he emigrated. His marriage at the age of eighteen reinforced his decision to emigrate to the Americas. Consequently, in 1918 Sukagawa joined a group of contract laborers to work in the coffee plantations of São Paulo, bound by a six-month labor agreement. Only half the cost of his passage on the Japanese vessel *Sanuki-maru* was paid for by government subsidies. Thus, Sukagawa arrived at the port of Santos with only his clothes and a few personal possessions. Assigned to work as a laborer at the Cafelandia plantation, Sukagawa was shocked to learn that the newly arrived immigrants could not save as much as the Morioka Immigration Company promised. He was also repelled by the poor living conditions on the plantation, particularly the "vermin infested shacks" in which the colonists were housed. Using Okinawan contacts in São Paulo City and Buenos Aires as an immigrant network and for financial support, Sukagawa fled Cafelandia after only nine weeks and traveled to Buenos Aires. Aided by Okinawans in the capital city, who gave him free lodging and meals until he was able to find work, this ambitious immigrant worked as a blacksmith's helper for two years. During that time he saved 1,300 pesos. He then located 12.5 acres in the Florencio Varela district, which he rented for 30 pesos per acre annually. Sukagawa built a rudimentary dwelling on the land and began life as a farmer. Within two years he was able to "call" his wife and two sons to Argentina. He moved to better land in the Burazco district, where he raised garden produce on a plot twice as large as his previous holding. In 1932 this hardworking truck gardener was able to purchase for 25,000 pesos the 12.5 acres of land he had previously rented, with the help of a loan from the local Okinawan association to augment his 15,000-peso down payment. Enjoying good prices for his produce in the expanding Buenos Aires market, Sukagawa was able to pay off his loan in five years and build a six-room house. Later, he purchased a Chevrolet pickup truck and a Mercury sedan, sure indicators of the material success he had attained since his arrival in Argentina three decades before.[16]

Other Japanese immigrants experienced more modest success. Many of the small shop owners in Buenos Aires, for example, continued to live in small apartments above their shops, and relatively few were ever able to afford an automobile. One such individual was Bitaro Miyashiro, an Okinawan born in Ogimi in 1908. He immigrated directly to Argentina in

1928, having been called by a relative living in Buenos Aires. The twenty-year-old Issei left his life as a farmer in Okinawa, intending to earn money and then return to help alleviate the financial problems of his father. Miyashiro arrived in Argentina virtually without possessions after using his life savings of 500 yen to pay for his passage. The young immigrant quickly found work in an Okinawan-owned dry cleaning establishment, where he worked for two years before earning enough money to open his own shop in partnership with a fellow Okinawan. Miyashiro was able to dissolve the partnership in 1938 and acquire sole ownership of his business in the Barrio Olivas district of Buenos Aires. In 1938, after a decade of hard work in Argentina, he had sufficient funds to travel to Okinawa to marry. Thereafter, he continued to work up to twelve hours a day, six days a week in his shop with two employees and his family members to make a success of his business. Miyashiro did not feel he was secure enough financially before World War II to buy the building in which his shop and dwelling were situated. He would be forced to wait until the early 1950s to consider purchasing his shop and the four-room apartment that then housed his family of four. Miyashiro, like so many Issei, could have returned to Japan with some significant savings at any time before World War II. Nevertheless, after a decade of disciplined work and financial struggle, he had built a secure life in Argentina that he wanted to share with his family.

In many ways, Miyashiro's story is typical of Japanese immigrants in Argentina as well as throughout Latin America. They did not enjoy spectacular success, but their modest middle-class existence was far better materially than they could have ever hoped for in Japan. Thus the sojourner mentality was overcome by the reality of better opportunities in the Americas. Although Sukagawa and Miyashiro and many others made new lives in Buenos Aires, there were small groups of Issei who began to settle in the provincial cities of Argentina during the 1920s as well.

By the late 1930s, significant numbers of Japanese worked in communities created in the province of Santa Fé. Most Issei were employed as small business owners in the cities of Rosario and Santa Fé because they could not accumulate sufficient capital to acquire even small plots of the increasingly higher priced farming land. Japanese immigrant associations in this province were quite active, sponsoring many social events and such sports activities as soccer, baseball, and track and field. Native Argentines played alongside their Japanese teammates, thus enhancing the relations between the two groups. Similar Japanese communities were established in the provinces of Córdoba, Tucumán, Salta, Chaco, and Corrientes, each numbering perhaps 200 to 300 in population.[17]

In direct contrast to the other nations of Latin America, Argentina did not impose significant restrictions on Japanese immigration during the 1930s. Nevertheless, passports issued to the Japanese averaged only 267 annually during the 1930s.[18] These numbers would have surely been larger if some form of immigrant subsidies and inexpensive land were more readily available. As it was, nearly all Japanese immigrants during the peak years of immigration were "called." Statistics for the Japanese population in Argentina at the end of the 1930s are problematic. Two estimates were published by the Japanese Ministry of Overseas Affairs in 1938. The lower estimate reported 5,838 settlers (3,977 male and 1,861 female); the higher one reported 7,095 (4,994 male, 2,101 female).[19] Although far smaller than its counterparts in Brazil and Peru, the Japanese community was well established economically and socially as World War II approached. Probably because of its small size, the difficulty in calling new immigrants, and its largely urban concentration in Buenos Aires, the Japanese community in Argentina was less prone than its counterparts elsewhere in Latin America to remain socially separate from the rest of the population. As we shall see, because of the pro-Axis orientation of the Argentine government during the World War II years and because of the patterns of immigration and settlement before the war, the Japanese Argentines did not suffer the devastating problems of internment, relocation, and severe restrictions of organizational activities that were common throughout much of the rest of Latin America.

Early Japanese Settlement in Bolivia

Although Japanese immigration to Bolivia until after World War II was not substantial, the cultural and economic precedents for later colonization efforts were successfully established by Issei pioneers between 1908 and 1938. Cheap Indian and mestizo labor, especially in mining, discouraged large-scale Japanese immigration to this Andean nation. Additional deterrents were the general lack of demand for plantation labor after the collapse of the rubber boom just prior to World War I and the absence of an immigration subsidy program similar to that in Brazil. In these respects, the climate for Japanese immigration to Bolivia mirrored that of Chile, where Indian and mestizo labor supplied the haciendas and the mines with sufficient workers. Yet it might have been possible for the Bolivian government to attract Japanese agricultural colonists after immigration restrictions closed off most of the Western Hemisphere nations to immigration after 1934. This possibility, however, was negated by the debilitating Chaco War (1932–35) with Paraguay in which Bolivia lost significant territory on its eastern frontier. The trauma of the Chaco War and the severe impact of the Great Depression on Bolivia's export-oriented economy thus provoked major socioeconomic changes in Bolivian society, including the emergence of a radicalized labor and peasant movement. The socialist-oriented governments of military presidents David Toro and German Busch during the late 1930s were primarily occupied with these domestic issues and with redefining the nature of Bolivian politics. Thus a well-articulated immigration policy was a very low priority of the government in the aftermath of the Chaco War.[20] Barely more than 500 Japanese would settle in Bolivia prior to 1938.

As noted, the first Japanese settlers were rubber workers who migrated from Peru seeking higher wages than sugar plantation labor offered. At the peak of the rubber boom in 1908, Michitaro Shindo, an agent of the financially troubled Meiji Immigration Company, headed a scheme to bring 5,000 Japanese rubber workers to eastern Bolivia during the next five years. This plan was never realized due to the company's bankruptcy and the lack immigration subsidies. In the end, only 120 Japanese rubber workers immigrated to Tambopata during the first year of the project.[21] Life in the forests of eastern Bolivia was lonely but profitable for these Japanese *seringeros* (rubber gatherers), who often earned three to four times what their counterparts in the sugar plantations of Peru were paid. They supplemented their diet with vegetables grown in small garden plots near their crude huts. Fishing and hunting often provided both a valued diversion and additional variety to diets. With the end of the rubber boom, however, the *seringeros* drifted into larger towns and cities such as Santa Cruz, La Paz, Oruro, and Potosí. Okinawans, who first began arriving in Bolivia in 1906, settled primarily in Riberalta.[22]

From interviews conducted with members of the Japanese community in 1956, Tigner notes that very few Japanese were able to call new immigrants to Bolivia before 1938 because of the strict regulations imposed upon the caller and the undeveloped state of immigrant networks, owing to the small size of the colony. Early Japanese residents of Bolivia informed Tigner that the records of Japanese immigration were poor because before 1915 no registration of immigrants occurred on the Bolivian frontier. Moreover, many of the early Japanese had transmigrated illegally from Peru, making proper record-keeping even more difficult. In any event, Tigner offers the estimate of only fifty-four called Japanese immigrants before 1941, based on the recollections of early immigrants and the information provided by the Japanese Association of Bolivia, founded in La Paz in 1923.[23] Thus many Issei married Bolivian women instead.

Japan and Bolivia signed a commercial treaty in 1914 that allowed Japanese cotton textiles, porcelain, paper products, and perfumes, among other items, to be imported into Bolivia, where they eventually became staples of the Japanese retail trade. On 4 February 1918, Bolivia appointed Víctor Muñoz Reyes as its envoy to Japan. The first efforts to establish an immigration agreement between Japan and Bolivia were initiated during the tenure of Muñoz Reyes, but they did not come to fruition. This may have resulted in part from Tokyo's decision not to establish a legation in Bolivia, where its interests were relatively minor.[24]

Since there was no Japanese diplomatic presence in Bolivia until November 1940, when a translator and a Japanese army officer were sent to La Paz to open a small post, the Japanese Association based in La Paz served as the unofficial branch of the Japanese legation in Peru. The association kept the legation informed of the activities of Japanese residents in Bolivia and maintained records of births, deaths, and marriages. Most significantly, it also provided financial assistance to newly arrived or needy Japanese residents and often secured employment for them.[25]

In 1915, nearly two-thirds of Japanese Bolivians made their living in agriculture in the Beni and Madre de Dios river valleys and in the immediate vicinity of the town of Riberalta.[26] Some of these Issei were subsistence farmers working new land, but most were rubber workers still employed in that declining industry. Later, many of them who had abandoned rubber gathering would begin establishing truck-farming operations in the Beni and Santa Cruz areas, very much in the pattern of the Japanese on the outskirts of Buenos Aires and those near São Paulo. As was the case with the Japanese Peruvians, many Issei would soon abandon the land and begin making a living as small merchants. The "monopoly" held by Peruvians and so-called *turcos,* or largely Christian Lebanese merchants, was successfully challenged in 1914 by Denju Horiuchi, the first prominent Issei entrepreneur in Riberalta. Soon other Japanese merchants opened small shops selling cigarettes, cheese, butter, rice, dried meat, and other food products not generally offered by the traditional merchants in the region.[27] Because of its proximity to the declining rubber plantations, Riberalta became the focus of Japanese settlement throughout the 1920s. By mid-decade, 262 of the 604 Japanese residing in Bolivia were residents of Riberalta.

The larger municipalities of La Paz and Santa Cruz claimed seventy-two and seventy-seven Japanese residents, respectively. At this time, the number of Japanese working in agriculture was nearly matched by those operating their own small shops or bazaars. Significant numbers were becoming barbers, carpenters, and owners of their own cafés.[28] By the mid-1930s, the Japanese were doing very well in La Paz. Operating in the center of the city in an area known as the *barrio comerico* (commercial district), the Japanese were owners of fifteen small stores, seven restaurants, five hair salons, and a textile factory. In 1935 the Japanese traders formed the La Paz Nihonjin Shogyo Kumiai (Japanese Trade Union in La Paz). These traders imported textiles, silk, wool, and toys from Japan and sold them in La Paz and other regional cities. The total value of these imports in 1938 was a sizable 5.8 million yen.[29]

Before the 1930s, most of the Japanese in Bolivia were establishing economically stable households and earning enough to live increasingly secure lives. On occasion, such as the great Kanto earthquake of 1923 in Japan, the Japanese community raised a substantial relief fund to be sent to the victims in their homeland. Similar financial efforts were made in support of the Bolivian government in the Chaco War and Japan's military operations in China in 1937. Yet the economic progress of the Japanese Bolivians was not sufficient to allow most male Issei to call wives from Japan or return to their homeland to marry. Recorded annual Japanese immigration to Bolivia never exceeded the 36 immigrants who arrived in 1936. Indeed, Japanese immigration throughout the 1930s totaled only 167 legal immigrants. Although the sources conflict, by the end of the 1930s there were approximately 600 people of Japanese ancestry. Of these, 306 were born in Japan, 7 had transmigrated from Peru, and 213 were Bolivian Nisei.[30]

With so few called immigrants, the Issei pioneers in Bolivia were simply unable to recreate the Japanese immigrant families that characterized the Japanese of Brazil and Peru. The gender balance among the first of Bolivia's Issei was one of the most unfavorable for endogamy in Latin America. For example, among the 604 Issei residing in Bolivia in 1923, only 49, or 8 percent, were women. Significantly, high rates of marriage with native Bolivians by the predominantly male Issei were common throughout the years before 1938. Statistics for the rates of intermarriage for the pre–World II period are not available. But Tigner reported in 1956 that "assimilation of Okinawans and *Naichi-jin* has progressed farther in Bolivia than any of the other Latin American Republics."[31] In that year, Tigner noted, 76 percent of the Okinawan Issei and 83.5 percent of the Naichi-jin were married to Bolivian women. No Japanese woman was recorded at that time to have married a native Bolivian. As one might surmise, nearly all of the Bolivian Nisei had intermarried with the Bolivian population at the time of Tigner's study. Cultural adaptation was thus occurring among these second-generation immigrants at a pace far more rapid than in the main receiver nations. The Bolivian Nisei were surpassing those of Mexico and Argentina in this regard as well.

Based on his interviews with Bolivian Issei who had married native women during the pre–World War II period, Tigner concluded that most of these Japanese immigrants had married lower-middle-class to lower-class women who were either illiterate or semiliterate. The marriages tended to survive only so long as the Issei remained successful in business and provided the lifestyle expected by their Bolivian wives at the time of their marriage. Usually little effort was made by the Bolivian women to learn Japanese, so Spanish was commonly spoken in the home and the children rarely learned Japanese. Compounding the difficulty of maintaining the immigrants' cultural identity through at least two generations was the absence of Japanese language schools in Bolivia. The small and dispersed Issei population, high rates of intermarriage, and the lack of funding from the Japanese Association of Bolivia seem to have been the principal reasons preventing their establishment.[32]

The biographies of two Okinawan Issei, Kajo Maeshiro and Eizo Tamashiro, offer useful insights into the common experiences of the Japanese pioneers in Bolivia. Maeshiro was born in 1914 into a poor farming family. After the death of his mother while Maeshiro was still a young child, his father immigrated to Peru in 1922 and left him in the care of an uncle. Working on his uncle's farm and attending elementary school while his father established himself as the owner of a small café in Lima, the young Okinawan eventually joined his father in Peru in 1932. The cost of passage was subsidized by the Japanese government. Toiling in his father's café in Lima while quickly learning Spanish, Maeshiro soon went to work as a salesman in a Lima bazaar. After three years, he accepted an offer to manage a similar bazaar in La Paz, Bolivia, in 1936. Soon he went into partnership with another Okinawan as co-owner of a bazaar in Oruro. Maeshiro did well enough in this venture and later the bakery business to call a Japanese wife in 1940. He also succeeded in a short stint as the principal owner of a 250-acre farm near Araca, nearly 200 miles from La Paz, and a bakery and tearoom in La Paz that he opened after the conclusion of World War II. Like many of the moderately successful Japanese of Bolivia and Argentina, Maeshiro achieved a secure middle-class lifestyle, primarily in urban commerce, after only slightly more than a decade of residence in Bolivia. His average monthly earnings in 1956 were a substantial, if not spectacular, $500 per month. He employed twelve people in his business at that time but still worked ten-hour days every day of the week. Nevertheless, he owned his business outright and had plans to build a house in La Paz for his family, which now included four daughters and one son. All of the children were raised as Roman Catholics, and all their godparents were Bolivians. With no Japanese schools in Bolivia, the Maeshiro family expressed the hope of sending their children (the oldest was ten) to high school in Japan. However, none spoke Japanese with any fluency and most had Bolivian playmates and reflected more the social mores of their native country than that of their parents.[33]

Eizo Tamashiro, born in Nago, Okinawa, in 1906, attained an elementary and middle-school education but was only able to earn a small wage as a mechanic in Tokyo before immigrating in desperation to Bolivia in 1931. Displaying the classic sojourner mentality, Tamashiro sought only to "work, save, and return" to his homeland after his immigrant stay in South America. Arriving in Bolivia with only two suitcases of clothes and 150 yen, he worked in a grocery store in La Paz for three years before moving temporarily to Córdoba, in western Argentina. Joined by his two brothers, he worked for three years as a waiter until returning to La Paz, where the brothers pooled their resources to open a tearoom and begin a small construction business. Selling their business during World War II to avoid its possible confiscation, the Tamashiro brothers "sheltered" their savings in a 3,500-acre farming operation forty miles from La Paz. The farm was later traded outright for another tearoom establishment in La Paz after the war. By 1952 Eizo Tamashiro was able to go it alone in his business venture by investing $10,000 in a soft-drink bottling plant in La Paz. Employing more than thirty people, all of whom were Bolivians, the business earned Tamashiro a substantial yearly profit of $22,500. Married to an Okinawan "picture bride" in 1940, Tamashiro raised his two children, a daughter who was nine and a son who was four when his wife died in 1951. The Issei businessman did not appear to be overly concerned that his children receive their high school education in Japan or that they marry fellow Japanese. Significantly, despite his success in business in Bolivia and a very comfortable lifestyle, which included an active social life involving hunting and baseball games with both Japanese and Bolivian friends, Tamashiro expressed plans to eventually return to Okinawa to be with his aging father during his last years.[34]

Both Okinawans like Maeshiro and Tamashiro as well as Naichi-jin in Bolivia demonstrated the same dedicated work ethic and quiet ambition for a better life so typical of the Issei in the larger receiver nations. The Bolivian Issei succeeded, however, without the elaborate immigrant networks—schools, active local associations, and direct funding from the Japanese government—that aided their counterparts in Peru and Brazil. With a relatively dispersed population in Bolivia, the Issei were either on their own or formed partnerships with friends or family members, as the Tamashiros had done. Their relatively small numbers and the social integration of the Japanese Bolivians seem to explain why they confronted so little discrimination prior to 1938. Consequently, the Bolivian government never established immigration restrictions against the Japanese during the 1930s. An open immigration policy thus made possible the post–World War II colonization program in Bolivia.

La Colmena: The First Japanese Colony in Paraguay

With its abundance of land and small population, landlocked Paraguay might seem to have been ideal for Japanese immigration and colonization in the twentieth century. Yet because of the devastating long-term impact of regional wars, immigration from all sources remained slight until the late 1950s. The first Japanese immigrants would not arrive until 1936, when the small Japanese colony of La Colmena was established 81 miles southeast of Asunción.

Colonization programs for European immigrants during the nineteenth and early twentieth century in Paraguay were not particularly successful. Attempts by English and Australian settlers in the late nineteenth century to create magnet colonies failed. During the 1920s, the first group of Mennonite refugees from the Ukraine and Canada began to settle in the remote, thinly populated Chaco region of western Paraguay. There they founded the Menno colony south of Puerto Casado. During the 1930s, German, Russian, and Polish Mennonites fled Nazi and Stalinist brutalities and established a second colony near Menno called Colonia Ferhiem. Mennonite refugees from World War II established a third settlement named Colonia Neuland.[35] Paraguay eventually became the home of one of the largest concentrations of Mennonite populations in the world by the 1960s. The Mennonite settlements, although successful, were not accompanied by significant additional immigration from more traditional sources. Other than these colonization efforts, only a trickle of immigrants from Spain, Italy, and Germany settled on land still dominated by the Guaraní (Paraguay's indigenous people) and mestizo culture that reflected little of European lifestyles. For example, between 1905 and 1925, only 13,300 immigrants established new lives in Paraguay.[36] Thus, only by the early 1930s was Paraguay's population restored to its level prior to the War of the Triple Alliance (1864–70). The La Colmena colony was a direct result of the restrictive immigration law passed by the Brazilian government in 1934. Japan was immediately compelled to search for new lands for its would-be immigrants in Paraguay.[37] Discussions leading to the establishment of La Colmena began in 1934 and involved the Japanese, Brazilian, and Paraguayan governments as well as colonization companies based in Japan. In early 1936, the Paraguayan government agreed to admit 100 Japanese families for the purpose of establishing the pilot colony. The Japanese company that was administering the colonization program wanted a site with reasonable access to rail lines and roads linking the colonists to Asunción. These transportation links were completed, however, only after feeder roads were constructed with great effort by the colonists during the first four years of settlement. (As late as 1992, when I conducted field research in La Colmena, the road network in the immediate vicinity of the town was difficult to traverse after heavy rains.) Moreover, the soils in the La Colmena settlement also did not prove to be as fertile as originally hoped because of their sandy texture, which could not tolerate long-term cultivation.

None of these problems was fully anticipated when the first small group of Japanese arrived in La Colmena in May 1936 to survey the land, design the roads, and mark the boundaries of newly created properties.[38] The colony was divided into six zones, with the small creeks within the settlement acting as natural boundaries. Within these zones, 485 agricultural lots were created, varying in size from 18 to 76 acres, depending upon the quality of the land and the topography. La Colmena's planners tried to distribute land fairly to each colonist with regard to fertility, availability of running water, and access to the community's proposed roads. A town center was also planned to include an administration building, hospital, schools, and a central market.[39] La Colmena's design appears to owe much to the pattern of settlement and land distribution already well established in the Japanese colonies in the Brazilian states of São Paulo and Paraná. Indeed, twelve of the first families to settle in this new Paraguayan community were Issei who migrated from the "frontier zones" of Brazil.[40]

The first large group of colonists began arriving in La Colmena in October 1936. Over the course of the next five years, approximately 138 families numbering 844 individuals established the nucleus of the colony. Fifteen families served as administrators and school teachers and in other support roles. The agricultural colonists were drawn from prefectures throughout Japan and from Brazil. These "agricultural colonists," in reality, lacked real farming experience. Like the first colonists in Brazil in 1908, fewer than half were "full time" farmers before they decided to immigrate.[41] The colony survived during these first difficult years, according to some of the original colonists, because of a disciplined sense of common purpose and the strong direction of an "authoritarian company administration that directed colony life and represented a tangible link with the mother country."[42] One visitor to the colony in 1937 noted, "'The colonists were not yet free, but they did not understand the meaning of freedom. They planted what they were told to plant, when they were told to plant, and where they were told to plant it. Accordingly their crops thrived, and in this way they must thrive also.'"[43] Despite this observation, the La Colmena colonization company made some bad decisions that alienated many of the colonists during the first years of operation. Colonists were required to contribute their labor to community projects such as road building and the construction of light industrial facilities. Some of these projects were poorly planned and were eventually abandoned. Moreover, the agricultural planning process for La Colmena was based on the successful programs developed in the Brazilian colonies during the previous two decades. Differences in climate and topography, however, soon proved these methods to be ineffective in this region of Paraguay.[44]

As they did in Brazil, the first Japanese colonists in Paraguay made a concerted effort to maintain strong cultural ties with Japan for themselves and their children. During the first year, the colonists built a school that initially employed a Paraguayan teacher and Paraguayan students along with their own children. This school was established under Paraguayan law and did not offer the cultural instruction that the Japanese colonists sought for their children. Consequently, the colonists soon created a parallel system of schooling that offered instruction in Japanese culture and language and was staffed by a teacher from Japan who arrived in 1937. At times during the first years of settlement, the colonists of La Colmena operated three separate Japanese schools at great difficulty and expense. Their children often found it difficult to spend the additional time in school to study Japanese language and culture and to meet their work obligations as well.

La Colmena's first Japanese colonists also tried to retain a spiritual bond with their homeland. As late as the end of the 1960s, 80 percent of the family heads in the colony claimed they were Buddhists and 5 percent expressed an affiliation with Shintoism. Household and village shrines, including one containing a stone from a Shinto shrine at Ise, Japan, were constructed in La Colmena during the colony's first years. Moreover, religious festivals commemorating the origin of Japan (*Meijei-setsu*) and the emperor's birthday (*Tencho-setsu*) were regularly observed until World War II brought an end to these expressions of Japanese tradition. The war would have far-reaching and negative implications for the preservation of Japanese cultural values in La Colmena.[45]

The Immigrants of Chile and Colombia

As we have seen, little available land and ample Indian and mestizo labor in the mining industry dampened Japanese colonization efforts in Chile from their very beginnings in the early twentieth century. During the years between 1908 and 1925, the "lack of opportunities" and a strong anti-immigrant bias, mirroring a similar trend in the United States, diverted many prospective Japanese immigrants to the other main receiver nations in South America. To put this in perspective, in 1907, 99 percent of Chile's agricultural labor force was native born and only 4 percent of the nation's industrial workers were foreigners.[46] Increased labor unrest between 1910 and the early 1930s led Chile's ruling elites to falsely blame the "'waves of human scum thrown upon our beaches by foreign countries'" for these emerging social problems. The Russian Revolution soon prompted the enactment of a residency law that permitted the government to prohibit entry and deport foreigners who were deemed potentially subversive.[47] Tokyo, clearly seeking to establish a sound basis for expanding trade relations with this Pacific Rim nation, opened a diplomatic mission in Santiago in 1911. Nevertheless, despite Japan's intent to increase immigration along with its expanding commercial ties with Santiago, only 194 Japanese immigrated to Chile from 1908 to 1925.[48] This number represented only a small increase over the original group of 126 Issei who immigrated to Chile with such high hopes in 1903.

These hopes went unrealized, as few opportunities for landholding ever materialized. Brian Loveman describes Chilean agriculture before World War II as a political and social "enclave" that was concentrated in Chile's rich Central Valley. There, 60 to 75 percent of Chile's rural labor force was "culturally isolated on the vast haciendas that dominated the countryside." This "captive labor force" meant that no temporary labor contracts for Japanese immigrants, which were so commonplace in Brazil and Peru, were necessary for Chilean agriculture to prosper. Moreover, land was so concentrated in the hands of Chile's rural elites that only 2.7 percent of *hacendados* owned 80 percent of the agricultural land in the Central Valley.[49] These landholding patterns remained in place until the early 1960s, thus depriving all but the wealthiest immigrants from any nation of a reasonable opportunity to build new lives in agriculture. Clearly, few Japanese immigrants were willing to struggle against these constraints when far greater opportunities were available in Brazil throughout this era.

Lacking the need for foreign laborers, and despite the insignificant number of Japanese entering the nation, the Chilean government, clearly following the lead of the United States, banned Asian immigration in 1925.[50] Small numbers of Japanese immigrants would continue to enter Chile until the end of the 1930s, however, as the Chilean government (apparently) permitted the calling of 171 relatives of Issei who had established a stable economic status.[51] The Chilean census of 1940 listed 948 Japanese.[52] The accuracy of these statistics from an ethnic perspective is questionable, however, since between one-third and one-half of all Issei males married Chilean women. The wives of these Issei, according to the evidence gathered in interviews by Tigner, were primarily working-class mestizas who frequently disdained Japanese traditions and raised their children with a heavy emphasis upon native customs. The few reasonably financially secure Issei who could afford to call Japanese wives frequently elected to send their children to Japan for schooling because of a lack of Japanese schools in Chile. The small number and dispersed settlement patterns of the Japanese prevented the establishment of the kinds of associations that bound other overseas Japanese communities to their homeland and to one another. It was not until 1939 that a Japanese elementary school was opened in Santiago. Even then, classes in the Japanese language and culture were offered only two days a week in three-hour sessions. The school was closed during World War II and never reopened.[53] The Japanese in Chile primarily made their livelihoods as proprietors of small shops, café owners, barbers, and launderers. A few Issei rented small plots and worked as truck gardeners or floriculturists, while others worked as tradesmen such as carpenters. As was the case with the Issei in the rest of Latin America, few were able to enter the professions because of language and cultural barriers. More than in any other nation in Latin America, the Issei of Chile suffered continuing economic hardships. Tigner noted that the standard of living of the Japanese in Chile, particularly the Okinawans, was the lowest in Latin America. The few Okinawans in Chile, for example, were making a meager living operating "third class barbershops" in the poorest neighborhoods of Santiago, Valparaíso, and San Antonio.[54]

When in November 1940 the Japanese government gathered representatives of the Japanese overseas at a conference to help celebrate the putative 2,600th anniversary of the accession of Emperor Jimmu, Chozan Ota, the representative from Chile, lamented that the Chilean Nisei were growing up without an opportunity to receive a genuine Japanese education or an appreciation for the culture of their ancestors. Ota noted that Issei volunteers and parents were attempting to provide the necessary instruction, but this training rarely exceeded two to three hours per week.[55] These candid comments by Ota at this prestigious conference reflect the desperation of an immigrant leader who saw his beloved cultural traditions ebbing away among the isolated and dispersed Japanese in Chile. These problems would only worsen with World War II and its aftermath.

Although not as severe as the hardships the Japanese faced in Chile, similar circumstances confronted the small colony of Japanese immigrants who began arriving in very limited numbers in the 1920s in Colombia. Japanese colonization prospects in Colombia appeared to be favorable in the two decades after World War I. Unlike Brazil, where the production of coffee was dominated by the vast plantations of the south, in Colombia this increasingly important commodity was raised on small and medium-size farms in the highland areas. This type of family-owned farm accounted for 75 percent of the nearly 200,000 coffee producers in Colombia by the late 1930s. In the Cauca Valley, the region where the first Japanese colony was established, small growers were clearing the forests and planting coffee in increasing numbers just as the Japanese were settling in the district. But unlike Brazil, where the planters were employing large numbers of newly arrived Japanese immigrants in the coffee fields, the large coffee estate owners in Colombia chose not to seek foreign labor to augment their labor force. Thus the transition from contract laborer to free landholder, which proved to be so successful in Brazil, did not materialize in Colombia. If the Japanese government had subsidized small coffee-farming operations for the early Colombian Issei, this type of agriculture probably would have been ideal for the hardworking Japanese immigrants.[56] Indeed, Nola Reinhardt's research on family farming in Colombia indicates that Japanese wage laborers could have possibly filled the acute short-term labor needs on the larger coffee haciendas. But Colombian *hacendados* were not as aggressive as the Brazilian plantation owners in meeting their labor needs. Reinhardt's research points to the continuing economic viability of small-family coffee units well into the late 1930s. Clearly, opportunities would have been there for the Japanese had they chosen to open new coffee lands in western Colombia.[57]

The Japanese consuls general in Panama and Peru first proposed the idea of Japanese immigration and colonization in Colombia to the Ministry of Foreign Affairs in the mid-1920s. Before then, there had been no significant Japanese presence in Colombia, with only twenty Japanese entering the country from Panama, Peru, and Cuba in the decade after World War I. Official immigration directly from Japan was very small, with only five passports being issued by Tokyo before 1928.[58] Finally, one year later, the Overseas Development Company (KKKK), which was very active in Brazil at that time, purchased 500 acres of land in the province of Cauca, near Cali, for the purpose of establishing a magnet colony in Colombia. The first Japanese contingent there was composed of five families from the prefectures of Fukuoka, Yamaguchi, and Fukushima. They arrived in November 1929 and settled near the town of Corinto, in the heart of the Cauca Valley. Two more separate groups of colonists arrived in 1930. The colonists were supposed to have practical farming experience and were expected to work at least three years for the KKKK in the vicinity of Corinto. The colonization company paid for the colonists' passage as well as their expenses for the first fifteen days in Colombia, until farming and the building of their dwellings could begin. Very soon, the KKKK allowed the colonists to buy their own land, and after a short period of unsuccessfully experimenting with fruit trees, potatoes, beans, corn, and cotton, the colonists settled on a cash-crop bean called *shiro-kintoki* (white beans). This crop became the main source of revenue for the colony over the course of the next two decades. Profits from the sale of the beans were kept by the administrative agents of the KKKK, who returned a small portion of the revenues back to the colonists as their needs required.[59] The basic daily requirements of the colonists were provided by a company store at reasonable prices.[60]

By 1936 the colonists were joined by approximately 100 additional Japanese immigrants. As happened with members of the La Colmena colony in Paraguay, they did not adapt well to the demands of local agriculture. Because of the exhaustion of the land and the low price of the beans by the end of the 1930s, some of the original colonists began leaving the community, establishing independent farming operations nearby.

The difficult economic conditions in the Cauca Valley community prompted the colonists to form an agricultural cooperative for the purpose of managing bean production and importing needed farm machinery. The cooperative worked reasonably well until it was abolished by the Colombian government soon after the attack on Pearl Harbor. The colonists were then placed under severe restrictions by the Colombian government and encouraged to farm individually.[61] It was only after the war that the Japanese in Colombia began enjoying some degree of economic success. Then they were able to form a Japanese agricultural association and market their produce more efficiently. This association not only helped maintain reasonable price levels for their products but enhanced the integration of the Japanese in Colombia into local civic and social affairs.[62] This process was further enhanced by their high rates of intermarriage with native Colombians, for reasons similar to those in Chile and Argentina. Like the Chilean and Colombian colonists, they were outside the mainstream of Japanese immigration in South America and confronted great difficulties in maintaining the high degree of cultural identity and solidarity characteristic of the larger receiver nations.

The Japanese of Central America and Cuba

After the opening of the Panama Canal in 1914, the Japanese government tried to establish better trade relations and immigration agreements with

Central American governments, but these efforts brought meager results. Gardiner notes, "Prior to the 1930s, Japanese trade with Central America was so inconsequential that it frequently eluded statistical records."[63] Panama was an exception to this trend because Japanese merchant and passenger vessels frequently stopped there before continuing their journeys to the west coast of South America. The overwhelming commercial and military dominance of the United States in Central America discouraged Japanese penetration of these small markets. Formal diplomatic relations with the other Central American republics were not established until July 1935, when the Japanese minister to Mexico, Yoshiatsu Hori, presented his credentials to the presidents of Guatemala, Honduras, El Salvador, Nicaragua, and Costa Rica.[64]

Well before Tokyo opened diplomatic ties with the Central American nations, these countries, with the exception of Panama, took steps to limit the access of Japanese immigrants to their shores. This appears to be a reflection of Washington's influence, which was perhaps motivated by the fear of cross-border migration of Japanese immigrants to the southwestern United States. As will be recalled, the U.S. State Department pressured the government of Porfirio Díaz in Mexico to limit Japanese immigration for this reason after the Gentlemen's Agreement. Costa Rica restricted Asian immigration in 1896 and Guatemala did the same in 1909. Panama did prevent persons of the "yellow race" from immigrating in 1926. However, the Japanese were exempted from this law only two years later when it became clear that the legislation would undermine Panama's importance as a transit stop for Japanese bound for South America. By the 1930s, all Central American nations except Panama limited Japanese access. As a result, only a few dozen Japanese immigrants settled in Central American nations other than Panama, and these Issei transmigrated from Panama.

With the beginning of the construction of the Panama Canal in 1904, Japanese began entering Panama. By 1905 there were approximately 30 Japanese in the country, many of whom were employed cutting the hair of the thousands of construction workers on the canal. After the completion of the canal in 1914, more Japanese continued to immigrate, primarily because Panama was on the transit route to Peru. Still, the number of legal immigrants remained small, with only 415 immigrants being recorded by the Japanese Foreign Office as entering Panama through 1938.[65] The Issei of Panama found work during these years in the same activities as their compatriots elsewhere in Latin America. They labored as fishermen, small farmers, barbers, and café managers. Some did well enough to become relatively prominent members of their communities.

Like Brazil and Peru, Cuba depended on African slaves as the primary labor force in the sugar industry until abolition in 1886. Also mirroring events in Peru, Cuban sugar planters, anticipating the end of slavery as early as the 1840s, eventually contracted 125,000 Chinese coolies to work in the cane fields, sugar mills, and railroad construction projects and as urban domestics before abolition.[66] With motives very similar to those of the Brazilian coffee planters, Cuban leaders also sought to increase white European immigration to augment the labor force and "whiten" Cuban society during the last four decades of the nineteenth century. Arriving mainly from Spain, these European immigrants nearly doubled the white labor force during the last years of slavery and Chinese coolie labor.[67] This influx of European immigrants transformed Cuba's labor force, but it was still not substantial enough by 1880 to discourage Cuban leaders from considering the possibility of importing Japanese laborers as well. In that year, a Spanish diplomat in Tokyo approached the Japanese Foreign Ministry with the offer of a treaty of immigration, similar to the earlier accord with China that brought thousands of coolies to cane fields and sugar mills. Recognizing the horrific conditions under which the Chinese labored in Cuba, Tokyo rejected the treaty overture.[68]

For the next two decades, as it went through the political and social turmoil of racial conflict and revolution, Cuba lacked appeal for Japanese immigrants. The first Japanese immigrant would thus not arrive in Cuba until 1903. Cuba's first Issei, Kietaro Ohira, transmigrated from Mexico, as would many Japanese who settled in Cuba in the ensuing decades. At least 60 Japanese would abandon Mexico for Cuba during the most violent years of the Mexican Revolution (1910–16), eventually finding work in the Cuban sugar mills.[69] With Cuba and the Philippines virtual protectorates of the United States after the Spanish American War, Tokyo now encouraged Japanese immigration to both destinations in the hope that the Japanese could eventually transmigrate to the United States.[70] But it would not be until 1916, well after the Gentlemen's Agreement limited Japanese immigration to the United States, that the first significant contingent of 76 Japanese would emigrate directly from Japan to Cuba. Thereafter, 610 Japanese would follow in their footsteps until the end of the 1930s.[71]

The Issei of Cuba did not long remain as laborers in the poorly paid and seasonal work of the sugar industry. The sugar planters of Trinidad and Santa Clara in western Cuba treated the Japanese as poorly as their counterparts were treated in Peru. Badly paid or cheated out of their contracted wages, many quickly left the cane fields and mills to open lightly capitalized barbershops, cafés, or speciality stores in Cuba's towns and cities. This transition, however, was met in some cases with firm resistance by Cuban business owners. For example, although there were no more than sixty Japanese-owned barbershops in Cuba by the mid-1920s, the Cuban barber's association devised a certification exam that disqualified all but ten Issei barbers on the island.[72] Clearly, the same resentment frequently expressed by business owners against the Japanese in the larger receiver nations was also experienced even when the Japanese population was quite small.

The most successful venture begun by Japanese agriculturalists in Cuba was a farming cooperative established on the Isle of Pines during the 1930s. Working the island's marginal soils, the Japanese began a successful produce-farming operation that was primarily directed at consumers in the United States. Raising tomatoes, peppers, eggplant, and a variety of fruits, the farmers did well individually until the Great Depression weakened the U.S. market and threatened their livelihood. The Japanese on the island responded to the crisis by forming the Matsushima Cooperative of Japanese Agriculturalists in 1934. Approximately seventy Japanese farmers pooled their resources to form the cooperative. Their efforts stabilized production and prices and allowed the Japanese on the island to weather the Depression and maintain a reasonably secure lifestyle. The cooperative would continue to operate until World War II, when it was dissolved by Cuban authorities.[73]

Although the Japanese in Cuba did reasonably well economically, the island held few real opportunities for them, compared with Brazil or Peru, before the 1930s. Few Japanese immigrants were willing to labor in the cane fields when opportunities were far more expansive elsewhere in Latin America. The best land in Cuba was monopolized by the large sugar firms, many of which were dominated by U.S. capital. Moreover, the large number of Spanish immigrants who arrived during the late nineteenth and early twentieth centuries provided stiff competition for the Japanese who tried to establish small businesses. This had also been true of the Chinese who toiled in the cane fields long before the first Japanese arrived.

✿ ✿ ✿

As we have seen, the Japanese diaspora in Latin America before World War II was quite uneven. Brazil, Peru, Mexico, and Argentina drew the most Japanese, for obvious reasons. Subsidized immigration and better economic opportunities were by far the most important considerations of immigrants who only wanted to make money as quickly as possible and return to their native land. When the Japanese immigrated to Bolivia, Paraguay, Chile, Colombia, Panama, and Cuba, they demonstrated the same discipline and resolve to succeed that was evident everywhere they settled in Latin America.

But because they were so few in number, they were unable to sustain the cultural traditions of their homeland through schools and associations like those that were so influential in Brazil and Peru. Intermarriage rates were thus very high, and the Japanese family was not maintained through the Yobiyose system as it was in the larger receiver nations. Still, as was true in Bolivia and Paraguay, these immigrant pioneers would establish a foundation that would provide a basis for important post–World War II colonization projects that emphasized ethnic solidarity and Japanese cultural traditions.

THE IMPACT OF THE ASIAN WAR, 1938–52

> We were thrown out of our apartment we rented . . . right after
> we arrived in Mexico City. A few families rented an apartment
> together, where each family cooked its own meals. The room soon
> became sooty and the owner told us to get out, saying the Japa-
> nese were so filthy.
> —A Japanese immigrant recalling the relocation of Nikkei to
>   Mexico City during World War II, 1983

The fate of its people in the Americas was of little consequence to the Japanese government as it moved inexorably toward total war after 1937. The
more than 400,000 people of Japanese descent residing in the United States,
Canada, and Latin America were isolated and, in many cases, victimized as
a result of Tokyo's decision to wage war. Clearly, the welfare of the nearly
quarter of a million Japanese Latin Americans was a very small stake in
Tokyo's policy making (see table 3).

Tokyo did make some efforts to reach out to the Japanese in Latin America
as war with the United States grew more probable. This initiative, however,
seemed to be prompted more by Japan's need to plan for a militarized colonization of Asia than concern for its nationals in the Americas. In November 1940, the Takumusho (Ministry of Overseas/Colonial Affairs) and the
Gaimusho (Ministry of Foreign Affairs) cosponsored a conference of the
overseas Japanese on the occasion of the 2,600th year since Japan became
a "nation" under the reign of Emperor Jimmu. It was called the Kaigai
Takushoku Daihyosha Kaigi (Conference of the Representatives of Overseas Colonization). Delegates to the conference were divided into four groups
depending on whether they represented the South Seas, Manchuria, North
America, or Central and South America. The conference was to establish
procedures for further overseas immigration and colonization based upon
the experiences of the Japanese in the Americas and in Manchuria. The

Table 3. Japanese Immigration to the Americas by Imperial Era, 1899–1941

	Meiji (1899–1912)	Taisho (1913–26)	Showa (1927–41)	Totals
Mexico	11,099	1,197	2,270	14,566
Panama	0	182	233	415
Cuba	4	419	249	672
Brazil	4,573	44,046	139,062	187,681
Peru	9,106	15,134	8,827	33,067
Argentina	22	1,321	4,055	5,398
Chile	135	189	174	498
Colombia	0	5	224	229
Bolivia	0	24	178	202
Venezuela	0	0	12	12
Uruguay	0	0	18	18
Paraguay	0	0	521	521
	24,939	62,517	155,823	243,279

Source: Data from Gaimusho Ryoji Iiju-bu, *Waga kokumin no kaigai hatten: Iiju hyakunen no ayumi* (Tokyo: Ministry of Foreign Affairs, 1971), 142–43.

Japanese government told the fifty representatives that the war in China and the Tripartite Treaty with Germany and Italy would surely result in "difficulties" for the Japanese overseas. Tokyo urged the delegates to inform their fellow "pioneers" to prepare for these difficulties with "great determination." Despite this plea, the delegates from Latin America were told that the Japanese colonization of Manchuria was one of the priorities of the Tokyo's foreign policy and that they should respect the importance of that colonization venture. Additionally, they were instructed to be ready, both "mentally and materially," to confront more difficulties because of that foreign policy. Lastly, they were encouraged to visit their hometowns and tell their relatives how they themselves had fared as immigrants in America.[1]

Clearly, the Japanese in the Americas were beyond Tokyo's imagined sphere of influence and increasingly removed from Japan's protective diplomatic pressures as the conflict in Asia escalated. The war and Japan's devastating defeat changed nearly everything for the Japanese Latin Americans. Many were interned or removed from their homes to more "secure" areas, and more than 2,000 were deported from Latin America and interned in the United States. Most suffered devastating financial losses from which it was very difficult to recover. Most profoundly, the staunch loyalty of many Japanese, particularly older Issei, to the invincible Japan of their memories and their firm belief in the certainty of a return to their ancestral homeland evolved, in some extreme cases, into denial that Japan had lost the war, while for most it prompted disillusionment and a search for a new vision of a lifetime in Latin America. What was left of the sojourner mentality was forsaken in the ashes of Japan's defeat. In its place, the Issei substituted a new hope—the security and prosperity of their children and grandchildren in a Latin American setting. This chapter will discuss the experience of the Japanese Latin Americans in the context of the Asian war and its immediate aftermath. A more in-depth analysis of the deeply compelling story of Peru's Japanese during this era will be offered in chapter 6.

The Japanese of Latin America Endure World War II

As war threatened, the Roosevelt administration began constructing a hemispheric defense initiative during the late 1930s to meet what it saw as the threat of German and Japanese espionage, sabotage, and military operations in Latin America. This cooperative hemispheric defense involving the close collaboration of the Latin American nations with the United States was a clear revision of the unilateral emphasis of previous U.S. policies.

At the Eighth International Conference of American States in Lima in December 1938, U.S. Secretary of State Cordell Hull made the first initiative for joint military operations. The resulting Declaration of Lima approved joint action to defend the states of the region from outside attack. Hull recalled in his memoirs how convinced Washington was of the dire threat of the Axis to hemispheric security. "To me the danger to the Western Hemisphere was real and imminent. It was not limited to the possibility of military invasion. It was more acute in its indirect form of propaganda, penetration, organizing political parties, buying some adherents, and blackmailing others. We had seen this method employed with great success in Austria and the Sudetenland. The same technique was obvious in Latin America."[2] Central to evolving U.S. war plans was the defense of the Panama Canal and the security of Mexico and the Caribbean nations from Axis penetration. With the fall of France and the imminent danger of the defeat of Britain in the summer of 1940, Chief of Staff George C. Marshall and Chief of Naval Operations Harold R. Stark became convinced of direct Nazi-inspired threats to the governments of Mexico and Brazil, and some planners proposed the possibility of "limited military operations in Mexico," if the situation required.[3]

These planners envisioned an Axis threat in Latin America that would seek not to conquer territory but rather to exploit Latin American political instability to foster "'upheavals'" and anti-American attitudes and create economic dependence on the Axis powers.[4] Tokyo's policy makers and its diplomats stationed in Latin America tried to carry out these actions in the eighteen months before the attack on Pearl Harbor.

Tokyo's risky policies in Latin America were, of course, closely linked to its military objectives in Asia. It is not surprising that Japanese political leaders showed minimal concern for the impact of these policies on Latin America's Japanese. After all, Tokyo's quest for an Asian empire and economic autonomy was creating significant hardship in the homeland. Confronting the cutoff of strategic war materials from the United States and the possibility that Japanese assets would be frozen by Washington, the Imperial Navy took the extraordinary step of transferring its sheltered funds from the United States to Latin American banks.

Well before the details of the Pearl Harbor attack were finalized, however, contingency plans were being made through Japanese diplomatic channels in Latin America for the gathering of intelligence that would aid the war effort. Washington was fully aware of these efforts because of the interception of Japanese diplomatic message traffic made possible by the MAGIC operation begun before Pearl Harbor. This counterintelligence effort was critical in shaping the policy of the United States and Latin American nations toward their Japanese populations from early 1941 onward. Mexico and Panama were major arenas for this emerging struggle.

Despite the bellicose threats of Japanese diplomatic personnel in Latin America, the naval and military threat to the Western Hemisphere was largely an empty one. But few military leaders in the United States and Latin America were prepared to dismiss this possibility after the raid on Pearl Harbor took place. The job of intelligence officers was to plan for the worst, and as a consequence, the Japanese of Latin America as well as its German and Italian population would figure prominently in their defense equation.

Preparing for War: The Impact in Mexico and Panama

Mexico was the primary focus of Japanese Latin American intelligence initiatives because of its proximity to the United States and its valuable strategic mineral reserves. Tokyo sought answers to questions about the war readiness of U.S. armed forces, about Washington's intent to ally with the European powers in the event of an attack on their Southeast Asian possessions, and about the possibility of securing strategic materials from the Latin American nations in the event of conflict with the United States. The Japanese government was also concerned with monitoring ship movements through the Panama Canal and undermining the diplomatic unity largely secured by the Good Neighbor Policy in the Western Hemisphere.[5]

From the mid-1930s until the attack on Pearl Harbor on 7 December 1941, Japan tried to secure large shipments of petroleum, scrap iron, and mercury from Mexico. This endeavor met with significant success before the war began. Japan developed economic interests in two petroleum companies, Compañía Mexicana de Petróleos la Laguna, S.A., and Compañía Petrolera Veracruzana, S.A. The Japanese Mexican businessman Kizo Tsuru served on the boards of both companies, which had close ties to prominent political leaders in Mexico. In 1939 the government of Lázaro Cárdenas briefly considered the possibility of constructing, with Japanese funding, a pipeline linking the Gulf Coast oil fields to the west coast outlet at Salina Cruz to facilitate increased petroleum exports to Japan. As late as October 1940, U.S. diplomatic officials were reporting that Japanese petroleum engineers working in Mexico appeared to be unfamiliar with basic petroleum engineering principles and speculated that they were really attempting to plan for the establishment of bases in the nation's northwest.[6] Also, the expropriation of U.S. and British petroleum companies by the Cárdenas regime in 1938 and the Mexican president's willingness to court German and Japanese markets for the newly created state-owned Mexico oil industry caused significant security concerns in Washington.

These concerns were not unfounded. In February 1941, Japanese foreign minister Yasuki Matsuoka instructed his diplomatic officials in Mexico City to organize Japanese residents, "including newspapermen and business firms for the purpose of gathering information." Care was to be taken so as "not to give cause for suspicion of espionage activities."[7] In early June 1941, Matsuoka told Yoshiaki Miura, Japan's ambassador in Mexico City, that 100,000 yen had been appropriated to be "used in Mexico City to collect intelligence concerning the United States." Matsuoka thought that Mexico City was "the natural geographical center for an intelligence base" and the "nerve center of an intelligence network spanning the United States and the Latin American nations." Miura went to Houston and New Orleans to plan for an espionage network. Other Japanese diplomats journeyed to Panama and Rio de Janeiro for the same purpose.[8]

Most troubling for the future of the Japanese in Mexico was Tokyo's initial interest in recruiting them for intelligence-gathering purposes. Japanese officials would eventually conclude, however, that the hardworking fishermen and farmers of Mexico's northwest and Baja California Norte were not members of the *inteligencia* and would have limited utility as espionage agents.[9] This still did not discourage Ambassador Miura from proposing some grand espionage schemes in conjunction with his military attaché, Yoshiaki Nishi. As the time of the attack on Pearl Harbor approached, Mexican public opinion and the decidedly pro-American position of the Manuel Ávila Camacho regime in Mexico (1940–46) made the development of a Japanese espionage network allied with German and Italian agents extremely difficult. Japanese diplomatic officials, anticipating the approaching danger for its nationals in Mexico, took limited measures to prepare the Japanese for war.

During July 1941, Miura held meetings with representatives of the Federation of Japanese Associations in Mexico for the purpose of coordinating security planning for the Japanese colony. Nine administrative areas throughout the nation were established, and one liaison official from the Japanese community in each region was named to report on security planning to the legation in Mexico City. Beyond these minimal measures, little substantive additional action to ensure the well-being of Mexico's Japanese was taken by Tokyo in the months before the outbreak of war. Anticipating the seizure of Japanese assets in Mexico, Miura did suggest to the leaders of the Japanese community that those Japanese married to Mexican nationals should transfer their properties to their spouses as soon as possible.[10]

Japanese and Axis intelligence in Mexico and throughout Latin America from July 1940 until the end of World War II was countered by the U.S. Federal Bureau of Investigation (FBI), headed by J. Edgar Hoover; the Office of Strategic Services (OSS), led by Colonel William Donovan; and the Office of Naval Intelligence (ONI). The FBI was given primary responsibility for counterintelligence in the Western Hemisphere in a presidential decree by Roosevelt in July 1940. Hoover had his FBI agents fan out throughout Latin America, where they went to work in U.S. embassies as "legal attachés" or under similar diplomatic cover. The State Department and the Immigration and Naturalization Service (INS) also played central roles during the war in the coordination and implementation of Washington's policy toward the Japanese Latin Americans.

The quality of U.S. counterintelligence concerning the Japanese was uneven at best. At times it represented nothing more sophisticated than the simple recapitulation of undigested rumors or complete falsehoods. The FBI was at its best in identifying and compiling data on key leaders of Japanese associations and businesses in Latin America. This information was presented in impressive binders with multicolored maps and tables purporting to show areas of Japanese and other Axis activities. These binders were sent directly to President Roosevelt and such principal advisers as Harry Hopkins.[11] But the reporting remained at a general level, with initial reports of alleged Japanese espionage activities rarely ever confirmed by agents in the field. In May 1941, for example, the U.S. Navy, concerned about the vulnerability of Baja California's long and remote coastline, sent Marine Corps Captain Norman Hussa to survey the possibility of Japanese military operations in that area. Hussa's estimation that the situation was "alarming" prompted the placement of two American-born Japanese in Baja to serve in a counterintelligence capacity. Soon other non-Japanese agents were stationed in Tijuana, Mexicali, Ensenada, Nogales, and Laredo. Immediately after Pearl Harbor, dozens of agents were sent to Mexico to monitor transportation centers and coastal sites and to establish liaisons with the nation's security agencies. Their reports often relied on information gathered from paid Mexican informants who were not on salary but were compensated on the basis of the information provided. As in many other cases in Latin America involving Axis nationals during the war era, this type of intelligence gathering rewarded opportunistic reporting of unsubstantiated rumors and outright falsehoods by paid informants. A recent analysis of the FBI's counterintelligence operations in Mexico is highly critical of the bureau's efforts. Commenting on the "lack of depth" of Hoover's reports, María Emilia Paz concludes, "if U.S. authorities had relied on this source of information only, they would have been in a rather poor situation."[12]

Most of Panama's small colony of 400 Japanese were located in the cities of Colón and Panama. Overwhelmingly male, they established small businesses, particularly barbershops, once they settled into their urban surroundings. Panama limited Asian immigration in the early twentieth century, as racial animosity toward both the far larger Chinese population and the Japanese mounted. Despite the opening of a Japanese legation in Panama in the late 1930s, Tokyo's diplomatic pressure was not sufficient to prevent the inclusion of Article 23 of the Panamanian Constitution of 1940 banning the immigration of the "yellow race." Increasing concern for the security of the Panama Canal prompted Washington to urge the Panamanian government to enact this measure and even stronger future policies to curtail the freedom of the nation's small Japanese colony. For example, a measure that closed the fishing industry to all foreigners, enacted in 1938, became the model for the denial of all business licenses to Panamanian residents whose fellow nationals were now prohibited from immigrating into Panama. This measure was clearly aimed at the Japanese and became an important precedent for the seizure of Japanese properties even before Pearl Harbor. Anticipating probable confiscation, Tokyo's legation in Panama urged the Japanese in Panama to adopt the same approach as their compatriots in Mexico and transfer their holdings to Panamanian citizens. Facing the near certainty of the loss of their hard-earned properties, nearly 10 percent of Panama's Japanese population left Panama for Peru in the months immediately preceding Pearl Harbor.[13]

Panama's seizure of Japanese businesses in the vicinity of the canal began almost as soon as President Ricardo Adolfo de la Guardia assumed office after his bloodless coup in mid-1941. On 29 October, business permits for Japanese-owned trading companies, small stores, and barbershops were canceled despite the protests of the 'Japanese minister in Panama, actions that appear to be directly related to intercepted messages from Minister Akiyama to Tokyo providing reports on the passage of U.S. Navy warships through the canal during September and early October. Akiyama's cables also provided highly detailed information regarding the construction of military installations in the Canal Zone. For example, one transmission of 2 October accurately reported the acquisition and camouflaging by the U.S. Navy of petroleum supply tanks at Boca on the Pacific side of the Canal Zone. Four days later, another message correctly reported the conversion of five civilian airfields to military aviation facilities by the U.S. Army. Significantly, this same report noted that several other proposed airfield sites were rejected because of the poor condition of the terrain.[14] U.S. authorities urged the Panamanian government to intern nation's Japanese in the event of war. It was agreed at these meetings that Panama would arrest the Japanese outside the Canal Zone and intern them on Taboga Island. Washington agreed to pay all expenses of the internment program and any subsequent related damage claims. These internment decisions, made in Panama nearly two months before the Pearl Harbor attack, paralleled those taken by the United States, Canada, and some other Latin American nations soon after Pearl Harbor.[15]

Japanese Relocation and Internment in the Americas: An Overview

What must be remembered about the experience of the Japanese in the Americas during this period is that their misfortune was part of a world war with such high stakes and massive suffering that the rights and welfare of innocent immigrants of an enemy nation were often given small consideration. Yet the principles of freedom that were being defended by the Allies were disregarded in respect to Japanese, Germans, and Italians by leaders in the United States, Canada, and Latin America. In Latin American nations, few Japanese were citizens, and human rights guarantees for the population as a whole were weak at best. In the case of Peru, for example, one former internee described the policy of the Peruvian government as a form of "ethnic cleansing," because it sought to rid the nation of all of its nearly 25,000 Japanese residents. No attempt will be made here to discuss in detail the internment programs in the United States and Canada. But it will be useful to consider the North American relocation and internment program as the context for the unfortunate experience of Japanese Latin Americans during this era. More than 2,000 Japanese Latin Americans were temporarily jailed at the behest of the U.S. government and then brought to the United States for confinement. Mexico interned a very small number of perceived "spies" for threats to the government at Perote in Veracruz. Other nations simply sent the Japanese to the United States or confined them. Brazil and Paraguay restricted them to their existing colonies while vastly limiting their liberties and often confiscating or exploiting their properties and physically abusing them. Hawaii interned only a tiny fraction of its large and economically essential Japanese population.[16]

A vast literature exists on the topic of the North American internment program, with the work of Roger Daniels being the centerpiece of this research.[17] The motives for the relocation and internment programs in the Western Hemisphere and in Australia seem to have been fourfold. First, security and the perceived fear of espionage and sabotage after Pearl Harbor was clearly a primary concern in all areas. There were debates within the security forces and governments of the United States and Canada about the loyalty of the Japanese before Pearl Harbor. Only U.S. Attorney General Francis Biddle held out for limited internment. While the discussions were continuing, the first secretary of the U.S. embassy in Mexico reported to Washington soon after Pearl Harbor that the Mexicans were very critical of Washington's delay in beginning its relocation program.[18] Mexico and Canada began their relocation before the United States, and once the war began, relocation and internment proceeded rapidly in both nations. General John DeWitt, the army's West Coast commander, for example, advised Washington, "'There isn't such a thing as a loyal Japanese.'"[19] California governor Earl Warren, bowing to the persistent anti-Japanese sentiment in California and acting on his own beliefs, was a strong advocate as well. No such discussion was ever held in Latin America. The Japanese had long been regarded as threats in all countries except Argentina. Second, after many U.S. citizens were caught in Japanese-held territories after Pearl Harbor, the idea of an exchange program—bartering Japanese Latin Americans for captured U.S. officials, business owners, and their families—was soon proposed by Washington.[20] Third, nearly everywhere in North America, the Caribbean, and South America, the property and wealth of the Japanese were coveted by those who sought to use relocation as an opportunity for personal gain. Fourth, the Pacific war was underscored by deeply ingrained racism and feelings of superiority and cultural exclusiveness on both sides. These attitudes motivated the relocation and internment programs everywhere in the hemisphere and led some Japanese internees, for example, to reject any possibility that Japan was capable of being defeated.

A curious suggestion in the midst of this planning for the internment of the Japanese in the hemisphere was Franklin D. Roosevelt's idea that the Japanese of the west coast of South America be interned on a small, remote island in the Galapagos. FDR asked his advisers, "'Is it really true that the climate of the Galapagos is delightful all year round?'" If so, the president mused, the only real expenses for the internees would be food, tents, clothing, and cooking utensils. Roosevelt noted that the Galapagos setting would be "'practically inaccessible to any German rescuing ship,'" but strangely, he made no mention of such a danger from Japanese naval forces.[21]

In early 1942, 110,000 of the 127,000 Japanese in the United States were interned in ten relocation centers established by the newly created War Relocation Authority (WRA). An additional 3,000 were arrested by various security agencies and held by the INS. Canada's 23,000 Japanese, more than 95 percent of whom were residing in British Columbia, were relocated in makeshift camps. They were assigned to work details in Manitoba and Alberta, and some were eventually sent to Ontario and Quebec.[22] In Canada there was a concerted attempt to permanently relocate the Japanese population away from British Columbia. This was a highly "successful" initiative. The Japanese in the United States became dispersed as a matter of their terms of release and economic opportunities, rather than because of a fixed policy by Washington. Only in Mexico, among the Latin American nations, would there be such a mass relocation of the Japanese population as a result of the war. It should be stressed that the United States was not only prepared to intern its own Japanese but intended to do the same with as many Japanese Latin Americans as possible. Early in the war, Washington was either prepared to subsidize the internment programs in Latin America or to intern as many West Coast Japanese Latin Americans in the United States as wartime logistics would allow. This grand internment scheme was soon seen as impossible because of the logistical problems of shipping and housing.

Created on 1 September 1939, the State Department's Special War Problems Division assumed the task of attempting to arrange for the exchange of Japanese in the Americas for U.S. citizens held by Tokyo. Numerous other agencies, including the FBI, the Justice Department, and the INS were also involved in the eventual deportation and internment in the United States of 2,118 Japanese Latin Americans. As we shall see, the vast majority of these deportees were Japanese Peruvians. (A more comprehensive discussion of the deportation and internment program will be offered in chapter 6). Resolution 20 of the Foreign Ministers Conference in Rio de Janeiro in January 1942 validated the internment program when it called for "the detention and expulsion of dangerous Axis aliens." The term *dangerous* was never defined and was left to U.S. officials and poorly trained Latin American police forces to determine. By September 1943, the Justice Department, on the advice of its agents in Latin America, arranged for the acceptance of 283 Japanese from Chile, 130 from Bolivia, 92 from Paraguay, 23 from Uruguay, and 24 from Venezuela.[23] After late 1943, the deportations and internments dropped off considerably as the perceived Japanese threat to Latin America subsided. Most of the Japanese were interned at three camps in Seagoville, Kenedy, and Crystal City in Texas. Some were interned for a time at a camp in Santa Fe, New Mexico. It should be noted also that the Japanese were interned with German and Italian internees at the Crystal City facility.

The Japanese deportees from Latin America were brought to the United States as "enemy aliens," their passports having been confiscated at the Panama staging area. Many Nisei who were interned were, of course, Latin American nationals. Even security officials in Panama noted that this was a clever ploy by the U.S. security forces, which allowed Washington to ship all but a few hundred internees to Japan during and after the war. Tokyo protested the internment program from the beginning, calling the Japanese Latin Americans "prisoners of war." Both Washington's and Tokyo's tactics undermined any attempt by the warring powers to negotiate better conditions for the Latin American Japanese during the war.

Now let us turn to a more detailed analysis of the circumstances of the Japanese Latin Americans during the war years and after.

Mexico's Japanese in Wartime: Relocation and Cultural Consolidation

Mexico's Japanese were a tiny fraction of the nation's population, numbering approximately 5,100, at the time of Pearl Harbor. The largest concentrations of Japanese were in Baja California, Sonora, and the Federal District, or Mexico City. U.S. intelligence estimated that more than 1,000 Japanese resided in Baja California Norte. These immigrants had always been important to the United States for reasons of security. Because of their close proximity to the border and Mexico's long and vulnerable west coast, with its many isolated harbors and potential military staging areas, the Japanese in that country would be watched more closely by counterespionage personnel than any other Latin American Japanese population except that of Panama. Despite the logistical limitations of the Japanese navy to conduct full-scale operations against the west coast of the Americas, such an attack was perceived as very possible by U.S. intelligence. Soon after Pearl Harbor, an OSS report on Mexico stated, "'Mexico is tremendously vulnerable from the Gulf and the Pacific.'" In an ironic reference to the United States' war with Mexico and the French invasion in the 1860s, the report went on to speculate, "'As experience has proved, a country can be taken quickly by occupying its key sea ports. This applies to a high degree with Mexico.'" The report noted that Mexico's six major Gulf and Pacific ports "'would be all an invading force would need.'" This overstated and naive report concluded that a "'great danger to our safety'" was posed by this possibility.[24] Any danger was removed when Mexico broke diplomatic relations with Tokyo and quickly closed the Japanese legation in Mexico City. When the diplomats and military attachés, particularly Ambassador Miura, who had been so aggressive with his espionage schemes prior to 7 December 1941, were removed from Mexico, what was left were primarily the simple farmers and merchants who posed no real danger to the security of Mexico or the United States. Nevertheless, U.S. security concerns were not diminished with the expulsion of Japanese diplomatic officials.

Washington's worries about a Japanese invasion of the United States from Mexico date from the beginnings of Japanese naval power in the early twentieth century. The fear of a possible Japanese attempt to establish a naval base in Baja California at Magdalena Bay in 1911–12 led to the Lodge Corollary of the Monroe Doctrine, which warned of the "grave concern" to the United States of the establishment of a naval base that would threaten the nation "anywhere in the Americas." Before the attack on Pearl Harbor, when U.S. intelligence intercepted Japanese coded messages indicating Mexico would be the center of a Latin American espionage network, Washington was duly alarmed. But what Washington could not yet know was that Japan would not have the capability of integrating its intelligence efforts with Germany and Italy when both of those nations' spy networks were broken in Mexico in 1942.[25]

There is no clear evidence that Japan ever seriously sought to invade Mexico in great force. Such an operation was beyond its military capabilities. Nevertheless, it was impossible for Washington to discount this possibility in the days after Pearl Harbor. Moreover, Washington's concerns over the security of the Panama Canal and the use of Japanese diplomats in Mexico to coordinate information gathering about ship movements through this vital waterway would mandate that the Japanese in key border areas in Mexico, and particularly Baja California Norte, be subject to nearly immediate relocation to Guadalajara and Mexico City. This would have a profound impact on the lives of the Japanese Mexicans in the postwar era.

Isolated cotton farmers would become successful urban business owners with well-integrated associations and schools after the war. Just as in the United States and Canada, relocation in Mexico would change their lives and those of their children profoundly.

On 11 February 1942, Japanese diplomats who were still in Mexico added to the woes of their immigrant compatriots by staging a public demonstration on the emperor's birthday. Moreover, General Salvador Sánchez, chief of Mexico's presidential staff, had a cordial dinner with the Japanese naval attaché even after relations had been severed with Japan and while the attaché, Captain Hamanaka, was awaiting deportation. At this cordial dinner, Hamanaka, perhaps after consuming some spirits, commented to General Sánchez that he would be back within a year, entering the port of Acapulco in command of his battleship. Hamanaka was also working with German agents in Mexico, attempting to determine the extent of damage to U.S. warships at Pearl Harbor.[26] This meeting alarmed and enraged Washington, and soon afterwards these diplomats were removed to the United States. At the same time, Japanese diplomats, particularly those in neutral Chile, were constantly reminding Latin American government officials of their successes and their military capability to attack the west coast of South America. Of course, this was just diplomatic bluster, but U.S. officials could not yet accept it as such, and policy toward the Japanese Mexicans was quickly being formulated. As Paz concludes, "It was assumed that Japan already possessed the necessary information on Mexico's Pacific Coast and was just waiting for the right moment to attack."[27]

It is important to understand that the situation of the Japanese in Mexico, in a critical way, was unique with regard to relations between Mexico and the United States. It would seem logical that a large number of the Japanese in Mexico, perhaps the entire population, could have been interned in the United States. Problems of shipping that plagued the internment of the Japanese of South America would not have been a factor since rail lines from Baja and northern California to internment centers in the southwest United States would have made this a relatively simple process. Ultimately, only a handful of the Japanese in Mexico were interned in the United States or in Mexico as immediate threats. Indeed, only fourteen Japanese supposedly threatened the United States, one of whom, in a fit of braggadocio, wrote a letter to a friend threatening to assassinate President Roosevelt by "corrugating his testicles" and commented, "I despise Roosevelt's white hair." The young Japanese salesman added, "I have given up all hope of returning to Japan and becoming a soldier." This letter was written and intercepted one month before Pearl Harbor. The young, patriotic, but eccentric dreamer was later interned in Mexico's detention facility at Perote in the state of Veracruz.[28]

✿   ✿   ✿

In the end, however, Mexico was not prepared to cooperate closely with Washington on the Japanese internment issue or on mutual defense plans on the West Coast. Mexico's Minister of Defense, former president Lázaro Cárdenas, whose nationalistic program during the 1930s had tested the Good Neighbor Policy greatly, was utterly opposed to having U.S. troops stationed on Mexican soil at any time during the war. Some U.S. troops would enter Mexico briefly as part of joint Mexican and U.S. Western Command operations, but these were largely ceremonial.[29] Attempts throughout the war to establish U.S. bases in Mexico like those in Brazil, Peru, Panama, and other Latin American nations never materialized.[30] Quite simply, the course of troubled relations between Mexico and the United States was at the root of this problem. Only Mexico, among the Latin American nations, had been invaded by the United States, with the subsequent loss of more than half its national territory. The Mexican government, even during wartime, felt a need to maintain a symbolic distance from Washington. Moreover, corruption and bribery in both Mexico and the United States often undercut attempts by the United States to have the Mexican government act more aggressively against Japan and the Axis in general. J. Edgar Hoover, frustrated by the failure of the government to root out all aspects of Axis espionage, would lament as late as 1944 that "only against the Japanese had concerted action been taken."[31] In this sense, Hoover was both right and wrong. The Mexican government quickly blunted the Japanese espionage campaign by expelling Tokyo's diplomats, who were the primary espionage actors. One of these spies who was not expelled, according to the FBI, was Benjamin Sutton, a 1913 graduate of West Point who was soon thereafter discharged from the U.S. Army for "embezzlement." Later, Sutton spent time in Sing Sing prison. In June 1942, it was reported that he met with the governor of the state of Durango in an effort to undermine U.S. influence in the state. The FBI claimed that Sutton worked for both German and Japanese intelligence and had visited Kobe, Japan, before the war. Little is known about what Sutton accomplished in Mexico, but he was not arrested by Mexican authorities. He later died under mysterious circumstances in Mexico after the war.[32]

Some high officials of the Ávila Camacho regime were friends of the leaders of the Japanese community in Mexico. This situation was unique to Mexico and would prove to be very helpful to the Japanese in that country as the war progressed. Still, many Japanese would suffer, as their U.S. counterparts did, with the loss of valuable property and physical and emotional harassment.

As war with the United States approached in late 1941, some Japanese families in Mexico became alarmed and recalled their children from Japan, where they were being educated in secondary schools. Some families did not act quickly enough, and their children were caught in wartime Japan. Separated families thus became one of the first hardships of the war. The Portuguese legation, with which the Japanese had little contact before the war, assumed the task of overseeing the treatment of the immigrants. That treatment included travel limitations, banning of meetings of more than ten Japanese, and the freezing of Japanese bank deposits two days after Pearl Harbor. The disposition of these frozen bank deposits in Mexico after the war became a troublesome issue, as it was nearly everywhere in Latin America. Many Japanese lost their life savings because of corruption in the Mexican government.[33]

The Mexican government's official policy in the wake of Pearl Harbor was the evacuation of all Japanese and other Axis nationals within 200 kilometers of the Pacific coast and 100 kilometers of the U.S.-Mexican border. These uprooted Japanese were to be relocated to Mexico City or Guadalajara but not interned. Most chose to go to Mexico City, where there were more Japanese contacts than in the nation's "second city," Guadalajara. These immigrants were not interned in camps but were allowed to travel relatively freely throughout both cities. They were forced, however, to improvise in strange and threatening urban settings for housing, employment, and schooling for their children. Most of the Axis aliens deemed as truly "dangerous" were confined at Perote, the vast majority of these being Germans and Italians. The relocation of Mexico's Japanese to the nation's central urban core was primarily a measure to make their supervision by the Mexican government more feasible.[34] Since Mexico's Defense Ministry records are closed to all but a handful of scholars, it is not yet possible to determine if internment of the Japanese was ever seriously considered in the aftermath of Pearl Harbor. An examination of the nation's Foreign Ministry records reveals no evidence pointing to the Mexican government's intention to emulate the United States' internment policy. Indeed, despite regular reports from U.S. intelligence agencies in Mexico that certain Japanese were clear "security risks," often no action was taken on these reports.[35] Given unreliable records regarding the total number of Japanese relocated to central Mexico, we must rely on the careful estimates of Minoru Izawa, who suggests that as many as 80 percent of the population was uprooted.[36]

The Japanese of Baja California Norte were the first to be removed from their homes in fishing villages and farms. In a rapid relocation that mirrored those of the West Coast Japanese in the United States, the removal was accomplished during the first weeks of January 1942. The order to relocate came just as one of the most abundant cotton crops in years was about to be harvested. It is interesting to note that many of these Japanese in Baja California Norte did not blame the Mexican government for their forced relocation but rather blamed the United States. The FBI received reports of angry Japanese who claimed that San Diego soon would be in ashes. These reports were never verified.[37] Given only five days notice, the Japanese were forced to dispose of their valuable property. A significant number of cotton farmers were forced to leave before being paid for that part of the crop already delivered. Mexicali's Japanese Association helped move a significant portion of the population by means of chartered trucks paid for by the association.[38] Unlike the Japanese in the United States and Canada who were transported by the government to their internment camps, the Japanese Mexicans in Baja California Norte lost their property and then were compelled to pay for their own transportation to an uncertain future hundreds of miles away. At least they did not end up behind barbed wire guarded by machine guns.

As might be expected, the evacuation from Baja California Norte was carefully supervised, comprehensive, and rapid. In other states, the whims of government officials, bribery, and the influential connections of the Japanese immigrants themselves sometimes allowed them to remain in their homes. This was particularly true of a few older Issei veterans of the Mexican Revolution who called upon old comrades in arms in local government positions to afford them special consideration. In the state of Chiapas, where the first Japanese colony in Latin America was established, no Japanese were uprooted.[39]

The opportunities for abuse of the evacuees by Mexican government personnel counterbalanced the *mordida* (bribe) safety valve for other relocated Japanese. In one especially egregious case in the state of Chihuahua, the state treasurer, Tomás Valles, had fifty-seven of the Japanese who had been living in Ciudad Juárez transported to his ranch near Villa Aldama, where they were forced to work virtually as slaves. Without adequate housing or food, these unfortunates were "paid" less than 50 cents per day for their labor. Finally, the sad fate of these evacuees was brought to the attention of the Portuguese legation by the Bokuto Kyoei-kai (Japanese Committee of Mutual Aid), and these "forced laborers" were allowed to leave the Valles ranch, after which most of them very likely migrated to Mexico City.[40]

Mexico's Japanese Committee of Mutual Aid played a central role in the resettlement of the evacuated immigrants. Approximately $15,000 was given to the committee by the Japanese government through its naval attaché. Another $16,000 was raised through various means to finance the resettlement of the Baja California Japanese and others from northern Mexico. The Mexican government took no role in housing its Japanese at any stage of the relocation process. Prominent members of the committee found temporary housing in an abandoned school in Mexico City and on a ranch near Contreras owned by Sanshiro Matsumoto. This ranch housed as many as 900 Japanese during the early stages of the resettlement process. Some of the more fortunate evacuees were allowed by the Ávila Camacho regime to draw $60 per month on their frozen bank accounts for living expenses.[41] On behalf of those less fortunate, with little money and no prospect for immediate employment, the committee met with President Ávila Camacho and arranged for the establishment of a 662-acre farm cooperative in Temixco, in the state of Morelos. Purchased by wealthy Japanese and turned over to the committee, the cooperative eventually housed and fed 350 Japanese, who grew rice and other foodstuffs during the war. Wisely, in order to avoid suspicions of espionage by the government or Mexican locals, the committee asked that an agent of the Ministry of the Interior be stationed at the camp.[42] The willingness of President Ávila Camacho to meet with members of the committee was a rare example of a Latin American leader directly cooperating with Japanese community leaders for purposes of their welfare during the war. As we shall see, such cooperation would have been unthinkable for President Vargas of Brazil or President Prado of Peru. President Ávila Camacho, despite the strong objections of Washington, also allowed Mexico's relocated Japanese to establish five schools for the children of evacuees during the war. Also funded in large measure by wealthy Japanese members of the committee, these schools operated openly throughout the war.[43] As is well known, the U.S. government established Japanese schools that operated in English within its internment camps. All other Latin American nations would either ban or greatly restrict Japanese educational facilities in wartime.

Again, although an ally of the United States, Mexico chose to adopt an independent policy regarding its small Japanese population. Still, as might be expected, the Japanese were the target of harassment and extortion by Mexicans seeking to use the war as an opportunity for profit. As happened in Peru, Mexicans provided false information to government and U.S. agents in Mexico regarding "fifth column" activities. The Japanese were frequently forced to pay bribes to avoid arrest by low-level Mexican security officials. A clear dichotomy existed regarding the Mexican government's relationship with its Japanese. At the street level, poorly paid police exploited the Japanese. At the uppermost levels of government, the immigrants were frequently "protected" by government officials. Watanabe concludes, "Many immigrants believe that the Mexican Government harbored them from Japanese-baiting Americans and the hostile public."[44] In two prominent cases, Watanabe's conclusion is supported by government policy. Former president Cárdenas, when he was Mexico's military commander, refused to allow the apprehension of nine suspected "spies" in Baja California Norte by a U.S. Army patrol in January 1942. The suspects were soon freed and allowed to travel to Mexico City to begin new lives.[45] In the second instance, President Ávila Camacho held fast to his agreement with the Committee of Mutual Aid regarding the Temixco farm and refused to allow local peasants to seize the property under the provisions of the agrarian reform laws of the 1930s. Ironically, it will be recalled that Japanese cotton farmers lost their properties to invading peasants before the war. In the midst of the conflict, they were now being protected by the Mexican government.[46] This simply would never have happened in any other Latin American nation, with the exception of neutral Chile and Argentina. Ultimately, former presidents Pascual Ortíz Rubio and Cárdenas as well as President Ávila Camacho were motivated by Mexican nationalism and the importance of personal relationships with Japanese leaders that often superseded wartime cooperation with the United States.

Japan's surrender in August 1945 left the Japanese in Mexico in a state of dismay and confusion. As with Japanese communities throughout Latin America, there were many who simply refused to believe that their beloved homeland had lost the war. Young superpatriots in Mexico, like those in Brazil and Peru, formed the Kokusui Doshi-kai (Japanese Nationalist Comrades Society). As late as May 1946, when the son of a very influential member of the Japanese community in Mexico returned from Japan to report on the truth of the defeat, he and his family became the target of threats and intimidation. He was accused of being a spy for the United States and a traitor to Japan. As late as 1981, the Nationalist Comrades Society still had two members, and there were other nonmembers who still believed in Japan's victory after visiting reconstructed Japan decades later.[47] Bitter divisions over the questions of Japan's defeat plagued the Japanese community long after the end of the war. But an equally important issue was the question of how the relocated Japanese in Mexico City and Guadalajara would reconstruct their lives. Most knew they would likely never return to Japan permanently. Watanabe aptly characterizes the attitude of most immigrants with his conclusion: "After the defeat . . . they finally made up their minds they would bury their bones in Mexico."[48] Would they return to their original homes in rural Mexico or make new lives in the large cities? Most chose to stay, especially the former residents of Baja California Norte who had lost nearly everything in the war. Many of the Issei were too old to begin all over again after the war. They had also appreciated the convenience and communal spirit of living together with other Japanese after their isolated lives in northern and western Mexico. Now they could meet on a daily basis with new friends their own age, speak in Japanese, and relieve their loneliness. For the younger Issei, the education of their children was a central issue. The opening of Japanese schools during the war by the Ávila Camacho administration established a cultural magnet that kept many of these younger Japanese parents in Mexico City for the sake of their children. Not least, vastly greater economic opportunities were available to the relocated Japanese in Mexico City and Guadalajara than where they had made their original homes. Many of these Japanese were to become successful industrialists, business owners, and professionals in the postwar years. Three decades after the war, more than half of all Japanese in Mexico resided in the nation's capital, whereas less than 20 percent did so prior to Pearl Harbor.[49]

Many of those Japanese who had adopted Mexican citizenship, intermarried with Mexican women, or had close connections with the local authorities before the war were able to retain their properties and return to their homes in the war's aftermath. In the end, World War II, with the permanent relocation of one of every two Japanese in Mexico, profoundly altered the outlook and makeup of the Japanese community. The pain of lost properties after lifetimes of work could not be forgotten. But a vibrant Japanese urban community arose from this painful experience, altering dramatically the lives of many Japanese who were no longer close neighbors of the United States, which had viewed them as such serious security threats during the war.

Brazil's Japanese: The End of a Dream

The Brazilian government of Getulio Vargas after 1938 followed a policy of *nacionalização* (nationalization) whose aim was for the descendants of foreigners "to speak the national language and to understand that Brazil is their home country." This was one of the central features of Vargas's Estado Nôvo. This, of course, conflicted directly with the Japanese immigrants' sojourner mentality and their desire to raise their children in the Japanese culture. Interviews in 1994 with two Nisei who experienced the government crackdown on Japanese schools confirmed the hardship this caused. Both noted how their parents organized "hidden classes," using carefully concealed Japanese textbooks. Despite altering the location of the classes on a regular basis to avoid detection, they were eventually discovered and the Japanese texts confiscated.[50] These hidden classes were held in the woods near the Japanese settlements, in warehouses, or in other concealed places. This nationalization policy was codified by a decree on 25 August 1939, only days before the beginning of World War II, that prohibited all foreign languages from being spoken in public places. One Nisei woman, who later became a successful financial officer in São Paulo, remembered these restrictions with sadness. "'My parents told me not to say a word of Japanese outside the home or the police would arrest me. Whenever I walked past a sign in Japanese, I would avert my eyes.'"[51] Any manifestation of Japanese, German, or Italian "spirit" was thus prohibited by a law that foolishly sought to suppress national identity and culture and to replace it with *espirito de Brasildade* (Brazilian spirit). By late 1938, all foreign schools were closed completely. When Germany attacked Poland on 1 September 1939, the colony of Bastos was immediately searched by Brazilian police. Little evidence of Brazilian-based education was found by government officials, and they reported that newly born Japanese babies were being registered with the Japanese consulate as citizens of Japan. The struggle for loyalty of identity between the culture of Brazil and that of Japan would become increasingly intense as the Pacific War approached.[52]

What were the primary characteristics of the Japanese community in Brazil during the war years? According to the census of 1940, the Japanese population of Brazil was 248,848, or 6 percent of the Brazilian population of over 41 million. More than 90 percent of the Japanese lived in São Paulo State. Because less than 3 percent of the Issei were known to have intermarried with native Brazilians, the Japanese population of Brazil was more homogeneous than other Japanese communities in Latin America. Moreover, the 104,355 Nisei among this group were considered subjects of the emperor of Japan by that country's law. Still overwhelmingly rural, more than 85 percent of the Japanese in Brazil were working as farmers, most of them on the colonies established during the 1920s. The Japanese farmers were more than eight times as productive as their Brazilian counterparts, producing 8 percent of Brazil's agricultural output as the war approached. Brazilian planters were still wedded to coffee as the prestige crop and not the varied produce crops that the Japanese agriculturalists produced almost exclusively and in ever increasing amounts. Unlike their counterparts in Peru, the Brazilian Japanese had not yet entered commerce in large numbers. This would be a post–World War II trend.

As in Peru, where violence against the Japanese was intense in 1940, anti-

Japanese sentiment arose in Brazil well before Pearl Harbor. By mid-1940, the police were harassing the Japanese on the slightest pretext. For example, in March 1940 near Tres Barras, in the state of Paraná, a truckload of light-hearted young Japanese baseball players returning from a game and singing songs in Japanese were stopped and arrested by the local police for "rioting."[53]

This type of incident was nearly a daily occurrence in Brazil during the war. Thus it is important to make clear that for the Japanese Brazilians, who identified more closely than any other colony in Latin America with Japanese culture, World War II was a devastating trauma. In their largely self-contained colonies, most Brazilian Issei retained hopes of returning to the glorious Japan of their childhood. There were many who simply refused to accept Japan's military defeat. The Japanese community in Brazil was to remain bitterly divided over the question of loyalty to Japan, the reality of Japan's military defeat, and their relationship with the Brazilian government that had gone to war with their beloved homeland. These divisions would torment the Japanese of Brazil until 1952. No other Japanese community in Latin America, except that of Peru, would suffer as much.

The population of Brazil's Japanese community of almost 250,000 during World War II was second only to the militarized colony in Manchuria. Thus its sheer size made deportation or large-scale internment an impossibility. There was a forced relocation of some 1,000 families, or 4,000 people, from the Santos area and the São Paulo littoral to Paranaguá in July 1943. This was one part of a relocation process that caused the uprooting of some 10,000 Japanese, Germans, and Italians at this time.[54] The relatively remote nature of the colonies also reduced the "perceived" security risk. The primary exception was the Japanese agricultural colony in the Amazon state of Pará. Long falsely rumored to have been planning military operations in the region, the Japanese there were removed to a government regulated area at Tomé-Açu, near Belém. Like the Japanese in Hawaii and those in California, Brazil's Japanese community was now an integral component of the nation's agricultural economy. The Japanese made important contributions of rice, cotton, sugar, produce, and, particularly, silk, which were essential to Brazil's and the Allies' wartime economy. Many Japanese farmers made a good deal of money as a result of the war. Ironically, these financial gains later caused many of them to feel guilt because they had profited from the war effort.

Brazil was a close ally of the United States and a leader of the hemispheric defense program. The Vargas government cooperated in the security effort by arresting and detaining leaders of the Japanese community for periods of time. Gatherings of more than three Japanese were prohibited. The bank accounts of most Japanese without powerful friends were frozen, and the immigrant leaders were not allowed to remain directors of businesses or corporations. Brazilian "temporary" managers were often appointed to operate their companies on a regular salary, as was commonly done in Peru. The opportunities for fraud under these conditions were, of course, substantial. Many Japanese Brazilians suffered great economic hardship as a result of these laws. There is evidence of exploitation and brutality in addition to these legal measures. Interviews by Sayaka Funada-Classen in 1994 and other Japanese historians writing on the war years in Brazil confirm that cases of police brutality were common. Searches of Japanese houses by the police sometimes led to theft of property, beatings, and in rare cases, slayings of immigrants who resisted the authorities.[55] As noted, the Japanese were often forced to remain mute in public places. Even the Nisei in the São Paulo City vicinity who often learned Portuguese were prohibited from using their native tongue.

The Japanese Brazilians also suffered emotionally, as so many did during the terrible war years. Not knowing the status of their families in war-torn Japan, many felt guilt that they were escaping the sacrifices that their compatriots were making for their beloved nation.[56] With the closure of all Japanese language newspapers after Pearl Harbor, the immigrant community had no firsthand knowledge of the course of the war. Their only source of news from home was Radio Japan, which began broadcasting in 1937 to South America. As would be expected, after the beginning of the war with China, Radio Japan became even more propagandistic. Broadcasting directly from Imperial Headquarters in Tokyo, it continually presented favorable views of the war to the Japanese Brazilians. Even though the Brazilian police tried to confiscate all Japanese radios, a few were retained and their owners became "radio directors" who provided the only source of news from Japan. They often exaggerated the reports of Japanese successes in the war in order to appear more important to their neighbors. The isolated Japanese in the interior colonies were thus sadly misled about the course of the war. Alone as they were, they had only Radio Japan, rumor, and government-controlled Brazilian newspapers as sources of information. Few believed what was printed in the Brazilian press, even if they could read Portuguese, particularly after Brazil declared war on Germany and Italy in late August 1942. Brazil would wait until June 1945 to declare war on Japan. Still, the Japanese were confined by the same restrictions as German and Italian immigrants. They were not allowed to congregate in groups or travel significant distances, their newspapers and periodicals were closed, their radios were confiscated, and their schools were shut down.[57]

As we know, most Japanese even before the war wanted to return to Japan to live out their lives. Once the war commenced, a deep belief in a Japanese victory led many relatively newly arrived Japanese immigrants to seek active resettlement in China or the recently captured Japanese islands in the Pacific. Before 1943, the younger immigrants began to dream and talk about life in Japan after their nation's "shining victory." Immediately after the outbreak of the Pacific War, however, most of the inhabitants of Bastos, Brazil's largest, most successful, and most heavily subsidized colony, located in western São Paulo State, expressed their wish to be resettled in Hainan Island or other newly acquired Japanese territories. The same report noted, however, that those veteran immigrants whose children were educated in Brazil, who had good positions socially and economically, and who had expectations of good treatment by Brazilian authorities after the war were inclined to prefer staying in Brazil. Perhaps their attitudes were being shaped by their Nisei children, who tended, even in the colonies, to have a greater identification with Brazil, the only home they had ever known.[58]

✿ ✿ ✿

As the Pacific War wore on and circumstantial evidence of declining Japanese military fortunes accumulated, there arose in many Japanese communities in Brazil and throughout Latin America two bitter factions. The Kachigumi (victory group) refused to believe that Japan was being defeated. The opposing and often scorned faction was the Makegumi (defeat group), which accepted the reality of Japan's defeat but rarely admitted it in public. As we shall see, both groups were victims of violence, but the Makegumi faction would be the primary target of violence and hatred by an extremist clique known as Shindo Renmei (Way of the Subjects of the Emperor's League), composed of some former soldiers in the Japanese army and other fanatically nationalistic immigrants who were never prepared to accept the truth of their nation's failure in war. Adding to the difficulty of achieving a true awareness of the course of the war was the Brazilian government's ban on the use of the Japanese language in public places. Although in the remote Japanese colonies it was not effective, the ban still added to the fear, confusion, isolation, doubt, and heartache of Brazil's anxiety-ridden Japanese community. As noted earlier, the Brazilian military and police added to the alienation of the Japanese community. The authorities would routinely conduct searches for suspect material. The finding of firearms, old military uniforms, or clothing resembling the same, and particularly pictures of the emperor would quickly lead to the arrest of innocents who had made the mistake of not burning or burying often treasured family heirlooms. In Karen Tei Yamashita's well-researched historical novel portraying life in the real

Japanese colony of Esperança, in western São Paulo State, the novel's narrator, Ichiro Uno, laments, "'Truthfully, people like me in Esperança did not know what to make of the war. We felt torn and confused that we had lost dearest ties to our family and friends far away.'"[59]

There are good reasons why the Brazilian government dealt in a repressive manner with the Japanese community. Unlike the Chilean government, which remained neutral, or the Argentine, which actually had pro-Axis sympathies, the Brazilian government did a diplomatic about-face after 1940. Always opportunistic, Getulio Vargas turned away from his profascist stance in the months before Pearl Harbor and became Washington's closest ally in Latin America. Significant for hemispheric defense was Brazil's willingness to provide critically important air bases for the United States in the northeast. In return for far more Lend Lease aid than any other Latin American nation and financing for the nation's first steel mill at Volta Redonda, Brazil sent an army division known as the Força Expedecionária Brasileira, or FEB (Brazilian Expeditionary Force), to Italy to fight with the U.S. Fifth Army in the tough battle for Monte Castelo. The FEB was a nationalistic effort, with troops raised from all of Brazil's states.[60]

Given the isolated status of Brazil's Japanese and their strong ties to the home country, one might imagine there would be no participation in the war effort by members of that community. Such was not the case. Kiyoshi Sakai, who was sent to the Italian front near Monte Castelo in 1944, later reported that there were at least 8 other Nisei soldiers in his battalion, suggesting that there may have been quite a few more in other FEB units. At least 8 Japanese Brazilians in the Italian campaign were killed in combat that saw 1,500 casualties suffered by the FEB. More needs to be learned about the recruiting process for this Brazilian division, which fought bravely in one of the most difficult theaters in World War II. What is clear is that Japanese American soldiers of the famed 442 Regiment, which was the most decorated combat unit for the U.S. Army during World War II, fought on or near the same Italian battlefields as their Nisei counterparts from Brazil. The Japanese Brazilian recruits were very likely drawn from the colonies, which were then cut off from mainstream Brazilian society and prohibited from making open expressions of the Japanese way of life. Members of the 442 enlisted from the U.S. internment camps where their families had been sent in the months immediately following Pearl Harbor. Unquestionably, the Nisei of both Brazil and the United States were not only overcoming the deep prejudices of the adopted nations of their parents but were willing to make the ultimate sacrifice for the nations where they were still unwanted.[61]

As might be expected, the usual sensationalist anti-Japanese propaganda appeared during the war. Typical of this propaganda was a pamphlet entitled "The Japanese Offensive in Brazil," by the journalist Souza de Moraes, which claimed that the Japanese of Brazil were there only to provide Japan's material needs for the war. He argued there were extensive Japanese espionage networks in the United States, Peru, and Brazil and went so far as to assert that the "militarized" Japanese colony in Brazil was actually planning an attack on the city of São Paulo. This inflammatory pamphlet was accompanied by the now-familiar stereotypes of Japanese in the "art work" throughout the publication: exaggerated depictions of wide mouths with huge teeth and squinting eyes peering out from beneath the caps of stoic Japanese army officers.[62] Journalistic sensationalism was quite common during the war, and such publications appeared all over Latin America as the conflict unfolded. The allegations of a Japanese attack on São Paulo, for example, mirrored those of the baseless rumor of a pending attack on Lima, Peru, in early 1942. The FBI and other intelligence agencies in Brazil were flooded with reports of this nature throughout the war.

The climate of fear and suspicion was thus high in Brazil despite the remote nature of the primary Japanese presence in São Paulo. With this in mind, a number of key ideas need to be pondered. Yes, the Brazilian Japanese were not interned. And yes, they were not relocated en masse, as were their compatriots in Canada, the United States, and Mexico. They were not deported, as were significant numbers of their Peruvian counterparts, nor was their property seized, as happened in other Japanese communities in the hemisphere. But life in the huge Japanese community of Brazil during the war was a period of continual turmoil, and there was a kind of deep "survivor" guilt felt by loyal Issei who wanted to be a part of Japan's war effort. Many wanted to leave Brazil and resettle in the captured lands that the Japanese army had conquered. Added to this was the troubling loss of contact with a homeland that they increasingly felt was lost to them forever after the Pacific War.

There can be little question of the loyalty of most Brazilian Issei to the emperor and their firm belief in the inevitability of a Japanese victory. What then can be said of their overt support for Japan's war effort? Allegations of espionage and sabotage abounded in the Brazilian press. U.S. intelligence agencies seemed to do a better job in Brazil than they did in Mexico. The FBI reported in June 1942 that a Japanese espionage ring, operating principally out of Chile and Argentina, was also gathering information in Brazil. The FBI speculated that despite the expulsion of Japanese diplomats from Brazil soon after Pearl Harbor, the information about Allied military operations in the country was "detailed to the extreme." J. Edgar Hoover, in a personal letter to Major General Edwin M. Watson, President Roosevelt's secretary, surmised that Japanese code books must still be in use in Brazil. The information supposedly being transmitted, however, was being gathered from the public record of U.S. newspapers, magazines, and other publications.[63]

Although flawed in some important ways, a report that was perhaps the most realistic assessment of the Japanese in Brazil during the Pacific War by a U.S. government agency was presented in early 1942, although not by the FBI but rather by its rival, the OSS. In a highly detailed, anonymous review that included all other nations with a significant immigrant presence, this summary noted: "The military danger of the Japanese in Brazil to the Allied cause is only a potential one. As things stand, military participation by Brazil's Japanese on the Axis side is not anticipated. However, if Axis armies should make a landing in South America, the Japanese could be expected to join with them where possible to draw off defending troops at more distant places." The memorandum goes on to speculate that Japanese immigrants in Brazil would likely cooperate with Italian and German immigrants should an invasion occur. Given the remote and insular nature of the Japanese immigrants in their colonies, this scenario now seems highly unlikely.[64]

James L. Tigner's original conclusions regarding the impact of the war on Japanese Brazilians, based on interviews with Brazilian law enforcement officials and Japanese throughout Brazil in 1951, are now being modified. Let us turn to these questions. There existed nationalistic secret Japanese societies during the war. These groups did engage in acts of terrorism and sabotage but almost exclusively against other Japanese and not against the Brazilian government or native Brazilians.[65] Originally, Tigner concluded that the Japanese of Brazil had such "blind faith" in a Japanese victory and the subsequent occupation of Brazil and the United States by Japanese military forces that antigovernment subversive activity was not necessary. Tokyo saw widespread subversive activity in Latin America by its "subjects" as generally leading to greater restrictions and harsher treatment, which it hoped to avoid, particularly in South America, where its military interests were not critical. Groups such as the Black Dragon, a secret but nonmilitant nationalist society, early in the war gave way to the powerful and highly controversial Shindo Renmei, secretly established in 1944 as Japan's military fate seemed increasingly certain. The organization was discovered by Brazilian police in 1945, but its terrorist activities and exploitation of Japanese immigrants in Brazil continued until a decade after the war's end.

Shindo Renmei's actions mark a painful episode in the history of the Japanese in Latin America. At least 15 Japanese were killed and 21 injured by Shindo Renmei militants, and 9 cases of arson were reported. The actual figures probably are far higher because many Japanese feared reporting terrorist organizations to the Brazilian police.[66] The reported leader of Shindo Renmei was a former lieutenant colonel in the Japanese army named Junji Kikkawa. Later, the Association of Ex-Japanese Servicemen of Brazil joined the Shindo Renmei. Total membership in the organization exceeded 50,000, and some reports estimated its membership at twice that figure. These figures were probably inflated by including total households. The position adopted by the leaders of this organization as U.S. forces advanced on the home islands of Japan was that Tokyo was preparing a huge trap to "lure" enemy forces into a slaughter by Japan's ground, sea, and air forces. These beliefs were held in the context of Japan's previous invincibility in war and the rampant nationalism of Shindo Renmei. The *kamikaze* (divine wind) had saved Japan in one of its most critical moments in history when an invasion from China was looming. Admiral Togo had done the same to the Russian fleet in 1905. Now it was anticipated that the U.S. fleet would meet the same fate. Thus, in the minds of the Shindo Renmei members, a last-minute victory would again be achieved.[67]

With Japan's defeat, this nationalist group turned to the intimidation and blatant exploitation of both the victory and the defeat groups. As documented by the Brazilian police, assassinations of defeat-group leaders continued until 1947. The first victim of the assassinations was the leader of the Bastos industrial cooperative. Later, newspaper officials who did not follow the victory position were targeted. One of the most prominent of those killed was Paulo Morita, an interpreter and head of the Japanese Section of the Swedish consulate in São Paulo City. Morita was murdered in January 1947, the last assassination conducted by the Shindo Renmei "Special Attack Group." In the midst of the Shindo Renmei violence, in August 1946, two Brazilian deputies in the national assembly introduced legislation banning the future entry of Japanese into Brazil. The measure failed, but it reflected the highly negative impact that terrorism, even among the Japanese, had on the government.

Along with the assassinations, this terrorist group conducted a campaign of economic exploitation of both those Japanese who firmly believed in a Japanese victory and those who were fearful of openly admitting defeat. "Emperor's medals" for loyal Brazilians were sold at enormous prices. Ship passages to a victorious Japan were sold. And most sadly, fraudulent deeds for real estate in the Philippines and Java were perpetrated on the passive and fearful immigrants.[68] Not until 1947 did the Brazilian police break Shindo Renmei's activities by a series of arrests, imprisonments, and deportations. But the divisions, fear, lost fortunes, and despair caused by its activities would linger long after the Pacific War ended. Funada-Classen's personal interviews with Japanese in Bastos in 1993 who endured the fear engendered by Shindo Renmei confirm a lingering bitterness of its legacy. One resident of Bastos told her, "*Shindo* were those without land or jobs. I did not say Japan had lost the war, even though I knew this was the truth, for fear of being killed."[69] Comments such as this seem to confirm the relative rootlessness of many members of Shindo Renmei. What was even more discouraging was that some members of assassination teams were violence-prone Nisei youths with a badly misdirected sense of morality. As Tigner notes, Shindo Renmei and the divisions between the victory and the defeat groups would lead to devastating consequences. "Lifelong friendships had been severed, children were estranged from their families, and business partnerships dissolved."[70] The last vestiges of Shindo Renmei would linger until 1955, when 100 demonstrators in São Paulo City would petition the Japanese consulate for repatriation to a victorious Japan. Nowhere else among the postwar Japanese communities of Latin America would the pain of the war linger as long. Only the deported Japanese from Peru and other Latin American nations would suffer such lasting turmoil.

Research during the last two decades offers new insights into the Shindo Renmei phenomenon in Brazil. Chiyoko Mita argues that Shindo Renmei was a reflection of the inner conflicts facing the Issei and Nisei generations in Brazil with regard to their increasingly fragile cultural identities. The strong emphasis on Brazilian national identity begun by the Vargas regime in 1937 served to further isolate young Japanese Brazilians from their cultural heritage, especially when Japanese schools were closed and the public use of the Japanese language was prohibited. Takashi Maeyama interprets the return movement to Japan, which was exploited by the worst elements of Shindo Renmei, as a reflection of the understandable response to the Vargas regime's strong challenge to their cultural identity. Toomo Handa concludes that the bans on assembly, free speech, and schooling left Brazil's Japanese feeling totally rejected by Brazilian society. These feelings fostered fear, resentment, and anger, which were manifested in their extreme form by the actions of Shindo Renmei militants.[71]

The violence and divisions in the Japanese Brazilian community, while extremely painful, did not fundamentally retard its development as an emerging and integral part of Brazilian society in the decades after World War II. Many successful Japanese who accepted Japan's defeat, however reluctantly, began to plan for the rest of their lives in Brazil. These Issei and smaller numbers of Nisei were the core of the Japanese Brazilian middle class that would emerge so prominently during the two decades after World War II.

After achieving economic stability in Brazil, they understood they would never have such security or commensurate status if they returned to Japan. Moreover, they knew that war-torn Japan could likely never offer them the social security payments to which they were entitled, even if they spent their last days in the homeland. Maeyama notes that almost immediately after the war, some prominent Japanese formed the Nihon Sensai Doho Kyuen-kai (Committee for the Relief of the War Victims in Japan) and began to systematically send funds and subsistence materials to the devastated home Japanese. "In so doing," Maeyama argues, "they came at last to abandon their identification with their home society."[72]

Successful coffee farmers and a small number of professionals and business owners were the first to completely abandon the sojourner mentality. Decades later this group would claim, "We are the ancestors in Brazil," because in their minds they had reestablished the Ie spiritual presence in Brazil. They saw themselves as foundation builders for an entirely new community of Japanese beyond the homeland. It was somewhat audacious of them to regard themselves as such because this attitude was rarely held in Japan, even among the most successful people. Thus they had become as much Brazilian as they were Japanese. They referred to Brazil as *yokoku* (adopted country). In some cases, Maeyama reported, individuals would later visit Japan and bring back the ashes of their ancestors to Brazil. A member of a new sect in Brazil reported to Maeyama, "'I thought we had left politics and the gods behind in Japan, but now the gods are recovered.'"[73]

The Japanese discussed by Maeyama were favored economically by the war, and they began to form the nascent middle class both in the countryside and gradually in São Paulo City. The Japanese of Brazil, like their native counterparts, would begin migrating to São Paulo in greater numbers in the years immediately following the war. Some would become business owners, but many others would resume farming as truck gardeners in the suburbs of the great city, where they would soon come to dominate the produce market. Thus began the transition from countryside to city and from loyal subjects of the emperor to citizens of Brazil.

The Lesser Japanese Communities: An Overview

In Central America and the Caribbean, the lesser Japanese communities survived the Pacific War and its aftermath with differing degrees of dislocation and trauma. The entire Japanese population of Cuba, for example, was interned, not in special camps, but on the Isle of Pines prison island. The very small and isolated colony of Japanese at La Colmena in Paraguay was left in place, with minimal controls by the government. Bolivia would cooperate more closely with the United States and send a comparatively large number of its Japanese for internment in the southwest. The questions of Argentina's and Chile's neutrality (Chile only until 1943) would pose serious security problems for the United States. As Rout and Bratzel argue effectively, German agents were the real problem in these nations, especially in Argentina, which leaned toward the Axis cause throughout most of the war. Before 1943, Japan's chief diplomatic official endangered the nation's small Japanese community by threatening the Chilean government. He vowed military reprisals if Chile abandoned its neutrality and joined the Allies.[74]

The Japanese of Central America were the first to be interned, even before Pearl Harbor. Led primarily by pro-American authoritarian regimes closely linked to the Roosevelt administration, all five Central American nations declared war on Japan the day following Pearl Harbor. The five countries sent some of their Japanese to the United States for internment. Twenty-four of these Japanese remained in U.S. custody as late as January 1946.[75] Like other internees, Benjamin Tanabe of El Salvador placed his café in his Salvadoran wife's name to protect the property. Another evacuee, from Nicaragua, argued vehemently that he was loyal to his adopted country and the Allied cause. As proof, he cited his veteran's status in the U.S. Navy, but apparently his service did not matter to U.S. or Nicaraguan security agents. Costa Rica, although more democratically inclined than the rest of the Central American nations, arrested all of its Japanese population, confiscated their property, and auctioned off the colony's agricultural machinery. The Japanese of Costa Rica, ironically, had originally been invited to that nation as cotton farmers in the hopes of increasing the nation's output of this valuable commodity. Again, as the work of Thomas Leonard demonstrates, German aliens were the key issue in these nations, and very few Japanese names ever appeared on the "Proclaimed List." Not until 1951 would the Central American nations renew diplomatic relations with Japan. The relatively few Japanese in these countries at the beginning of the war found Central America very unwelcoming in the war's aftermath, and many sought their futures elsewhere.[76]

The other main concentration of Japanese in the Caribbean before World War II was in Cuba. As noted earlier, all male Japanese were incarcerated during World War II, we can assume, at the behest of the United States because Cuba was in such close proximity to key military and strategic areas. The Japanese of the Isle of Pines had arrived primarily between 1915 and 1930 and soon established small produce farms that had a direct market in Havana. The acculturation of the Japanese was mixed, some of the men married Cuban women, and racial toleration of the Japanese was generally favorable. The Japanese of Cuba, as elsewhere, viewed education as essential and sent many of their children to the American school on the Isle of Pines. Nevertheless, the Japanese farmers were widely distributed on the Isle of Pines, and there was only one Japanese association to help the poor and the ill. The number of Japanese in Cuba reached its maximum at about 1,000 in the early 1930s and declined to less than 600 by the late 1950s. Changes in the attitude of the Nisei to small farming and the negative experience of the war may well have influenced a transmigration to Havana or the Dominican Republic. Little is known about the conditions of the incarceration of Japanese males during the war, but it is clear that this internment disrupted families and may well have influenced the abandonment of the Isle of Pines in the decade after the war.[77]

The Paraguayan government took control of La Colmena, its only Japanese colony, in early 1942 and prohibited meetings of any kind. Isolated as it was, La Colmena mirrored the remote colonies of Brazil, where the Japanese residents knew very little about the actual course of the war. La Colmena's colonists were driven by nationalistic feelings, prayed for Japan's victory, and raised money for the war effort before the Paraguayan government banned such activities. Norman Stewart notes that the shock of Japan's defeat was profound among the La Colmena Japanese. "Spiritual convictions were deeply shaken by defeat . . . [and] subsequently all public demonstration of Oriental faith vanished, and shrine veneration, formerly attached to the founder's movement, disappeared."[78] Equally important was the reversal of roles of the Issei and Nisei in La Colmena as a result of the war. Stewart argues that the war "catalyzed the process of authority inversion" of the generations. Feelings of "loss" and "shame" on the part of the Issei because of Japan's failure made it seem to the pioneer generation that the assumption of authority by the Nisei was logical and necessary, according to Stewart. The advancing age of the Issei clearly accelerated the process of Nisei leadership, but once again the Pacific War and the realization of a permanent life in Paraguay forced the Issei to place their future hopes in their children rather than in returning to Japan. The Japanese of La Colmena began to rebuild for their future in Paraguay in July 1948 with the creation of the Nokyo-kumiai (Agricultural Cooperative Union), which would be the foundation for farm production in the decades following the war years. By the early 1950s, membership in the cooperative had risen to nearly 80 percent of La Colmena's farm families. Generational leadership change and institution building thus became the most prominent ways in which Paraguay's small Japanese community adapted to the aftermath of World War II.[79]

Bolivia was very important to the United States during the war because of its large reserves of tin. Previously, the United States had secured tin ore from Malaya and was thus forced to shift to a Bolivian market as the Pacific War approached. In 1940, Washington signed an agreement with the Bolivian government to purchase 18,000 tons of tin, almost half the total amount of Bolivian exports. Additionally, Bolivia's tungsten and rubber were highly valuable to the United States after the war began. At the beginning of the war, there were approximately 600 Japanese in Bolivia, and they posed little threat to U.S. strategic interests.[80]

This Japanese population was given little direct attention by Allied counterintelligence during the war. Yet, in an apparent attempt to compensate for counterintelligence's lack of background knowledge or capable field personnel, nearly one-sixth of Bolivia's Japanese community was deported to the United States for internment. Thus, despite Bolivia's geographic setting as a landlocked nation, distant from Japan, and despite having limited contact with Tokyo before the war, comparatively large numbers of Japanese Bolivians had their lives disrupted by deportation. Early in the war, the United States targeted 146 of them for internment, 83 of whom were nondiplomatic personnel. The number of Japanese Bolivians interned in the United States would climb to more than 100 by war's end. Some would remain interned until late 1946. One desperate Bolivian woman with a Japanese husband wrote a personal letter to President Truman for his release. Five others, some of the last to leave the internment camp in Santa Fe, New Mexico, wrote directly to the Department of Justice appealing for their release in March 1946. Their letter, written with the assistance of supporters in the United States, stated that "other than being a Japanese alien residing in Bolivia, we are still unable to determine why we were taken away from Bolivia and interned in Santa Fe."[81] One of the leaders was Tomás Fujiike, who at the time of his deportation was president of the Japanese Association of La Paz. The Japanese Association, like all other formal immigrant organizations, was closed by 1943.[82]

After the war, in August 1948, the Association of Okinawans in Bolivia was created in La Paz for the express purpose of raising financial relief funds for the people of their home island. Less inclined than some of their compatriots to hold fast to a belief in Japanese victory long after the war, the mainland Japanese and Okinawans in Bolivia sought to rebuild their community organizations with the intent of establishing permanent and prosperous residence in their adopted nation. In 1951 the immigrants created the Japanese Bolivian Cultural Association in La Paz in an attempt to better integrate the community into the nation's mainstream culture. Significantly, a non-Japanese Bolivian, the son of a former Bolivian consul in Japan, was named vice president of the association. The Japanese in Bolivia recovered so well from the war that their nation would become the focus for renewed immigration from Okinawa in the early 1950s. Ironically, the U.S. government, which had seen fit to deport one of every six Japanese Bolivians during the war, during the 1950s saw Bolivia as a partial solution to the devastating economic conditions in Okinawa. Details of this colonization process await us in chapter 7.

Chile, with its long, unprotected coastline, chose to remain neutral until 1943, largely because of the perceived threat of military attack from Japan. This was not an idle fear in the mind of Chile's leaders, for Japanese diplomats in that nation were rattling sabers continuously in an effort to keep Chile neutral. For its part, the FBI paid great attention to Chile's small Japanese population of less than 1,000, which was concentrated in the smaller towns of the northern mining districts.[83] Here American copper firms controlled production and bowed to the U.S. government to keep copper prices fixed during the war. Thus the prosperity enjoyed by some Japanese cotton growers in Brazil as a result of the war was not experienced by the Japanese shopkeepers and other immigrants associated with the mining industry in Chile during the war. Some estimates place the loss to the Chilean economy because of the frozen copper prices at $100 million to $500 million during World War II.[84]

As the war progressed, the FBI and other intelligence sources envisioned the establishment of a Japanese base on Easter Island, more than a thousand miles from Chile's coastline. Other scenarios placed Japanese invaders at nearly every major port on the Chilean coast as late as 1943. As might be expected of a neutral nation, Chile did not intern its small Japanese population. Once Chile broke relations with Japan in 1943, many key Japanese warships and carrier planes lay at the bottom of the Coral Sea, off Midway Island, and below the waters of the Philippine Sea. Still, the most important Axis espionage ring outside of Argentina existed in Chile. With its significant population of Germans in the south, Chile was a happy hunting ground for German agents. Radio relay stations, which were also of value to the Japanese, were established by the Germans and operated without great interference by Chilean security personnel until 1943. Moreover, Chile's successful presidential candidate, Juan Antonio Ríos, solicited funds from the German government and was offered campaign funding by Tokyo. Not to be outdone, the United States and Great Britain considered matching these funds, but President Roosevelt blocked the issue for fear of a negative impact on the Good Neighbor Policy if the bribery was discovered. In so doing, he rebuffed OSS chief William Donovan, who maintained that the election of Carlos Ibáñez, a candidate favored by the Axis, would endanger the war effort. Donovan argued, "'Steps should be taken by all means available, including bribery, if necessary, that the armed forces would not support a coup d'etat by Ibáñez.'"[85]

The Japanese likewise sought to influence the Chilean election by donating 500,000 pesos to Ibáñez. Tokyo also approved the use of funds to influence Chilean newspapers with liberal donations, but this did not seem to help Tokyo's cause.[86] With the subsequent election of the more pro-Allied Ríos, the Japanese ambassador in Chile, Kiyoshi Yamagata, proposed that a coup d'etat be funded to topple the government. This audacious scheme never materialized. But by November 1942, the Japanese ambassador told a Chilean member of the government, "'The only reason the Japanese Navy is not rushing against Chile is because Japan respects Chile's [neutral] position.'" Yamagata would later cable Tokyo and actually request an invasion of Chile when it was about to break diplomatic relations in 1943.[87] But, of course, by this time Japan was in retreat, and the Japanese ambassador only spread deeper suspicions among those in the counterintelligence community who were reading his coded cables.

Ironically, Chile's Japanese actually benefited from the audacity of Japan's diplomatic personnel because their threats helped maintain Chilean neutrality, and thus the immigrants avoided deportation and internment. Yet all over Latin America the actions of officials such as Yamagata gave the impression that all Japanese community leaders and even the "little people," as one diplomat in Peru referred to them, were targets and often victims of Allied counterintelligence.

After the war, Chile's Japanese continued to live the quiet lives that were their norm before the conflict, but they did not often prosper in Chile's class-oriented and troubled society. Instead, the small Japanese population in the copper and coal mining districts and in the rural areas got caught up in the problems of labor unrest inspired by the Communist Party's attempt to unionize miners and rural laborers. As Chile became a remote battleground in the cold war, Gabriel Gonzales Videla (1946–52) re-created the old conservative order that had existed before 1938. This situation allowed few new opportunities for the Japanese immigrants in landholding, and some drifted to the larger cities such as Santiago. Scattered as they were, the Japanese did not develop the communal spirit to the same degree as some of their Latin American counterparts. Many had intermarried with Chileans before the war, and group identity was limited. The Japanese had never found Chile a land of opportunity nor a country that welcomed them. Too many other desperately poor rural workers competed for cheap land, which the Japanese found in Brazil and, to a lesser extent, in Peru. The conservative order would cling desperately to their land. Such remained the case in the aftermath of World War II through the 1960s.

Argentina provides a very unusual case study of the Japanese of the World War II era. Here, a brief overview of how the Japanese in Argentina fared during the war years and after will be helpful. Additionally, we will look at related Japanese government activities in the most spy-ridden nation in all of the Americas during the world conflict. Argentina's neutrality was dictated by its long-standing diplomatic and commercial rivalry with the United States and by the favorable attitude toward the Axis adopted by Argentina's military leaders who took power in 1943. Since its economic preeminence in the 1890s, Argentina had thought of itself as a leader in Latin America that would counterbalance the growing influence of "Yankee imperialism." Even as relations between most of the Latin American nations and Japan badly deteriorated in the late 1930s as a result of Japan's invasion of China, Japanese-Argentine diplomatic ties remained cordial, and government officials of both nations formally celebrated four years of good relations in a grand public fashion in 1938. More significantly, Tokyo and Buenos Aires raised their diplomatic relations to ambassadorial status, and Argentina's first ambassador in Tokyo, Dr. Rodolfo Moreno, arrived in early 1941 during the presidency of Ramón Castillo.

As the Pacific War approached, Argentina's Japanese population numbered approximately 6,000, with many associations in the provinces and in Buenos Aires. The Japanese maintained a communal cultural spirit, most particularly in the nation's capital. A bilingual Japanese and Spanish school was opened in Buenos Aires, for instance, in 1938. The school would remain open during the war. In addition, four Japanese-language newspapers were publishing in Argentina when the war began, and they continued to remain open until 1944, when they were finally closed in response to immense pressure from the United States. In 1944, the Argentine government, now led by a group of army officers who took power in 1943, formally severed diplomatic relations with Japan. Argentina was the last Latin American nation to make this diplomatic break. Only with the formal declaration of war with Japan by Argentina in January 1945 was the bilingual Japanese school closed. A repatriation movement of the Japanese in Argentina was supervised by Teizo Ogawa in 1947. But few Japanese in Argentina had any real interest in returning to war-torn Japan. The sojourner outlook was converted to a new optimism in an Argentine future, not one in Japan. Ogawa, for instance, became president of the Argentine-Japanese Association in 1950, which became quite vibrant during the next decade, encouraging new Japanese immigration to Argentina rather than repatriation to Japan.

Finally, what can we say about the role the Japanese government played in Argentina during the war years that influenced the status of its immigrants in that distant nation? As it did throughout Latin America, Tokyo instructed its nondiplomatic personnel to maintain a low profile so as not to provoke more aggressive action by Allied counterintelligence agencies. Much of Japanese information-gathering in Argentina was done through the very active German espionage networks in that country. Rout and Bratzel discuss these German-led activities in great detail in their book *Shadow War*.[88] What is clear is that Tokyo saw little strategic importance in Argentina, given its distant location from Tokyo's military priorities.

The Nisei would emerge as prominent and active members of the Japanese community in Argentina in the postwar years as they did everywhere in Latin America. This was facilitated by the interruption of the education of many Argentine Nisei in Japan during the war years. The sons and daughters of Issei in Argentina and elsewhere were forced to adapt to the cultural milieu of their adopted lands. Some Nisei would take over the shops and cafés of their aging parents. Others began playing prominent roles in Japanese associations. Still, like the Nisei in the United States and elsewhere, they struggled with their identity as the café and tango culture of Argentina became more alluring.

From a comparative perspective, the Japanese Latin Americans enjoyed far less formal legal consideration from their governments than the Japanese in the United States during the war and its aftermath. It is true that the United States and Canada interned nearly their entire Japanese populations, both citizens and noncitizens. The Latin American nations, for the most part, did not. Nonetheless, based upon their cooperation with the United States' deportation and internment program, in which twelve Latin American nations sent some of their Japanese to camps in the United States, it is fair to say that the intent to intern was there, certainly in Central America as well as Peru. Had it been logistically possible, many of these Latin American nations, with the possible exceptions of Argentina and Brazil, would have interned their Japanese just as the United States and Canada did.

The mentality and material condition of the Latin American Japanese underwent a fundamental change as a result of World War II and its aftermath. The future of the Latin America Issei and their children was firmly rooted in their adopted nations because of Japan's defeat and its material devastation until the mid-1950s. The tenacity with which many Japanese Latin Americans clung to their distant image of a sacred, unique, and powerful nation is evidenced by Brazil's Japanese and by the views of World War II internees (which will be examined in chapter 6), who simply refused to accept the image of their beloved Japan in ashes after the war. These beliefs not only speak to the spirit of the Japanese immigrant but also to their cultural isolation nearly everywhere in Latin America. World War II would leave many Japanese Latin Americans destitute and homeless, particularly those deported to the United States for internment. The Issei were forced to try to rebuild their lives, but not all were able to do so.

The first-generation Japanese made the critical but really unavoidable decision to turn the leadership of the Japanese communities over to the Nisei. Many Issei continued to sacrifice, not in the faint hope of returning to Japan but rather to afford their children a better life in Latin America. Some Issei, such as the cotton farmers of Brazil, prospered from the war. They began to form the core of a new urbanized middle class that had not yet fully emerged in Brazil or most other Latin American nations. But even prosperity during the war had its cost for some Japanese Latin Americans. Guilt expressed by some as late as the 1990s that they prospered while their compatriots in Japan suffered the horrors of war is a testament to the firmly held bonds to the culture of the homeland. The challenge of building new lives posed perhaps the greatest obstacle for the Japanese Peruvians. They were the unwanted Japanese immigrants deported in greater numbers than any other Japanese community in Latin America during World War II.

This "picture bride" photograph of Mito Kataoka was sent to Jinkichi Tsuji, who transmigrated from Japan to the United States in 1911 and then to Mexico. The couple married soon after this photograph was sent and eventually settled in California. (Courtesy of Rebecca Tsuji and Jessica Barrientos)

A group of Nisei students sharing a light moment during their school day in Japan. Financially able Issei parents in the United States and Latin America often sent their children to Japan for part of their education. (Courtesy of Rebecca Tsuji and Jessica Barrientos)

Betty and Julie Tsuji, the daughters of Mito and Jinkichi Tsuji. Preservation of traditional Japanese dress and customs was a very important part of parenting for the Issei generation. (Courtesy of Rebecca Tsuji and Jessica Barrientos)

A schoolmaster with his class at the Escuela Japonesa in Puerto Maldonado, Peru, 1919. (Courtesy of the Museo Conmemorativa de Inmigración Japonesa en el Perú, MCIJP)

Japanese women and children working in the fields in Cañete, Peru, in the early 1920s. Japanese women did not typically work as field laborers in Peru because plantation owners preferred to use men. This contrasts with Brazilian coffee planters who favored families as the preferred work unit. (Courtesy of the Museo Conmemorativa de Inmigración Japonesa en el Perú, MCIJP).

Japanese Peruvian baseball team and its supporters on a Lima baseball diamond in 1935. Sports, especially baseball, were always an important part of the Japanese cultural tradition in Latin America. (Courtesy of the Museo Conmemorativa de Inmigración Japonesa en el Perú, MCIJP)

Koshiro Mukoyama and his wife Chiyoka with their sons Reiichiro Luis Ricardo (with his father) and Jorge. This photograph was taken in 1939 in Lima before the family was deported to the United States during World War II. Not shown is their daughter Teresa, who spent her early years in the internment camp at Crystal City, Texas and later at Seabrook, New Jersey, where the family worked at a produce processing facility. (Photograph courtesy of Teresa Masatani)

The Swedish motorship MS *Gripsholm,* which transported hundreds of Japanese Latin Americans to the United States for internment during World War II. The lack of sufficient shipping substantially limited the number of Japanese the U.S. and Latin American governments could intern during the war. (Courtesy of the United States National Archives and Records Service)

A solitary Japanese facing internment is lost in thought aboard the transport vessel MS *Gripsholm* in 1942. (Courtesy of the United States National Archives and Records Service)

The rabidly anti-Japanese Lima, Peru, newspaper *Mundo Grafico* carrying the headline "The Nationalist Response to the Japanese Danger Reaches throughout the Nation." The newspaper would continue to call for anti-Japanese measures even after World War II was over. (Courtesy of the Museo Conmemorativa de Inmigración Japonesa en el Perú, MCIJP)

Japanese theater group posing in 1943 before a performance at the Crystal City, Texas, internment camp. (Courtesy Betty Fly)

A Japanese father with his children and their traditional Paraguayan high-wheeled cart known as a *yvyrajere* in La Colmena, Paraguay, in 1995. (Photograph by Daniel Masterson)

Senhor Matsubara stands in front of one of the outbuildings on his *fazenda* (plantation) in the Brazilian state of Paraná. Matsubara once worked as a laborer on this plantation and was eventually able to acquire it from its Brazilian owner. (Photograph by Sayaka Funada-Classen)

Senhor Matsubara poses with his second wife, a native Brazilian, on the steps of the plantation house. (Photograph by Sayaka Funada-Classen)

Japanese school as it appeared in the mid-1990s in the pioneer Japanese colony of La Colmena, southeast of Asunción, Paraguay. (Photograph by Daniel Masterson)

The Centro Cultural Peruano-Japonés (Peruvian Japanese Cultural Center) is the focal point of Japanese Peruvian social and cultural activities. The center is located in central Lima on land donated to the Japanese Peruvian community as a gesture of conciliation by the Peruvian government for its deportation of Japanese Peruvians during World War II. Today it is largely frequented by the aging Issei and Nisei (first- and second-generation Japanese immigrants) in Peru. (Photograph by Daniel Masterson)

EXILES AND SURVIVORS:
THE JAPANESE PERUVIANS, 1938–52

I still need to know why Peruvians of Japanese ancestry were
interned in the U.S.A. I know my parents suffered and learned
hardship when they needed to start life anew in the United States.
—A Peruvian Nisei now residing in California, 1993

The Anti-Japanese Campaign

The experience of Peru's Japanese during World War II and its aftermath is
most compelling. But it should not be allowed to overshadow in the reader's
mind the trials and challenges of other Japanese Latin Americans, particularly those in Central America and Brazil, whose experiences have received
less attention. The consequences of the Great Depression and the concur-
rent emergence of nationalism and populist politics had a profoundly negative impact on the Japanese Peruvian community by the late 1930s. C.
Harvey Gardiner and Orazio Ciccarelli have carefully analyzed the multi-
faceted nature of the anti-Japanese movement and found that it was deeply
rooted in the economic and racial insecurities that dominated Peru as the
nation struggled to modernize. Gardiner notes the profound paradox of anti-
Japanese sentiment as it intensified in the late 1930s. Newspapers and political leaders continued to criticize the Japanese community because the
Japanese were unwilling to mix racially, or "Peruvianize." At the same time,
racial extremists considered the Japanese an inferior race that Peruvians
should shun.[1] *Anti-Asia,* a magazine that was first published in Peru in
December 1930, set the tone for more than fifteen years of press attacks on
the Japanese by both Peru's marginal periodicals, such as *La Sanción* (Sanc-
tion), *Blanco y Negro* (Black and White), and *Cascabel* (Little Bell), and its
leading newspapers, *La Prensa* (The Press) and *El Comerico* (Commerce).
These publications blamed the Japanese for increasing the severity of the

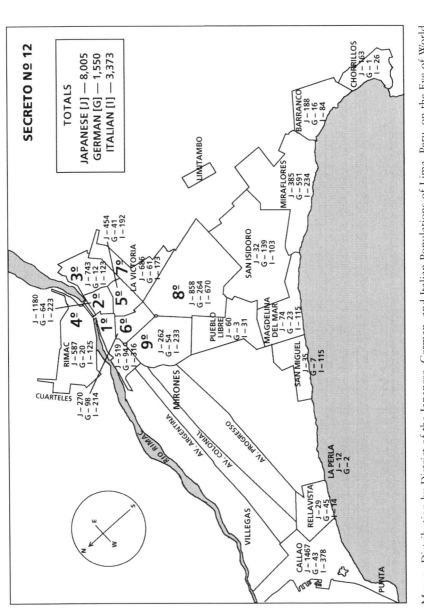

Map 3. Distribution by District of the Japanese, German, and Italian Populations of Lima, Peru, on the Eve of World War II. (Based on a Peruvian naval intelligence document housed in the Peruvian Naval Museum)

Depression by dishonest and illegal business practices, such as selling dis-ease-ridden and stolen goods. The magazine also continued to perpetuate the rumors that Japanese males were really soldiers ready to seize the government upon notice from Tokyo.[2] Rumors of militarized Japanese "fifth columns" would pervade the popular media in Peru throughout the pre–World War II years and would lead directly to the destructive anti-Japanese riots of May 1940. Deeply rooted racism against the Japanese clearly was embedded in a psychological matrix of fear of Japanese militarism and envy over the relative economic success of the Japanese in this troubled land.

Specific allegations of economic imperialism and unfair economic practices were consistently leveled against Japanese cotton producers. Although they controlled no more than 15 percent of national production, these efficient agriculturalists were portrayed as a dire threat to Peru's generally small- to medium-sized cotton producers. British economic interests were also served by limiting Japan's trade in low-cost textiles to Peru; England's former dominance in this lucrative enterprise was being challenged by Tokyo in the midst of the Depression. London thus allied itself with Peru's powerful Sociedad Agraria Nacional (National Agrarian Society) in promoting the anti-Japanese campaign in the economic sphere.[3] This alliance provided substantial dividends for the British when it led to the abrogation of the Peruvian-Japanese economic accord of 1924 by the Benavides administration in early October 1935. This opened the way for England's greater role in the cotton trade with the Japanese now excluded.

❀ ❀ ❀

When viewed in the context of the economic anxieties plaguing all sectors in Peru in the mid-1930s, the restrictive Brazilian immigration legislation of 1934 produced a profound reaction in the Andean nation. Despite the fact that more Japanese were leaving Peru than entering by the mid-1930s, anti-Japanese elements in that country feared that a significant portion of the thousands of Japanese immigrants who would have formerly settled in Brazil would now choose to immigrate to Peru. This misapprehension, of course, ignored the issue of subsidized immigration to Brazil, greater availability of land in Portuguese America, and the increasing government pressure to settle in Manchuria for the Japanese immigrants. But as we have repeatedly seen, logic and rationalism rarely guided immigration policy regarding the Japanese anywhere in the Americas.

Like the Vargas regime in Brazil, the Benavides administration responded to the imagined threat of increased Japanese immigration by enacting anti-Japanese and exclusionary legislation on the model of the U.S. Immigration

Act of 1924. In 1934 the Treaty of Commerce and Amity signed during the Leguía regime before the Japanese takeover of Manchuria was denounced by the Benavides government.[4] Written in secret by Benavides and his foreign minister, Alberto Ulloa, the Immigration Act of June 1936 placed a cap on the number of foreign nationals in Peru at 16,000. Reflecting the xenophobic nationalism rampant in Latin America at the time, the law made naturalization more difficult, requiring longer waiting periods for citizenship and placing other restrictions on resident aliens. Understandably, very few Issei were willing to abandon their sojourner mentality and adopt Peruvian citizenship, although the Japanese community comprised the largest number of foreign nationals in the country. Since their number already exceeded 16,000 in 1936, the Immigration Act of 1936 was tantamount to the total exclusion of future Japanese immigrants. Furthermore, the law prohibited foreigners from holding more than 20 percent of any urban or rural occupation. Clearly aimed at the Japanese, the legislation would not allow the Japanese to travel to their homeland and return as foreign nationals nor would it allow them to bring their families from their homeland. Significantly, they were also not allowed to transfer their businesses to their children, as was done in the United States after the alien land laws were enacted in the western states. Additional legislation during the following four years sought to strip the Japanese of nearly all legal and economic status. The most significant of these measures were a decree of 20 April 1937 that denied citizenship to Peruvian Nisei if they were born after 26 June 1936, and a November 1940 interpretation by the Peruvian Ministry of Foreign Relations that native-born Peruvians who had resided in their parent's nation for education or other reasons would be considered to have acquired another nationality and thus forfeited their Peruvian citizenship.[5] Additional decrees limited the number of foreigners who could be naturalized. Further legislation prohibited the publication of Japanese newspapers in Spanish translation. By late 1940, these restrictions and the intense anti-Japanese climate led to the demise of all but one Japanese language newspaper, *Lima Nippo*. These government measures effectively ended Japanese immigration to Peru forty years after the first contract laborers arrived to work on the coastal sugar plantations. In 1939 only twenty-four Japanese were issued passports to travel to Peru, and Japanese immigration would never be substantive again after World War II.[6] Had all these restrictions been consistently and strictly enforced, they would have immediately devastated the Japanese community. Although waning quickly after the invasion of China in 1937, Japanese diplomatic influence was still a moderating force in the treatment of their overseas compatriots. Still, this legislation established the framework for the Peruvian government's extreme measures after 1941. The most concerted government assault on the rights of the Japanese would not come until after the May 1940 riots and soon after Pearl Harbor, when the Prado government was assured of overwhelming popular support and the full cooperation of Washington in its anti-Japanese campaign.[7]

The late 1930s also witnessed the attempt by Peruvian political groups of both the right and the left to use the growing Japanese military threat as leverage to enlist the support of the United States for their causes. Claims of Japanese intentions to threaten the Panama Canal or to establish bases in the Galapagos Islands or the northern Peruvian port of Chimbote were consistently presented to the U.S. embassy in Lima in an effort to justify the government's anti-Japanese campaign. None of these claims could ever be verified by the embassy, but this still did not diminish Washington's continued fear of Japanese intentions on the west coast of South America.[8]

✿ ✿ ✿

Seiichi Higashide, a former retailer in the southern Peruvian city of Ica, understood very well the political capital to be gained by populist parties who adopted an anti-Japanese position. Higashide concluded: "From the standpoint of the older, established businesses the Japanese were seen as newcomers and unwanted intruders in the business community. . . . Among those who had to adjust to the Japanese shop owners, the most seriously affected were the owners of small, unstable businesses. The Japanese economic advances touched a sensitive spot among those of that stratum and brought forth a poisonous resentment."[9]

During the mid-1930s, the rightist Unión Revolucionaria (UR), formerly the political vehicle of the slain populist president Luis M. Sánchez Cerro, sought to broaden its political base among the economically hard-pressed small-merchant class that Higashide describes by adopting a pronounced anti-Japanese stance. Members of the UR undoubtedly participated in the anti-Japanese disturbances of 1930 and 1931 during Sánchez Cerro's highly nationalistic presidency.

The leftist Alianza Popular Revolucionaria Americana (APRA) party appealed to the same constituency and used the same tactics after 1938. APRA sought to solidify its support among small farmers, especially cotton growers and urban merchants who were in direct competition with Japanese businesses in Lima and Callao, by attacking the Japanese. Driven underground for more than a decade after one of its activists assassinated Sánchez Cerro in April 1933, APRA also sought desperately to play the anti-Japanese card to have the party legalized through the diplomatic intervention of the U.S. State Department. After 1938, APRA publicly and dramatically altered its previous anti-imperialist platform and expressed clear support for the Good Neighbor Policy. Touting themselves as the only truly democratic and anti-Axis political group in Peru, APRA leaders repeatedly approached U.S. diplomatic personnel from 1938 through the early World War II years, claiming they best understood the depth of the Japanese threat, could augment Washington's anti-Japanese campaign with their own party intelligence network, and were prepared to use force against the Japanese, if only the party could be legalized with the help of the United States. The thrust of the anti-Japanese *Aprista* initiative was familiar. Party leader Víctor Raul Haya de la Torre insisted that virtually the entire Japanese population of Peru was male adults, ignoring recent census figures that proved that 40 percent were children and females. Additionally, the APRA leader claimed that all the male Issei in Peru were army veterans and many were former officers and were prepared to overthrow the government when so ordered by Tokyo.[10] APRA's clandestine party newspaper *La Tribuna* sought to inflame public opinion against the Japanese with such bold-type slogans as "We do not want to be Japanese" and allegations that "The German and Japanese fifth columns are preparing an invasion of Peru."[11] *La Tribuna,* with anti-Japanese flyers enclosed, was distributed throughout Lima and Callao only ten days before the anti-Japanese riots of mid-May 1940.[12] Haya de la Torre even wrote directly to President Roosevelt in 1942 to repeat his allegations against the Japanese and appeal for the president's support for the party's legalization. Ultimately, the Prado administration's complete cooperation with the United States on the internment issue undercut APRA's bargaining power with Washington, and the party was not legalized until 1945. During the early World War II years, U.S. Ambassador R. Henry Norweb may well have used APRA informants to aid the anti-Japanese campaign. But Norweb knew that President Prado "was our best friend on the West Coast of South America," and he could not risk alienating that administration by supporting APRA's legalization. Norweb commented years later that Haya de la Torre was well aware that if APRA had engaged in violence or sabotage against the government out of frustration over its failed anti-Japanese gambit, the party leader "would have been ridden out of Peru on a rail."[13]

Much of the intelligence gathered by the Peruvian and U.S. governments regarding the Japanese Peruvians before the attack on Pearl Harbor was flawed or utter nonsense. A good deal of this false information was created in a climate of fear, envy, and racial hatred. As the war progressed, FBI and U.S. Army Intelligence officials gradually recognized this reality. Nevertheless, rumor and false reporting still often guided their reporting and policy making. One such report written soon after Pearl Harbor commented on long-prevailing attitudes toward the Japanese, reflecting views similar to those of some opportunistic Californians as the U.S. internment program was progressing. The intelligence official noted, "For every Japanese owner of a hardware or price goods store or barber shop, there are at least three Peruvian candidates [waiting] to take over their businesses."[14] Raymond Ickes, who was sent by the U.S. government to review the internment of Japanese Latin Americans in mid-1943, agreed with this assessment and warned the embassy staff in Caracas, Venezuela, not to follow the pattern of Peru, "'Where attempts have been made to send . . . lots of Japanese to the States merely because Peruvians wanted their businesses and not because there is any evidence against them.'" Decades later, Japanese-Peruvians who were deported remained convinced that the principle reason for their expulsion from Peru was the economic exploitation of successful Japanese merchants.[15] Thus, U.S. government officials were well aware of the cynical motivations of Peruvian government officials as late as early 1944 but were reluctant to address the problem with the Peruvian government because of their overriding concern for security. For example, J. Edgar Hoover's analysis of the Japanese community based upon flawed intelligence gathered before 7 December 1941 demonstrates why U.S. officials viewed Peru's Japanese in the same way they regarded their own Japanese population.

Accurately concluding that the Japanese were "thoroughly disliked by Peruvian officials from President Prado on down," Hoover then offered an assessment that was probably instrumental in shaping U.S. policy toward Peru's Japanese during World War II. His simplistic analysis divided the Japanese community into three main groups. The Nisei were judged to be of the "live and let live" mentality and not interested in the war but only in living peacefully in Peru. A second faction was referred to as the "emperor's group," largely composed of Issei who felt the war was not the emperor's doing but was the work of Japanese militarists. This group's "loyalty" was not considered "secure." A final segment was described as the very sizable "Military and Naval" group, veterans of military service in Japan who were "attempting to organize the Japanese colony on a military basis." Hoover specifically referred to rumors of a 6,000-man Japanese "suicide" squad that was purportedly being formed to lead attacks on critical installations in northern Peru. These reports had been preceded by memos sent to Roosevelt and Vice President Henry Wallace claiming that the "Japanese Colony is impenetrable in Peru" and that "they live and work like an organized army."[16]

In actuality, although accurate statistics for the percentage of military veterans among the Japanese are not available, it seems clear that the number was quite small. Many Japanese males immigrated to Peru and Latin America to avoid the "blood tax" or draft. But this fact was never understood by Peru or the United States because the intelligence services of both nations lacked Japanese-language capabilities. The reading of Japanese documents or questioning of most Issei proved to be very difficult because only one government official in Peru before and during World War II, U.S. embassy officer John K. Emmerson, understood Japanese. This appalling inability to gather reliable information led the FBI and other U.S. and Peruvian intelligence agencies to treat rumor and purposeful "disinformation" as fact. Emmerson, writing later of his experience in Peru, acknowledged as much: "In [Peru's] atmosphere of suspicion and distrust—where every Japanese barber was assumed to be an admiral in disguise and every Japanese tailor a constant recipient of secret orders from Tokyo . . . I became fascinated with the story of what they [Japanese] were really doing."[17]

The May 1940 Riots and the Deportation Program

Anti-Japanese violence had plagued the Japanese community during the 1930s but had not reached the scale of the May 1940 riots. The catalyst was an incident involving Tokihiro Furuya, a naturalized Peruvian with a Peruvian wife whom the Japanese consul in Lima tried to deport clandestinely to Japan as a dangerous espionage suspect. In the process of this botched effort, a Peruvian woman was badly beaten and later died. After word of this incident reached the newspapers, teenage Peruvian students at the Guadalupe School in Lima staged an anti-Japanese march through the city. Widespread rioting and looting of Japanese businesses and homes then erupted in Lima and Callao, while less serious disturbances broke out in the agricultural centers of Chancay and Huaral. Japanese Peruvians recalling the rioting years later attributed it to the nearly constant rumors and press reports of Japanese subversion and military activity in Peru. Luis Okamoto Yokoyama, a twenty-two-year-old Nisei at the time of the riots, and Yasuhiko Ohashi, an Issei who had resided in Peru for fourteen years before the disturbances, attributed the violence to the consistent press campaign against the Japanese. Both of their families suffered serious financial losses when their businesses were looted. Another Nisei, only four years old at the time, remembers that the looters broke into their family home and "stole everything, even the toilet."[18]

The two days of anti-Japanese rioting and looting cost the lives of ten

Japanese and injured hundreds more. Damage to 600 Japanese businesses and homes was estimated by the Japanese consul in Lima at a cost of $7 million. Peruvian police did little to stop the rioting during the first day, and only after strong protests from the Japanese embassy were the rioters dispersed with tear gas on 14 May. Many Japanese were forced to flee their homes and seek refuge in the Japanese schools in Lima, where the Central Japanese Association quickly organized their defense and subsequent recovery program. Still, nearly every Japanese business in Lima was either totally destroyed or badly damaged. Many Japanese families were homeless and sought shelter in Lima's Japanese Elementary School. Sixty-four Japanese families, including 316 individuals, faced losses so profound that they were forced to repatriate to Japan in July 1940. Tokyo lodged a strong protest with the Prado government in the aftermath of the riots and eventually gained partial payment, amounting to only 25 percent of the original damage claim.[19] The Japanese press also condemned the Peruvian government for its inaction against what Tokyo claimed was an "organized movement." *Nichi Nichi* (Day to Day), in characteristically jingoist fashion, suggested that a few Japanese warships take "'action against the offending country.'"[20]

Tokyo apparently viewed the May 1940 riots as a clear indication of the precarious status of Peru's Japanese. U.S. intelligence agents in Peru concluded, "The fear of mob action in anti-Japanese riots will in all likelihood prove a great deterrent to sabotage attempts on the part of the Japanese community. . . . inasmuch as the Japanese are especially unpopular with the Peruvians, any sabotage occurring in Peru would probably be blamed on the race and might serve as an excuse for further riots against the race." The FBI concluded six months after Pearl Harbor that the Japanese government already had discouraged the other Axis powers from instigating sabotage in Peru for fear of the potential violent backlash against the Japanese community.[21]

In the aftermath of the rioting, the Japanese community felt their isolation even more profoundly. Seiichi Higashide remembers when the Japanese left their own neighborhoods, they were often met with shouts of the epithet *chino macaco* (dirty Chinese). The poorly educated Peruvian masses still demeaned the Japanese by associating them with despised Chinese coolies. Higashide recalled: "We could only endure the situation with bone-felt painfulness. Now every Japanese in Peru, without exception, feared that anti-Japanese violence might again flare up at any time. Our days passed filled with anxiety and feelings of isolation."[22]

The allegations of Japanese militarism in Peru had international ramifications for the Lima government after a long-standing border dispute with Ecuador erupted into a brief border war between the two Andean nations in July 1941. Ecuador, completely desperate for U.S. intervention to prevent a total military defeat by its more powerful southern neighbor, "claimed that 3,000 Japanese troops were fighting for Peru." Lima quickly denied these charges, but U.S. military intelligence officers in the region gave them more consideration than they were due, given the history of the Peruvian government's paranoia regarding the arming of its Japanese population.[23] Indeed, it is worth noting that most Issei, because they were not naturalized, were not eligible for the armed forces academies and thus could not become officers. Conscription in Peru invariably was imposed almost exclusively on the Indian masses and not the urban middle class. Thus the Issei escaped military service. If Peru's Nisei wished to enter the armed forces officer corps, and there is little indication that they did, it is highly unlikely they would have been admitted to the service academies, given the strong anti-Japanese sentiment that emerged in the armed forces during the 1930s while Lieutenant Colonel Sánchez Cerro and General Oscar Benavides occupied the presidency. A review of the army's officer staff lists and graduating classes for Peru's military and naval academies for the period under review reveals nearly a complete absence of Japanese officers in those institutions. Significantly, no Japanese attended the military academies until after World War II.[24]

It is not surprising the Japanese were excluded from the armed forces. They also chose to avoid the risk of becoming involved in local or national institutions or politics, remaining active only in the Japanese community's associations. This sharply contrasts with the career path of European immigrants in the Peruvian army as well as in the militaries of Argentina, Brazil, and Chile, where Italian, Irish, German, and French immigrants and their children entered the officer corps quite freely. This was yet another example of the isolation of the Japanese from the mainstream of Peruvian society. As was overwhelmingly true of the Japanese in the Western Hemisphere, Peru's Japanese were without advocates in the nation's ruling institutions and were completely vulnerable after Pearl Harbor. Because the story of the Japanese Peruvian internment is so compelling, we will first turn to an analysis of this unfortunate episode before discussing the larger question of the how the vast majority of the nation's Japanese endured during the World War II years and their aftermath.

As we have seen, the pattern of arrest, relocation, and internment of the Japanese in the Americas drew upon the precedents established by the Mexican, Canadian, and U.S. governments. In Peru, the legal status of both the Issei and Nisei was weakened even more than in other nations by the anti-Japanese legislation of the late 1930s. Moreover, as C. Harvey Gardiner has noted, "the vulnerability of the alien in wartime was complete" because of the primacy of national security requirements under international law.[25] Gardiner's moving historical account of the arrest, deportation, and internment of the Japanese Peruvians in the United States is appropriately entitled *Pawns in a Triangle of Hate*. In the context of war, when the security of the hemisphere was, without question, the key issue governing the treatment of the Japanese, Peru's Japanese were also used as pawns by the Prado government to strengthen its domestic political base and gain military and economic concessions from the United States. For their part, a wide array of government agencies in the United States was involved in a program during the war to utilize Peruvian and other Japanese Latin American internees in a potential exchange for U.S. nationals caught in Japanese occupied territories after the hostilities began.[26] These questions will be initially addressed before we turn to issues of the alleged Japanese Peruvian security threat and the actual deportation and internment program.

The signing of the so-called Rio Protocol, officially ending hostilities between Peru and Ecuador in January 1942, was directly linked to Peruvian cooperation with Washington on the severing of relations with Tokyo and Japanese internment.[27] U.S. Ambassador Norweb viewed President Prado as "'our best friend on the West Coast of South America'" and proposed soon after Pearl Harbor to "assist the Peruvian government by making available information and suggestions based upon our handling of Japanese residents in the United States."[28] Thereafter, while the Prado government was deporting its Japanese aliens to the United States, Lima was able to persuade Washington to extend an Export-Import Bank loan to Peru that financed the nation's first steel processing plant at Chimbote. Moreover, despite not declaring war on the Axis until January 1945, Peru was one of the leading recipients of Lend Lease aid in South America. In March 1942, Washington extended Peru more than $29 million in Lend Lease armaments and munitions at a time when it was replenishing its military stocks after the Ecuador conflict.[29] This was the largest single transfer of Lend Lease aid in Spanish America during World War II. In return, the United States was given permission to construct and operate the El Pato air base at Talara in northern Peru to protect the sea approaches to the Panama Canal. Direct military ties between the U.S. and Peruvian armed forces were strengthened prior to and during the war.

On the domestic front, the Prado government came to the conclusion soon after Pearl Harbor that the deportation and internment in the United States of as many of the nation's Japanese as possible was both politically popular and expedient. Peru's Japanese, unlike their counterparts in Mexico, whose leaders had important advocates within the upper ranks of the government, lacked political influence. The immediate blacklisting and early deportation of Ikumatsu Okada, the "Cotton King" of the Chancay Valley, was clear evidence of this. In another instance, Prado's own Japanese cook in the presidential palace was unable to avoid deportation to the United States.[30] What must be understood, however, is that although some wealthy Japanese avoided deportation through bribery of Peruvian police officials, they were able to do so only because the internment program became so haphazard after 1943.

Initially, the Prado government considered a domestic internment program. Nelson Rockefeller, the coordinator of Inter-American Affairs, reported to President Roosevelt in October 1942 that Peru was considering interning at least 6,000 Japanese in camps but would need assistance from the United States. Some U.S. leaders suggested that the Japanese internees be put to work on road and agricultural projects under the supervision of U.S. technical advisers. But lack of effective monitoring of the project and the unwillingness of the Peruvian government to fund such a scheme doomed it from the beginning.[31] Prior to the Rockefeller report, Jorge Larrañaga, a former member of Peru's Financial and Economic Advisory Board, expressed the "anxious" sentiments of the Prado administration to government officials in Washington. He warned that Japanese shop owners could "'set the city of Lima on fire overnight'" and urged that all Japanese be placed in concentration camps as quickly as possible.[32] Even after plans for domestic internment were abandoned by the Prado government and a limited deportation program was begun in cooperation with the United States, Lima continued its efforts to rid itself of its Japanese until the last year of the war. The first ship, the *Etolin*, left Callao harbor in early April 1942 with 141 Japanese Peruvians, all male, aboard. As Gardiner notes, no legal charges had been brought against any of the deportees, and none had a police record. Most significantly, less than 5 percent were on the initial proclaimed list of suspect Japanese prepared by Peruvian and U.S. authorities. The *Etolin* made one stop in Colombia to pick up more Japanese deportees before it completed its voyage to San Francisco. Later voyages would take deportees to temporary camps in Panama before they debarked in New Orleans.[33]

The slow and haphazard process of the deportation pleased neither Peruvian nor U.S. authorities. For instance, when presenting his credentials to President Roosevelt in August 1944, Pedro Beltran, the newly appointed Peruvian ambassador, boldly requested that all Japanese be removed from Peru and interned in the United States before being eventually repatriated to Japan. He reportedly stressed the urgency of this matter to FDR, arguing, "'If we wait until the end of the war, feeling against the Japanese might not be as strong as it is at present.'" Beltran's efforts were so persistent that some Washington officials characterized him as a "'considerable nuisance.'"[34]

Beltran's cynical goal of ridding Peru of its Japanese with the cooperation of the United States was not as far-fetched as it might seem. A Japanese Peruvian interned in the United States during World War II decades later referred to Lima's deportation program as "Peru's version of ethnic cleansing."[35] Indeed, early in the war, Secretary of State Cordell Hull boldly but naively suggested that the United States should seriously consider the internment of all Japanese Latin Americans in the United States.[36] Hull's notion was prompted by Washington's perceived need to secure Japanese nationals in Latin America for a possible exchange program involving U.S. citizens caught in Japanese occupied territories in Asia. A proposed exchange of this sort was also supported by Armed Forces Chief of Staff George C. Marshall, who argued in December 1942 that 1,000 Japanese Peruvians be deported to the United States for use in an exchange for "'American civilian nationals now interned.'"[37] Such an exchange program achieved little progress, but this did not deter U.S. officials from pursuing it throughout the first years of the war with Japan.

A lack of shipping severely hampered the program from the beginning. Thus logistics and Japanese diplomatic pressure, not humanitarian considerations, appear to be the main reasons why far more than 1,800 Japanese Peruvians were not deported and interned. Under the pressures of war, the Roosevelt administration was willing to disregard the rights of U.S. citizens in establishing its own domestic policy of placing the Japanese in concentration camps. Domestic intelligence by the FBI in the United States was far better than that produced by the same agency in Peru. Yet still no evidence of a major threat to the security of the United States by Japanese Americans was ever uncovered by J. Edgar Hoover's agency. Without a factual basis, the U.S. internment program went forward anyway. On the other hand, as we have seen, rumors and false reports from Peru clearly influenced Washington's policy on the Japanese Peruvians at the highest levels of government. For instance, Vice President Wallace, drawing on State Department, FBI, and military intelligence reports, informed FDR in early 1942 that he was convinced that "'the Japanese plan [of attack on South America] would advance from Peru by Japs in that country against Guayaquil [Ecuador] and strategic nearby points, undoubtedly including Salinas, where the U.S. is now building an important base.'"[38] Wallace's invasion scenario may very well have been based on J. Edgar Hoover's imaginary 6,000-man "Japanese suicide squad." Framed in the context of war, the perceived security threat to strategic points in South America, as well as the United States' internment of its own Japanese as a precedent, it is clear why Washington showed little reluctance to use the Japanese Peruvians as pawns in violation of established principles of international law. Only in late 1944, when it became clear that Japanese Peruvian internees in the United States were not dangerous enemy aliens and that the military threat from Japan was rapidly ebbing, was the entire program reevaluated by Raymond Ickes, head of the Central and South American division of the alien enemy control unit of the Department of Justice. When Ickes completed his Latin American evaluation mission, no further deportations from Peru occurred, and those from other nations in the region effectively ended as well.[39]

The deportation and internment program was an administrative nightmare. Three U.S. government agencies—the departments of State and Justice and the Immigration and Naturalization Service—at various times were involved in the undertaking. The Special War Problems Division, created by the Department of State in 1939 to deal with complex war-related issues, assumed the most immediate control of the program. It would be administered by this agency, with inspection rights given to Spanish diplomatic officials in the U.S. internment camps, throughout the war. In the beginning, Japanese diplomatic officials were given first priority for removal from Peru. But very quickly the haphazard pattern of deportation for the Japanese Peruvians themselves was established.

Ultimately, the Peruvian government was primarily responsible for the gross injustices of the deportations. The so-called Proclaimed List, which was supposed to include the most influential leaders of the Japanese community who were deemed threats to national security, was riddled with errors. A lack of familiarity with the Japanese language created many of these problems. But poor intelligence, lazy police work, rampant corruption, and bribery shifted the burden of the deportations upon what John Emmerson called the "little people," often the late-arriving Okinawans who had not yet been able to achieve any stature. The general decree stipulating the Peruvian government's policy towards Axis nationals was issued on 22 January 1942. It called for the "immediate expulsion" from Peru of those individuals for whom there was "conclusive proof" that they had engaged in "anti-national activities."[40]

This "conclusive proof" was never found. In his memoirs, Emmerson recalled that after his nearly two years of intelligence work in Peru, "Nothing emerged to confirm the rumors constantly whispered to our legal, army, and naval attachés by their conscientious paid informants."[41] In the climate of fear and war, proof really did not matter. Thus Japanese families were relocated from some of Peru's north coast cities into the interior, the community's schools were prohibited from teaching the Japanese language and culture, the bank accounts of all the Japanese Peruvians were frozen, travel was restricted, gatherings of more than five Japanese were prohibited, the personal radios and telephones of many Japanese were confiscated, and publication of any Japanese newspapers was banned. The prohibition on meetings was particularly troubling for the Japanese community, which was so dependent upon group-oriented decision making in times of crisis. Most unfortunately, many families were torn apart at a time when the previously highly supportive Japanese community could not effectively come to their aid. Wives and children of first deportees, who were primarily male, were consequently often left to fend for themselves. This caused many of them to request deportation and internment in the camps in the United States in a desperate attempt to reunite their families. Wartime conditions for the Japanese in Peru were more difficult than anywhere else in Latin America. Nevertheless, as in the past with Peru's anti-Japanese legislation, these harsh measures were often compromised by all ranks of Peruvian government officials who were willing to look the other way for both the big and the small bribe.

✿ ✿ ✿

Who were these deportees and how can their unfortunate experience be characterized? John Emmerson's firsthand account of his own central role in the deportation process, Gardiner's compelling analysis, and the testimonials of the Japanese Peruvian internees gathered for this study tell a story of fear, prejudice, misunderstanding, victimization, and greed as the underlying causes of this episode. On the other hand, when the Japanese Peruvians remember this experience, their recollections are most frequently tales of courage and fortitude that are generally lacking in bitterness. Even while they seek redress for their internment experience, they say *"shikata ganai"* (it can't be helped). "These things happen in war" was the sentiment of thoughtful former Japanese Peruvian internees more than half a century later.[42]

Gardiner's analysis of the first shipment of deportees from Peru aboard the former Pacific passenger steamer *Etolin* tells us much about the pattern of the entire deportation and internment saga that would continue for more than two years. The first shipload of Japanese deportees was supposedly chosen from a "final and definitive list" of "dangerous individuals" prepared by the Peruvian Foreign Office in consultation with U.S. officials in Peru. Emmerson later stated, "Lacking incriminating evidence, we established the criteria of leadership and influence in the community to determine those

163

Japanese to be expelled."[43] Yet less than 10 of the 141 Japanese who left Peru on the *Etolin* on 5 April 1942 were on the Proclaimed List. Nearly half of them were, in Gardiner's words, "lowly employees" with little money and far less influence in the Japanese community. Almost all, as one might expect, were from the Lima-Callao metropolitan area. More than half had not married, and among those who had families, nearly all their families had already departed for Japan. There was only one Peruvian citizen among the group, a Nisei.

Since the vast majority of these deportees were born in Japan, Gardiner concludes that a significant number of the *Etolin* group may have been volunteers who wanted to return to Japan to escape a hostile Peru and be reunited with their families. Indeed, more than 900 Japanese Peruvians had previously indicated to the government that they were willing to be deported. They apparently saw deportation to the United States as the first stage in a repatriation process. After the *Etolin* departed, however, the Peruvian government and U.S. officials refused to allow these volunteers to leave the country unless they were the wives or children of men who had previously been deported. Those volunteers that were able to be shipped out were quite correct in their assumption that they would be returning to Japan, because when they entered the United States at San Francisco and were processed by INS officials, they were denied passports or visas. These unwanted Japanese were classified as "enemy aliens," which would be the status of all future Japanese Peruvian deportees and would assure that the vast majority would never return to Peru, would not be permitted to remain in the United States, and would eventually be deported once again to a devastated Japan. An INS official commenting at the time about this decision to deny the Japanese Peruvians visas concluded, "'Only in wartime could we get away with such fancy skullduggery.'"[44]

Once the first vessel had departed with deportees, Emmerson and other U.S. officials in Lima attempted to convince Peru's security forces to limit the arrests and deportations to only those "influential leaders" of the Japanese community who had been specifically selected for expulsion. Emmerson's efforts met largely with failure. As Japanese "suspects" were deported from Peru on such vessels as the *Gripsholm*, the *Shawnee*, and the *Frederick C. Johnson*, little effort was made to coordinate the deportations with the limited Proclaimed List. Japanese Peruvian women joined their men as "voluntary deportees" in mid-1943 and thereafter. Life aboard these aging vessels was very difficult. Unaccustomed to the food, many deportees became ill or ate little. Conditions were cramped and damp, and opportunities to seek fresh air and exercise on deck were limited.

Some of the male deportees were forced to live in tents or self-constructed barracks in the rainy jungle of the Panama Canal Zone while awaiting further transportation to the United States. In one case, a Japanese deportee was shot and seriously wounded as he tried to escape by scaling the barbed wire surrounding the make-shift camp.[45] As late as the sailing of the *Frederick C. Johnson,* the sixth vessel carrying deportees from the northern port of Talara in February 1943, Lima's chief of police largely ignored Emmerson's carefully prepared lists and "apparently emptied Lima's jails of miscellaneous vagrants and petty miscreants with Japanese faces and sent them off to Talara."[46] Emmerson personally freed these nonselectees in frustration during his inspection tour of the vessel.

Some Japanese Peruvians evaded deportation after they were solicited for bribes as high as 16,000 soles ($1,600) by a government ring involving, among others, the Lima chief of police and the prefect of the department of Lima. This scheme was so involved that it included the use of a rented hacienda near Lima where "protected" Japanese could be hidden. Lesser bribes of 100 soles ($10) were paid to police officials for temporary "safe conduct" passes that violated the government's restriction on Japanese travel. As one might imagine, the freezing of Japanese assets and the eventual liquidation of many Japanese properties offered much opportunity for enrichment by corrupt Peruvian officials. In one case, the director of Peru's Banco Minero was suspected of transferring the assets of a Japanese business to his wife.[47] It is, of course, impossible to determine how many Japanese were able to avoid deportation through the corrupt intercession of government officials. But it should be understood that some Japanese on the Proclaimed List paid protection money for extended periods and were still eventually deported. In all fairness, it must be said that some Peruvians, like some U.S. citizens, did come to the aid of the unfortunate Japanese deportees. A number worked as transitional managers of Japanese businesses that otherwise would have been sold at auction and lost forever. In other cases, it is clear that Peruvians chose not to betray Japanese who were on the Proclaimed List when it very well might have been beneficial for them to do so. As always, the story is never completely one-sided. Simple humanity often emerges in times of crisis.

All this should tell us that there was no regularity and certainly no justice with the process of deportation of the Japanese Peruvians. The plan of using them for a prisoner exchange did not fully materialize. Moreover, since some important Japanese community leaders avoided deportation, U.S. intelligence officials were never assured that their security concerns were being met by the Peruvian government. Indeed, the entire assumption by John Emmerson and his fellow security officials that the leaders of the Japanese community automatically should be regarded as the main security risk was flawed. Most of these leaders had been in Peru for several years and were primarily interested in consolidating their business holdings, ensuring the security of their families, and maintaining a low profile for a Japanese community that was increasingly threatened by violence. Japanese officials in Lima clearly understood this. When the Japanese chargé d'affaires in Lima, Masaki Yodakawa, was expelled from Peru on 24 January 1942, he reminded the Japanese community, "'No Japanese should forget his pride as a subject of the Empire.'" But Yodakawa went on to warn the Japanese Peruvians to "'be prudent in word and deed . . . obey Peruvian laws and officials . . . and maintain discretion and good sense.'"[48] Seiichi Higashide, writing later of his own deportation experience, reflected: "I could not think of any reasons [for my deportation orders]. I had not committed any crimes. I had not participated in any propaganda activities for the Japanese government and, of course, had not engaged in espionage or underground activities. I could not understand what criteria had been used to compile the [deportation] list."[49]

The *Frederick C. Johnson* departed from Callao on 11 October 1944 with the last contingent of twenty-two Japanese Peruvians. Characteristically, only three of the deportees were on the Proclaimed List, and two of these had avoided deportation for more than two and a half years. Sanitary and medical conditions aboard this vessel were perhaps worse than on any previous sailing, reflecting the nearly complete lack of regard for the basic health of the deportees by U.S. officials. Women and children outnumbered adult men by two to one on this sailing, many of them dependents of previously interned male family heads seeking reunions in the Crystal City internment camp in Texas.[50] Life in the various camps throughout the western United States proved to be a mixture of heartache and renewed strength, as the now homeless and stateless Japanese Peruvians struggled to begin life anew behind barbed wire in a strange land.

Internment and Its Aftermath

The U.S. government interned the Japanese Latin Americans as "enemy aliens" under the supervision of the INS in camps at Kooskia, Idaho; Missoula, Montana; Santa Fe, New Mexico; and Kenedy, Seagoville, and Crystal City, Texas. The INS had been transferred from the Labor Department to the Department of Justice before Pearl Harbor in anticipation of the need to deal with enemy aliens within the law enforcement framework of the federal government. Although Japanese Americans were interned in some of the same camps, including Crystal City, as the Japanese Peruvians, the War Relocation Authority (WRA) did not have jurisdiction over the displaced Japanese from the Andean nation.

After the initial voyages, which entered the United States at San Francisco, the deportees thereafter disembarked at New Orleans before a train ride to the camps. The transit and entry stage of the deportation and internment saga was characterized by the many indignities that "prisoners" typically have to undergo, including overcrowded passenger vessels, little privacy, poor food, lack of adequate sanitation facilities, and, for the men, strip searches. These deportees endured without complaint, but some never forgot. One of the Crystal City internees, for example, who rarely spoke of his experience to his children in their occasional "talk stories," did later painfully recall the "humiliation" of being forced to disrobe by U.S. officials upon entry at New Orleans.[51] Another, a merchant from the southern Peruvian city of Arequipa, put his intense feelings to verse while in transit to the United States. In his "Song of Farewell," the merchant lamented

> We bid our last farewell . . .
> We are the hostages
> Damn it, take us any place . . .
> What hard labor, the armed watch,
> We don't give a damn . . .
> Sadly there is no way to ward off
> Anxiety over our dear families
> Abandoned in the Peruvian land . . .
> Bear it, bear it, the raindrops whisper . . .[52]

The Kenedy, Seagoville, and Crystal City internment camps in Texas were the main confinement centers for the Japanese Peruvians. Kenedy, a former Civilian Conservation Corps facility on the outskirts of an agricultural community of nearly 3,000, housed Japanese, German, and Italian male deportees from Latin America. Seagoville, a former reformatory for women offenders built in 1940 near Dallas, primarily interned women. Crystal City, once a migrant labor camp and located just over a mile outside the town, 120 miles south of San Antonio, became the "family camp" for reunited Japanese, German, and Italian families from Latin America when it opened in December 1942.

Life in the internment camps for Japanese Peruvians mirrored conditions in the WRA camps for the Japanese Americans in many ways. This was particularly true of the "family camp" at Crystal City. Initially, the facilities were often crude barracks that were generally improved with better sanitation, recreational, and medical facilities as the populations of the camps increased and the Japanese internees became more assertive about their needs. The internees appear to have been well fed. A week's meals at the Kenedy internment camp in June 1943, for example, included a balanced diet that offered fish, beef, pasta, vegetables, and ample supplies of eggs, rice, and fruit.[53] The fried chicken that John Emmerson claimed the internees raved about in their letters to Peru, in which they reportedly encouraged other Japanese Peruvians to "'come on up and join us, it's not so bad here,'" was not in evidence.[54] Recreational facilities were provided in all the camps, but the days passed slowly for the single men in the internment centers other than Crystal City. This was especially true for men whose wives and children were still in Peru. Higashide, recalling his days at Camp Kenedy, remembered, "We had more than enough free time, and indeed passed much of our time aimlessly. All we could do was gather together in small groups to engage in foolish conversation, gamble, or participate in sports to keep us from boredom."[55] At times, the younger Japanese men in the camps engaged in small acts of resistance such as intentionally breaking chinaware after meals. Significantly, the male internees in the camps became divided by the degree of their loyalty to Japan as the news of Japan's military losses mounted. Higashide, for example, was criticized for being "pro-American" for criticizing resistance efforts in Camp Kenedy and was ostracized by the younger internees.[56]

Higashide and hundreds of other Peruvian Issei and Nisei who eventually found themselves interned at the Crystal City "family camp" were forced to use the experience as a basis for building new lives beyond Peru. Interned with Japanese from the United States and Hawaii, termed "mainland people" and the "Hawaiian contingent," respectively, along with Italian and German "enemy aliens" from Latin America, many of the Japanese Peruvians would remain at Crystal City until well after the war ended. Only 79 Japanese Peruvians (Peruvian citizens and their families) were permitted to return to their adopted land. The majority of the deported Japanese were either voluntarily or involuntarily "repatriated" to Japan. Eventually, 364 Japanese Peruvians successfully fought a legal struggle to remain in the United States. As Karen L. Riley has perceptively noted in her study of the camp schools at Crystal City, the INS publicly declared that it had no obligation to treat the Japanese Peruvians as anything other than enemy aliens bound by the rules of the Geneva Convention. Because many of those interned at Crystal City were viewed as "voluntary internees" who had decided to accept deportation and internment in order to reunite their families, the INS claimed, "'This country is not obligated by any international agreement to provide family camp care; families are not therefore entitled to such care.'"[57] Ironically, despite this disclaimer, the INS did in fact provide quite satisfactory family care at Crystal City, including significant autonomy in group decision making. The Japanese Self-Governing Association, for example, reflected the highly organized and integrated social networks established by the Japanese in both the United States and Latin America. It had fourteen divisions, including medical, housing, educational, community welfare, and security components. Higashide characterized the Self-Governing Association as "splendidly organized and superbly managed."[58]

Within the family camp that housed at various times between 3,000 and 4,000 internees, the Japanese were provided health services, schooling, recreational facilities, and ample opportunities to improve living conditions through gardening and the manufacture of many of the products they required for daily life. Unlike in the Kenedy Camp, Japanese male family heads detained early in the war appear to have kept quite busy in meaningful tasks during their internment. This was less true of those who arrived after late 1943, when most of the best "jobs" were taken. Two Peruvian Issei internees interviewed in Lima in May 1990, for example, remembered conditions at Crystal City as "good enough," particularly since one enjoyed his work as the postmaster for the Japanese internees and the other was occupied in the camp's canteen.[59] These conditions can be explained by the clear concern that U.S. officials had for potential reprisals by the Japanese against U.S. citizens interned in Asia. This was made quite clear in a confidential circular distributed to INS employees in late April 1943 that stated, "'a grave responsibility rests upon each of us because of the bid we constantly make for reciprocity in securing equally fair treatment of *OUR* civil and military prisoners held in the custody of enemy nations.'"[60]

The opportunity to be constantly with children their own age, the ample recreational facilities, and the high-quality schooling offered at Crystal City appear to explain why some Peruvian Nisei who responded to a questionnaire prepared for this study recalled their experience as being "fun," with a spirit of adventure. Libby Maoki-Yamamoto, whose father managed a store in Chiclayo, Peru, before her entire family was eventually interned in Crystal City, recalled that the "children in the camp really didn't suffer [because] their parents adopted the attitude of *kodomo no tame ni* [for the sake of the children]." Maoki-Yamamoto recognized later how well her parents shielded her from the deep anxieties they had about their uncertain future. Ironically, she also remembered well how strongly allegiance to the Japanese cultural heritage was imbued into the education of the Nisei in the Crystal City school.[61] This is not unlike the recollections of some young American Nisei in the WRA camps throughout the western states. Other Nisei, perhaps reflecting the views of their parents, remembered the experience as being marked by "no privacy, no comforts of the [Peruvian] home that was left behind, only one trunk of belongings, and [not being] allowed to roam freely."[62] The constant theme running through the responses of the former Crystal City internees, however, is the uncertainty about their futures and the utter frustration of being unable to reunite family members who had been left behind in Peru or who had "repatriated" to Japan. Higashide recalls the fate of some Japanese Peruvians who were separated for more than ten years after the war because the Andean nation would not permit any deported Japanese to return until the early 1950s. The ever perceptive Higashide recalled in his memoirs that the Japanese at Crystal City were really like "birds in a cage," materially well provided for but denied freedom or even a secure knowledge of when they could begin rebuilding their lives.[63]

As the war in the Pacific drew to a close with the invasion of Okinawa and the highly destructive bombing raids of the home islands, news of Japan's impending defeat began to divide the Japanese Peruvian internees in the United States. As in Peru and even in Japanese internment camps in Australia, two primary factions emerged: the Kachigumi (also called Gambari) group, which refused to acknowledge the military failure of their homeland and sought repatriation to Japan, and the Makegumi group, which accepted this harsh reality and was divided about rebuilding their lives in Peru, returning with reluctance to a shattered homeland, or trying to remain in the United States.[64] Higashide described the intensity of the division among the Crystal City internees at this time. The former Ica merchant saw the Kachigumi group as mainly individuals who had "received a thorough indoctrination in militarist ideology in Japan and had been confined to the closed off Japanese community in Peru."[65] Many of these individuals, according to Higashide, "rejected advice from their parents and words of persuasion from their children, and simply returned to Japan."[66] These staunchly patriotic Japanese returned to Japan as the camps were beginning to close in late 1945 and early 1946. Those internees like Higashide, who dreaded returning to a devastated Japan with his wife and with five young children to raise, were regarded by the Kachigumi group as "great fools who . . . were pitied or detested, and were laughed at even to our faces."[67]

Of course, not all the internees who chose to return to Japan from the internment camps were fanatical nationalists. The sojourner mentality remained a powerful force in the minds of many of these internees. The parents of Higashide's wife, for example, saw postwar repatriation as possibly the last chance they would have to return to their homeland. Others wanted to join their wives and children who had been sent away from Peru for their safety after the May 1940 riots. One Peruvian Issei, Alberto Bunken Tosa, after laboring thirty-five years in Peru and losing assets of nearly $110,000, simply felt he had no choice but to return to Japan. Such was also the case with the former Japanese Peruvian farmer Katsuo Nakasone, who bleakly informed INS officials, "'all my property are confiscated by the Peruvian government'."[68] These voluntary repatriations were ideal for U.S. officials, who simply wanted to rid themselves of internees that posed increasingly difficult legal and social problems after Japan's defeat. Secretary of State Dean Acheson characterized the attitude of most U.S. government officials in December 1945, when discussing the future of the "Japs" from Latin America: "I understand that we have no evidence against them, and don't want to be stuck with them."[69] Nevertheless, the resolution of the fate of the internees proved to be a protracted and difficult process.

The stories of some of the Japanese Peruvian internees who were deported to Japan are only now being told. Well before Japan's defeat, the United States tried to ensure that the internees would not be allowed to return to any nation in the Western Hemisphere by the adoption of Resolution 7 at the Mexico City Conference on the Problems of War and Peace in the early spring of 1945. The resolution recommended that "'any person whose deportation was necessary for reasons of security of the continent'" should be prevented from "'further residing in this hemisphere if such residence should be prejudicial to the future security or welfare of the Americas.'"[70] The enabling act that would implement this resolution in the United States was issued by Harry Truman in a presidential proclamation on 12 September 1945. It called for the removal of all enemy aliens from the hemisphere "'who are within the territory of the United States without admission under the immigration laws.'"[71] Of course, this provision applied to all the Japanese Peruvian internees whose passports and visas had been confiscated before they were forcibly interned as enemy aliens.

Some acquaintance with the experiences of those repatriated to Japan is essential to gaining a fuller understanding of the internment experience. Among them was a young Peruvian Nisei, Rikio Kubo, who was deported from Peru with his entire family in June 1942. The family was "repatriated" to Japan in early September 1943 aboard a Swedish registered vessel, the *Gripsholm,* which carried 484 Japanese Peruvian internees among its 1,340 Japanese "repatriates" from Mexico, Panama, Hawaii, Costa Rica, Nicaragua, Cuba, Ecuador, Guatemala, and Alaska. Leaving New York, the vessel made stops in Rio de Janeiro and Montevideo to pick up additional Japanese, including diplomats from Chile. At Goa, then a Portuguese territory in the Indian Ocean, the internees were transferred to the Japanese passenger ship *Teia-maru*. In early November, 1,107 of the internees were disembarked in Singapore, where they were ordered to work as "local personnel" to support the Japanese war effort. The vessel then stopped in Manila, where 49 adult male internees, including Kubo, were put to work at the Kure Arsenal with the 103rd Supply Division of the Japanese Imperial Army. Kubo was separated at this time from his parents and siblings, who continued on to Japan. After the invasion of the Philippines by Allied forces, Kubo and 300 other civilian workers were forced to retreat into the Sierra Madre mountains, where they remained until five months after the Japanese surrender in August 1945. On Christmas Day 1945, Kubo began "my second experience living behind barbed wire" when he was placed in the first of what was to be a series of prisoner-of-war camps. There he remained for eleven months. Finally, in late November 1946, this unfortunate internee was released and sent to Japan, "a place I had never seen before."[72]

The experience of Kimiko Saeki Matsubayashi was less dramatic but still reflective of the hardships of the repatriates to Japan. One of six children whose father "made a fortune" operating an auto body parts manufacturing plant in Lima, she recalled "growing up happily and enjoying a free life in Lima" before the family's deportation and internment in Crystal City during March 1944. The war's end left the Matsubayashi family uncertain about Japan's postwar fate. Realizing that Peru would not permit his return, Kimiko's father decided to take his family to Japan. Departing from Seattle, the repatriates sailed directly to Uraga, in Kanagawa Prefecture, where they found a devastated nation with massive food shortages. Finding temporary housing in an old school building, the Matsubayashi family survived during their first months in Japan by *takenoko seikatu* (life sustained by selling property). Selling nearly all of their precious belongings, including a wrist watch and their marriage rings, the Matsubayashi family was able to survive the worst of their initial months in Japan. They were helped by Kimiko's grandparents, who were farmers and were able to supply them with food on occasion. Then fifty years old, Kimiko's father was able to provide for his family by calling upon his early skills as a carpenter. Later he would open his own company, installing industrial machines, before his untimely death of cancer at the age of fifty-six.[73]

Adding immeasurably to the trials of the repatriation experience for many fiercely loyal Issei was the shocking revelation of Japan's defeat once they reached their devastated homeland. Sumi Utsushigawa Shimatsu wrote movingly of this experience nearly fifty years later: "Realization of defeat did not 'hit' many of the Issei, who clutched their undying loyalty and faith in their home country, until they landed in Uraga. There rows of Japanese women in white *kapogi* were bowing, apologizing over and over, '*sumi masen, sumi masen, . . . makemashita . . . honto ni sumi masen*' [I'm sorry, I'm sorry, . . . we lost . . . we are truly sorry]. The shock and disbelief on many of the Issei faces was a tragic scene. They could not believe that Japan would surrender."[74]

✿ ✿ ✿

Those who chose to reject repatriation to Japan and sought residence in the United States met with deep frustration. Higashide recalled that when he was petitioning to remain in the United States, he was interviewed by INS officials who were seeking to enforce this order while the Crystal City camp was slowly being emptied of its internees in 1946. Despite the sympathy of some INS officials who were aware that the Japanese Peruvians were victims of the Catch-22 policy of the U.S. government, Higashide remembered that the interviews always ended with "forced smiles" and demands for documents that the authorities knew full well did not exist.[75]

As might be expected, Peru cooperated fully with these efforts by Washington to exile all of its deportees to Japan. Lima strengthened its ties with Washington when it formally declared war on Japan on 12 February 1945 during the last months of the Prado administration. Even the election of a moderate reform president, José Luis Bustamante y Rivero in June 1945, did not alter the position of the Peruvian government regarding the return of the expelled Japanese. Haya de la Torre of the APRA party, now legalized and in a position of influence in the Bustamante government, continued to actively oppose the readmittance of any of the deportees. The newly appointed U.S. ambassador to Peru, William D. Pawley, supported the Peruvian government's position in some measure, a reflection, it appears, of his own racist sentiments. For example, in early 1946 Pawley characterized Peru's Japanese as "'this alien population in Peru [that] has reverted to its non-moral Asiatic cunning, unchecked by self respect.'"[76]

By January 1946, however, protests by the American Civil Liberties Union (ACLU) and the desire of some Latin American nations to allow their deported aliens to return forced a change in U.S. policy. Thereafter, the issue of deportations to Japan rested on the issue of the "security threat" the deportees posed and their eligibility for U.S. or Peruvian citizenship. Lima actively opposed the readmission of any Japanese Peruvians without citizenship, even taking its case before the United Nations. As previously indicated, Peru reluctantly admitted 79 Japanese Peruvians and their dependents who held citizenship status in the immediate postwar years. Between November

1945 and June 1946, more than 900 Japanese Peruvian deportees were sent to Japan either by choice or in the belief that they had no chance to reenter Peru or to remain in the United States and petition for citizenship.[77] In some cases, families that were separated by deportations appealed directly to President Truman for relief. Emilia de Kaneshige, a Peruvian mother of five whose husband had been deported to the United States, wrote the president in October 1945. Claiming that the departure of her Japanese husband "has produced distress and planted sorrow and desolation in his family," Señora Kaneshige said her husband was only deported because he was Japanese, even though "by nature and sympathy he was more Peruvian than Japanese." The letter closed with the expressed hope that she might obtain the "grace" of President Truman.[78] Numerous other letters of this sort were written either by the internees or their families in Peru. The Truman administration was not moved to change its policy as a result of these appeals.

For 364 of the internees, their fate took another course, primarily because of the efforts of California ACLU attorneys Wayne M. Collins and A. L. Wirin. Because of protracted lawsuits filed by Collins on their behalf, the last of the Japanese Peruvian Crystal City internees were able to remain in the United States, where throughout 1946 most were paroled to labor at the Seabrook Farms near Bridgeton, New Jersey, a truck farming and food freezing plant that had previously used a workforce of German prisoners of war. The Seabrook experience proved trying for many Crystal City "survivors" who remained in the United States. But it provided the bridge to new lives in the United States once the protracted struggle to achieve "legal" alien status and access to citizenship was finally achieved in 1954. A small group of Peruvian internees stayed on in the area to lead productive lives. Among these were Ginzo Murono and his wife and children. Deported from Peru in 1943, after building a successful retail business in Lima, Murono was first sent to the Kenedy camp in Texas. Later the Murono's youngest son, Seiki, was born in the Crystal City camp. In the years that followed, the Muronos raised three children in Seabrook, with Ginzo first working as a gardener and then a laborer in the plant, on wages that did not exceed five dollars a day. Stressing education and sports as a socializing activity, the Muronos saw their children prosper at nearby Bridgeton High School and in their subsequent careers. Seiki was a star athlete at the local high school and in college. Choosing banking as a career, he became a senior vice president of Chase Manhattan Bank.[79]

Arriving at Seabrook when she was only five years old, after being deported from Peru and interned in Crystal City, Teresa M. Mukoyama Masatani saw her parents endure hardship in both the United States and

Venezuela before she returned to Seabrook to eventually play a leading role in creating the Seabrook Educational and Cultural Center, which today houses perhaps the most valuable repository of records of the Japanese Peruvians' experience in the United States after their internment.[80]

Arturo Shibayama was another of these Japanese Peruvian "survivors." As a former Crystal City internee in his late teens, he worked twelve hours a day, seven days a week, on rotating shifts at Seabrook to help his family in its transition to life in the United States. Like the Higashide family, the Shibayamas subsequently moved to Chicago, where Arturo was living when he was drafted into the U.S. Army during the Korean War. In a decision fraught with deep irony, his petition for U.S. citizenship while serving in the U.S. Army was denied because of his status as an "illegal alien." Shibayama would not attain his citizenship until 1970, after years of frustration and poor advice from U.S. government agencies. In the midst of this struggle, in desperation, Shibayama even arranged a brief stay in Canada and made a "legal" reentry into the United States to "validate" his petition for citizenship. Shibayama did much to earn his long-delayed citizenship, and when years later he was "accused" by the hypercritical comedian Don Rickles on a Las Vegas stage of being Japanese, he replied with the loud approval of the night club audience, "No, I am an American."[81]

The Japanese Who Endured in Peru

For the more than 20,000 Japanese Peruvians who avoided deportation to the United States, the World War II years and their aftermath were a constant battle against fear and economic hardship. Mary Fukumoto refers to this era as one of "confusion and hardship."[82] Some Japanese fled the Lima area and sought refuge in remote areas of Peru's interior. Although statistics are not available, it is clear that some Japanese Peruvians transmigrated to Argentina or Brazil, where anti-Japanese attitudes were far less severe. Heads of families, particularly those on the Proclaimed List, were frequently forced to go into hiding for long periods of time and leave their families to fend for themselves. Those that lost their businesses were commonly compelled to go to work for other commercial establishments, seek employment as waiters or laborers, or take up new ventures such as horticulture.[83] The Peruvian government expropriated Japanese businesses and farms by the cancellation of all land leases held by Axis nationals during May and June 1942. Only those Japanese who were able to transfer legal ownership of their holdings to their Nisei children or place property in the hands of a reliable intermediary were able to save their assets. This was the case with Kame

Kina, who had fortunately anticipated troubled times and had deeded his Rimac Valley cotton holdings to his Nisei son. Most other Japanese agriculturalists were not as fortunate. Prosperous Japanese cotton growers in the Chancay, Rimac, Lurín, and Pachacamac valleys near Lima, for example, had their productive properties seized by the government. Their only recourse was to drift to Lima and try to survive, like so many other Japanese, as small shop owners in a hostile environment. But this course was also fraught with difficulties. In the case of Ryshin Onaga, his highly successful Lima wholesale establishment was ordered into receivership by the Peruvian government. A Peruvian *interventor* was appointed by the government to manage the business during the war. Finally, in 1945 the government seized the business outright and eventually compensated Onaga, by his estimation, for only 15 percent of its original value.[84] Many Japanese-owned stores were confiscated immediately and were then "auctioned off to the highest bidder." The proceeds of these auctions were supposedly placed in an escrow fund, where they remained "frozen" for more than a decade. In actuality, compensation was rarely ever forthcoming. Interestingly, smaller neighborhood businesses such as bazaars and cafés were often not seized because they exclusively served the needs of the middle-class patrons.[85] Since all Japanese schools were ordered closed after Pearl Harbor, home schooling and clandestine schools continued the education of the Nisei in the Japanese language and traditions.[86]

Throughout the war, the Lima press continued its attacks on the nation's beleaguered Japanese colony. As it had done in the past, *Mundo Grafico* (Graphic World) was in the forefront of this anti-Japanese campaign. For example, its 8 January 1944 issue reflected the virulent racism motivating its campaign when it claimed that the "Japanese and [small colony of] Jews were sharing the monopoly of our Industry and Commerce." Decrying the "visible affluence of the Jews" in the midst of the Holocaust and claiming that the two groups were conspiring to dominate Peru's wartime economy even while the Japanese were being divested of their property, *Mundo Grafico* reflected the very worst aspects of the racist xenophobia that had reached its height during World War II.[87] Understandably, when the first few Japanese Peruvians who held citizenship began to return to Peru from Crystal City in November of 1945, *Mundo Grafico* proclaimed in bold type that "The Leaders of the Japanese Fifth Column are returning to Peru."[88] As in the past, the false reports of subversive activities after the war helped maintain the climate of hatred against the Japanese. On the other hand, after the surrender of Japan, the nationalism and unscrupulous practices of some of the younger Issei in Peru offered seeming justification for the continued ostracism of Peru's Japanese.

The inability of the younger Peruvian Issei in the internment camps to comprehend or accept Japan's defeat mirrored a broader nationalistic, pro-Japan mentality that emerged in both Brazil and Peru in the immediate aftermath of Tokyo's surrender. As we have already seen, in Brazil the underground nationalist movement known as Shindo Renmei was marked by fanaticism and terrorist tactics designed to intimidate those Japanese who accepted the reality of Japan's defeat and wanted to get on with the task of rebuilding their lives. Influenced by Shindo Renmei, fervent pro-Japan nationalists in Peru formed the Aikoku Doshi-kai (Society of the Japanese Patriots of Peru). Far less radical than its counterpart in Brazil, Aikoku Doshi-kai nevertheless proved very damaging to the Japanese community's recovery from the turmoil of the war years. Employing false photographs and documents purportedly "proving" that Japan had won the war, criminal elements within the Japanese community were convincing naive diehard patriots to advance them large sums of money in hopes of returning to their victorious homeland.[89] Aikoku Doshi-kai was mainly concentrated in the Lima-Callao metropolitan era but also initially had branches in Huaral and Huancayo. This patriotic league, which never numbered more than 500 members and was predominately Okinawan, nevertheless exploited the loyalty to the emperor and tradition of their beloved Japan of some of Peru's most desperate Japanese. Aikoku Doshi-kai operated as many as fourteen clandestine schools in Lima and Callao in which Nisei and Sansei were "indoctrinated in the spirit of old Japan."[90] Some of these schools continued to function as late as 1952.

The Aikoku Doshi-kai phenomenon can be explained, to a significant degree, by the enduring sojourner mentality of Peru's most recent immigrants who arrived just prior to World War II. For some of them, the concept of never being able to return to the Japan they once knew was too difficult to comprehend. For the vast majority who were able to accept reality and go on with their lives, Aikoku Doshi-kai continued to make their struggles more difficult because it perpetuated anti-Japanese attitudes well beyond the end of the war. An attempt by the Okinawan community to form a mutual aid society immediately after the war, for example, was thwarted by the Peruvian government because of its association with Aikoku Doshi-kai. The Okinawan Association was finally created in 1948, after ending its affiliation with the patriotic league. Aikoku Doshi-kai also continued to draw the attention of FBI agents in Peru, whose reports to the Truman administration

in 1946 may well have influenced U.S. policy on Japanese Peruvian internees and their return to Peru.[91] It seemed to justify in the minds of Peruvian
political leaders the necessity of maintaining an anti-Japanese campaign.

Even after the government of General Manuel A. Odría reestablished
diplomatic relations with Japan, and Tokyo reopened its consulate in Lima
in June 1952, Peru's Japanese remained the target of intense discrimination.
Japanese immigration to Peru was still prohibited, and many Japanese who
had traveled to Japan before the war or who were exiled were still denied
the right to rejoin families separated by the conflict. A number of these desperate Japanese journeyed to Brazil or Bolivia and subsequently entered Peru
illegally.[92] Some of these "illegals" were apprehended, jailed, and deported
permanently. Those Japanese who finally made the decision to take the major
step of adopting Peruvian citizenship were frustrated as well. For example,
after completing field research in Peru in 1952 to determine the potential
for future Japanese immigration to that nation, James L. Tigner noted, "Since
most *naichi-jin* and Okinawan *Issei* are resigned to spending the rest of their
days in Peru, many have applied recently for naturalization. All applications
thus far have been rejected, and have been returned [by the Odría govern-
ment] bearing the notation, 'not assimilable.'"[93]

World War II and its aftermath was a time of devastation and torment
for millions. Thus the injustices experienced by Peru's Japanese have gone
largely unnoticed in the midst of this vast crucible of suffering. Just as in
the United States, it was very difficult for Peru's Japanese to accept the reality that they were unwanted in their adopted homeland. In the end, however, a determination to rebuild their lives, not bitterness, best characterized
the prevailing attitudes of Japanese Peruvians, whether they began anew in
Peru, the United States, or Japan. With Japan's defeat, however difficult it
was for many of them to accept, came the fundamental realization that for
those who remained in Peru, this often hostile land would be their permanent home. This thought alone drove them to soon reconstruct the social
and economic bonds that had served the Japanese community so well before World War II badly disrupted their lives.

NEW *COLONIAS* AND THE OLDER
NIKKEI COMMUNITIES, 1952–70

The Japanese are known for their honesty, diligence, and respect
for the law. It is because of these admirable qualities that they have
endeared themselves to the Argentine people.
—President Juan Domingo Perón of Argentina, 1952

For nearly two decades after Japan resumed emigration in 1952, only one
Latin American nation received substantial numbers of Japanese settlers.
Many of the immigrants were from war-torn Okinawa, which was now
administratively separate from Japan and under direct U.S. military rule. The
U.S. government strongly encouraged this immigration because of the economic difficulties of the Okinawan people and the need to acquire space for
the military bases Washington intended to build on the island. Tokyo continued to encourage immigration for the same reasons it had before the war.
The uncertain economic conditions in Japan through the early 1960s prompted this policy. The traditional attraction of Brazil, with its very large Japanese community, drew nearly 50,000 additional immigrants between 1952
and the mid-1960s. Both Bolivia and Paraguay, heretofore the host of only
a few hundred immigrants, became the focus of highly ambitious colonization programs aimed at settling mainland Japanese and displaced Okinawans
in newly established rural *colonias*. This grand design never fully materialized, primarily because of the rapid recovery of the Japanese economy, the
perceived need to rebuild Japan by its people, and the formal peace with
the United States and subsequent financial aid, particularly after the Korean
War began. Indeed the Japanese economic recovery was so complete that
the era of Japanese immigration to Latin America effectively ended by the
mid-1960s. Meanwhile, with no new significant immigration to establish
fresh cultural links to Japan, the older Japanese enclaves in Brazil, Mexico,

Peru, and the smaller receiver nations saw the Nisei and Sansei generations assume leadership roles in their communities. With the sojourner mentality no longer dominant and the Issei generation rapidly aging, the younger members of the Japanese communities in Latin America began to merge their cultural identities with the societies in which they lived. Now Japanese Brazilians, for example, would increasingly refer to themselves as Brazilian Nikkei-jin, or Japanese who accept a dual cultural identity. Only Argentina and the Dominican Republic among the lesser receiver nations admitted more than 1,000 Japanese during the postwar era. Many of these immigrants settled in new colonies in western Argentina, as their counterparts did in Bolivia and Paraguay.

Postwar Conditions in Japan's Mainland and Okinawa

Japan's rapid recovery from the devastation of the Pacific War during the Allied occupation (1945–52) and the ensuing two decades was the primary reason emigration from Japan was so meager during this era. By 1970, Japan boasted one of the leading economies of the world, thus negating the need for large-scale emigration, as was true in the decades prior to World War II. Economic conditions in Okinawa improved more slowly, and the Ryukyus continued to send immigrants to Latin America well into the late 1960s.

The Allied Council for Japan, the governing body for the conquered nation, was dominated from the beginning of the occupation by the U.S. military administration, headed by the overpowering personality of the Supreme Commander of the Allied Powers, General Douglas MacArthur. By the summer of 1947, one perceptive analyst argues, "The United States had little alternative but to promote Japan's recovery and its integration with the rest of Asia. And should the United States fail to fund such a program, the outcome would be calamitous."[1] Clearly, a rebuilt and economically health Japan was to be the centerpiece of Washington's Far Eastern policy in the emerging cold war. Agrarian reform was a key element of this program.

Initiated in October 1946, agrarian reform sought to reduce high tenancy rates and thereby implement a major redistribution of wealth in the agricultural sector. Initially the government purchased land from the original landowners and made it available to former tenants. The new owners then assumed payments to the government over a thirty-year period at an interest rate of only 3.2 percent. This program allowed even the poorest of farmers to own land, and absentee landlordism was made illegal. The program was generally successful.

The policy of the occupation government was equally successful in the labor sector. To promote democratic processes and further the distribution of wealth, a trade union law was enacted in December 1945 that legalized union activities. Collective bargaining and the right to strike were guaranteed for the first time. As a result of these measures, labor union membership soared, and the condition of the industrial working class improved dramatically. By 1970, there were nearly 59,000 unions operating in Japan, with a total membership of more than 11 million workers.[2]

Initially stimulated by the Korean War, Japanese industrialization continued to benefit from a well-educated and hardworking labor force and favorable business legislation, which primarily benefited the huge corporations that much resembled the pre–World War II *zaibatsu* (large business combines). Freed from the burden of military expenditures, Japan was able to invest heavily in research and development and in modern industrial infrastructure to replace that which had been shattered by the war. Unlike in the past, wages followed the rise in Japanese industry. By 1952, the pay of workers had recovered to the prewar level. During the 1960s, wages increased at an annual rate of 10 percent, surpassing the rise in the cost of living by 4.7 percent annually. In 1970 alone, wages increased 21.4 percent.[3] A nation of 104 million people by 1970, Japan was now able to feed itself with a much more productive agricultural sector and provide increasingly well paying jobs for a people who still had vivid memories of the horrible devastation of war. In the years before this recovery began to accelerate, however, immigration to Latin America was still seen as a viable option for Japanese.

With the successful Brazilian colonization projects as a stimulus, the Kaigai Kyokai Kabushiki Rengokai (Federation of Overseas Associations) was established in early 1945, and one year later the Kaigai Ijyushinko Kabushiki Gaisha (Overseas Immigration Promotion Association) was created to facilitate the colonization of Japanese immigrants by purchasing land, financing road-building projects, and making loans to prospective colonists. These two organizations, based in Japan with branches in Latin America, were merged in 1963 into the Kaigai Ijyu Jigyodan, or KIJ (Overseas Immigration Service), which became responsible for all Japanese immigrant affairs and particularly the colonization programs in Latin America.[4] By this date, however, Japanese emigration and colonization were no longer seen as government priorities because of the improving economy. Economic recovery in the Ryukyu Islands was not as rapid, and the post–World War II U.S. military occupation caused significantly more problems in Okinawa than was the case on the main islands.

✿ ✿ ✿

Migration from Okinawa was a significant component of overall Japanese immigration from the early 1900s onward. Brought under the full hegemony of Japan during the Meiji Restoration by decree in March 1879, the Okinawan people were required to pay high taxes and meet the obligations of the mainland Japanese, without the full citizenship rights of the Naichijin. Mitsugu Sakihara describes Tokyo's policy toward Okinawa before World War II as "the preservation of the traditional system as much as possible."[5] Essentially this meant that Tokyo would not try to replicate the rapid pace of social and economic change of the mainland but would introduce reform slowly. When, for example, the Japanese government initiated land reform in Okinawa in 1903, abolishing the communal ownership of land and creating private landholders for the first time, this initiative came thirty years after similar legislation on the mainland. Even then, the tax burden on the Okinawan farmers was so great that the cash payments they were required to make drove many of them into tenancy status after only a few years as private landholders. These economic troubles forced many Okinawans to seek relief through emigration. The initial Okinawan contingent, a group of 26 immigrants, went to Hawaii in January 1900 to work on the Ewa sugar plantation on Oahu. From this small group, immigration grew to 26,500 by 1927, with 10,119 going to Hawaii, 5,464 to Brazil, and 1,369 to Peru.[6] With the increasing immigration restrictions in North America and Latin America by the 1930s, Okinawans immigrated to the Philippines and the mandated Pacific islands until World War II. Additionally, by the late 1920s, 32,000 Okinawan youths were working in the industries of southern Japan, where their remittances to their families in Okinawa helped lessen the desperate poverty of the tax-burdened rural masses.[7] Emigration was thus truly a safety valve for the overpopulated and economically underdeveloped island chain until World War II. Before the devastation of the Pacific War, the population of the Ryukyu Islands stood at 742,174, which meant a density of 588 per square mile. Historically, however, less than 30 percent of the land on the Ryukyus was suitable for cultivation. As one would imagine, the average holdings of individual farmers was thus very small. As late as the 1960s, for example, the common size of holdings was between one-eighth and one-fourth of an acre.[8]

Farmers raising the four main groups of Okinawan agriculture—rice, sweet potatoes, soybeans, and sugarcane—were forced to rely on intensive agriculture involving terracing and highly sophisticated irrigation techniques, even while limited by their traditional hand tools, such as the *kuwa* (long-handled hoe), *dakkokuki* (treadle thresher), and *maguwa* (harrow). Okinawans also engaged in commercial fishing and limestone quarrying to earn a living. The *sekko* (stonecutter) was usually involved in a very small operation that generally included only himself and his sons or brothers. The *sekko* acquired only the rights to quarry the stone and not the land from which it was extracted, and his profits were usually quite small. Nearly all economic endeavors on Okinawa were limited this way, and the people of the islands engaged in a constant struggle to achieve a secure, economical lifestyle.[9] After 1941, these hardships increased dramatically, and for many Okinawans daily life became an often tragic struggle for survival.

World War II brought dislocation and death to many Okinawans because the Japanese government used the Ryukyu Island chain as a last bastion of defense of the home islands. When Tokyo decided to "sacrifice" Okinawans in the defense of the mainland, 120,000 of them became war casualties; they were caught with no place to hide from the invading Allied armies and the entrenched Japanese defenders. With the surrender of Japan, the Okinawa Prefecture was abolished by the occupying military forces of the United States, and the Ryukyu Islands would remain under Washington's rule until they were returned to Japan in 1972.

Particularly after the victory of the Chinese Communists in 1949, the Ryukyu Islands became a vitally important site for U.S. military bases during the cold war. Nearly 25 percent of the arable land on the large island of Okinawa was acquired by U.S. military administrators for that purpose. This loss of valuable arable land came at a time when the population of the islands had soared to more than 930,000 in 1965, a 25 percent increase since 1940.[10] As a result, there was virtually no chance for young Okinawans to make a decent living on the land in the postwar era. Moreover, despite shipments of surplus canned meats and pork and beans from the United States, Okinawans experienced significant food shortages. Not surprisingly, many of them were filled with resentment against the American officials because the military construction program was causing the loss of valuable farmland. What is more, Okinawan laborers, despite their improved wages, were still at the bottom of a pay scale that saw U.S. workers, Filipinos, and Japanese from the mainland earning significantly more. Finally, when the construction boom was over in the late 1950s, most Okinawan workers were laid off, with no real prospects for earning a meaningful livelihood.[11]

Consequently, in 1950 the United States Civil Administration of the Ryukyu Islands (USCAR) began a well-financed campaign to encourage emigration. USCAR officials looked to Latin America, especially Bolivia and to a lesser extent Paraguay, as potential settings for major colonization programs to resettle as many of the economically distressed islanders as possible. Toward this end, in July 1951, U.S. administrators on the islands contracted James L. Tigner to conduct a review of the existing Japanese and Okinawan communities in Latin America to determine where new communities of immigrants could be established.[12] After an extended period of field research, Tigner recommended the Santa Cruz area of Bolivia as the most favorable site. In the early 1950s there was no shortage of Okinawans willing to emigrate. In September 1951, 172,000 of them had applied for emigration permits, and most of these applications were for the South American nations.[13] As in the past, Brazil remained the main magnet for postwar Japanese immigration to Latin America because of opportunity, a very large Japanese population, and a history of relatively reasonable treatment by the Brazilian government. Many Japanese hoped to partake in what they expected would be Brazil's economic takeoff after World War II. Their hopes were often met with mixed results.

Brazil's Japanese and the False "Miracle"

As Japanese Brazilians emerged in the postwar era, they did not have to confront the great challenges of dislocation, deportation, and wide-scale confiscation of their property that people of Japanese descent in North America and in many communities in Latin America had suffered. In terms of population, the Brazilian Nikkei-jin remained the most formative Japanese community in Latin America, totaling 356,641 as reflected in the national census of 1950. The Nikkei remained overwhelmingly concentrated in southern Brazil, where 316,641, or about 96.2 percent, resided in the states of São Paulo and Paraná. Of these, 84 percent still remained in São Paulo State, where the Japanese colonists originally settled in the largest numbers. Nearly 40,000 were living in the state of Paraná at the time of the census. Despite efforts to settle the Japanese in colonies in the north and northeast regions of Brazil in decades past, these efforts were almost completely fruitless. Less than 1 percent of the Nikkei in Brazil were located in the fourteen states in these two main regions. Somewhat surprisingly, Brazil's southernmost state of Rio Grande do Sul, which might have offered opportunities for cattle raising or dairy farming, was of little attraction to the Japanese. Less than 500 resided there in 1950. Even further evidence of the unwillingness of the Nikkei-jin of Brazil to leave São Paulo State was the small number who made the important state of Rio de Janeiro their adopted home. Only 2,484 lived in this key region. Unlike Japanese in other Latin American nations, those of Brazil openly maintained their religious affiliations brought from Japan. Nearly half were classified as Buddhists. Agriculture still dominated their professions, with 53 percent classified in that activity or "kindred industries." Those engaged in commerce were approaching 10 percent, and as might be expected, most of the Japanese females were working in domestic service. The agricultural occupational base would evolve into a Japanese domination of the fruit and vegetable markets of São Paulo, where by the 1990s the Nikkei would produce 70 percent of these products for the domestic market.[14]

Brazil's Issei may have been regionally centralized, productive, and, at least in a religious sense, more culturally affiliated with their Japanese roots than other such communities in Latin America. Still, after the war, they were more divided as a group than their compatriots anywhere else in the hemisphere. As the internal struggles promoted by the fanatical campaign of Shindo Renmei demonstrate, Japanese Brazilians were actually in a state of civil war in the two years following World War II. Soon after the war, some members of the Brazilian Congress tried to pass legislation that would ban future Japanese immigration, largely in response to the violence and fanaticism of the Shindo Renmei movement. The legislation failed to pass, and it is reasonably safe to assume that this failure reflected the continuing demand for Japanese labor and the belief that postwar fanaticism was not reflective of the stable and productive history of the Japanese in Brazil up to that time. Still, the divisions wrought by Shindo Renmei, as Jeffrey Lesser as so aptly argued, prevented the Issei from "asserting themselves as an important component of the Brazilian nation."[15] As discussed with respect to other Japanese Latin American communities, the need for the Issei to accept their adopted homelands for themselves and their children was essential after the war. Return to Japan was simply not possible, and their children and grandchildren were increasingly becoming more Brazilian than Japanese in their outlook. The struggle to face this reality was by far the most intense in Brazil because the Japanese communities in that nation had enjoyed more autonomy than elsewhere in Latin America. Often isolated in the interior of Brazil, the Issei maintained very strong ties to the Japanese homeland. Takashi Maeyama noted that as late as the end of the 1940s many of the Issei still considered themselves *tabi-bito* (wayfarers) and that immigrants would say, "'We left our home in someone's care during our absence. We came here leaving everything behind, relatives, ancestors and god.'"[16] Once the struggle to end the campaign of denial by Shindo Renmei was over, the Japanese of this expansive nation could begin seeking the many opportunities of the promised "economic miracle" that Brazilian political leaders held out to the nation for more than three decades after the war. This promise was never realized. Brazil's civilian governments of the 1950s and early 1960s floundered because of poor economic planning, highly divisive politics, and unrealistic aims for the immediate future of the nation. These problems, and the tensions produced by the cold war and a perceived threat from the Brazilian left, prompted the military to seize power in 1964 and dominate the nation for the next three decades. Brazil was no longer an open and dynamic society but a closed dictatorship for more than a generation. But the Japanese, as they had everywhere else in Latin America, were still able to build vital lives for themselves more in the Brazilian social mainstream than ever before. Still, the Brazilian Nikkei-jin, Lesser notes, "were now Brazilian even as society at large continued to define them as Japanese."[17] What did this mean in terms of Japanese cultural traditions? Maeyama argues, "The gradual turn to permanent residence [in Brazil] resulted in discrediting and denigrating the 'return home idea.'" He noted that by the 1960s many Japanese Brazilians would say, "'We are the ancestors, or we the immigrants will be the ancestors of Brazil.'" In this sense, they meant that they were the foundation of something important, such as the idea of a new Japanese community outside of Japan. Japanese by the 1950s commonly came to call Brazil *yokoku* (adopted country). Maeyama contends that the Japanese in Brazil interpret immigration to include the transplanting of "kinship and familial principles and consequently the Brazilian nation is here understood in terms of *ie* [the community]."[18] Still, the Japanese government continued sending new immigrants to Brazil, even as the earlier immigrants began to accept another distinct identity. The violent and highly negative image of the Japanese among Brazilians provoked by the Shindo Renmei movement was in significant measure responsible for the banning of Japanese immigration by the Brazilian government until 1952. The reopening of immigration then was facilitated by Rio de Janeiro's formal peace treaty with Japan in April 1952.[19] Thereafter, Japanese-Brazilian relations steadily improved. Brazil sought to benefit from commercial relations with the expanding Japanese economy as the South American nation launched its ambition program of economic development during the next two decades. This program was highlighted by heavy investment in industry, agricultural diversification, and the symbolic movement of the nation's capital to Brasilia in the interior as an impetus for migration from the coastal regions. Much of this development was financed by deficit spending and huge foreign loans, which would initiate hyperinflation by the mid-1970s. Against this backdrop, the Japanese Brazilians, still largely concentrated in the state of São Paulo, began a steady migration from the interior colonies to metropolitan São Paulo. This migration pattern mirrored the massive urbanization that was happening throughout Brazil in the decades after 1950.

Some of the Japanese immigrants who arrived in the early 1950s settled in the established colonies such as Bastos and Tietê. A serious effort to establish Japanese colonies in the Amazon was even attempted with 324 families, totaling nearly 2,000 immigrants, between 1953 and 1955. Other colonization schemes were also launched in the northeast of Brazil.[20] During the late 1950s, a steady but not spectacular flow of Japanese immigrants went to Brazil. In 1959, for example, Brazil welcomed 7,041 Japanese. But the numbers began to decline in the early 1960s, never again to reach significant levels. In 1960, 6,832 Japanese immigrated to Brazil. Two years later, only 1,830 made this decision. In 1964, only 751 entered Brazil. Interestingly, 52 families, numbering 268 individuals, decided to leave Brazil in 1962 and resettle in the Dominican Republic.[21] By the mid-1960s, the era of Japanese migration to Brazil was essentially over.

Serving as a framework for Nikkei agriculture in São Paulo in the decades after the mid-1950s was the huge agriculture cooperative known as Cotia. This cooperative would be one of the largest in Latin America and greatly facilitated the marketing of Japanese agricultural products all over Brazil, but particularly in the São Paulo metropolitan area. Cotia helped new immigrants establish a viable economic base in the agricultural economy of Brazil, and its success demonstrated the highly organized and integrated nature of the Japanese community.[22] No cooperatives of this type and size were ever so successfully established by the Japanese in other Latin American nations. Japanese immigrant youth were also trained in industrial skills through the auspices of the Sangyo Kaihatsu Seinen Kai (Youth Groups for the Development of Industry). In 1955, a special school for training Japanese immigrant youth, particularly in the construction trades, was opened.[23] This and other programs for training and introducing Japanese immigrants to Brazilian society were in part subsidized by the Japanese government in the same tradition that led Tokyo to financially support the Japanese Brazilians in the 1920s and 1930s.

An important step in bringing the Japanese community in Brazil together after the great controversies of the war and its aftermath was the formation of the Committee to Aid the Victims of the War in Japan in 1947. This committee gained widespread support from the entire Japanese community in Brazil and gave them a sense of pride that they were aiding the people of their homeland at a time of great need. However, according to Maeyama, participating in the aid program was actually an act of separation from the home country, and the Japanese of Brazil "came at last to abandon their identification with their home society."[24]

A number of commissions were established over the course of the next decade that were designed to bring the Japanese community more closely together, as it was beginning to disperse from the rural colonies to metropolitan São Paulo and across the state of Paraná as well. Another goal of these groups was to encourage the collaboration of the Brazilian and Japanese governments in the hope that closer diplomatic and commercial ties would provide benefits for the Japanese Brazilian community. One of the most active of these groups was the San Pauro Nihon Bunka Kyokai (São Paulo Society for Japanese Culture), founded in 1958. One of its primary stated goals was the "education of the Nisei as future leaders of the Nikkei community in Brazil."[25]

At the center of Japanese intellectual and cultural life in Brazil is the Centro de Estudos Nipo-Brasileiro (Center of Japanese Brazilian Studies). Originally established as an intellectual center in 1948, by the 1960s it was the most respected cultural and academic center for the Japanese community. Over the past several decades, the center has compiled statistics on the Japanese Brazilians and sponsored as well as published valuable studies of the community by Japanese Brazilians and foreign scholars. Similar to the Japanese cultural center in Lima, Peru, it is far larger and more ambitious in its scope, as might be expected considering the size of the Nikkei population in Brazil.

Building upon these economic and cultural foundations, the Japanese of Brazil began to make the important transition from a primarily agricultural community to a far more diversified population. More Issei would venture into commerce and would encourage their children to seek quality educations and venture into the professions. In this ambition the Issei would generally find great satisfaction throughout the ensuing decades. By contrast, the Japanese of Bolivia, numbering only a small fraction of their counterparts in Brazil, would have a less promising future.

New *Colonias* in Bolivia

By 1952 there were 1,044 individuals of Okinawan and mainland Japanese ancestry residing in 241 households in Bolivia. Most of them had established residence before the war and were scattered mainly in the five communities of Riberalta, Santa Cruz, Potosí, Cochabamba Tarija, and Trinidad. Of this group, 288 were Issei, only 49 of whom were female, and the remaining 756 were Nisei. More than half of the households (133) were engaged in small business enterprises, and the remainder worked in agriculture. Because of the small number of female Issei, 197 male Issei, or more than two-thirds of the first generation males, had Bolivian wives.[26] Despite their small number, the qualities of these early immigrants impressed Bolivian political leaders. In the wake of the Bolivian Revolution of 1952, the government was seeking stable, hardworking individuals to begin rebuilding the nation. The land-reform program begun in 1953 aided this process, as it encouraged colonization of new lands by both relocated Bolivian peasants and immigrants. Mennonite colonists from Paraguay, Canada, and Mexico, for example, also settled in the Santa Cruz area during this same period. By the mid-1960s, 15,000 Bolivian and immigrant families, numbering 64,000 individuals, had been settled in the Santa Cruz region as a result of government agrarian reform and colonization projects.[27] Underscoring the Bolivian land-reform program was U.S. economic aid, which was the highest per capita in the world from 1952 to 1958. Fearing the Bolivian social revolution would take a leftward course, like regimes in Guatemala and Guyana, the United States gave generously to the Andean nation.[28]

Briefly, between 1954 and the mid-1960s, four agricultural colonies for both mainland Japanese and Okinawan settlers were established in eastern Bolivia, in the general vicinity of the city of Santa Cruz. Like the Brazilian government of Getulio Vargas in the early 1930s, the governments of Víctor Paz Estenssoro and his successors either made sizable grants of free land or purchased substantial tracts of arable land for these agricultural colonies at bargain prices. Much of this land was wooded and required significant labor to clear it for planting, but it was generally fertile and proved productive for the colonists. The colonies established between 1954 and 1961 ranged in size from the Carranda settlement of only 1,200 acres to the huge colony of San Juan de Yapacaní, whose expanse of hundreds of thousands of acres became home to more than 1,500 families from mainland Japan and Okinawa. These colonies were all agricultural settlements raising rice, sugarcane, corn, bananas, and sweet potatoes. The Okinawan farmers initially practiced largely subsistence agriculture, but as the colonies matured, agricultural cooperatives were created with the aid of Bolivian and U.S. agencies. Kozy K. Amemiya's extensive interviews in the colonies confirms that despite the assistance, the formative years of this colonization experiment were fraught with hardship.[29] An overview of the development of these colonies, with special emphasis on the Japanese colony of San Juan de Yapacaní, will help place Okinawan and Japanese immigration to Bolivia in perspective.

Okinawan and Japanese inhabitants of the Santa Cruz and Beni areas in Bolivia provided an important cultural and economic foundation for the new immigrants by creating the Uruma Agricultural and Industrial Society in 1949. Founded by 16 Okinawans from Santa Cruz, Beni, and Riberalta under the leadership of José (Kame) Akamine, a resident of Santa Cruz for thirty-nine years, and Juan Gushy, who was president of the Okinawan Association of Riberalta, the Uruma Society purchased 2,500 acres of land forty-five miles east of Santa Cruz City to be used as part of the site for the new immigrant colony. To facilitate the colonization program, USCAR authorities in September 1952 allocated $160,000 to subsidize the cost of transportation for 400 Okinawan immigrants. Additionally, an Emigration Bank was established in the Ryukyu Islands with U.S. funding. It initially provided $93,000 to provide loans to immigrants for a ten-year term at 6 percent interest. Once the first large contingent was preparing to immigrate to the Santa Cruz site, the U.S. Department of State allocated an additional $194,000 to the Uruma Society to meet the "startup" costs for the immigrants.

This generous funding program for the Bolivian colonization project represented the best financed project of its kind in the history of Japanese immigration to Latin America.[30] Clearly, the U.S. government recognized the growing potential for unrest on the Island of Okinawa if some measures to relieve population pressures and related economic distress were not undertaken. The Bolivian government also cooperated fully with this initiative. In June 1953, President Estenssoro authorized the colonization of as many as 3,000 Okinawan families in the Santa Cruz region.[31] Following the approval of the Bolivian government, two administrators from the islands were sent to the Santa Cruz area to work with U.S. and Bolivian officials to approve the Uruma Society site for the colonization project. Final approval was facilitated by the recent completion of a highway from Santa Cruz to Cochabamba and two railroad lines in the nearby vicinity. The marketing of the agricultural products raised by the immigrants in the proposed colony thus seemed far more assured than in the more remote colonies created in Brazil and Paraguay before World War II.[32]

The first group of 269 Okinawan immigrants arrived at the Uruma site in mid-June 1954, after a two-month sea journey and a one-week railroad trek from the Brazilian port of Santos across South America to Santa Cruz. These colonists were joined by an additional 128 who arrived one month later. The organizers of the colonization project, following the Brazilian model, encouraged the immigration of entire families. The first colonists were mostly skilled farmers but also included tradesmen, medical personnel, and a school teacher.[33] Nevertheless, they confronted devastating problems from the first days of their Bolivian undertaking. Tigner notes only that the new site in the Ñuflo de Chávez area near Santa Cruz proved "untenable" because of an outbreak of disease and severe drought during the first months of the venture. The colonists then moved to another site.[34] Years later, the extent of these first colonists' hardships became more widely known as they talked with researcher Amemiya about the devastating "Uruma" disease that took the lives of 15 colonists and sickened 80 more. The cause was never discovered by U.S. and Bolivian medical personnel who, according to some of the remaining colonists, were more interested in analyzing blood samples than treating the sick.[35] As additional problems arose, such as flooding and an infestation of rats, it was discovered that the site of the colony rested on the floodplain of the Rio Grande. The settlement was eventually moved by the colonists in mid-1955 to the present site of Okinawa Colony Number 1, as it was called when it was eventually settled permanently.[36]

Despite the extensive experience of earlier Japanese colonization programs in Brazil, Colombia, and Paraguay, the planners for the colonies in Bolivia still not did establish consistent initial criteria for the farm size, the location of dwellings, establishment of service centers, or access to water and roads. Most of these decisions were made on the basis of existing conditions in the settlements, and in many cases they were altered to respond to changing circumstances. Generally, the farm sizes were in the 125-acre range, which was the maximum size approved by the Bolivian government. Most of this land was wooded and required clearing by the colonists before extensive farming could take place. The Okinawan colonists were able clear their properties at a rate of 20 to 25 acres per year with the help of Bolivian laborers. This supplemental labor was possible because of the high rate of capitalization of the project by Ryukyuan, U.S., and Bolivian government agencies. Relatively soon, some of the most enterprising and hardworking colonists were farming their maximum holdings and looking for additional land. Curiously, provisions were not made in some of the original colonies for the purchase of additional land because new plots were to be reserved for future colonists. Thus, the more successful colonists either rented land that was not being exploited by other colonists or they purchased more remote plots from Bolivians to increase their holdings.[37]

In the case of what came to be called Okinawa Colony Number 2, founded in 1954, the colonists erected houses on their own plots, rather than living in compound homes as the earliest settlers had done. Roads and other infrastructure projects were constructed communally. In 1956 the Okinawa Agricultural Corporation was formed in Bolivia, under the leadership of Buntoku Shinazato, to aid in the marketing of the rice, corn, and sugarcane raised in the colony. Okinawa Colony Number 2 was self-sustaining in its food requirements as early as 1957. As a result of its capitalization, the colony had at its disposal eight tractors, two trucks, and a jeep and was preparing to begin construction of a sawmill by early 1958. At the end of the decade, the colony boasted 815 inhabitants and five schools offering educational programs to 338 children. Instruction, however, was only offered in Spanish. A church was also being erected in the community. Tigner reported that in the first six years of the community's existence twenty-three marriages had been performed, three of them to Bolivian women. The population of the colony was increased by 156 births during those years. Thus, new Ryukyuan families were being started in a community environment that was far different from those of the first Japanese and Okinawan immigrants to Bolivia four decades before. Significantly, Tigner noted that many of the inhabitants of Okinawa Colony Number 2 wanted to acquire Bolivian citizenship, and none wished to return to their homeland.[38] This optimistic assessment by Tigner seems to have been premature. Continued uncertainty over crop prices and marketing, in addition to the very slow improvement in the road system in the Santa Cruz region until the early 1970s, appears to have left many of the colonists concerned and unhappy about their futures in Bolivia. These colonies experienced significant transmigration to Brazil and Peru in the years after 1970.

The other Okinawan colonies established in the mid-1950s followed largely similar patterns of development. One of the principal problems was finding qualified teachers to staff the schools. Understandably, recreational facilities for the children were often given low priority as the colonies were being constructed. Unlike the Brazilian colonies of the 1930s that were consistently supported by funding and subsidies from the Japanese government, there did not appear to be any determined effort on the part of U.S. administrators in Okinawa to promote the Bolivian colonization project after 1960. Perhaps this reflected improved economic conditions on the islands, and it may explain why immigration never reached the tens of thousands of colonists originally envisioned by U.S., Bolivian, and Okinawan planners. During the eight years from 1954 to 1961, Okinawan immigration totaled 2,431, or an average of 303 immigrants a year.[39] Nevertheless, the pattern of postwar immigration to Bolivia was established. Consequently, in the mid-1950s, one of the largest colonies in the history of Japanese immigration to Latin America was created at San Juan de Yapacaní near Santa Cruz. It is this colony that will be examined in the greatest depth.

This colony has been studied extensively by scholars from Japan, Bolivia, and the United States since its formation.[40] San Juan de Yapacaní has attracted so much scholarly attention because it represents one of the most ambitious efforts in the post–World War II era to settle Japanese immigrants in an isolated agricultural setting. It was another attempt to replicate the successful colonization programs in Brazil before 1941.

Toshimitsu Nishikawa, a Japanese immigration promoter who had earlier directed his efforts to the sugarcane fields of Java, was instrumental in making the initial investigations and contacts with the Bolivian government regarding the establishment of the San Juan de Yapacaní colony. Nishikawa hoped to bring Japanese immigrants to the Santa Cruz region to begin producing sugarcane for export. Fifteen Japanese families, numbering 98 persons, settled on the land set aside for the colony a year before the final immigration agreement was signed by the Japanese and Bolivian governments in August 1956. The contract called for the admission of 1,000 families (5,000 persons) in the initial five years. This was later to be expanded to 5,000 families over a nine-year period. The immigrants were to "dedicate themselves to professions in agriculture and animal husbandry and to demonstrate industry, honor, and aptitude for work."[41]

The amount of land granted by the Bolivian government for the San Juan de Yapacaní colony was 87,198 acres of mostly wooded terrain, 129 kilometers from the city of Santa Cruz. Each Japanese household that settled in the colony was given a land grant of 110 acres, which was in compliance with the limits of the Bolivian agrarian reform law of 1953. Originally, 590 of these 110-acre tracts were surveyed, and within the first eight years of settlement, 269 of these holdings were occupied by Japanese colonists.[42] Most of the immigrants who established new homes in San Juan de Yapacaní arrived during these first eight years of settlement. The peak years were 1958, when 438 colonists began life in the community, and 1961, which saw the arrival of an additional 626 settlers. After 1963, when Japanese immigration in general all but ceased, only 38 new colonists left Japan for the colony near Santa Cruz. This ambitious experiment in Japanese colonization of Bolivia's remote *oriente* thus attracted 319 families, including more than 1,600 individuals, before 1970 and only a handful thereafter.[43] As with the Okinawan colonies, immigration never achieved the scale that was originally envisioned by Japanese, Bolivian, and U.S. planners. Still, like earlier Japanese colonies in Brazil and, as we shall see, contemporary settlement projects in Paraguay, San Juan de Yapacaní represented one of the last efforts on the part of the Japanese government to transplant its immigrants on the soil of Latin America.

The Japanese colonists of San Juan de Yapacaní were true pioneers. Like homesteaders in the western United States after the Civil War, they were given free land in the colony by the Bolivian government with the stipulation that they live on their tract for a least two years while clearing and

cultivating at least half of the holding.[44] The colonists were required, however, to repay the KIJ for the cost of passage, and the Bolivian government
required the immigrant family to possess start-up capital of at least $500.
This was substantially less than the $1,500 required by the Brazilian gov-
ernment at this time and helps explain why the colonists chose Bolivia over
Brazil, which was the first choice of many of the immigrants.[45] Most of the
immigrants came from Nagasaki, Kumamoto, and Fukuoka prefectures, the
same areas that were the traditional source of immigrants since the beginnings of the Japanese diaspora nearly a century before. Stephen Thompson,
an anthropologist at the University of Illinois who did extensive fieldwork
in San Juan de Yapacaní in the mid-1960s, found that despite the regulation by the Bolivian government that the immigrants have agricultural skills,
only 115 of 262 household heads listed their previous occupation in Japan
as "farmer." Laborers (69), coal miners (27), and small business owners (23)
comprised the bulk of the remaining colonists. Thompson suggests that the
actual number of coal miners may have been higher, since this occupation
was considered a low-status job in Japan at the time, and some of the
interviewees may not have been truthful in their responses. Moreover,
significant labor strife in the mines during the late 1950s and early 1960s
clearly prompted immigrants to leave the mines, many of which were closing, for better opportunities abroad.[46]

Thompson found that among those who characterized themselves as farmers, many were still unable to gain access to enough land in Japan even after the agrarian reform law. The abolition of primogeniture soon after World
War II, while a progressive measure, resulted in the troublesome fragmen-
tation of existing small holdings. This led to continued emigration from some
of Japan's marginal agricultural centers such as Kuroki, a small agricultural
community in Fukuoka Prefecture that supplied a number of colonists to
San Juan de Yapacaní. Significantly, Thompson found that 40 percent of the
colonists lived outside Japan for at least two years before coming to Bolivia.
Nearly 30 percent of the family heads in the colony immigrated to Manchuria before World War II and were repatriated after Japan's surrender.
Others had resided in the Philippines, Taiwan, China, Saipan, and Java.[47]

Very similar to nearly all pioneering Japanese communities in Latin
America, San Juan de Yapacaní by the mid-1960s still experienced a significant gender imbalance. Of its 1,651 residents, 903 were males and 748 females. Although not as unfavorable as the gender inequality during the early
years of immigration in Bolivia or Peru and Mexico, it had significant implications for the future of the colony. Like the immigration pattern of

the Japanese in Brazil, temporary or "false" marriages that were arranged merely to meet Bolivian and Japanese requirements also occurred in the San Juan de Yapacaní colony. Thompson noted from his interviews in the colony that there seemed little possibility that Japanese women would be willing to travel to Bolivia to begin a difficult life on the frontier. Although intermarriage with Bolivian women was still not common in San Juan de Yapacaní, it appeared in the 1960s to be inevitable for many of the colony's young bachelors. Still, there was resistance to intermarrying. The term *genshi-jin* (primitive native) was frequently used by colonists and their children to describe their often illiterate Bolivian neighbors.[48]

Many aspects of the traditional Japanese family, which seemed likely to fragment because of the ready availability of new land in San Juan de Yapacaní, in fact were remaining at least temporarily intact in the colony. Instead of young men striking out on their own to establish new households and farming units, the difficulty of finding Japanese mates and, even more importantly, the acute labor shortage in the area actually contributed to an average family size that was larger in 1964 than it had been at the time of the founding of the colony in 1956.[49] The traditional extended family of Japan, of course, was in the minority, since most of the colonists were younger and their fathers or older brothers had not emigrated.

The religious beliefs of the colonists reflected patterns established by the earlier immigrants to Brazil studied by Reichl. As will be recalled, Reichl had noted significant modification of Shinto and Buddhist religious ritual among Japanese immigrants. Ancestor worship in particular was nearly abandoned in the distant colonies of southern Brazil. Thompson's interviews revealed that 32 percent of the 262 household heads in the community declared themselves Buddhist, an equal number described their beliefs as Catholic, 6 percent were of the Shinto faith, and 17 percent were of the modern Buddhist sect called Soka Gakkai, which is practiced in Japan today. Of the Catholics, well more than half converted to that faith after immigrating to Bolivia. The anthropologist noted, however, the superficial nature of their conversion, commenting that few attended mass on a regular basis. It must be added that many Latin Americans, as "cultural Catholics," rarely attend mass either. Thompson also characterized the Buddhists in the colony as "distinguished by a general indifference to religion." There were no Buddhist or Shinto priests in San Juan de Yapacaní by the mid-1960s, nor were *kamidana,* or Shinto family shrines, evident in the community in any significant numbers. Thompson noted that, "with the exception of the native-born Japanese Catholics and the *Soka Gakkai* members, the colonists display remarkable apathy toward religion." He concluded that the "absence of Shinto deities and of Shinto and Buddhist clergy and the removal by thousands of miles from the resting place of their ancestors had created a religious void which some have attempted to fill by converting to Catholicism."[50] Thompson's conclusions regarding the apathy demonstrated by the colonists at San Juan de Yapacaní are consistent with that which is felt by many young people in Japan today. Nevertheless, most troubling for the colonists of San Juan de Yapacaní was that their religious beliefs, however superficially they were expressed, were a source of factionalism in the community. For example, the main school of the colony was turned over by Bolivian authorities to Jesuit administrators in 1963. Soon, all non-Catholic personnel in the school were purged. This prompted a concerted protest by the Soka Gakkai faction in the community.

Upon studying the San Juan de Yapacaní colony during its first decade of existence, Thompson offered a pessimistic conclusion regarding community solidarity in this still remote settlement. Noting that "factionalism and discord are rampant in San Juan," he argued that members of the community lacked a "pervasive kinship network," were "too heterogeneous" in their religious beliefs, and were too widely dispersed and dependent on local labor to develop bonds similar to those in the homeland. For example, two attempts at establishing an agricultural cooperative in the community failed during its first decade.[51]

Were these problems just inevitable "growing pains" for a pioneer community confronting long odds in the remote east of Bolivia? The ultimate success of the Japanese agricultural colonies in Brazil cannot be used as a valid point of comparison because they benefited from a vast network of support systems generated by the very large Japanese community in that country. (Brazil's Japanese colonies also took decades to develop, and many mistakes were made, causing much hardship. Additionally, the Japanese immigrants in Bolivia had to compete for development materials that were in short supply in the decades after World War II.) Moreover, there have been ample examples of failed agricultural colonies in other parts of Bolivia over the course of the past half century.[52] San Juan de Yapacaní was a functioning Japanese settlement for decades after its founding in 1956. Nevertheless, out-migration to Japan, Argentina, Brazil, and Peru was quite substantial after 1970.[53] Clearly, times were different from the 1930s, when Japanese colonists were forced to stay rooted to their original settlement because of the conditions in Japan and the costs of transportation. The Bolivian colonies continued to struggle because of these new realities.

The Japanese in Eastern Paraguay

The presence of the colony at La Colmena in Paraguay, like the scattered Japanese settlements in Bolivia before World War II, helped stimulate a much more ambitious colonization program in Paraguay in the decade after 1954. Japanese immigrants came to Paraguay during the first decade of the thirty-four-year dictatorship of General Alfredo Stroessner (1954–88). Though repressive and at times quite brutal, the Stroessner era brought stability and sustained economic growth after the years of turmoil marked by the Chaco War and the Civil War of 1947. Stroessner, who was a native of Encarnación, one of the larger cities of eastern Paraguay, actively encouraged Japanese immigration in his home region as a means of developing the vulnerable border area with Argentina. Like the Paz Estenssoro regime in Bolivia during the 1950s, Stroessner benefited from generous U.S. economic aid because he portrayed himself as a staunch anticommunist in the formative days of the cold war. The pinnacle of Stroessner's development programs in eastern Paraguay was reached with the completion of the giant Itaipú hydroelectric project as a joint venture with Brazil. The dam, the largest in the world, generated significant economic activity in the very area where the Japanese had begun to settle a decade earlier. This development project stood in sharp contrast to the limited opportunities confronting the Ryukyuan and Japanese immigrants to the Santa Cruz region of Bolivia during the same era and largely explains why Paraguay attracted 6,539 immigrants during the two decades before 1970, while the Santa Cruz region saw only about 25 percent of that total settle.[54]

Before turning to a discussion of the new Japanese colonies established in southeastern Paraguay after 1954, it will be helpful to examine the evolution of the La Colmena colony. On a site visit to La Colmena in 1992, I found a community that appeared stable but by no means prosperous. La Colmena was no longer exclusively an enclave of Japanese immigrants and their descendants; many native Paraguayans were evident in the community as landholding residents or agricultural laborers employed by the Japanese. Indeed, by the mid-1960s the Japanese were actually a distinct minority of La Colmena's population, as native Paraguayans entered the community in significant numbers after World War II. Economic assistance programs sponsored by the Japanese government were evident throughout the community and were an important component of La Colmena's economic viability. Patterns similar to the cultural evolution of the San Juan de Yapacaní colony's agricultural labor, economic individualism, and religious beliefs appeared evident in this Paraguayan community. These patterns were carefully analyzed by Norman Stewart in the 1960s in his valuable study of the La Colmena colony.[55]

By the late 1950s, La Colmena's Japanese population had actually declined to 716 from 1,372 in 1941. As happened in Bolivia, out-migration occurred largely to Argentina and Brazil. This decline can be attributed to the colonists' limited success in agriculture. Throughout the quarter century after World War II, the Japanese grew cotton, rice, corn, soybeans, peanuts, onions, and even tobacco. None of these, however, proved to be a valuable and reliable source of cash that would sustain the colonists and allow for expansion and further capitalization of their holdings. Furthermore, little mechanization of agriculture occurred in La Colmena. As late as 1992, there were very few trucks or tractors in the community, and the high-wheeled carts called *yuyajeres* were still the principal mode of transport. It is understandable that only a few of the Issei in the community were able to expand beyond the 100-acre plots originally assigned to them. Like other colonies in Bolivia, La Colmena was never fully successful in establishing a viable agricultural cooperative. This was reflective of the growing individualistic nature of Japanese farmers on their dispersed homesteads.

Still, Issei families like the Yamaokas were able to build modestly successful lives and raise families. The older Yamaokas settled in the community in the 1940s and raised seven children on a farm of only 150 acres. In the early 1960s, their homestead was a modest four-room dwelling of mud and bamboo, typical of the structures in La Colmena. The oldest son married a Japanese woman and settled nearby. The elder Yamaokas owned a few cows, pigs, and chickens and raised rice in the wetlands created by a small stream on their property. Their main cash crop was cotton, and from these activities and some small crafts they doggedly continued their lives in rural Paraguay.

As time went on, Japanese cultural traditions slowly eroded in La Colmena. The waning of cultural traits was reflected in the daily diet of the colonists. Stewart noted that by the mid-1960s only 15 percent of the Japanese in La Colmena consumed a primarily Japanese diet. Traditional foods such as *soba, sukiyaki,* and *shoyu* were cooked only on special occasions. More fundamental aspects of Japanese culture, such as family structure and religious beliefs, also underwent significant change.[56]

At least through the early 1960s, colonists in La Colmena were determined and successful in maintaining the "racial integrity" of the community. Stewart noted that "feelings against intermarriage [with native Paraguayans] have been particularly strong." In 1959, only two Japanese-Paraguayan couples were residing in the colony, and no Japanese woman had taken a

Paraguayan husband. The Japanese of La Colmena still brought the wife of the eldest son into his family's household, and there were instances of younger sons establishing "branch families" on new lands. But limited economic opportunity and the need for labor reduced the instances of branch families being established. The most striking change in the traditional Japanese family structure in the community was the erosion of hierarchy, obligation, and cooperation that is so fundamental to family unity in Japan. Most significantly, the Nisei generation assumed leadership of the affairs of the colony even before the Issei would have logically passed on their responsibilities because of age. "Loss of pride" and "feelings of shame" on the part of La Colmena's Issei as a result of Japan's defeat in World War II prompted their retreat from leadership roles soon after World War II.[57] It must also be understood, however, that the Issei parents in Paraguay and elsewhere in Latin America badly needed the language and social skills of their children to help them meet the challenges of life before as well as after the war. Thus, they were torn between their emotional need for their children to learn Japanese culture and their practical need for the Nisei to assume some of the economic burdens.

Japanese religious expression in La Colmena underwent the same transformation as has been discussed in respect to Brazil and the San Juan de Yapacaní colony. The Japanese of La Colmena were quite diverse in their religious beliefs by the mid-1960s. Although Buddhism and Shintoism were the predominant forms of religious expression, the colony included Catholics, Protestants, and Evangelicals who migrated from Brazil. Stewart noted that World War II and the "shock of Japan's surrender" greatly influenced religious beliefs in the colony. Thereafter, no public displays of Buddhist or Shinto beliefs occurred, village shrines disappeared, and those in the household gradually assumed less importance. Most fundamentally, religious rituals were rarely integrated into family life even during times of crisis. The erosion of traditional religious practices may have been profound. Nevertheless, colonists in La Colmena attributed the "salvation of the colony" to the pervasive feelings of harmony with the environment that fostered a "tranquility of spirit" among the colonists during even the most difficult times.[58]

The colonists of La Colmena made a concerted effort to stop the erosion of traditional Japanese values when they established the Bunka Kyokai (Japanese Cultural Association) in 1957. This organization was intended to be exclusively Japanese and included the entire Japanese community. The Bunka Kyokai coordinated the activities of an athletic club formed in 1946 and youth groups established in 1954. Japanese language classes, dances, and sports such as baseball, sumo wrestling, and *shogi* chess were promoted by the association. Baseball teams from La Colmena, for example, were outfitted in attractive uniforms and played highly competitive games with teams from the Japanese colonies in eastern Paraguay once they were established in the late 1950s. For the older Issei men, conversation, a hot bath, and a good smoke seemed to be the most common form of relaxation. For the younger Nisei, hunting and fishing were frequent forms of recreation. Social activities for Issei women were more limited and centered primarily on the home and family.

These efforts to build a solid social foundation for the community were successful to only a limited degree; La Colmena continued to lose settlers throughout the 1950s. The colony's declining Japanese population adversely affected its only Japanese language school, the Yazawa Gakuen. Some parents were reluctant to send their children to the school because of labor obligations. For others, the financial burden of supporting the school proved onerous. No secondary school was established in the community, and few Japanese teachers were employed by the community to teach Nisei children the language and culture of their parents. Those Nisei students who wanted to attend high school were forced to do so in Asunción, at great sacrifice to their parents. A university education was all but impossible for the vast majority of Nisei in La Colmena.[59] Recognizing that the continued isolation of the settlers was undermining the cultural solidarity of the colony, community leaders in 1953 formed the Compañía Nipo-Paraguayo de Colonización (Japanese-Paraguayan Colonization Company) to promote new Japanese immigration to Paraguay. Their efforts to convince Paraguayan and Japanese leaders of the value of future immigration to Paraguay were successful. Community leaders from La Colmena served as advisers for the planning of new colonies in eastern Paraguay. Unfortunately, the new immigration after 1954 benefited the La Colmena colony very little because only a few new colonists settled in the community.[60] The renewed Japanese colonization campaign near Encarnación, while never reaching the scale originally envisioned by its Japanese and Paraguayan promoters, proved to be far more substantial than the pilot colony at La Colmena.

The Stroessner regime, seeking to develop the fertile lands on the border with Argentina, welcomed the initiative of the Japanese government to settle the hardworking and productive Japanese in this historically sensitive area. Private property at two sites called Chaves and Fram in the department of Itapúa was acquired by the Paraguayan government in 1956 for two colonies to be settled by Japanese immigrants. As with the four main colonies to be established in the region, these colonies developed far more rapidly because of the mechanization of agriculture and easier access to markets.

For example, by 1960, 369 families (2,363 individuals) were already settled in the Fram colony, nearly twice as many colonists as La Colmena claimed at its peak in 1941. The early success of the Chaves and Fram settlements prompted the creation of a third colony at Alto Paraná in 1958. Discussions between Japanese and Paraguayan authorities leading to the founding of Alto Paraná were complex. At first both nations attempted to arrive at an arrangement wherein the Japanese government would help construct a railroad from Asunción to Puerto Guaira on the Brazilian border, as a prelude to the settlement of at least 100,000 Japanese in colonies situated near the transportation link. This ambitious partnership never materialized but was instead replaced by an agreement that called for the Bank of Japan to loan Paraguay the funds to purchase nine Japanese-made river gunboats, in return for permission by the Stroessner regime to admit 85,000 Japanese immigrants over the course of the ensuing thirty years.[61]

The enthusiasm for Japanese colonization to Paraguay was so pervasive that it even prompted a poorly planned scheme by American businessman Clarence Johnson to reintroduce contract labor to South America. Japanese immigrants were brought to a site near the town of San Juan Caballero and Amambaí, where 131 families were settled between 1957 and 1966. Originally conceived by Johnson and his investors as the foundation of a coffee empire in eastern Paraguay, the San Juan Caballero settlement soon was reduced to subsistence farming when the coffee trees were damaged by frost and the operation ran out of funds. Eventually, the Japanese of San Juan Caballero left the settlement and drifted to Argentina or Brazil. This failed experiment represented the last attempt to bring Japanese contract laborers to Latin America. The demise of the San Juan Caballero settlement is reflective of the failure of nearly all efforts to bind Japanese immigrants to the land in Latin America. That Johnson would attempt this scheme in Paraguay, where so much free land was being made available by the Paraguayan government, demonstrates his gross misunderstanding of conditions in Paraguay and the desires of the Japanese immigrants.[62]

The vast difference between the settlement of the original colony at La Colmena and those at Chaves, Fram, and Alto Paraná was the level of economic assistance provided by the Japanese government to the settlers in the Encarnación colonies. Settlers in the three colonies were granted about the same amount of land as the La Colmena pioneers. Each immigrant in Chaves, Fram, and Alto Paraná received approximately a 100-acre grant. But the Japanese government extended the colonists credit for tractors, jeeps, imported bulldozers, and other construction equipment for the building of badly needed roads. Moreover, the soils in the Itapúa region were more fertile than those in La Colmena, and soon the colonists were growing enough cash crops such as soybeans and corn to begin exporting their surpluses to Argentina, Europe, and Japan. In contrast to La Colmena, four agricultural cooperatives functioned effectively in the Chaves and Fram colonies, providing the use of trucks, jeeps, and storage facilities in Encarnación to their members. It seems that the leadership of these communities was able to generate support for the cooperatives when it was clear that the Japanese government was willing to offer generous aid. This was never the case in La Colmena. From the beginnings of the colonization campaign in Brazil during the early twentieth century, the Japanese government hoped that its overseas colonists would help provide necessary foodstuffs to the homeland. This was finally being realized with the new colonies in eastern Paraguay.[63] Ironically, these exports from Latin America came at a time when Japanese agriculture was finally meeting the needs of the homeland.

Significantly, the mechanization of agriculture and the nearly immediate success of the agricultural colonies near Encarnación helped assure the ethnic solidarity of the communities. Unlike San Juan de Yapacaní in Bolivia and La Colmena, native labor to clear fields and assist in the harvesting of crops was not as badly needed in these communities. The rapid increase in the price of land in the Chaves and Fram colonies also prevented most local Paraguayans from integrating the communities as landholders as they had done at La Colmena. The history of the Ishigaki family, one of the pioneers of the Fram colony, is suggestive of the differences between the La Colmena settlers and those Issei in eastern Paraguay.

The head of the Ishigaki family was a Japanese army veteran who settled at the Fram site before it officially was turned over by the Paraguayan government to the Japanese colonization company. With only his fourteen-year-old son and his wife, he purchased a 125-acre parcel from the Paraguayan government for the equivalent of only $150. Within a few years after roads had been built and new parcels surveyed, the value of his land had increased ten-fold. The Ishigakis farmed 60 of its 100 acres, raising soybeans and corn that were processed by machines from the cooperative and transported in trucks to Encarnación at harvest time. The family grew a variety of vegetables for their own consumption. Tung and grapefruit trees added diversity and additional income to the farm operation. Clearly, the senior Ishigaki would not have been able to prosper in La Colmena with only one son to assist him.[64]

Among the Issei settlers in the Encarnación colonies, education was a high priority. By the early 1960s, eleven schools were in operation. Still, the schools were staffed by Paraguayan teachers and had not yet begun teaching Japanese language or culture courses. Wallace Keiderling's fieldwork in the colonies confirmed the persistence of what seemed to be traditional Japanese customs, except for religious expression, during the first years of their existence. In particular, Japanese foods remained predominant in the immigrant's diet, and patterns of dress had not yet been modified along Paraguayan styles, as had occurred in La Colmena.[65]

These colonies in eastern Paraguay continued to attract support from the Japanese government for the next three decades. Additional agricultural colonies would be founded in the region, with the new Pirapó colony north of Encarnación being the most substantial. Pirapó was established in 1960 on 185,000 acres by the Japanese government-sponsored Settlement Revival Company. Aided by the mechanization of agriculture, the settlers in Pirapó raised soybeans and wheat as the main staples and supplemented their efforts by raising cattle, rice, and various fruits. Pirapó would thrive, and by the early 1990s a substantial town center was the focus of the bustling colony.[66] It boasted well-organized Japanese youth activities when visited by *National Geographic* reporters in 1992. By that year Japan would be the leading source of foreign aid to the Paraguayan government, with economic assistance continuing to flow to the Japanese colonies near Encarnación and to a lesser extent La Colmena.[67]

Understandably, after the late 1950s there was significant migration from La Colmena and the eastern colonies to Asunción and Encarnación. At least a third of the Japanese immigrants to Paraguay did not have agricultural backgrounds despite the stated requirements of the Japanese and Paraguayan governments. By the mid-1960s, more than 300 of these urbanites were settled in Asunción, and some were already migrating to Encarnación. Finding livelihoods very similar to the Japanese of other Latin American nations, the Paraguayan immigrants in particular opened restaurants and hotels, while others engaged in small-scale commerce. In Encarnación some of the urban migrants opened dry cleaners, a watch repair shop, and a beauty parlor. The Takimoto family, for example, after two unsuccessful years as colonists in the Fram colony, decided to sell their holding and move to Encarnación. With six children, four of whom were old enough to help in their new enterprise, the Takimotos opened a small hotel that soon became a gathering place for Japanese visitors to the city. With its restaurant serving excellent Japanese food, the hotel also attracted Paraguayans interested in Japanese cuisine.[68] The urban presence of the Japanese in Paraguay became quite significant in ensuing decades. At present, one of the most attractive buildings in Asunción is the Japanese cultural center. After 1970, the migration of the Nisei and Sansei to Asunción and Encarnación as well as to Japan accelerated. This pattern of migration from new agricultural colonies to the major Latin American cities was a small component of the massive migration to the cities by the rural peasantry throughout Latin America after 1960.

Although the literature on the Nikkei in Paraguay is scarce, population estimates for the colonies and urban areas are available. The total Nikkei population of Paraguay was estimated to be 5,744 in 1995. Residing in the three main urban centers of Asunción, Encarnación, and Ciudad del Este were 1,823, mostly occupied in commerce and retail sales. The Pirapó colony boasted the largest concentration of Nikkei with 1,358 inhabitants. The Fram colony's population had remained relatively stable since its founding in the mid-1950s with slightly over 700 colonists. La Colmena's core group of Nikkei numbered only 317 by the mid-1990s. Slightly more than 1,500 Nikkei could be found in rural settings, mainly in eastern Paraguay. There had been no significant immigration from Japan since the early 1960s, but the transmigration of Nikkei from the countryside to the cities continued. Reliable statistics for the migration of the Paraguayan Nikkei to Japan are not yet available. The urbanizing trend of Paraguay's Nikkei was mirrored in Argentina.[69]

The Japanese Immigrant in Buenos Aires and on the Pampas

The post–World War II experience of the Japanese in Argentina mirrored Brazil's but on a much smaller scale. New colonies were created in western Argentina following the pattern of the settlements in Paraguay and Bolivia. Additionally, the Japanese population in the Buenos Aires metropolitan region, like those Nikkei-jin in São Paulo, generally prospered in an economic environment made uncertain by the nationalist polices of the populist *caudillo* (strong leader) Juan Domingo Perón (1946–55). During Perón's first administration, his five-year plan launched in 1947 called for the admission of 250,000 immigrants to work primarily in agriculture and industry. Argentina permitted Yobiyose immigration from Japan as early as 1947, thus becoming the only Latin American nation to admit Japanese immigrants before formal immigration from the homeland was reinstated in 1952.[70] Agricultural workers were particularly needed in the labor force. In fact, 600,000 immigrants would enter Argentina in the period 1947–51. The vast majority of these were European immigrants, but Argentina's doors continued to remain open to the Japanese, as they had since the early twentieth century. What continued to discourage large-scale Japanese immigration to the fertile pampas, however, was an unfavorable land-tenure system. Usually only tenancy was possible on those lands that were readily accessible to transportation and markets.[71] This was true until small-scale colonization programs were begun in the late 1950s. Perón's pro-labor policies had minimal impact on the Japanese of Buenos Aires, who were primarily independent business owners, not workers. The former army colonel's agricultural policies were another matter. Despite his authoritarian populist regime, he never attempted a comprehensive agrarian reform program, which would have broken up the huge *estancias* (agricultural estates) dominating the pampas. The overthrow of Perón in 1955 precipitated a long period of civil-military unrest and economic instability that made Argentina unattractive to further Japanese immigration after 1960.

Immigrant arrivals from Japan and Okinawa during the mid-1950s totaled approximately 4,300. Significantly, more than 90 percent of the immigrant Okinawans paid for their own passage to Argentina; no contract immigration or colonization projects were undertaken until the late 1950s.[72] Thus, although no significant special subsidized programs encouraged Japanese and Okinawan immigration, Argentina still ranked third among the Latin American nations, behind Brazil and Paraguay, as a receiver of Japanese and Okinawan peoples in the postwar period.[73] As was true before World War II, most Naichi-jin and Okinawans established permanent homes in the greater Buenos Aires metropolitan area because of the limited opportunities in agriculture. By the late 1960s, more than 80 percent of these Japanese made their living in Argentina's largest city, typically as operators of dry cleaners, as floriculturists, or as truck gardeners. Of the nearly 800 dry cleaners in the capital city in the early 1950s, for example, more than 500 were owned by Naichi-jin or Okinawan immigrants. On average, these dry cleaners grossed 100,000 Argentine pesos per year, resulting in a net income of about $3,000. Because the price of urban real estate escalated rapidly during the high inflation of the Perón years, Japanese shop owners continued to live in modest apartments above their businesses. Dry cleaning operators and floriculturists were tightly organized in trade associations that maintained uniform price levels and regulated wages of employees. Most Japanese businesses hired native Argentines, particularly women, in their shops and found it beneficial to actively participate in these trade associations. Their involvement with other Argentine business owners aided in the widespread acceptance of the Japanese in the Buenos Aires commercial world.[74]

The Japanese in Argentina were less inclined to support the continued active operation of their language schools after World War II. Closed in 1945, these schools were allowed by the Argentine government to reopen in March 1947. Subsequently, five elementary schools commenced operations in Buenos Aires, in the metropolitan districts of Burazco and Escobar, and in the provincial cities of Córdoba and Vicente Casares. Enrollment in these schools continued to remain small. Inflation and the lack of permanent facilities throughout the 1950s restricted instruction to private homes, with tuition costs having risen four times higher than they had been before World War II. Instruction remained largely the same as it was before the war, with an emphasis on traditional Japanese cultural topics and language instruction. As in Paraguay and Bolivia, and unlike Brazil before 1970, the Issei and Nisei generations in Argentina rarely attended secondary school or attained a university degree. Few Japanese families were financially able or inclined to have their children educated in Japan. The urbanized and cosmopolitan Japanese and Okinawans in Argentina adopted the Roman Catholic faith in greater numbers than their counterparts in other South American nations. Nevertheless, these converts, like so many Japanese immigrant converts to Catholicism in Latin America, did not actively practice their faith. Interestingly, despite a degree of cultural assimilation that exceeded that of any other Japanese community in South America, Argentina's Japanese rarely chose to become Argentine citizens after World War II. Despite the liberalization of Argentine citizenship requirements by the Perón regime, less than 5 percent of the Japanese and Okinawans seemed interested enough in voting rights or holding office to file for citizenship in the two decades following the war. One of the most important examples of the Japanese community's cultural identity during this era was the continued publication and relatively wide readership of Japanese language newspapers. The Okinawan *La Plata Hochi* (La Plata News) was published twice weekly and served a readership of 3,000. The two Naichi-jin newspapers, *Pan América* and *Aikoku Nippo* (Fatherland News), appeared two and three times a week, respectively, and had a combined readership of 4,600. All of these newspapers were published in Buenos Aires, where the vast majority of the nation's Japanese resided. As the number of Issei readers capable of reading these publications began to decline after 1960, the Nisei and Sansei were less supportive of this important aspect of cultural communication.[75]

On matters relating directly to the homeland, the Japanese Argentines were capable of organizing effectively. For example, in response to the desperate conditions in Japan and Okinawa following the Pacific War, the Naichi-jin and Okinawan community in Argentina created the Comité de Ayuda la Victima de Guerra en el Japón (Committee for Assistance of Victims of the War in Japan), which functioned for five years supplying money, clothes, and food for the needy in both the home islands of Japan and Okinawa. Such organized fund-raising clearly aided in the process of "calling" relatives from Japan and Okinawa after the war. This was necessary because until colonization projects were undertaken in the late 1950s, no travel subsidies were available for those immigrating to Argentina. With regard to the Okinawans, for example, by the mid-1950s, 1,377 immigrants had been called from the islands. Unlike the Japanese communities in Mexico or Peru, which received no significant new immigration after the war, the Nikkei community was able to reunite family members, including first cousins, under Argentine law. The Japanese community in Argentina thus increased in size to about 15,000 at the end of the 1960s and retained close ties to the homeland at a time when cultural assimilation was advancing rapidly in every other Latin American nation, with the exception of Brazil.[76]

Although Japanese and Argentine authorities did not attempt to officially establish agricultural colonies on the pampas before World War II, as we have seen, the migration of the pioneer Issei from metropolitan Buenos Aires farms to settlements in the hinterlands created a rural presence that encouraged colonization efforts after 1950. The number of Japanese settlers living in Argentina's western provinces was only about 10 percent of the nation's total by the mid-1960s. Nevertheless, the steady, if not overwhelming, migration of Japanese immigrants from Peru, Bolivia, and Paraguay since the early twentieth century augmented official immigration to Argentina and helped create a consumer market for the specialty products of Japanese agriculturalists. The colonists who began arriving in the 1950s, like those in Bolivia, were also able to benefit from the social and economic support networks that were already in place after nearly five decades of a Japanese presence in Argentina. Indeed, Japanese and Okinawans in Argentina were primarily responsible for encouraging the colonization program in the absence of official Argentine or Japanese government initiatives before 1957. With these favorable conditions in mind, Tokyo began negotiating with the Argentine government in 1957 to settle as many as 400 Japanese families in the western provinces of Mendoza and Misiones. By the end of 1965, 25 families had established homesteads at the Andes colony, located fourteen kilometers southwest of the town of General Alvear in Mendoza. A larger colony of 100 families was established during this period in the far western province of Misiones, across the Rio Paraná from the Japanese settlements in Paraguay.[77] The Misiones colony represents the most ambitious colonization effort in Argentina in the post–World War II era. A brief review of the formative years of this colony will add a useful agrarian perspective to the primarily urban image of the Japanese in Argentina.

After exploring and rejecting settlement possibilities in the Argentine province of Chaco, members of the Japanese contingent, who came from nearly all prefectures in Japan, agreed on the site in Misiones Province in close proximity to the colonies in Alto Paraná and Fram, across the Rio Paraná in Paraguay. The site known as Gauhapé was marked by rolling terrain as well as a hot and humid climate. This suited the preferences of the Japanese colonists, since these conditions closely replicated circumstances in their home prefectures. Fieldwork by geographer Robert C. Eidt in the Misiones colony in the mid-1960s confirmed that the Japanese colonists welcomed the isolated setting. Eidt noted, "Experience in Misiones has demonstrated that pioneer settlements operate most successfully when foreign groups are broadly supervised while being permitted to remain intact. [Misiones] is a remote region in which foreign settlers have been allowed to maintain their cultural identity."[78] Japanese settlers in the nearby communities of Jardín América, Dos de Mayo, Obrerá, and Loreto, in the vicinity of the town of Posadas, actually participated in the selection of the site and aided the newcomers on their arrival.

The 100 Japanese families were settled on 6,800 acres of privately owned land that was purchased from a firm in Buenos Aires. Gauhapé lay between the thriving German settlements of Puerto Rico and Monte Carlo, which served as markets for Japanese agricultural products until river transport to the rail terminus at Posadas to the south could be established. Unlike the La Colmena and San Juan de Yapacaní colonies, where the settlers' holdings were not always laid out to give easy access to roads or water, the Gauhapé settlement was configured in 75-acre plots in what was known as the *waldhufendorf* (upland wooded) settlement form, a pattern that was utilized in the nearby German settlements. Using this surveying technique, the Gauhapé colony featured elongated plots that followed ridgelines and streams. Roads were constructed along stream patterns. In this way, each Japanese household had access to both water, varying soils, and transportation. This facilitated the immediate raising of livestock as well as the irrigation of plots and marketing of agricultural commodities.[79]

As was the case in nearly all the Japanese colonies of South America, a sizable share of the colonists in the Gauhapé settlement (30 percent) did not have farming experience. Still, they were able to adapt well, with the help of Japanese from other rural areas of Argentina and from colonists who were brought in from Santa Cruz, Bolivia, and the Dominican Republic. A small study group of the original pioneers who traveled to California to learn subtropical agricultural techniques also assisted. The establishment of a Japanese government-funded cooperative in 1960 aided in the opening of these new lands in Gauhapé. This cooperative quickly opened a 40-acre experimental farm and purchased tractors and livestock to be sold at bargain prices to the settlers. The Japanese initially planted tobacco as a quick source of revenue but then made the transition to traditional crops such as corn, rice, manioc, soybeans, tea, and vegetables. Eventually, after enough land was cleared, the Gauhapé colonists began raising oranges and tung trees like their counterparts in the Japanese colonies across the Rio Paraná in Paraguay.

Crop diversification, which was characteristic of nearly all post–World War II Japanese colonies, assured the financial stability of the Gauhapé colony until the severe inflationary crisis of the mid to late 1960s began to cause significant hardship in the community. Expressing sentiments similar to those of the San Juan de Yapacaní colonists nearly ten years after Gauhapé was founded, these pioneer Shin-issei, as post–World War II immigrants were known, were most distressed with the poor educational facilities provided by the Argentine government. At that time the settlement was still too small and the resources of the colonists too limited to consider opening their own Japanese language school. If one considers, as Eidt notes, that the Japanese of Gauhapé were very concerned with demonstrating at least a public front of adopting some native Argentine traditions, then the delay in opening a Japanese school may have been cultural as well. Terming it a "voluntary program of change," Eidt observed that the Japanese women of Gauhapé stopped carrying their babies on their backs and wearing kimonos in public. Argentine forms of housing were adapted for their dwellings, and their diets quickly were integrated with pork, ham, pasta, and dairy products. This degree of cultural adaptation in Gauhapé seems to have been conditioned by the proximity to a diverse range of European settlers in the region and an awareness of the difficulties of isolated colonies in other nations in South America.[80]

Japanese in the Cauca Valley of Colombia and the Dominican Republic

As previously noted, the only Japanese presence in Colombia before World War II was the small settlement of Japanese families near the town of Corinto in the Cauca Valley. After the war, the colony continued to prosper despite adverse government decisions on the marketing of the colony's principal crop and the endemic political strife that plagued Colombia after 1948. These adverse circumstances notwithstanding, the Cauca Valley Japanese by the late 1960s were some of the most prosperous colonists in Latin America because of the mechanization of agriculture, the full participation of the community in a viable agricultural cooperative, and creative land-use methods that diverged from established patterns of Japanese colonies elsewhere in Latin America.

What was most significant about the colonists in the Cauca Valley was their resourcefulness and independence. With no support from the Colombian or Japanese governments, the settlers migrated between 1945 and 1948 to a new settlement site thirty-five miles north of the original colony at Corinto. The decision to move was prompted by the continuing ill-feelings of Colombians toward the Japanese that lingered after World War II. Also encouraging the colonists to relocate was the promise of cheaper land. Uncertain of the new land's fertility, the colonists chose to rent the property for a three-year growing cycle and then, if necessary, move their agricultural operations to new lands that required clearing by the same slash-and-burn methods used so extensively in Bolivia and Paraguay. Planting the same profitable *shiro-kintoki* bean that allowed them to prosper in Corinto, the Japanese at their new colony at Palmira became the leading bean producers in the Cauca Valley by 1950. Unfortunately, the Colombian government in 1951 chose to import cheaper beans from Chile and the United States, a measure that threatened the livelihoods of the Cauca Valley Japanese. Once again the colonists responded successfully to a crisis by creating the Sociedad de Agricultures Japoneses (Japanese Farmers Society). All fifty-six of the families in the colony joined the society, which immediately worked to diversify agricultural production through crop experimentation, market analysis, and agronomy classes. Soon two varieties of corn and soybeans were being planted to supplement the *shiro-kintoki* bean. Profits from these crops were so substantial that by the mid-1950s the colony owned 237 tractors, 79 combines, and 120 trucks, valued at $1.25 million. The Palmira colony was thus one of the most heavily mechanized agricultural settlements of Japanese immigrants in all of Latin America. With this machinery, the Japanese of the Cauca Valley were able to clear new land easily and keep costs down by continuing to rent new cropland. Such an approach to land tenure was unique among the Japanese agricultural colonists in post–World War II Latin America. Throughout the worst years of *la violencia*, the Japanese were able to maintain the security of their operations through their own vigilance committee and by hiring local police to serve as armed guards. The Cauca Valley Japanese demonstrated a degree of courage rarely matched by other Japanese immigrants in Latin America. Culturally isolated in the Cauca Valley, they not only endured but prospered in perhaps the most dangerous area anywhere in Latin America after World War II. By the beginning of the twenty-first century, 1,000 people of Japanese descent were living in Colombia. Some, who were not still farming in the Cauca Valley, had migrated to Barranquilla, where they tended to intermarry with native Colombians.[81]

The short-lived Japanese colonization episode in the Dominican Republic had its roots in the massacre of 25,000 Haitian men, women, and children with the direct support of the dictator Rafael Léonidas Trujillo in October 1937. Fostered by Trujillo's racial diatribes against his eastern neighbors, despite his own partial Haitian heritage, this brutal measure was part of the dictator's campaign to "whiten" (*blanquear*) Dominican society by exiling blacks and inviting immigrant groups to settle on the island. Unlike the Brazilian racial theorists of the late nineteenth century, who preached racial harmony and assimilation, Trujillo's violent and race-oriented policies instead clearly established his reputation as one of the most ruthless dictators in all of Latin America. In failed efforts to mollify his growing critics in the ensuing decades of his dictatorship, Trujillo attempted to cultivate an image as a humanitarian by inviting and giving land to Jewish refugees from Germany and Austria and Spanish exiles fleeing the dictatorship of General Francisco Franco. Viennese Jews, for example, settled near the northern coastal town of Sosúa.[82] As Trujillo faced repeated attempts to overthrow his regime into the 1950s, he clung to this politically motivated immigration policy and added a geopolitical twist regarding the Japanese. Like the Paraguayan dictator Stroessner, who attempted to use Japanese settlers near Encarnación as a "buffer" against his Argentine neighbors, Trujillo invited Japanese immigrants to settle near the border with Haiti in a clear effort to discourage further Haitian immigration in this critical area.

The ill-starred Japanese colonization venture to the Dominican Republic began in 1956 with promises from the Trujillo regime of housing, land, living allowances, and the construction of a transportation infrastructure for the Japanese immigrant farmers who were to settle on the Haitian border. Unlike the Argentine, Bolivian, and Paraguayan colonization projects, which were reasonably well planned by Japanese officials and agents of the host countries, the Dominican venture lacked proper research and preparation. Still, the Japanese government, in a policy that later was to be termed *kimin,* or "throwing away" people, appeared eager to initiate even a poorly planned project. Over the course of the next four years, 250 families, or 1,300 Japanese, entered the Dominican Republic.

The Japanese settled in six colonies during the brief colonization effort. The most prominent of these were the Jarabacoa and the Constanza colonies, located in La Vega Province in the central region of the Dominican Republic, and the Alta Gracia colony in the southwest, near the Haitian border. The Dominican government wanted the Japanese immigrants to raise coffee and tea on the fertile soils along the border with Haiti. But the Japanese were more interested in raising cash crops that would bring them an immediate return, rather than wait the five to six years for the coffee trees to mature. Initially, the Japanese established truck gardens, raising vegetables for the local market. But soon production exceeded the local demand, and the market price of the cash crops declined significantly. The discouraged immigrants were not prepared to invest the time and sacrifice that the early immigrants to Brazil had made in coffee production, augmented by smaller outputs of vegetables grown in the coffee groves. With Japan's improving economy and the uncertain political climate after Trujillo's assassination in May 1961, most of the Dominican Republic's Japanese colonists decided to abandon the project and return home or seek opportunities elsewhere in Latin America. In the end, only 230 individuals from the original 1,300 decided to stay, after receiving grants and subsidies from the Dominican government to aid their farming operations. Nearly half of the immigrants (611) returned to Japan in 1961, and 376 migrated to other nations in Latin America. Only a small contingent remained in the Dominican Republic over the course of the next three decades in the aftermath of the most abject failure by Japanese immigrants to colonize since the Chiapas colony in Mexico in 1897. Some three decades later, some of these colonists would actually begin legal action for what they claimed were the false promises of both the Japanese and Dominican governments regarding the opportunities on the Caribbean island. Some of the Dominican Republic Japanese may have gone to Mexico, since the Japanese community in that nation was making a successful transition after the dislocation of the war years.[83]

Nikkei in New Settings: The Japanese in Postwar Mexico

The Japanese in Mexico continued to rebuild their lives after the war in their new homes in and near Mexico City and Guadalajara. A minority returned to their rural roots after the relocation of the war years. Approximately 70 percent of the Japanese of Baja California Norte, for example, remained in their new homes in the Federal District. From a broader perspective, 56 percent of all the Japanese residing in Mexico by the early 1970s lived in the capital city, as compared with only 16.5 percent in 1925.[84] The changing demographics of the Japanese in Mexico were nearly unprecedented in the Americas. Only the wartime relocation of Canada's Japanese from coastal British Columbia produced as profound and as lasting an impact on the immigrant community's attitudes as the resettlement of Mexico's Nikkei.

In Canada, 90 percent of the Japanese lived in British Columbia before World War II. By 1961, only 36 percent were residing in that west coast province. Two decades after the war concluded, more Japanese were living in Toronto than in the former heart of Japanese life, Vancouver.[85]

In the case of Mexico, resettlement seems to have had positive implications for those who remained in their new homes. Most of Mexico's Nikkei-jin in the postwar period established secure lives in urban commerce, industry, or commercial agriculture. As in Peru, because of restrictive laws passed during the 1930s, the Japanese community of Mexico was not revitalized by new immigration after World War II. Indeed, Japanese immigration statistics indicate the issuance of only twenty passports to Mexico after the war.[86] Nevertheless, the Nikkei-jin benefited from the so-called economic miracle generated by the policies of the ruling Partido Revolucionario Institucional (Party of the Institutional Revolution), known as the PRI, during this era. The PRI heavily emphasized industrialization, infrastructure development, and the promotion of commercial agriculture. The emphasis on building a probusiness environment with the support of the PRI's increasingly better educated leadership suited the Japanese commercial community very well.[87]

A number of Mexican Issei and Nisei became leaders of their respective business communities during this time. For instance, Teikichi Iwadate, whose family was relocated to the Federal District during World War II, became the pioneer producer of commercial soya products from a modern factory located in San Luis Potosí. Another Mexican Issei, Kizo Tsuru, whose company was confiscated during the war, subsequently became one of Mexico's leading producers of citrus fruits. Sanshiro Matsumoto, one of the Issei pioneers who settled in Mexico in 1910, rebuilt his floricultural business in Colima after the war with the aid of his sons and grandsons and became one of the largest suppliers of flowers in the region.[88]

Mexico's Issei went in two separate cultural directions in the postwar era. The relatively few who returned to their former homes in Baja California Norte and northern Mexico forfeited their opportunity to become part of a close-knit and culturally active Japanese community that was developing in Mexico City. Those Issei and their families who returned to their original homes usually did so because they were drawn back by their high social status in their former towns and villages and to landholdings that were not confiscated by the government during the war. The Mexican government frequently did not seize the landholdings of Japanese who married native women.[89]

The Issei who stayed in Mexico City and Guadalajara after the war did so for three primary reasons. Many were too old to begin anew on lands from which they had been so quickly expelled. Then, too, many aging Issei soon became accustomed to the regular social contact and numerous traditional cultural activities of Mexico City's evolving Japanese community. Ironically, they now felt more "at home" than ever before. Finally, Mexico City offered the Nisei, in particular, the opportunity to educate their children in high-quality schools that were staffed by professionally trained teachers, many of whom were from Japan. These schools taught the younger Nisei and Sansei the Japanese language and culture in rigorous learning environments.

Although no centralized "Japan Town" setting in Mexico City was established after the war, cultural activities primarily evolved around the Nichiboku Kyokai (Mexican Japanese Association) and the Japanese schools. The Mexican-Japanese Association grew to include over 500 Japanese families after it was formed in 1961. The association promoted good relations between the Mexican and Japanese governments, hosted visiting Japanese diplomats and dignitaries, and organized cultural and sporting events such as baseball games and sumo wrestling tournaments. Elderly Issei especially benefited from the association because it provided a "home away from home" at the Nichiboku Bunka Kaikan (Mexican Japanese Cultural Center). Housed on nearly five acres in Mexico City, the cultural center boasted offices and meeting rooms, a banquet hall for 500 people, a highly profitable Japanese restaurant, and sports facilities including tennis and volleyball courts, baseball and soccer fields, and playground areas for young Sansei. The cultural center was built with funds donated by the Japanese government when Mexico released the assets it had seized during World War II. Interestingly, a similar cultural center was built in Lima at about the same time with money the Peruvian government paid as a form of "redress" for the deportation of its Japanese residents. The Mexican-Japanese Association, like its sister organization in Peru after World War II, helped the Japanese embassy gather census information on the Japanese community.[90]

When the Liceo Mexicano Japonés (Mexican Japanese School) opened in the late 1970s, after more than a decade of organizational activity, it marked the culmination of the Japanese community's efforts in Mexico City to centralize its educational facilities in one well-funded setting. The school, located in the fashionable suburb of Pedregal, soon enrolled more than 1,000 students from kindergarten through secondary school and became one of the most prestigious schools in the nation. Both Mexican and Nikkei-jin students attended the school, along with the children of Japanese diplomats and business owners residing in Mexico. Fieldwork by Chizuko Watanabe concludes that Japanese parents sent their children to the school to "maintain their ethnic identity and pride, implant a spiritual heritage that they claim is the basis for success, and to establish close ties with Nikkei-jin children who live in distant areas." The majority of classes at the school were offered in Spanish, but ten hours of study per week were required in the Japanese language. Classes also were held in Japanese calligraphy, art, and music, in addition to the tea ceremony, judo, and karate. The school hosted a number of picnics and athletic events during the year, which afforded parents and children their best opportunities to socialize. Other voluntary associations that proved to be important to the Japanese in Mexico after the war were the Kenjin Kai (Prefectural Association), the Bokuto Sogo Fujo-kai (Association for Mutual Aid), and the Nisei-kai (Nisei Association).[91]

These organizations were typical of other groupings among the Japanese of Latin America. They united immigrants from the same prefectures in Japan, offered aid to needy immigrants, and provided social and educational opportunities for the Nisei in Mexico. The Grupo Sansei (Sansei Group), which was known by its Spanish, not its Japanese name, brought the third generation of Japanese Mexicans together in the period from the early 1970s onward. Its membership grew to 500 young Nikkei-jin, mostly students, by the early 1980s. With branch associations in Guadalajara, San Luis Potosí, Hermisillo, and Mexicali, the Grupo Sansei was the most important organization for young ethnic Japanese, just at a time when third-generation Nikkei where experiencing significant pressure to acculturate elsewhere in Latin America. The organization's activities included sports events, disco parties, and an annual national convention that drew Sansei from all parts of Mexico. The Mexican Sansei also sent representatives to the Convention of Panamerican Nikkei, which began to be held periodically beginning in the early 1980s throughout the Americas. The Grupo Sansei appears to have been one of the most highly organized Sansei associations in all of Latin America. While it embraced many aspects of modern Western culture within the context of the strictly Japanese social network, another organization, the Kokusui Doshi-kai (Japanese Nationalist Comrades Society), clung to traditional prewar Japanese values. Mirroring the views of the other ultra-nationalist movements in Peru and Brazil after the war, this association was, nevertheless, far less militant. Its original 352 members refused to accept Japan's defeat and continued to celebrate traditional Japanese holidays in public ceremonies well into the 1970s. By that time, its membership had dwindled to only a few members, and its activities were rarely noticed by the Japanese community.[92]

Watanabe observed that Mexican Issei, unlike their counterparts in the United States, Brazil, and Peru, generally mastered the native tongue. The

Japanese communities in Mexico before World War II were "small and scattered," and the Japanese immigrants needed to know Spanish to survive. After the war, the relocated Japanese spoke Spanish in the household but were then able to provide Japanese language training to the younger Nisei and Sansei as the school system improved. The vast majority of Japanese Mexicans also adopted at least the most overt forms of Roman Catholic religious expression. Their children were baptized and given Catholic names, and the holy days, rituals, and customs celebrated by Mexican Catholics were observed. Nevertheless, as was certainly true of the Japanese throughout Latin America, particularly the newcomers to Bolivia and Paraguay after World War II, a syncretism blending Catholic and Buddhist rituals was quite common. For example, during her visits to Japanese households, Watanabe noted, "An average family altar consisted of a statuette of Christ, a picture of the Virgin of Guadalupe, Buddhist name tablets for deceased members of the household, Buddhist incense, candles and fresh flowers." The adoption of Mexican cultural traits with regard to diet, housing, clothing, mannerisms, and even facial expressions was also far advanced, according to Watanabe.[93]

While the Nikkei-jin during this era acted in many ways as Mexicans, they tried to avoid close social contact or intermarriage with the native peoples. Watanabe, observing the Mexican Nikkei community, concluded that they "seem to be erecting an ideological barrier around themselves to delay assimilation at all levels." As elsewhere in Latin America, and despite their Spanish language skills, Mexico's Nikkei-jin strove to maintain their strong Japanese identity, and thus their motivation to make cultural adaptations was quite weak.[94] Another impediment to assimilation was the growing class consciousness of Mexico's Japanese in the postwar years. Often desperately poor when they first arrived in Mexico in the early twentieth century, the Japanese by the late 1960s were primarily middle to upper-middle class. Although not broadly discriminated against, as was the case in the United States, Canada, Peru, and to a lesser extent Brazil, they were nonetheless denied entrance to the nation's elite social and political circles.

Thus, as Watanabe concluded, this reality of social stratification tended to promote a conservative cultural outlook because "they fear 'downward' mobility by mingling with Mexicans of lower status." Mixed marriages were not only disdained but were avoided because they might diminish the economic resources of the family and lead to an erosion of social standing. These attitudes slowed the rate of cultural adaptation in Mexico City and Guadalajara significantly in the three decades after the war. The Japanese who returned to their prewar homes in the north and west of Mexico very likely were not as constrained by these attitudes regarding racial and ethnic solidarity. But sufficient information about the lifestyles of the Nikkei-jin in rural areas is lacking. Given the small Japanese population in Mexico, which numbered little more than 12,000 by the early 1980s, this small community was sure to have increasing difficulty in maintaining the racial and cultural solidarity in future decades that it had achieved in central Mexico since World War II.[95] This dilemma, however, certainly was not unique to the Japanese Mexicans but was shared by every other Nikkei-jin community in Latin America.

Toshiro Katagiri's life in Mexico offers evidence of the strength of cultural bonds with Japan in the face of this dilemma. Born in a small farming village in Nagano Prefecture, Katagiri left Japan at the age of fourteen to join his sister in Mexicali in 1927. After working for a time in his brother-in-law's bottling plant, he turned to cotton farming where he prospered, only to have his land seized by agents of the Mexican agrarian reform program in the mid-1930s. Starting over on another farming site near the Colorado River, Katagiri soon was able to afford to bring a picture bride from his home village in Nagano to Mexico in 1938. The war, however, forced the Katagiri family's relocation to Mexico City in January 1942. The resilient immigrant survived in Mexico City by working briefly as a plasterer, carpenter, and gardener, until he finally settled on the occupation of floriculturist in the nearby state of Morelos. Eventually, the Katagiri family grew to include four daughters and five sons, and they returned to Mexico City to raise gladiolas and carnations on plots of land that were leased for three-year growing cycles. As his business grew more successful, Katagiri, practicing his strongly felt filial obligations, invited his aging parents who had been living with his brother in Brazil to live with them. In 1966, Katagiri sponsored the immigration of a young Issei who had learned the flower nursery business in California. The young immigrant convinced Katagiri to shift to greenhouse production of chrysanthemums. By the late 1970s, the Katagiris, with the help of the young Issei who had married one of his daughters, were the leading chrysanthemum growers in Mexico. With a comfortable income and eighteen grandchildren, Katagiri returned to Japan for the first time in forty-four years in 1970. Thereafter, he made regular visits to Japan as a tourist, businessman, and loyal Issei who planned to retire in his homeland with his wife after leaving their flower business to their children. This may not have been easy. Katagiri thought of his flowers as "his children" and rose every morning at 3 A.M. to cut and prepare them for the market.[96] Katagiri's resolve in the face of nearly lifelong adversity was not unusual among the Japanese of Mexico. Similar examples of enduring courage were also common among the post–World War II Nikkei community in Peru.

Rebuilding New Lives: Peru's Nikkei-jin, 1952–70

During the two decades after 1952, Peru's Nikkei-jin recovered from the tragic dislocation of World War II to again grow and prosper as these courageous immigrants had done before Pearl Harbor. Initially, these were not easy years for them in Peru. The military dictatorship of General Manuel A. Odría (1948–56) and his civilian successor Manuel Prado y Ugarteche (1956–62), who directed the deportation of the Japanese during the war, remained hostile to the Japanese community. As we have seen, less than 100 of the 1,800 Japanese Peruvians deported to the United States during World War II were allowed to return. The Odría administration did restore diplomatic relations with Japan in April 1952 and permitted the reopening of Tokyo's consular office in Lima two months later. After these diplomatic channels were reestablished, Peru's Nikkei-jin were able to gain the passage of legislation in March 1954 calling for compensation for some of the properties seized by the Peruvian government during the war. Among the most prominent of these properties was a Japanese school in Lima. Despite these positive measures, the Odría regime did not essentially modify a policy that remained largely hostile to the Japanese community. For example, prominent sports figures, such as soccer player Luis Okada and cyclist Teófilo Toda, were barred from participating in international competitions. More significantly, Peru did not revise the highly restrictive immigration legislation of the 1930s that all but ended Japanese migration to the Andean nation. Thus, unlike Brazil, Peru discouraged Japanese immigration after the war. Indeed, Brazil, Bolivia, Paraguay, and even Argentina seemed far more inviting places to immigrate to than Peru, where the Nikkei-jin had been treated badly since the 1930s. Fewer than 800 new immigrants entered Peru from Japan in the years 1951–70. The legacy of discrimination, maltreatment, and abuse reflected in the 1940 riots and the deportation program remained uppermost in the minds of many potential immigrants.[97]

Still, there were many Peruvian Nisei who wanted to return to Peru to rejoin their families after nearly a decade of residence in Japan. These were former students who had traveled to Japan before World War II to study. Some of these Nisei immigrated to Brazil and Bolivia and entered Peru illegally in order to be reunited with their parents and siblings. In one unfortunate case, twelve Nisei were arrested and jailed along with some of their family members residing in Peru. They were subsequently deported to Bolivia. The Odría government routinely denied requests by Japanese who wanted to return, claiming they had lost their right to reside in Peru by leaving in the prewar era. Potential Japanese immigrants were universally denied admittance on the grounds that they "could not be assimilated." As late as 1958, the second Prado administration attempted to deny voting rights to second-generation descendants of Chinese and Japanese immigrants. Thanks to the efforts of Peruvian constitutional scholars, this legislation was never enacted.[98] What made this situation so troubling for the still beleaguered Nikkei-jin was that Peru's diplomatic relations with Japan were improving rapidly, even while their status in the Andean nation remained low. For example, when Tokyo was seeking admission to the United Nations in 1956, the famed Peruvian diplomat Victor Andres Belaúnde, while presiding in the Security Council, actively supported Japan's application for admission. In a statement fraught with the deepest irony, Belaúnde claimed a "'close relationship has always existed between the Government of Peru and the Government of Japan . . . and there have been and are many Japanese settlers living in Peru contributing to its economic development, obeying Peruvian laws and adapting themselves to the outlook, ideals and customs of our nation.'"[99] Diplomatic convenience or hypocrisy aside, clearly the status of the Nikkei-jin in Peru remained low in the decade following the war, as old resentments and prejudices continued to direct a highly negative government policy toward a people who had been residing in the nation for more than half a century.

As the Japanese economy began to prosper during the 1960s and 1970s, successive Peruvian governments sought better relations with Tokyo and consequently treated Peru's Nikkei-jin with increased deference. Prado, accompanied by his wife and daughter, conveniently forgot his past denunciations of Peru's Japanese during a state visit to Japan in 1961. This visit in part may have been made possible by Peru's decision in 1960 to soften its steadfast opposition to further Japanese immigration. Lima was now willing to allow the limited admittance of the immediate relatives of Japanese residing in Peru. Following this visit, significant Japanese funds were invested in a fertilizer plant in Chimbote, in an irrigation and electrification project in Tacna, and in the expansion of port facilities in southern Peru.[100] Nevertheless, only 150 Japanese were subsequently admitted as a result of the new immigration legislation.[101] Whether this low number was a result of the past policies of the Peruvian government toward its Japanese, the dramatic decline of the appeal of Peru to the Japanese immigrant, or both is not clear.

Despite renewed Japanese investment and a softening of the Peruvian government's policy toward the Japanese, improving conditions for Peru's Nikkei-jin were clearly a result of their own resolute efforts in the postwar years. As in the past, small venture capitalists in agriculture and commerce, mutual aid associations, and schools and newspapers were the backbone of Japanese economic stability and cultural solidarity. Japanese cotton farmers in the Chancay Valley, for example, regrouped in January 1961 to form the Asociación Fraternal Japonesa de Valle Chancay (Japanese Fraternal Association of the Chancay Valley). Other Japanese agriculturalists began raising chickens in the late 1940s, and within little more than a decade nearly 70 percent of the producers in this growing industry were Peruvian Nikkei-jin. The professional and regional fraternal Japanese associations so familiar to the community before World War II soon reappeared in the postwar era. For example, the Sociedad Mutualista Japonesa de Libertad (Mutual Society of the Japanese of La Libertad) in northern Peru was created in 1951. Similar fraternal associations were founded in Chiclayo, Huancayo, Tarma, Cañete, and Callao over the course of the next decade.[102]

Japanese magazines and newspapers such as the *Peru Shimpo* (Peru Progress), *Sakura* (Cherry Blossom), *Nikko* (Sun), and *Juventud Nisei* (Nisei Youth) began publication within ten years after Japan's defeat. These publications provided the still very insular Japanese Peruvian community nearly daily news of Nikkei activities, thus helping restore a sense of cultural solidarity after the troubled war years. Increasingly, however, these periodicals were published in Spanish; the Nisei and Sansei generations lost touch with Japanese language skills because of the changing nature of Japanese education in Peru. Although La Victoria, established in 1948 as one of the first successful postwar schools for Nikkei-jin, offered classes in Spanish, English, and Japanese, most Nisei and Sansei were "fundamentally educated as Peruvians" after World War II.[103]

Not conflicted by the sojourner mentality of their parents, the Nisei, like their counterparts elsewhere in the Americas, primarily spoke the native language of the country, ate the food of their homeland, and accepted most aspects of the cultural life of Peruvian society. In some cases the Nisei chose to have their own children educated in the elite foreign community schools, such as the Abraham Lincoln School, the Roosevelt School, or the British Primary School. Almost all attended Peruvian universities instead of those in Japan. Some students were sent to the United States or Europe to complete their education.[104] Thus the earlier practice by the Issei of sending their children to Japan for secondary and university education all but ended. For most parents there seemed to be little choice in this matter, for few of the Nisei had sufficient language skills to adjust to living in Japan. Indeed, by one estimate in the late 1960s, 90 percent of Japanese Peruvians lacked a command of conversational Japanese. The Japanese government responded to this seeming loss of cultural contact with the homeland by subsidizing

Japanese language instruction in Peru, sending Japanese instructors, textbooks, and language-training materials.[105] These efforts did not significantly change the course of the inevitable acculturation of Peru's Nisei to the Spanish language. As the Issei generation passed on the leadership of the Japanese community in Peru to their children during the 1950s, the Nisei made the understandable choice to accept their Peruvian nationality. Nevertheless, as they did in Mexico, the Nikkei-jin still chose to associate primarily among themselves.

As a cultural, recreational, and scholarly focus for the Japanese community's activities, the Centro Cultural Peruano-Japonés (Peruvian Japanese Cultural Center) proved to be a magnet drawing the community even more tightly together, in much the same manner as the Liceo Mexicano Japonés functioned in Mexico City for Mexican Nikkei-jin. The Jinnai Center became a particularly important gathering place for Peru's aging Issei, who regularly met to paint, play cards, or attend the many cultural events held at the facility.

With no new immigration of consequence, Peru's Japanese community grew modestly during this time. When the community conducted its first comprehensive self-census in 1966, the tabulators counted 32,002 Nikkei-jin on their rolls. Significantly, the historical gender imbalance favoring males had largely disappeared by 1966. Nearly half, or 15,452 of those listed on the census rolls, were females. Peru's Japanese remained heavily concentrated in the Lima metropolitan region, with nearly 85 percent of the Nikkei-jin population residing in the Lima-Callao area. By 1966, only 18 percent were Issei, while the Nisei comprised 43 percent of the community. Reflecting the longer Japanese presence in Peru than in other Latin American nations, the third generation, or Sansei, were nearly as numerous as the second generation, numbering 38 percent of the community. There were also 376 fourth-generation Japanese (Yonsei) residing in Peru at this time, or about 1 percent of the community. Peru's Issei were aging by the mid-1960s. Only 18 percent were under fifty years of age, while 45 percent were sixty years old or older. The Nisei were entering their most productive years, with more than 60 percent ranging in age from twenty to fifty. The Sansei, as one would imagine, were almost exclusively youngsters, with 90 percent of them being nineteen years of age or younger. While Peru's Nikkei-jin still overwhelmingly continued to engage in small-scale commerce as their livelihood, significant numbers of Nisei had entered the professions, and women had joined these ranks in increasing numbers. More than 1,500 of the Japanese community listed themselves as professionals, with doctors, dentists, accountants, and engineers being well represented. Few of them chose to enter the legal profession. As in the past, most owned small shops, stores, or cafés. About 15 percent of the community engaged in agriculture, mainly in the vicinity of Huaral, Cañete, Chiclayo, Trujillo, and Puerto Maldonado. Smaller numbers were entering manufacturing, but this sector would grow significantly after 1970.[106]

What can be said of those Japanese who established lives in the provinces, away from Lima-Callao, the main cultural focus of the Japanese community in Peru? A study by Luis Rocca Torres in the northern Peruvian department of Lambayeque offers valuable insights into the lives of those Nikkei-jin set apart from the main Japanese community in Lima.[107] The national census of 1941 listed 181 Japanese living in Lambayeque. Primarily dwelling in the city of Chiclayo, these Nikkei-jin made their living mainly as small-scale merchants. During World War II, 46 of them, including many of the community's leaders, were deported to the United States and interned in Crystal City. Only 4 of these deportees were able to return to Peru after the war. Among these returnees were Fusakichi Oyama Kumakawa, his wife, and their two sons, who were born in the Crystal City camp during the war. Some of Lambayeque's Japanese left their original homes and went "underground." Following the conflict, they resettled in other parts of Lambayeque after they changed their names and established new identities.[108]

After the war, many of Lambayeque's Issei were fifty years old or older and having lost their small businesses during the conflict were forced to begin life anew as agricultural laborers or barbers, as they had done during their first years in Peru. Additionally, as was true elsewhere in Peru, the small Issei community had to contend with the loss of such critically important cultural institutions as the Colegio Japonés, Chiclayo's only Japanese school. Eighty students were enrolled at the time of its closure in 1942. The school did not reopen after the war. Thereafter, Nisei and Sansei were educated in the public and private schools of Lambayeque with little Japanese language training or formal exposure to their ancestors' cultural traditions. Moreover, as elsewhere in Peru and the rest of Latin America, many older Issei were traumatized by Japan's defeat and the realization that they would not likely return to the Japan of their memories and imagination. There was some evidence of the Issei's willingness to embrace the culture of their adopted homeland. Soon after the war, some of Lambayeque's Issei adopted Peruvian citizenship. Interestingly, two Issei, aged seventy and sixty-five, were baptized as Catholics and then married in the church of Santa Lucía de Ferreñafe. This marriage formalized a common-law arrangement that had satisfied the couple in the prewar era.[109]

Still, the older immigrants found strength in their familiar cultural groups.

In Lambayeque, the main social network for the Nikkei-jin was the Sociedad Japonesa de Chiclayo. But in the postwar era, the leadership of this society passed to the Nisei, and they were far more likely than their parents to integrate themselves into the economic and social mainstream of life in the local community. For example, one of the principal directors of the society in the postwar years was Makoto Nakasaki Nakadio, who was also a leader in the local chamber of commerce and numerous other prominent social and cultural associations in Chiclayo. Reflecting the same cultural patterns of relatively small and isolated Japanese populations in Mexico before World War II, the Nisei in Lambayeque were far more willing to intermarry with native Peruvians after 1945. Thirty-five percent of all marriages involving a Japanese were exogamous prior to World War II. Four decades later, nearly two out of three marriages in Lambayeque were mixed. Occupational patterns also changed dramatically. Rejecting the commercial life of their parents, increasing numbers of Nisei in Lambayeque joined the professions, particularly after 1970.[110] Clearly, the patterns of cultural assimilation seemed to have accelerated far more quickly in the smaller Japanese communities away from Lima. This issue will be examined more fully in the final chapter of this study.

As noted, most of the Nikkei-jin in Peru were able to rebuild their lives in the decades after World War II with substantial success, as did those who remained in the United States after being deported during World War II. The stories of the Kato and Higashide families are compelling. Robert (Roberto) Kato, a Nisei born in Peru in 1935, was seven years old when he was deported with his family to the United States during the war. "Life must have been extremely difficult for my parents during the post–World War II years," he recalled. His parents were in their late forties, with no English skills or work experience. After moving to Los Angeles, his father worked as a dishwasher in a downtown restaurant, while his mother labored as a maid. But Kato remembered that "my parents pushed me through college." He had no bitterness in his later years. Nearly sixty, Kato reported, "I harbor no ill-feelings toward Japan or Peru or even the United States. I am proud of my heritage. I am equally proud that I am an American."[111]

After their difficult years at Seabrook Farms in New Jersey, the Higashide family, which then included six children, decided to "start from zero again" in 1949 on Chicago's North Side. Living in a tiny three-room apartment, as Seiichi Higashide described it, his family's first three years in Chicago were "a time of complete and ultimate poverty." Moving from one temporary laboring job to another and burdened by his lack of facility in English, Higashide was nevertheless able to feed and house his family. Still, the feeling of isolation in such a large city, though Chicago's postwar Japanese population was significant, was difficult.[112] With Higashide and his wife both working and caring for the family, they eventually were able to purchase an apartment building with the financial assistance of the Japanese Trust Association. Living in the basement of this building and working tirelessly to take care of the numerous demands of their eighteen tenants, the Higashides began building a secure and prosperous life for themselves. By the late 1960s, they were involved in the ownership of five apartment buildings on Chicago's North Side valued at more than $250,000. Still longing to return to Japan where his aging father anxiously awaited his return, Higashide nevertheless decided that he and his family were once again going to adapt to another culture. The Higashide children were educated in the Chicago public schools and graduated from fine local universities. This educational process, of course, facilitated their Americanization and widened an already existing gap between the attitudes of their Issei parents and their own, more individualistic outlook. Higashide wisely recognized this and noted that unlike Peru and certainly Japan, the United States is a society that "reaches out toward unlimited progress . . . [and] where the past is ruthlessly abandoned if it would impede progress." Using a contemporary analogy, Higashide viewed American society as a "multi-staged rocket which expels its earlier stages of power to fly off into the openness of space." Higashide candidly admitted that he and his wife were "amazed" that the youngest of their highly successful children who were born in the United States had not "abandoned" them. The strength of their traditional Japanese family ties was clearly enhanced by their early years of struggle in Chicago. Knowing the inevitability of the Americanization of their children and accepting this demanding reality of life in America, Higashide and his wife became American citizens in 1958. In his later years, he expressed pride and satisfaction at his highly diverse cultural background. Characteristically, before moving to Hawaii to retire in the 1970s, the Higashides turned their apartment buildings into temporary homes for students from Japan, Taiwan, Korea, South America, Iran, and Hawaii.[113] The experience of many of Peru's Japanese during the decades following World War II was clearly one of hardship and renewal, as it was for the Japanese throughout Latin America after the trauma of war.

NIKKEI COMMUNITIES IN TRANSITION: NIKKEI-JIN IN PERU, BRAZIL, MEXICO, AND JAPAN

> In Brazil, which is very young, traditions are not so heavy, one feels freer here.
> —Brazilian abstract artist Tomie Ohtake, 1993

Japan, during its economic recovery after World War II, began paying some attention to Latin American nations as trading partners, but these trade levels were not significant, compared with its growing commerce with the United States and Europe. To some degree, the Japanese economic resurgence before the slow-down in the 1990s had a "trickle down" impact on Latin America and the Nikkei communities in these nations. What must be taken into account, however, is that while the Japanese economy was thriving, nearly all Latin American nations were suffering during the 1980s, perhaps the worst economic decade since the Great Depression in that region. The international debt crisis and poorly managed statist economies led nearly every nation, except Mexico during its brief oil boom, to suffer through a serious economic decline. In this dismal economic climate, the Japanese were disinclined to invest significantly in Latin America. Very few yen found their way into the Latin American economies during the dark economic days of the early 1980s. The Japan International Cooperation Agency (JICA), the Japanese development agency for Latin America, was of some significant help in the smaller Japanese communities, such as in Paraguay, especially in the more recently established communities in the eastern part of that nation. But overall, the Nikkei-jin of Latin America did not partake noticeably in the Japanese "miracle," except for many younger Japanese who migrated to Japan itself for work. Let us turn to a closer examination of three Nikkei communities.

As the Nikkei communities of Latin America entered the twenty-first century, there were more than 1.5 million residents of Japanese descent in Peru, Brazil, Mexico, and the rest of Latin America. Brazil is the home of more people of Japanese origin than any nation outside Japan itself. In mid-1999, Peru's Japanese celebrated the 100th anniversary of the first permanent settlement of their compatriots in a Latin American nation. Peru's Nisei president, Alberto Fujimori, presided over celebrations that included a visit from the princess of Japan. Mexico's smaller community of approximately 15,000 Japanese has adapted well to the many challenges of life in that nation during the boom-and-bust years after 1970 in their relocated homes in metropolitan Mexico City and Guadalajara. Clearly, these three Japanese communities in Latin America have come of age. It would have been unimaginable to conceive of a Japanese president of any country in Latin America, much less Peru, at any time prior to Fujimori's election in 1990. Many of the older Japanese immigrants in Peru, Brazil, and Mexico have become well-established and prosperous citizens, rebuilding their lives after the war years. Yet all is not well with the younger Nikkei-jin in these nations. Their futures are clouded by political troubles and lack of economic opportunity. Perhaps as many as a quarter of a million have chosen to follow the sojourner's tradition of the Japanese pioneers in Latin America and have gone as "temporary guest workers" to Japan for the same reasons their ancestors left Japan, to find better futures outside their home countries. Only as the first years of the twenty-first century pass will the consequences of this phenomenon for the Japanese communities in both nations become apparent.

The years after 1970 marked an era of turmoil and promise for the Japanese of North America as well. Of course, this was the era of the Civil Rights Movement and the Vietnam War. The vast changes in the militancy of minorities in the United States helped the Japanese there and in Canada begin to seek redress for their internment during World War II. This would be a painful process because many of the older generation did not want to renew the memories of the war years, while the Nisei, in general, sought justice. The Japanese by this time were considered a "model minority" in the United States, but they were still more militant than in the past.[1] This redress was finally achieved when the Reagan administration, in the Civil Liberties Act of 1988, acknowledged "the fundamental injustice of the evacuation, relocation and internment of United States citizens and permanent resident aliens during World War II." The U.S. Congress officially apologized on behalf of the people of the nation for the treatment of Japanese Americans and their incalculable losses and suffering and offered

$20,000 in compensation to all Japanese Americans living at the time of the passage of the act.[2] In the struggle to achieve justice, the Japanese Latin Americans, mostly Peruvians, were not participants in the process. A political and tactical decision was made by the leaders of the redress movement in the United States to focus on the Japanese in the United States so as not to legally complicate the issue. Thus the Japanese of Latin America continued to struggle into the twenty-first century for a rectification of the injustice of their own deportation and internment. We will discuss the struggle for redress in some detail as this chapter draws to a close.

Peru's Nikkei and the Nisei *Caudillo*

After more than nine decades of confronting highly negative attitudes by the Peruvian people, the Japanese Peruvians achieved a place of prominence because of the election of the highly forceful Nisei president, Alberto Fujimori. During the two decades before his surprise election, however, they continued to quietly rebuild their lives and achieve modest levels of prosperity, even while the Peruvian economy went into a steady decline. The promise of substantial aid from one of the most powerful economies in the world as a result of the Fujimori leadership turned the minds of many native Peruvians to see the Japanese community as an avenue to long-delayed progress against crushing poverty in Peru. Just as important, Fujimori, as the first of a new breed of "elected dictators" in Latin America, accomplished what few thought possible in the early 1990s, the defeat of the vicious terrorist front, Sendero Luminoso (Shining Path). He also quickly and painfully privatized a state-dominated economy that was in utter shambles when he assumed office in April 1990.

Fujimori ruled Peru like the typical Spanish *caudillo* but with the confidence and resolve of the leaders who transformed Japan during the Meiji era. However, his forceful and often questionable legal methods, rampant corruption, and penchant for *continuismo* (continuing in power) eventually led to his abandonment of the Peruvian presidency and self-imposed exile in Japan after a decade in office.

The Japanese-born president's parents arrived in Peru from Kumamoto Prefecture in 1934. His father, Naiochi Fujimori, was born in 1897 and his mother, Mutsue Fujimori Inomoto, in 1912. Alberto was born in 1939. The family then moved to the Lima barrio of La Victoria, where they were to spend the decade of the 1940s living very quietly. In those days, the Fujimoris lived in a very tough part of La Victoria. Their humble, quiet lifestyle apparently worked in their favor, and they avoided deportation during the war years. Alberto was educated in Peru's public schools, including the University of San Marcos and the Agricultural University at La Molina. He also spent two years in the United States in the early 1970s at the University of Wisconsin. With preparation in mathematics, agronomy, and agricultural engineering, Fujimori would soon teach at La Molina and after attaining his doctorate would eventually rise to the position of rector of the university. He used this post as president of a university as the unlikely foundation for his campaign for president of the country in 1990. In the perspective of the times, however, this preparation was appealing to many Peruvians. Fujimori was a Japanese *tecnico,* a hardworking and pragmatic engineer who could bring logical solutions to Peru's enormous problems. After the terrible chaos and bungling policies of the Alan García administration (1985–90), a no-nonsense man of color and a well-educated nonpolitician was exactly what the Peruvian electorate preferred.[3]

Interestingly, when the now powerful executive was first running for office, leaders of the Nikkei community opposed his candidacy on the grounds that it would raise the low profile of the Japanese to a point where they would suffer abuse or become targets of terrorists and political enemies of Fujimori.[4] Even though Fujimori ruled Peru longer than any other president in the nation's history, except Augusto Leguía (1919–30), nevertheless, he was still only one member of a community that now numbers well over 50,000.[5] We now turn to an analysis of Peru's Japanese in the years after 1970.

From First to Fifth Generation in Peru

The period after 1970 in Peru was a terribly turbulent time for the Japanese and for all Peruvians. A military government led by General Juan Velasco Alvarado seized power in October 1968 and remained in place until 1980. It instituted a series of radical social and economic reforms that transformed the Peruvian state's relationship to the private sector and restricted civil liberties. Large businesses, particularly those that were foreign owned, were the main target of the Velasco reforms. But a Law of Social Property instituted in the early 1970s attempted to create a mixed socialist economy that allowed the workers to share in the profits of medium-sized businesses. This reform was a failure, like most of the military government's programs, and it had a negative impact on Japanese businesses with more than ten employees. The agrarian reforms decreed in the early years of the military government radically transformed a semifeudal landholding system but little altered the situation of the few Nikkei cotton farmers, whose holdings had either been lost during the war or were reestablished as small operations in the department of Huaral, near Lima.

As was made clear earlier, the majority of the Japanese in Peru were still small business owners who were overwhelmingly based in Lima. Thus they tended to survive the rigors of the Velasco years. Vastly helping the status of the Nikkei was the attempt on the part of the Velasco government to seek closer ties with Tokyo as the military regime tried to distance itself from the United States. This was part of an overall independent foreign policy that saw the regime begin trade ties and weapons purchases from the Soviet Union and recognize Castro's Cuba. Trade relations with Japan assumed even greater importance, and the Velasco regime began to import significant amounts of machinery and chemicals from the now vibrant Japanese economy. For its part, Japan imported mainly minerals, especially copper, forest products, cotton, wool, and petroleum. Peru was even able to enjoy a small favorable balance of trade with Japan during the early Velasco years. The military government went further and tried to establish military ties with the Japanese Defense Force. Velasco invited a contingent of Japanese marines to Peru to perform operations with their counterparts. In 1973, Peru and Japan concluded a century of diplomatic ties with great fanfare.

Trade relations between these two nations were encouraged by Peru's membership in the new Andean Common Market, which seemed to hold promise for Japanese business owners.[6] As a result of these closer ties, Japan sent badly needed aid during a terrible earthquake in northern Peru in 1970. Additionally, Tokyo sent technical assistants to aid the inexperienced Peruvian military administrators in their attempt to implement the wide-ranging reforms that were faltering by the mid-1970s.[7] Velasco was eased from power after a grave illness in 1975. He was replaced by the more moderate General Francisco Morales Bermúdez, who reversed many of the more radical reforms but still left a largely state-dominated economy intact.[8] Trade relations with Japan remained ongoing but went into decline during the corrupt and badly managed economy of President Alan García. For example, by the end of the García administration, inflation soared above 7,000 percent. Even against this economic backdrop, by the 1980s the leading automobile manufacturers such as Toyota, Nissan, and Honda began operating in Peru. At the beginning of the Fujimori administration in 1990, Toyota sold one out of every six automobiles in Peru.[9] It goes without saying that vibrant trade ties with the home country had a very positive impact on the fortunes of Peru's Japanese, but not until the later Fujimori years. New careers for managers, salesmen, and other middlemen in the Japanese companies that began opening branches in Peru would have to wait, as the nation endured terrible times during the 1980s and early 1990s.

After the military government returned power to the very civilian it ousted in 1980, Fernando Belaúnde Terry, there followed a decade of inept and corrupt leadership by Belaúnde and his successor Alan García that led during the late 1980s to a shattered economy, opening the path to the terrorism of Sendero Luminoso. In a number of instances, Japanese business owners were the targets of Senderista attacks, as the group sought to tear down Peru's social and economic fabric and replace it with a complex and distorted mixture of Maoist ideology, terror against the peasantry, and the personality cult of Senderista leader Abimael Guzmán Reynoso. Not surprisingly, Sendero failed to convert the peasantry to its ideology, and it was strongly opposed by peasant self-defense brigades known as Rondas Campesinas. By the late 1980s, the terrorists were driven to abandon Maoist tactics and begin an urban bombing campaign in Lima, similar to that of the Irish Republican Army.

The Peruvian Nikkei-jin: A Profile

The election of a Nisei president in Peru in 1990 marked the first time an immigrant of Japanese heritage achieved such high office anywhere outside Japan. Mary Fukumoto concedes that Fujimori's election marked a new positive feeling for Japanese immigrants in Peru. But just as important, Fujimori campaigned as a *paisano,* a man of color and of the new Indian and mestizo voters who were enfranchised by the voting reforms of the Velasco years. Contrasting greatly with the elite and often absent novelist Mario Vargas Llosa, Fujimori's opponent in the presidential campaign, the Nisei began a presidential "dynasty" of historic proportions. But his first two years in office were marked by a drastic austerity program dubbed "Fujishock" and by bloodshed and terror of unprecedented proportions in Lima. The urban terror campaign by Sendero Luminoso nearly brought the newly elected Fujimori government to its knees until the capture in October 1992 of Guzmán Reynoso in his Lima safe house. Ironically, the former professor at La Molina was in a literal death struggle with Guzmán Reynoso, a former professor of philosophy at a technical university in the remote mountain province of Ayachucho. The technocrat prevailed, and the reputation of the *caudillo* as a man who could save Peru was established. From then on, Fujimori would adopt a personal, hands-on style that often weakened institutions that should have been being rebuilt after the decline of Sendero Luminoso. Thereafter, Fujimori was able to slowly reclaim Peru from terrorism and economic disaster, but at the expense of the human rights of many innocent Peruvians who were inadvertently caught up in the struggle. As always, violence and the return to social and political stability had its price. In the case of Peru's Japanese, it was the lives of the youngest that were most greatly changed. The most important aspect to consider about these violent years is how they robbed most young Peruvians of hope for the future. As will be discussed in detail in this chapter, this led significant numbers of Nisei and Sansei to abandon Peru for newly created opportunities as "guest workers" in factories in Japan. This phenomenon was also replicated in Brazil, whose economy was equally troubled and denied talented and well-educated Japanese the chance to succeed in their homeland.

There are some other important similarities between these two groups of immigrants. Each of the Nisei, Sansei, and Yonsei generations have undergone the hard decisions associated with cultural adaptation and have placed a very high priority upon education. Finally, as well-educated as both the Peruvian and Brazilian second, third, and fourth generations are, they are deeply frustrated that their educations have gone for naught in lands plagued by economic hardship. These are only the most prominent similarities between the two Japanese communities. Many, more subtle nuances will be noted as we examine more closely the most important Japanese communities in Latin America.

We are extremely fortunate to have data from careful surveys conducted in 1966 and 1989 by leaders of the Nikkei community in Peru. Each of these censuses had significantly high response rates and is far more reliable than official government data. Moreover, the Peruvian government would have had no reason to ask questions that were important to Nikkei leaders concerned with issues of cultural adaptation and adherence to traditional Japanese values. Japanese Peruvian academics conducted the two self-censuses. The far more thorough 1989 census was directed by the sociologist Amelia Morimoto and achieved a response rate of more than 90 percent. An extremely valuable compilation of the data for the 1989 census is contained in a booklet edited by Morimoto.[10] No such detailed summary exists for the 1966 census, but the researchers for the later survey drew heavily on that data on a comparative basis.[11]

Not as carefully drawn as the 1989 survey, the 1966 census does not deal in useful detail with such key cultural issues as retention of Japanese language skills through the generations, traditional diet, songs, religion, and other primary parameters of cultural identity. Recognizing this, Morimoto and her staff of 116 included these critical questions in the 1989 survey (see table 4).

Table 4. Japanese Peruvian Population in 1989 by Age and Generation

Age (Years)	Generation					Total
	First	Second	Third	Fourth	Fifth	
0–4	4	83	1,323	2,156	79	3,645
5–9	10	118	2,456	1,764	44	4,392
10–14	5	143	3,695	1,273	25	5,141
15–19	8	158	4,204	619	7	4,996
20–24	7	298	3,672	238	1	4,216
25–29	15	436	2,737	79	1	3,268
30–34	69	858	1,848	25	0	2,800
35–39	97	1,591	1,114	4	1	2,807
40–44	69	2,234	504	2	0	2,809
45–49	70	2,587	177	1	0	2,835
50–54	68	2,664	58	2	0	2,792
55–59	96	2,009	25	1	0	2,131
60–64	104	1,202	7	0	0	1,313
65–69	133	583	2	0	0	718
70–74	353	176	0	0	0	529
75–79	538	34	0	0	0	572
80–84	390	6	0	0	0	396
85–89	199	0	0	0	0	199
90–94	55	0	0	0	0	55
95–99	16	0	0	0	0	16
Older than 99	0	0	0	0	0	0
No information	5	12	4	1	0	22
	2,311	15,192	21,826	6,165	158	45,652
% of total	5.06	33.28	47.81	13.50	0.35	99.98

Source: Amelia Morimoto, ed., *Población de origen Japones en Perú: Perfil actual* (Lima: Commission Celebrating the 90th Anniversary of the Japanese in Peru, 1991), 44.

Before we begin to examine the 1989 census, some discussion of the improvement in the quality of education and related youth activities, the Japanese press, and the growth of associations may be helpful. Two schools in particular raised the standards of education, requiring graduates to be bilingual in Spanish and Japanese and adding a variety of courses in fields previously neglected. The first of these was the Colegio Cooperativa de la Unión (Cooperative Union School), located in the district of Pueblo Libre, where many Japanese made their residence. The second was the Centro Nikkei de Estudios Superiores (Nikkei Center of Higher Studies). Schools in the provinces also raised their standards and expanded the programs of extracurricular activities to help keep a healthy interchange going between the various youth groups.[12] Among the activities offered for the female students were dance and singing classes. Traditional sports such as soccer as well as track and field were generally included. But by far the most popular sport was baseball, introduced to Peru by the Japanese and played almost exclusively by their young people. As popular as baseball has been in Japan for the past many decades, the same can be said for the sport among the Nikkei-jin in Peru and throughout Latin America. It was not unusual for leaders of the Japanese community and even visiting dignitaries from Japan to present awards to winning teams in the regularly scheduled competitions.

The Japanese press and scholarly community have also become more active in the last decades, generally offering bilingual editions of magazines and newspapers. *Peru Shimpo* and *Sakura,* which began publishing in the 1950s, were later joined by *El Japón, El Día, El Nisei, Fuji* (Purple), and *Puente* (Bridge).[13] The Japanese press, which brought the Peruvian Nikkei together with news from the community and Japan, except during the war years, gradually became more vibrant than it had ever been. Led by the work of Morimoto and Fukumoto, very valuable studies of the Japanese community appeared in the 1990s. Demonstrating the growing maturity of the scholarship on the Japanese was Luis Rocca Torres's excellent regional study of the Japanese in Lambayeque.[14] This work added immensely to our understanding of Peru's Nikkei, and more quality work is in process as of this writing.

The Japanese Association of Peru has experienced a significant drop in membership since the 1970s. Nevertheless, at least one in four members of the Japanese community still regularly attends major functions of the association. Given the diverse activities of today's young people and their frequent disdain for activities of the old generation, this is still a significant number and reflects the close-knit nature of the Nikkei community. Yet even in regions remote from Lima, such as the department of Lambayeque and particularly the city of Chiclayo, the Nikkei have tended to remain well organized and bound together even when their populations were quite small, and intermarriage with Peruvian natives has become the norm. The Sociedad Japonesa de Chiclayo made major adjustments to the changing racial and cultural nature of the Japanese community in this northern Peruvian city. Yet as recently as the mid-1990s, the Japanese there sought to revive their traditions by establishing a mutual aid society known as the Sociedad Japonesa de Auxilos Mutuos de Chiclayo (Japanese Society for Mutual Assistance of Chiclayo). Under the leadership of their president, Oscar Uchiyama, this society has held well-attended social gatherings, sought to document the history of the Japanese of Lambayeque, and generally kept alive the feelings of community that were being lost through the generations.[15] There are eighteen additional regional Japanese associations, even in far southern Peru at Ica and Pisco, where the number of Japanese has always been very small.

The Japanese community of Peru is so well organized that it has hosted large conventions of Nikkei from across the Americas on a number of occasions. At the Eighth Convention of Panamerican Nikkei held in Lima in 1995, for example, President Fujimori addressed the plenary session and summarized his views of people of Japanese heritage everywhere in the Americas. Fujimori's comments deserve being quoted at length: "Two feelings are combined inside the hearts of those who belong to the *Nikkei* communities in our countries: the respect for the cultural traditions of our parents, and the deep love for the land that welcomed them and where they were born. Between the respect and love for our ancestors and the spiritual and material roots taken in our countries we have built our homes and forged our professions in which our hard work and the honesty of our values have always distinguished us. I belong to the melting of these values."[16]

The first Panamerican Nikkei conference was held in Mexico in 1981. Since then, conferences have been held every two years throughout the Americas: Peru (1983), Brazil (1985), Argentina (1987), the United States (Los Angeles, 1989), Paraguay (1991), Canada (1993), Peru (1995), Mexico (1997), Chile (1999), and the United States (New York, 2001). They are attended by people of Japanese heritage from nearly every country in the Americas and reflect their common cultural bond and their powerful need to collectively share their experiences in their own nations of origin. On the other hand, many of the attendees at these conventions are of mixed Japanese and Latin American heritage, and this Nikkei identity was addressed in a commentary by Mary Fukumoto for a review of the 1995 convention in Peru. Fukumoto discussed the issue of "racial identity" that is important to consider when we discuss the nature of Japanese identity in Peru with respect to the 1989 census: "The *Nikkei* community of Peru has become a very heterogeneous group. There are, in addition to the *Issei,* four generations of their descendants with a significant degree of racial mixing. Whereas some *Nikkei* have maintained themselves 'racially pure' from one generation to the next, others have married outside the group. These Japanese tend to lose their Japanese cultural characteristics more easily. Thus the *Nikkei* community of Peru is extremely complex."[17] As noted in the preface of this book, the issue of Nikkei identity was addressed again by prominent scholars at the 2001 New York conference. There a working definition of *Nikkei* was established.

The Nisei of Peru have created their own active association, and it has played an integral role in the education of the Sansei, now the largest segment of the Nikkei population in the country. More will be said later of the aging Nisei and their place in the Nikkei community. Let us turn now to an examination of Peru's Nikkei as they entered the 1990s.

For the 1989 census, a twenty-three item questionnaire with many sub-topics was the main instrument, but interviews were also employed. The census was announced in the Japanese press, and questionnaires were distributed to more than sixty institutions that had direct contact with the Japanese community. The census counted 45,644 Peruvians of Japanese heritage, which represents an increase of 13,622 from 1966, or 45.2 percent in twenty-three years. Gender remained evenly balanced at 22,485 males and 23,137 females. By 1989 little more than one in twenty of the Japanese were Issei, one-third were Nisei, and almost half (47.8 percent) were Sansei. Indeed, the largest age group, 29 percent, was fourteen- to nineteen-year-olds. As far as age goes, the Nikkei were dominated by teenagers! This has vast implications for the Japanese community when these teenagers form their identities as young adults in the context of their Japanese heritage. The Japanese population was now even more centralized in Lima, Callao, Chancay, Huaral, Huacho, and Cañete. This part of the population totaled 38,492. Thus more than eight of every ten persons of Japanese heritage now resided in or near Lima. The most populated neighborhood was the now well-to-do barrio of La Victoria. The remaining 15 percent outside Lima were scattered in the various departments, with La Libertad being the home of 1,633, or only slightly more than 3 percent.[18] Importantly, Okinawans composed the largest group from a single prefecture, reaching nearly half of the total at 21,253. From the beginnings of immigration to Peru, Okinawans have always been a significant component. The census certainly confirms this dominance by Okinawans, who, as previously noted, have tended to form their own associations and have not always been treated equally by immigrants from the home islands of Japan.[19]

Even during the terrible economic crisis of 1989, the employment rate among the Japanese was almost 95 percent. As a result of the improvements in education and the softening of attitudes toward the Japanese, the rise in the professions among the Nikkei-jin was dramatic. Professionals listed in the census now totaled 1,754, with nearly 250 doctors, more than 300 engineers, and nearly equal numbers of teachers, accountants, and pharmacists. Lawyers, architects, economists, dentists, and biologists were also beginning to emerge. The Japanese were now entering industry in significant numbers for the first time in their history in Peru. One in ten was now engaged in some form of industrial activity, but nearly half of these were bakers. Very small numbers were engaged in mining and the fabrication of metals. Thus the Nikkei-jin remained mainly in commerce and the services, with nearly 60 percent making their living as the Japanese immigrants had tended to do since their earliest settlement in Peru. Those engaged in agriculture continued to decline in numbers, with little more than one in twenty working in the fields. The Velasco land reforms and Peru's distorted economy may be the principal reason for this decline.[20]

In addition to Fujimori, who attained the nation's highest elective office, a number of Peru's Nikkei-jin have gained distinction in their occupations. To name only a few examples of Nikkei who have gained national reputations, there is the painter and photographer Venacio Shinki, who works with themes of Japanese identity as well as Peruvian subjects; and Alejandro Tamashiro, president and editor of the popular magazine *Puente*. One of the very few Nikkei-jin in national security affairs is General Marco Miyashiro. A Sansei, this national police general was heavily involved in the capture of Sendero Luminoso's leader Guzmán Reynoso in 1992. A decade later he headed the Antiterroist Division of Peru's National Police. Perhaps the most curious mesh of Japanese and ancient Hispanic cultures is the career of the Nisei bullfighter Ricardo Mitsuyu, who became one of the leading matadors in Peru. After Fujimori dissolved the Peruvian Congress in 1992 in an unsuccessful attempt to rule by decree, more Nikkei-jin emerged on the political scene as a new congress was elected that was not predictably dominated by members of the president's once small political party, Cambio Noventa (Change 1990). Thus, only in Peru, and to a lesser extent in Brazil, would the Japanese enter the formerly forbidding world of politics. As we have seen, the Issei predominantly refused even to become citizens of their adopted homes. Attitudes about participation in politics have clearly changed among the Issei's children and grandchildren in at least these two Latin American nations. But the question remains, how "Japanese" are the offspring of Peru's original Japanese immigrants?

The central issue of how the census defines *Japanese* is addressed by Morimoto. Noting that exactitude regarding *mestazaje,* or race mixture, and cultural adaptation is nearly impossible for the history of the Japanese and their descendants in Peru, the census does, nevertheless, attempt to arrive at some estimate by using social and institutional criteria. Because certain social institutions established by the Issei in Peru heavily discourage membership by those who have married non-Japanese partners, the census estimated an institutional or "social nucleus" of the Nikkei population at nearly one-third, or 32 percent. Another 28 percent had a "familiar connection" with these social networks, meaning that they would participate or support their general activities. The remaining 40 percent had no connections with these social networks at all. Question 20 of the census asks specifically about intermarriage with non-Japanese, Brazilian Japanese, or native Peruvians.

One can conclude from these data that among the generations the Sansei tended to have the highest rate of intermarriage with native Peruvians.[21]

Sociologist Fukumoto paid special attention to the diet, dress, and cultural rituals of Peru's Nikkei-jin through the generations in her review of the 1989 census. It is not possible to deal with these customs in detail, but some examples will be discussed. According to what the respondents in 1989 replied regarding diet, Peru's Nikkei-jin usually combine native Peruvian foods with at least one traditional Japanese meal per week. At least 70 percent eat Japanese food on a somewhat regular basis. Rice and vegetables, of course, are still the main staple of their diet. A special dish prepared primarily for festive occasions is *sekihan*, cooked with a special rice known as *mochigome*. Okinawans regularly eat a daily dish of soup with rice and some pork. This meat is very popular among the Okinawans in Peru, as is a native rice drink known as *awamori*. For everyday wear, the Japanese dress in the Western style, but the kimono and two types of sandals known as *zori* and *geta* are worn very frequently in the home. As in Japan, the Nikkei-jin of Peru are impeccable in their personal hygiene. The public bath is still very popular for men, as it has always been in Japan. Many still engage in Japanese rituals regarding birth and coming of age, celebrated for Japanese boys at sixteen and Okinawan boys at thirteen. This is quite interesting, considering that the overwhelming response, 92 percent, for religious preference on the census was Roman Catholic. This conjunction is most evident during marriage and funeral ceremonies. For instance, a Catholic wedding may be accompanied by certain Japanese rituals, such as gifts of *sake* and *mochigome*. Traditional foods are also served at funerals. A very popular festival among the Okinawans in Peru is called Shiimii-sai (festival of the dead), celebrated during the third new moon of the year. Other lesser festivals and rituals are still observed by many older Japanese, according to Fukumoto. Particularly important is traditional Japanese music, dance, and song. Children are taught Japanese songs in school, and adults frequently sing them on special occasions. A folk dance known as *ondo* is often performed at special occasions, with the most popular musical instruments being the *shamisen,* a form of banjo, and the *shakuhachi,* a flute made of bamboo.[22] It remains to be seen whether the young Nikkei-jin will continue to practice these customs as they reach adulthood in the twenty-first century. But given their long tradition in Peru, the chance of this happening seems encouraging.

The census does offer projections regarding the future population of Peru with some Japanese heritage. The Japanese community is viewed as growing slowly, at a rate of less than 1 percent per year. At the beginning of the new century, it was estimated to be 51,374, and by 2016, as far ahead as projections were made, 56,123. These figures are low compared with those listed by the Japanese Foreign Ministry, which placed the number of Japanese in Peru in 1999 at approximately 80,000. The projections of the census may have been too conservative in this context and the criteria for defining ethnic Japanese different than those of the Foreign Ministry. Still, Peru is the second leading Japanese community by population in Latin America.[23] What, of course, was not taken into account in the 1989 census was the migration, primarily by Sansei, to Japan to work as temporary laborers. How many of these Sansei will leave Peru permanently for Japan, the United States, or Europe still is in question. This depends on the internal situation in Peru and the social bonds created during the migration process. It is to the question of migrants from nations with smaller Japanese populations that we now turn. We will deal with the much larger Brazilian migration in detail when we discuss the contemporary Japanese Brazilians.

A New Generation of Sojourners

Although the Japanese Peruvians and Japanese Brazilians comprise the largest components of sojourners to Japan after 1989, it is important to understand that Nikkei-jin from Argentina, Bolivia, and Paraguay have also reversed the immigrant path of Issei pioneers as well. A brief overview of the attitudes of all these migrants early in the immigration process will help place our discussion of the Peruvian and Brazilian sojourners in a clearer perspective. Sponsored by JICA, extensive interviews were conducted with more than 1,000 Japanese migrant worker informants ranging in age from sixteen to sixty-seven, between May and December 1991. The average age of these temporary immigrants was thirty-one, and males outnumbered females by more than two to one. As might be expected, most of the migrants were Japanese Brazilian (62.4 percent). Slightly more than 21 percent were from Peru, and those from Argentina comprised nearly 10 percent. The smaller population of Japanese in Paraguay and Bolivia were reflected in the relatively small percentage from these two nations, 3.2 percent and 2.2 percent, respectively. Most of these Nikkei workers had never been to Japan. As might be expected, single migrants (59.3 percent) were considerably more numerous than married ones (39.1 percent). Okinawa was the leading prefecture of ancestral origin, perhaps reflecting the less stable economic status of their families, compared with those from the mainland prefectures. Quite significantly, four of every ten of these migrants were university educated, yet eight of every ten were working in factories at the time of the survey. Clearly, most were underemployed in terms of their educational backgrounds, but like their ancestors who journeyed to Latin America, most originally came to Japan to save money and return home or to temporarily escape bad economic times at home.[24] As we shall see, within less than a decade, many of these "temporary sojourners" had established economic and social roots in Japan, which would make their return to Latin America increasingly questionable.

Quite simply, these Latin American Nikkei workers were earning good wages even as Japan was entering the long-lasting economic recession of the past decade. At the beginning of the 1990s, this group of informants was earning an average of $3,319 per month for males and $2,032 for females. This represents one of the highest wage scales for common labor anywhere in the world. It is no surprise then, that despite working in jobs well below their educational skills, seven of ten of these informants expressed "satisfaction" with their work status. Even more significantly, half of those questioned at this early stage of the migrant process felt that they had "adjusted" to life in Japan despite problems of discrimination that plagued a good number of them. In sum, only one-third of this group of 1,000 Nikkei workers said they wanted to return to Latin American homes when they saved enough money.[25] Only 17 percent claimed they wanted to return no matter what happened economically. Clearly, these sojourners were beginning to mirror the early pattern of their ancestors in Latin America.

The near collapse of Peru economically and politically in the early 1990s and the alteration of Japan's immigration laws to allow "ethnic Japanese" to enter the country as temporary workers prompted a significant migration of the nation's younger Nikkei-jin that emulated the Issei pioneers in a most ironic manner. These descendants of the first immigrants to Peru traveled to a highly prosperous Japan beginning in the late 1980s to accrue savings for a better life once they returned to Peru. In truth, some of them may never have had any intention of returning to a nation that before the mid-1990s appeared to have very little chance of offering a secure or prosperous future. Many native Peruvians also left for the same reasons and settled in the United States or Europe.

The precise numbers of these "new sojourners" are in dispute. Fukumoto claimed that by the mid-1990s, the number of Peruvian Japanese who had registered to travel to Japan approached 40,000. This estimate is very likely too high. The actual number may well have been increased by Peruvians with no Japanese heritage who carried forged papers and even some who went to such great lengths as to have their facial features altered by plastic surgery to find better opportunities in Japan. These "false Nikkei-jin" may have totaled one of every three migrants. How many of these "illegal" immigrants were permitted into Japan before the immigration laws were made more strict is, of course, impossible to estimate. Many were later deported when the Japanese recession hit in the mid-1990s.[26] Even so, as late as October 1998, while visiting Japan I observed some of these Peruvian immigrants who had very few of the physical characteristics of Japanese and who are referred to in Peru as *nikkei mestizos*. These people may have been the partners of Japanese migrants who are permitted to enter Japan as well. But in one case, such an individual was clearly the owner of a Peruvian restaurant in Yokohama with no Japanese co-owners or helpers to be seen. The *Japan Times* estimated that at least 250,000 Japanese Brazilian immigrants were residing in Japan as of late 1998. It was also estimated that the Brazilian Nikkei-jin were joined by 40,300 from Peru, 3,300 from Bolivia (presumably these were mostly Okinawans), 3,300 from Argentina, and 1,400 from Paraguay.[27] But it should be noted from the beginning that these ethnic Japanese from Latin America were culturally reflective of their Latin American homelands. Thus even their "race" did not free them from some very difficult times when they arrived in what is still a culturally rigid Japan.

This phenomenon should not really be that unexpected. Merry White opens her very important book about the Japanese overseas by quoting a Japanese children's chant, "*Iki wa yoi; kaeri wa kowai*" (leaving is good; but it is frightening to return). White argues that native Japanese business people and their families face a "crisis of return" once their overseas business stay is over: "This crisis—suffered by children in schools, mothers in the community, and fathers in the workplace—requires constant adjustment . . . by individuals and by families." She characterizes Japan as a nation with an outward-looking economy and a still inward-looking culture. Once individuals leave the all-important networks or social groups that are the fabric of Japanese culture for an extended period of time, even if they are Japanese, they pay a price. Threats of "spoiled identity, damaged career paths, and, most important of all, educational prospects" are, according to White, put greatly at risk by leaving Japan. She summarizes her argument in a wonderfully succinct manner: "The simplest criteria of being Japanese is to be born in Japan, to be of Japanese parents, to live in Japan, and speak Japanese. . . . [One must] be an active participant in relationships which clearly draw lines of responsibility and loyalty."[28]

With this in mind, it is understandable that the reception given Japanese from Latin America, who spoke little or no Japanese and were, particularly in the case of the Brazilians, far too animated in their outward manner, often forced them to make many of the same difficult cultural adjustments their ancestors were required to make when they settled in Latin America. But the issue of the new "guest workers" is becoming very complicated. Although the number of studies is growing, we do not yet have enough substantive research that looks closely at the long-term experiences of the Japanese Peruvians and Nikkei from Latin American nations other than Brazil. Fortunately, Takeyuki Tsuda, whose careful and comprehensive studies of Brazilian migrant workers in Japan appeared in 1988 and 1989, gives us a valuable framework for assessing not only the Brazilian experience but, by cautious inference, that of the other Latin American Nikkei-jin in Japan as well. As we shall see, there has developed among Brazilian Nikkei-jin a tendency to move toward permanent residence in Japan. Given the dire conditions of most Latin American economies during the late 1980s through the 1990s, it is likely that the Nikkei-jin from Peru, Bolivia, Argentina, and Paraguay have embraced this tendency as well.[29]

The wages paid to the Peruvian migrants in the days before Japan's economic difficulties in the late 1990s attracted highly educated Sansei with degrees from good universities, such as the University of Lima and the University of the Pacific. These new Dekasegi could earn more than $3,000 per month as factory workers. Considering the devastated condition of the Peruvian economy, where professionals and even high-ranking military officers were earning less than $200 per month, these highly attractive wages drew young Japanese whose families were not severely hard pressed financially, even in the midst of Peru's crisis. Most of the migrants took factory jobs in the Kanto region of Tokyo or Nagoya. The majority of the sojourners, as might be expected, were males. In 1991 nearly eight out of ten were males, nearly nine out of ten were from Lima, and seven out of ten were of mixed Japanese and native Peruvian heritage. More than half of these guest workers were graduates of Peru's universities, and most held high school diplomas.[30]

The impact on this massive out-migration of young Nikkei-jin on the Japanese community's social fabric was quite harmful. The Okinawan associations in the Peruvian provinces suffered a severe drop in membership. Important Japanese associations, such as the Estadio de la Unión, Centro Nikkei de Estudios Superiores, and the Asosiación Nikkei de Callao, suffered the same fate. Attendance at Japanese schools and Peru's universities declined as young people abandoned the immediate course of education for "quick money" in Japan. Japanese marriages also became very difficult because many potential male and, to a lesser extent, female partners had left the country. Often such social events as dances, team sports, and the like were abandoned for lack of potential participants. One young Japanese, when interviewed in 1992, characterized the young Nikkei community as "'paralyzed because all of our people have gone to Japan.'"[31]

The impact of this migration on existing Japanese families was also highly disruptive. Sometimes young fathers left their families to earn money in Japan. In the historic tradition of detached families brought about by immigration, problems of loneliness, depression, infidelity, and even drug use emerged. For the tight-knit Japanese family in Peru, however, these problems took on greater dimensions. In any event, life in Peru in the early 1990s was extremely hard, given the constant threats of terrorism, street crime, and, until the late 1990s, a badly faltering economy. So Japanese families paid a high social price for survival in dangerously difficult times in Peru.

From a positive perspective, like their ancestors before them, these sojourners remitted significant sums of money to their families back home when it was, in many cases, badly needed. A good number of Nikkei parents reported that their sons and daughters returned from Japan with a greater sense of "discipline" learned in the hardworking and conformist society of their forebears. Their children learned a great deal about Japanese culture, and they became more cosmopolitan in their outlook. Many young migrants simply enjoyed activities open to them in Japan that did not exist in Peru. One young person from Chimbote in northern Peru claimed that life in Japan was enjoyable. The anonymous interviewee said, "'In Japan we could live the good life. We could go bowling, skiing, and do things not possible in Peru.'" Another, from Lima, claimed that with the high wages earned in Japan he could buy gifts for his family and particularly his girlfriend that he could never afford or that were not available in Peru.[32] Are these sentiments so different from those of the early Issei pioneers in Peru who wanted to return to Japan dressed in "golden brocade"? Clearly they are not, and the Dekasegi mentality unquestionably endures through the generations in this Andean land.

As the Peruvian economy significantly improved in the late 1990s, many of these new sojourners returned to resume their lives in their homeland. But for at least a quarter of a million Japanese Latin Americans residing in Japan at this time, what has emerged is a distinct immigrant culture in such places as Tokyo, Yokohama, Nagoya, and other large Japanese cities. Some immigrants, like their ancestors in Peru, have opened cafés, bars, and other establishments that appear to be prosperous. By the graciousness of my Japanese hosts during a visit to Japan in 1998, I was able to enjoy excellent Peruvian cuisine in a Yokohama restaurant and later listen to samba music and watch taped soap operas from home in a Japanese Brazilian establishment with a standing-room-only crowd in attendance. Does Peru now face the dilemma of a dual culture of young Japanese who have found Japan more attractive, despite its recent economic problems, than their home country? And are those who have returned home content or disappointed with their experience? These questions need be addressed in the context of how the Japanese Latin Americans will be regarded in this century, based on the cultural attitudes toward these migrants as they exist today. Although comprehensive research remains to be done on the Peruvian Nikkei-jin of the type that is now becoming available on the Japanese Brazilian immigrants, it is fair to say that fieldwork Sayaka Funada-Classen and I have done in Japan point to significant similarities in the experience of both groups. Japanese from Peru tend to be more conservative and less animated than those from Brazil, and that has helped them adjust somewhat easier than their Brazilian counterparts. But both groups have faced significant discrimination initially that seems to be lessening as Japan adjusts to its Latin American Nikkei-jin population after more than a decade of their migrant labor in Japan. In terms of what Tsuda calls "structural embeddedness," the tendency of migrant workers to extend their stays indefinitely and eventually contemplate permanent residence in Japan, it can be said that it is likely that some and perhaps many Peruvian guest workers share the views of the far more numerous Japanese Brazilians. Much more research needs to be completed on this topic to arrive at a more definitive conclusion. The discussion of the Brazilian Nikkei-jin will be useful in placing these attitudes in a clearer framework.

Brazil's Nikkei-jin and the Failure of the Economic "Miracle"

Brazil's Nikkei-jin and the vast majority of the natives saw their hopes fade for the realization of the Brazilian economic "miracle" and the nation's rise to world-power status during the twenty-one years of military rule from 1964 until 1985. The weight of the world's largest international debt generated by an economic mentality of "debt-led growth," the petroleum crises of the 1970s, and an incredibly distorted distribution of wealth dashed the hopes of all but a few of Brazil's wealthiest elite during these years. Significantly, this failure laid the groundwork for Brazil's new Dekasegi, who continue to leave Brazil by the thousands for a better economic future in Japan.

Tellingly, despite being one of the largest nations in the world with an equally large economy, Brazil's ranks 105th in the world in per capita income, behind even Paraguay, Surinam, and Gabon. As Joseph Page notes in his wonderfully engaging portrait of the Brazilian people, the nation's self-deprecating jokers were fond of referring to their nation as "Belinda," a

THE JAPANESE IN LATIN AMERICA

blend of the economic capacity of Belgium and the desperate want of India.[33] In this land that has a stereotypical image of warm, openly emotional, and sentimental people, whose passions are samba, soccer, and a spontaneous lifestyle, there exists a tragic dichotomy. For example, Brazil's treatment of its poor children is a national tragedy. The nation's "street kids," uneducated and surviving by behavior that often includes theft and violence, has proven to be a great scar on the nation's image as a friendly and carefree society. The government's lack of a firm resolve to educate its poor masses has created a street culture of homeless and semi-homeless young people, who are often viewed with disdain, anger, and alarm by most of Brazil's middle class and elite. Many of Brazil's poor are migrants or descendants of migrants from the nation's impoverished northeast. This region, from the great famine of the 1870s until the present, has been unable to support its population because of the poor quality of the land and the often uneven rainfall. The land made available to the Japanese immigrants in the states of São Paulo and Paraná was not within the economic reach of these very poor peasants. The only alternative for many of them was to settle in the teeming *favelas* (shanty towns) of Rio de Janeiro and São Paulo, where life continues to be enormously hard. As a consequence, these people tend to look away as police prey on street kids to demonstrate their decisive action against Brazil's appalling rate of street crime. For example, in 1992 alone, the state of Rio de Janeiro saw 424 of its children murdered in street crime or by the police. In the mid-1990s, it was estimated that every day 4 children were homicide victims in the city of Rio de Janeiro.[34]

Notwithstanding this bleak overall picture, Brazil's middle class enjoyed generally good opportunities through the early 1980s before the near utter collapse at the end of the decade. The middle class did well, particularly in the southern states of Rio de Janeiro, São Paulo, and Rio Grande do Sul. These were the states that house the vast majority of Brazil's immigrants: Italians, Germans, East Europeans, Middle Easterners, Russians, and, of course, Japanese.

Despite the large Nikkei population in Brazil, Japan has not traded or invested as aggressively in Brazil since the 1970s as one might imagine. Restrained by the uncertainty of the nation's economic swings and persistent inflation, the Japanese government and private investors have remained generally cautious. Still, the total volume of trade and investment by Japan in Brazil exceeds that in any other Latin American nation. Toyota established operations in Brazil as early as 1955. Soon thereafter Japanese investment was channeled into small-scale steel and shipbuilding partnerships with the Brazilian government. During the 1960s and early 1970s, Japanese electronics firms such as Toshiba and Nippon Electric opened branches in Brazil as well. After 1970, as Japan's economy rapidly expanded and the need for raw materials soared, interest in Brazil began to peak. In addition to substantial investments in paper and pulp, $1 billion bought a 49 percent share in the huge Alunorte aluminum refining operation in the Amazon. Japanese investors also purchased nearly half of Cerrado, an agricultural initiative in the state of Minas Gerais. Japan's total investment in Brazil for the period 1951–90 reached $6.5 billion, well over half of all investment in Latin America but less than 3 percent of Japan's total overseas investments. As Japan continued to require agricultural and paper products from Brazil in the 1980s, the South American nation continued to maintain a modest trade surplus with its Asian partner, which at the end of the decade amounted to nearly $2 billion. The Japanese recession and Brazil's own severe economic difficulties in the 1990s reduced Brazil's trade surplus by half by 1997.[35]

After 1970, Japanese companies in Brazil afforded a greater opportunity to the Brazilian Nikkei-jin for substantive employment than anywhere else in Latin America. And JICA was very active in the Brazilian agricultural sector, supporting rural development projects that aided the Brazilian Nikkei-jin. For the most part, however, the Japanese generally fell back on their own resources, especially their increasingly better schooling. Brazil's young Japanese, as might be expected, were highly educated. In 1988, for example, 17 percent of the students at the highly regarded University of São Paulo were Japanese. The common joke among native Brazilian university students was that to gain admission to the university, one not only had to boast good grades and entrance scores but it was also necessary to "kill a Japanese."[36] Augmenting their education was a traditionally strong work ethic that helped the Japanese attain relative economic success in the broader national Brazilian context. Nonetheless, this would only continue until the late 1980s, by which time Brazil's economy was in shambles. Then Brazil's economic crisis forced the Nisei, Sansei, and some Yonsei to seek a new future in Japan. Like most Brazilians during these years, these young Japanese had lost faith in the ability of their nation's leaders to ever deliver on the promise of a meaningful and prosperous life.

Having migrated in large numbers from the interior *colonias* of São Paulo State to the environs of the vast metropolis of São Paulo City, Japanese agriculturalists now dominated truck farming and produce production for the great city. Cotia, a Japanese-administered farm cooperative, boasted 20,000 members and operated in fourteen Brazilian states. Ranking twenty-sixth among all Brazilian economic ventures by income, Cotia, by far the most successful farm cooperative in all of Latin America, raised much of

Brazil's fruits, vegetables, and grains.[37] Thus many Japanese immigrants had in large measure remained rooted in the agricultural setting where they began their venture in Brazil more than eight decades before. These are only some aspects of the success story of Japanese Brazilians. Many others have prospered in finance, industry, the arts, and occasionally in politics. We will leave their story until later, after we provide an in-depth profile of the Japanese immigrant in the contemporary era.

Japanese immigration to Brazil after 1970 declined to only a few hundred per year, down from an average of about 1,000 per year during the early to late 1960s. From the 1980s onward, there would be occasional immigrants who chose to leave a very prosperous Japan for personal as well as financial reasons, but as might be expected, they were very few in number.

Brazil's Nikkei-jin: A Demographic Overview

The Japanese Brazilians conducted two major censuses of the Nikkei population in that nation, one in 1958 and the other thirty years later under the auspices of the Centro de Estudos Nipo-Brasileiro in São Paulo. These two projects mesh nicely with the 1966 and 1989 censuses conducted by the Japanese Peruvians. As of 1988 there were 1,288,000 Nikkei in Brazil. It can be assumed that these numbers have now exceeded 1.4 million. The Japanese accounted for slightly less than 1 percent of the Brazilian population of 141.5 million. The overwhelming majority of the Japanese lived in Brazil's southeast, as had been the case from the beginnings of immigration in the early twentieth century. Nearly 80 percent of the Nikkei resided in that region as of 1988. Those that lived in the south, especially in the state of Paraná, comprised 11.7 percent of the population; about 4 percent lived in the central west; 2.7 percent in the north; and 2.3 percent in the northeast. Understandably, 72 percent of the Nikkei-jin population in Brazil lived in São Paulo State and, significantly, 26.6 percent in the city of São Paulo. A comparison of the data from the 1958 census showed very little change in the location of the Japanese population in Brazil over the course of three decades. There had been some slight movement to the north, northeast, and central west, but it was not in any way substantial.[38]

Far more important than the change from one region to another was the movement from the rural sector to the cities of Brazil. In 1958, 55 percent of the Nikkei lived in the countryside and 45 percent in the cities. By 1988 this figure had changed dramatically. These three decades saw their population in urban areas soar to 89 percent and those in the rural areas plummet to less than 11 percent. During the early years of this migration, it is useful to note, the Nikkei population living in the city of São Paulo increased eighteen times, from 3,467 in 1939 to 62,000 twenty years later. By the late 1970s, one-third of all the Nikkei in Brazil lived in the São Paulo metropolitan area. This change reflected the overall massive migration to the cities in Brazil during this period but was far more pronounced among the Nikkei population than other immigrant groups and native Brazilians. Second-, third-, and fourth-generation Japanese in Brazil were clearly making the decision to abandon the colonies of the Issei pioneers and begin more socially integrated lives in commerce, industry, and the professions. Heavy Japanese enrollment in Brazil's best universities since the 1958 survey was clear evidence of this trend.

As in Peru, during the last several decades, the Nikkei population of Brazil was becoming younger. The largest age group as of 1988 was the fifteen and under category, comprising 31.5 percent of the population. The cohort from sixteen to thirty followed, with nearly 23 percent. Taking these two groups together, more than half of Brazil's Nikkei were thirty and under. This demographic reality had vast implications for the future in Brazil, since these young Japanese were growing up and being educated in a society in clear economic decline. Those university-educated Japanese in the sixteen-to-thirty age group were finding far less opportunities for advancement in Brazil, and this clearly explains their willingness to seek opportunities in Japan, where they were less fettered with family obligations or careers of long standing. Additionally, these young Brazilian Nikkei-jin were more able to do the hard and dirty factory work required of them in Japan. They were also more likely to be willing to take risks, look for new adventures, and try to establish a monetary base for their futures, much like their Issei forebears in Brazil decades before. Among other age groups, the thirty-one-to-forty-five category included nearly 20 percent of the Nikkei-jin, and the forty-six-to-sixty group encompassed 15 percent.[39]

Like the Nikkei of Peru and, as we shall see, of Mexico, the Issei generation in Brazil was on the verge of passing away by 1988. Little more than one in ten (12.1 percent) of Brazil's Nikkei were first generation. Thus the predominant influence of the traditional ways of the homeland was ebbing away as the original Japanese pioneers in the tropics were living out the last of their lives. Their children (Nisei) were now not even in the majority, comprising 31 percent of the population. The grandchildren of the Issei, as in Peru, were now the largest group in Brazil, accounting for nearly 42 percent of the Nikkei population. Most of these grandchildren were under thirty years of age. Fourth-generation Japanese, or Yonsei, slightly exceeded the number of Issei, at 13 percent. Gosei, or fifth-generation Japanese, were beginning to appear on the census roles, although their numbers accounted for less than 1 percent of the population.[40]

The question of how culturally and spiritually Japanese were these third-, fourth-, and fifth-generation Nikkei-jin is not easy to answer. The Brazilian studies were not as thorough in this respect as was the 1989 self-census in Peru, where that nation's far smaller Japanese population was easier to evaluate in depth. One important measure of the Nikkei's adherence to Japanese customs was marriage patterns. As might be expected from the strong influence of their Issei parents, intermarriage among the Nisei was rare. Only 6 percent of the second-generation Japanese in Brazil married a non-Japanese, as reported in the 1988 census. In contrast, 40 percent of their children, the Sansei, took non-Japanese spouses. The Yonsei intermarried at a rate even higher, more than 60 percent. Understandably, there are significant differences in intermarriage rates by region. In southern Brazil, which has the largest concentration of Nikkei population, there was a much greater tendency to marry within the group. In the north and northeast of Brazil, where few Nikkei reside, intermarriage rates approach seven out of every ten unions. In the states of São Paulo and Paraná, the traditional strongholds of Nikkei culture, the exact opposite has occurred, with more than 75 percent of all marriages remaining within the Japanese group. More availability of Japanese partners, the strong pressure of Issei and Nisei parents to prevent their children from "marrying down" with native Brazilians, and the influx of more Japanese immigrants in these two states after World War II explain this far higher tendency for endogamy.[41]

Changing patterns in the use of the Japanese language and adherence to traditional religious beliefs also underwent significant changes from the 1950s, when measured in the late 1980s. In 1988 only 6 percent of the Nikkei spoke only Japanese, 20 percent spoke both Portuguese and Japanese, and well more than half of the population (56 percent) was only able to speak Brazil's native language. As might be expected, the figures for the rural areas varied significantly in the exclusive use of Japanese. In the interior communities of the states of São Paulo and Paraná and in the smaller communities in the north of Brazil, more than one of every five (21.7 percent) spoke only Japanese. Still, almost half (47 percent) could only speak Portuguese. Clearly, as the Nisei and Sansei generations matured, they were losing their Japanese language skills, despite the many Japanese language schools and cultural programs in contemporary Brazil. To illustrate the rapid loss of these language skills through the generations, compare the 1958 self-census, which indicated that 60.5 percent of those Japanese residing in the rural areas still spoke only Japanese, long after World War II and before the massive migration to Brazil's major cities had reached its peak. Even then, 45 percent of the Nikkei in the cities still were capable of speaking only their native language.[42]

By the late 1980s, six out of every ten Japanese Brazilians called themselves Roman Catholic. This figure is low compared with that of Peru and might reflect the long adherence to Buddhist, Shinto, and other Japanese sects by Brazil's rural-based Japanese before the great migrations to the cities after 1960. As late as 1988, one out of every four Nikkei still adhered to traditional or newly emerging Japanese religious beliefs.[43]

Occupational patterns reflected the changes in demographics that had occurred since the late 1950s. The 1988 survey conducted by the Centro de Estudos Nipo-Brasileiro found that the Nikkei worked primarily in management and office work, with 28 percent listing these occupations. Business and sales, which one can assume represents a large number of small shopkeepers, as in Peru and other Latin American nations, accounted for one in every five Nikkei careers. Sixteen percent worked in professional and technical fields and approximately 10 percent in the service industries and manufacturing. What is most remarkable is that the Japanese who tilled the soil had nearly vanished by the late 1980s. Now only 10 percent of the Nikkei claimed their occupations as farmers or fishermen. In contrast, in 1958, 55.9 percent were toiling, as they had been for generations, in agriculture and fisheries (a very small number in the latter category).[44] The transition to urban careers, which took less than a decade for most Nikkei in Peru, was now nearly complete after eight decades in Brazil. Thirty years before, less than 10 percent of all Nikkei in Brazil worked in management and sales; within three decades this number had nearly tripled to account for the greatest number of all the professions among the Nikkei. It can be assumed that a significant share of Brazil's small number of agriculturalists were making a good living as members of Cotia or as the prosperous truck farmers feeding the masses of São Paulo. These demographic changes were profound, and their impact on Brazil's increasingly younger, urbanized, and more sophisticated Nikkei were significant.

What attitudes among the Nikkei in Brazil underlay these demographic changes? Some representative examples were gathered by Sayaka Funada-Classen during fieldwork in successful rural colonies of Bastos and Mogi das Cruzes in São Paulo State and in Cambara in the state of Paraná during January and February of 1994. She interviewed Issei who had immigrated to Brazil during the 1920s and 1930s and were thus the recognized leaders of their rural colonies by the mid-1990s. Regarding their life goals in Brazil, the respondents largely voiced attitudes that were reflective of post–

World War II realities. For example, many argued that they were so busy making a good living to assure a better life for their children that they had little time to think about their own futures. As with nearly all first-generation immigrants in Brazil and the rest of Latin American, the Issei in these three colonies placed great emphasis on the education of their children. One Issei interviewee claimed, "Although we have never told our children where to go or what to do, they studied very hard in school." These Issei pioneers placed great emphasis on endogamy and were proud that their children did not intermarry with what they referred to as *gajin* (foreigners), meaning, in this context, native Brazilians. One Issei volunteered, "If our grandchildren were of mixed race, I would not feel like favoring them." The first-generation leaders of these communities worried about the increasing pressure facing Sansei men to marry Brazilian women. One noted, "Recently many *gajin* parents want their daughters to marry with Japanese men because their social status is rising, they work hard, will not divorce, and are good providers." Nikkei men "need to be careful" was the obvious conclusion of this respondent. Finally, what distressed these immigrant pioneers greatly was the loss of Japanese language skills among their grandchildren in particular. "We talk with our grandchildren in Japanese, but they seem not to understand us at all" was typical of the lament by many of these Issei. They understood that their sons and daughters had not remained fluent in Japanese because "we sent them off to the cities to study," where they spoke Portuguese predominantly. These Issei recognized that their children were culturally "Brazilian." Nevertheless, they looked forward with great trepidation to the day when there would be gatherings of Nikkei where only Portuguese and not Japanese would be spoken. Even now, one Issei sadly commented, "If you don't use Portuguese, young people will not come to even small gatherings. . . . If the Japanese cannot speak Japanese, what will happen?"[45] These attitudes were voiced even as many Japanese Brazilians were not only leaving the countryside but Brazil itself for better opportunities in Japan. Still, Brazil drew some new Issei in the mid to late 1980s for reasons often different from those of the first Issei in the early decades of the twentieth century.

The Last Japanese Immigrants? The New Issei of the 1980s

Even while Japan prospered as never before, small numbers of Japanese chose to immigrate to Brazil for reasons somewhat different from their predecessors. Among the total of approximately 53,000 who immigrated to Brazil after World War II, 95 percent did so before 1973. The last year of any significant Japanese immigration to Brazil was 1983. Interestingly, these migrants went predominantly into agricultural, while others entered the engineering and commercial fields. A limited number arrived to do missionary work in support of the new Japanese religions in Brazil. Significantly, the picture bride system was still functioning well into the 1980s, with the religiously based International Women's Training Center in Tokyo serving as one of the clearinghouses enabling young Japanese women to correspond with prospective husbands and prepare themselves to eventually travel to Brazil to meet them. Other motivations to immigration included interest in experimental agricultural ventures or technical work supported by JICA and a spirit of adventure among young Japanese who wanted to experience a society less constrained by tradition than their own.[46]

As noted, religion and missionary work was a factor for Japanese immigration both before and particularly after 1970. Approximately thirty Japanese religious groups have engaged in missionary work in Brazil. Besides the traditional Buddhist and Shinto advocates, the other principal religions include Tenri-kyo, PL Kyodan, Soka Gakkai, Makuya, and, most recently, Risshokoseikai. Except for PL Kyodan, which claims a significant number of native Brazilian adherents, these newer Japanese religions have relatively few members. According to Kochi Mori, the rapid urbanization of Brazil's Nikkei since World War II has weakened family ties, increased individualistic tendencies, and fostered rapid class mobility. These changes brought increased stress to the lives of Brazil's Nikkei, especially women who were now being required to work outside the home for the first time. These factors tended to increase the membership in both traditional and nontraditional religions as a means of attaining a better sense of emotional and spiritual well-being. As of 1988, Mori calculated that among the Nikkei-jin, 60 percent claimed to be Roman Catholic, 3 percent declared Protestant affiliations, 25 percent listed the Nikkei or Japanese religions prominent in Brazil, and 13 percent said they had no religious affiliation. Of the religions mentioned, Tenri-kyo is primarily a rural-based religion in western Japan, with headquarters in Nara. Arriving from that environment, its members adapted well to the lifestyle of the isolated rural colonies of the early Japanese Brazilian experience. With the rise of urbanization after World War II, this faith made a successful transition to the cities. To some degree this was also true of Makuya. Some young members of this religion were sent to Israel to work on a kibbutz as early as 1962. Brazil and Paraguay also became natural sites for the overseas promulgation of this religion, given the growing Nikkei-jin population in these two countries.[47]

One of the few later immigrants to Brazil was a preacher of the Makuya faith named Numata, who arrived in São Paulo in 1982 to lead the congregation in that city. Because of Brazil's increasingly restrictive immigration laws, Numata was not able to gain immigrant standing. He then turned to neighboring Paraguay and purchased an immigrant card that allowed him to travel to Brazil on a temporary three-month visa, which needed to be renewed in Paraguay. These restrictions did not prevent Numata from actively leading the Makuya faithful from a large and attractive house in São Paulo, presumably financed by the religion's members. In the late 1980s, this preacher hoped to have his son admitted to Brazil as a technically trained agricultural worker, the easiest way to gain admittance to Brazil over the course of the past few decades. Since Numata could not sponsor his own son because he lacked residency status in Brazil, another Makuya member, who farmed near Pilar do Sul, agreed to "call" the young man. It was hoped that Numata's son, after gaining residency status in Brazil, would "sponsor" his father and mother so they could establish permanent status in Brazil and leave Paraguay behind. Thus, because of Brazil's continued emphasis on skilled agricultural workers, the "calling process" would actually be reversed in this unusual case.[48]

As few as they were in number, Japanese immigrants to Brazil after 1980 continued to follow patterns established for decades by the Japanese immigrants who arrived before them. They made direct contributions to the Japanese community and its solidarity by providing needed services in key fields such as agriculture and religion. The efforts of these new immigrants augmented the positive accomplishments of earlier generations and perhaps helped strengthen the cultural bonds with Japan of the Sansei and Yonsei generations in Brazil.

Building the Institutions for Japanese Brazilian Solidarity

Since the early 1970s, Japanese Brazilians have continued the characteristic trend of the Japanese in Latin America and overseas in general to create organizations and fraternal societies based upon their geographic origins, occupations, educational activities, sports, social pursuits, and health care. In Brazil, these organizations abound. They are far too numerous to discuss in detail, but a discussion of the more prominent of these associations will be useful to an understanding of their diversity and importance to the Japanese communities throughout that country. The Centro de Estudos Nipo-Brasilciro, founded in 1948, became especially active after 1970 as a center for the study of Japanese immigration and cultural experiences in Brazil. As already mentioned, it was the agency that oversaw the 1988 census of the

Japanese in Brazil. Unquestionably, the best research being done today on Brazil's Nikkei is being undertaken at the center. In the early 1970s there were 350 schools teaching the Japanese language in Brazil, and by the late 1980s their activities were being coordinated by the Centro de Estudos do Lingua Japonesa. The Japanese Brazilians have taken the teaching of the Japanese language to second-, third-, and fourth-generation Nikkei-jin quite seriously, as they attempt to overcome some of the loss of this important connection with their traditional culture caused by the restrictions imposed in the decades after the late 1930s. In this vein, the primary agency for co-ordinating cultural activities associated with maintaining ties with traditional Japanese culture is the Sociedade Brasileira de Cultura Japonesa, known as Bunkyo. This organization and others were responsible for the opening in the late 1970s of the Museu Historico da Imigração Japonesa (Japanese Historical Immigration Museum), which was constructed to celebrate the 70th anniversary of the arrival of the first Japanese immigrants to Brazil in 1908. The 80th anniversary was celebrated with great fanfare in similar ceremonies in 1988.

By this time, health care and social activities had been given high prior-ity by the Brazilian Nikkei. With financial aid from the Japanese govern-ment, the well-staffed and modern Hospital Nipo-Brasileiro opened in Janu-ary 1984. Other health care facilities also have been established to safeguard the well-being of Brazilian Japanese children and the emotionally ill. The Brazilian Nikkei-jin also have formed associations for their numerous sport-ing activities, including golf, baseball, judo, karate, and sumo. For example, they hold an annual national championship of Japanese Brazilian baseball teams and boast their own baseball stadium in São Paulo.[49]

Unlike their Peruvian counterparts before Fujimori, the Japanese Brazil-ians have participated in politics at the local, regional, and national level. Some have served as government ministers, and others have held important elected posts in the state government. During the military governments in the early 1970s, the Japanese began to actively partake in politics as never before. João Sussumu Harada and Diogo Nomura from the state of São Paulo and Antonio Yoshio Ueno from Paraná were elected federal deputies. Shiro Kiyono, Antonio Morimoto, Jihei Noda, and Hachiro Shimomoto served in the São Paulo State legislature. Masao Tadano also won a seat in the Mato Grosso legislature.[50]

The political activism of the Nikkei began as early as 1945, when Hideo Onaga, who had long been a proponent of the full integration of Brazil's Japanese into the nation's societal mainstream, was asked to run for elec-tion as a federal deputy representing the nation's Japanese minority. Characteristically, Onaga refused, claiming he would only run as a Brazilian and not as a Japanese. Another Nisei, Kazuo Watanabe, who was born in the model Brazilian colony of Bastos in its formative years in the 1930s, spoke only Japanese until the age of six. In his later years he was named to a prestigious judicial position in the high court of São Paulo State. Watanabe, according to Joseph Page, also strongly opposes what they call "hyphenated Brazilians," accepting the inevitable assimilation of the third-, fourth-, and eventually fifth-generation Japanese through intermarriage and cultural adaptation.[51]

What have the Japanese contributed to Brazilian society, even as they struggled with their own identity? What of their futures in this nation of many immigrants and racial diversity? In many ways, they have significantly altered Brazilian agriculture, emphasizing new crops such as rice and a wide variety of vegetables and fruits. Changes in the Brazilian diet to include these foods are a direct result of Nikkei influence. The intensive desire of Japanese Brazilians for higher education for their children is in some significant measure responsible for higher budget allocations for university-level education, particularly in the state of São Paulo. Unfortunately, because many Japanese primary schools are private, grade school education in Brazil has continued to founder without a great deal of concern on the part of either the Japanese or native Brazilian middle class, which also relies on private primary education. Japanese martial arts and other forms of Nikkei popular culture, such as karaoke, have become part of Brazilian mainstream entertainment. Japanese Brazilians have distinguished themselves in all phases of business and banking as well. In the arts, painter Tomie Ohtake and filmmaker Tizuka Yamasaki have achieved international prominence.

Ohtake, an abstractionist, notes, "'The Japanese tradition is very strong in my blood, it is apt to surface at any moment and any manner.'" A Jun-nisei (those who were taken overseas when young), Ohtake took up painting somewhat late and held her first exhibition in São Paulo in 1957. As a Jun-nisei, Ohtake blends both Brazilian and Japanese themes in her art, which makes her work unique. This leading artist attributes much of her success to the more open attitudes of Brazilian culture. Ohtake gratefully recognizes, "'In Brazil, which is very young, traditions are not so heavy, one feels freer here.'"[52]

Tizuka Yamasaki is another talented Nisei woman who produced the documentary film *Gajin*. That film, based on the life of her grandmother, details the early immigrant experience in Brazil. A stickler for authenticity, Yamasaki was compelled to hire native Japanese actors for a number of the parts in the film because she found, to her dismay, that the Brazilian Nikkei-jin were far too demonstrative and expansive in their acting style. Somewhat of a rebel, Yamasaki left São Paulo to study in Brasilia and Niteroi and later worked with a prominent native Brazilian filmmaker. Yamasaki loves the Brazilian self-deprecatory sense of humor and laments that most Brazilian Nikkei find this form of personal release difficult.[53] Yamasaki, as an artist, is intimately aware of the personal and cultural issues that still are fundamental to the self-identities of the Brazilian Nikkei.

Cultural adaptation may be the position of some prominent Nisei like Hideo Onaga and Kazuo Watanabe, but there is evidence that many Sansei, like third- and fourth-generation immigrants everywhere, are developing a longing to understand and embrace their cultural roots more fully. Some third-generation Japanese in Brazil, for example, are expressing a desire for Japanese first names rather than the typical Brazilian names they were given at birth. Others are attending the many Japanese language schools with a degree of discipline that was rare among their Nisei parents. As with the Nisei everywhere in the Americas, the second-generation Japanese Brazilians felt some measure of guilt for the actions of the government of Japan during World War II. This is a burden that the Sansei do not share, and it seems to have freed many of them to embrace, at least to some degree, their heritage.

Some of Brazil's Sansei have not only embraced their cultural traditions in their South American homeland but, as we have noted, are beginning to create identities as the new Dekasegi, temporary immigrants to Japan. Their presence in the land of their ancestors very much clouds the future of the Japanese Brazilians as we enter the new century. Let us now turn to a close examination of the new immigrants that are changing the face of this community as never before.

Cyclical Immigration of the New Brazilian Dekasegi to Japan

When the young Nikkei-jin of Latin America began to migrate to Japan in the late 1980s, it was assumed that this was Dekasegi immigration and these sojourners were seeking only a temporary solution to their miserable economic opportunities. Like the Issei of the post–World War II era, there was always the hope of their returning permanently to their native Latin American homeland. Now preliminary research seems to indicate that for a good number of immigrant workers their stay in Japan may well be of indefinite duration. Takeyuki Tsuda's research among Japanese Brazilian immigrants in both Japan and Brazil has produced some valuable findings. Our discussion of these immigrant workers in Japan will rely heavily on Tsuda's research and the personal contacts with these immigrants by Funada-Classen during the 1990s.

The aging of Japan's population and a birth rate that dropped below 1.6 percent in the mid-1990s, coupled with the disdain that most Japanese young people have for "dirty, dangerous, and difficult" manual labor, has opened Japan to migrant workers. Among the higher paying jobs with larger Japanese companies, workers were being increasingly replaced by Japanese Brazilians and other Japanese from Latin America after the immigration laws were altered in the late 1980s. An important reason for admitting the Japanese from Brazil was the perceived "temporary" nature of their stay in Japan. A Japanese Foreign Ministry official interviewed by Tsuda explained, "'Most of the *nikkeijin* are living good lives [in South America]. . . . In fact, immigrants from Asia are much poorer and won't return home. In fact, they may end up residing in Japan by calling over their families and having children.'"[54] This Japanese immigration official clearly demonstrated a bias against all foreign workers establishing permanent residence in Japan. But he clearly misjudged how much the economic status of the Japanese in Latin America had eroded. What was also not clear to him was how "embedded," to use Tsuda's term, Japanese Brazilian immigrants would become in the society of their ancestors.

Under the new immigration laws, Nikkei-jin from Brazil and other South American nations can be admitted on "visitor" visas for periods of six months to three years. These visas, however, have no limitation on their renewal. Thus, many Japanese Brazilians have begun a period of cyclical migration that has brought them home to Brazil and back to Japan a number of times. This revolving-door process has, of course, badly disrupted their lives in Brazil, caused distrust among Brazilian employers regarding their potential long-term job status, and left many of the Brazilian Dekasegi in a form of cultural limbo.[55]

The Ministry of Justice's Bureau of Immigration Statistics has kept reasonably accurate records of the number of Japanese Brazilian migrants registered in Japan since the change in the immigration laws, and the projected increase in immigration is remarkable. The Justice Ministry only classifies the Brazilians as "foreign," but it can be assumed that the overwhelming majority are Brazilian Nikkei-jin. In 1989, 4,159 immigrants from Brazil entered Japan just as one of the new immigration laws was about to go into effect. By 1992, in the midst of the corruption and impeachment scandal involving President Fernando Collar de Mello (1990–92) and near economic chaos in Brazil, 147,803 were residing in Japan. Even more telling is that this number kept rising as Japan went into recession and Brazil experienced an economic upturn under the cautious leadership of President Fernando Henrique Cardoso (1993–2002). By 1996, 201,795 "temporary" immigrants were residing in most of Japan's major industrial cities.

Return rates to Brazil were low for the 1990s. For example, only 34,287 migrants returned home. And it is likely that for many of them their stay in Brazil would be short before they decided to return again to Japan to earn the very high wages available to them.[56] The estimates of the *Japan Times* that as many as a quarter of a million Japanese Brazilians were residing in Japan as the millennium drew to a close seemed to be on the mark. The Brazilian Nikkei-jin are now facing the new century in increasing numbers with the intention of making Japan their permanent home. Tsuda notes that what is clearly now happening among the Japanese immigrants is that a process of "cyclical" migration has become well established. As early as 1992, the Japanese government found that six out of every ten Brazilian Nikkei were repeat migrants. Thus the pattern of migration to Japan was established very early on and, according to Tsuda, as the years pass, these immigrant workers are becoming economically and socially "embedded" in their own networks established in Japan. These networks, like those established by immigrants everywhere, help reduce the pain of *saudade* (nostalgia or homesickness) for their Brazilian roots and make longer and, in many cases, permanent residence in Japan increasingly probable. It must be understood that if the trend continues, nearly one out of every five Brazilian Nikkei-jin will have abandoned their homeland for that of their ancestors. Funada-Classen had the opportunity to view firsthand the difficulties that many Brazilian Nikkei-jin and their children were having in adjusting to life in Japan when she worked in three public elementary schools in Okaka and Neyagawa cities in Osaka Prefecture from 1992 to 1994. She helped in these schools three days a week, teaching Japanese and supporting the study of Portuguese and Spanish. Counseling the parents of these young Nikkei-jin as well as the employers of Nikkei workers from Brazil in Hyogo Prefecture, she was struck by the difficult cultural transition that was required of the Latin American Nikkei, especially the older immigrants.

Despite these difficulties, there can be no question that the wage scales offered to the Brazilian Nikkei-jin are the single most important stimulus drawing them to Japan. Most Japanese Brazilians are reasonably well educated and would reject blue-collar jobs in Brazil. But in Japan they are able to make as much as ten times their yearly salary in Brazil, and many are able to save as much as $20,000 per year working in automobile plants, machine shops, and small businesses that demand long hours. This was made possible, as indicated earlier, because there is an acute shortage of unskilled labor in Japan due to the aging population and the unwillingness of the highly educated Japanese youth to accept a life of manual labor. This should be no mystery to those residing in any advanced industrialized country. This same phenomenon of well-educated, and sometimes semi-educated, youth disdaining the work of their parents and grandparents is common in the United States, Germany, and most Western European countries. Japanese parents have always valued education as the means of social mobility, and now Japan faces the dilemma of a labor shortage because these attitudes and demographics show no sign of abating even in the midst of the worst post-war recession in Japan's history.

Why should it be any different in Japan? The son of Irish immigrants, I was often told as a young college student working summers in the dirty and dangerous steel mills of southeast Chicago by my blue-collar supervisors, "Stay in college so you don't end up working thirty years in a place like this." Many of these steel workers, who were immigrants themselves, were very proud that they were able to finance as many as four of their own children's college educations. In this sense, Japan is no different. But in the steel mills of Chicago, Mexican migrant workers, African Americans, and immigrants still only a few decades removed from war-torn Europe became the predominant work force. In Japan, it has become the foreign immigrant, the Nikkei-jin from South America, South Asians, and even Iranians. At the top of this immigrant worker pyramid are the Brazilian and other Japanese Latin Americans. The Nikkei-jin get the highest-paying jobs and are the last to be fired because of their ethnic ties to their native Japanese employers. This does not shield them from cultural prejudice, but it places them further up the hierarchical scale than other immigrant workers who do not have this ethnic link. This may explain why the Nikkei-jin are more inclined to stay longer in Japan and even consider permanent residence through the repeated extensions of their visas.

After nearly a decade of Dekasegi immigration to Japan by Japanese Latin Americans, there is significant evidence that they are becoming better adjusted to Japanese society, and many intend to stay.[57] But the Nikkei-jin still face substantial difficulties. The immigrants have their own social circles, cafés, and neighborhoods. Thus they have established networks, as all long-term immigrants do. Many now look to Japan, not Brazil, for a better future. One example of this is the experience of Edson M. Tamada, a resident of the industrial city of Ida, where 1,700 Japanese Brazilians now reside. Tamada left Brazil at the age of seventeen after dropping out of school and found work in an auto parts factory in Ida. Today, he manages a binational food company with revenues of $16 million and a staff of seventy workers.

Tamada claimed the key to success for Brazilian immigrants in Japan is to embrace Japanese "'culture, customs, language—to integrate into the community, to create a new generation.'"[58]

Tsuda's analysis of the Japanese work force points to an increasing informality of the labor supply, much like in the United States. Japanese companies are now far more willing to rely on *hi-seishain* (temporary or casual workers) from the immigrant pool to avoid long-term obligations to foreign workers. Still, the temporary job market is so fluid, even during economic recession, that it is not difficult for the earlier Brazilian workers to move from one temporary job to another without a great degree of hardship.[59] Now, for those Nikkei-jin from Latin America who have brought their children to Japan, the situation has become more complex. Because it is so difficult for the children to adapt to the new schools, a change in jobs, even with a higher salary, does not offset the personal difficulties faced by the families. As their stay in Japan lengthens, their Spartan lifestyle and work ethic begins to soften, and as one would expect, they seek a better, more comfortable life. One of Tsuda's interviewees put it very well: "'At first I did as much work as possible, and tried to save as much as I could without spending it. I would never go out. But as you continue living in Japan, your priorities change and you begin to desire a more relaxed life. Eventually you lose your previous objectives and begin buying stuff and entertaining yourself. Now I go to Tokyo and see new regions of Japan. I eat out and meet new people.'"[60]

By the mid-1990s, perhaps as many as 80 percent of the Japanese Brazilian migrants were living with their families in Japan. Thus the pattern of family migration to Brazil eight decades before was being repeated in Japan with the Nisei and the Sansei in the last years of the twentieth century. In contrast to some reports, Tsuda asserts that the children of the Nikkei-jin were beginning to adapt rather well to Japanese schools because they quickly learned Japanese and soon were speaking it quite well. Tsuda is willing to venture even further on the issue of the cultural assimilation of immigrant children. He argues that after several years in Japan, "The result is a rapid assimilation that affects not only individual personality and behavioral patterns, but ethnic identity. . . . Many of the younger children come to believe that they are completely Japanese and come to identify exclusively with Japan."[61] Funada-Classen is not nearly as optimistic about the future of the Nikkei-jin migrants and their families in Japan. She noted that the children of immigrants may soon adjust well in the elementary school environment, but the challenges they face will increase dramatically in junior high school and beyond. There the young Nikkei-jin will confront the intense competition for entry into the better high schools and universities that is so necessary for highly regarded careers. As the Nikkei-jin move through the school system in Japan, many will not have the sophisticated Japanese language skills needed to perform well on the demanding exams. Moreover, many are losing (or never acquired) a proficiency in Portuguese or Spanish. Many now find themselves between two cultures, as their Issei ancestors did in Latin America before World War II. Their adjustment will come with time. But for now, the implications for the present generations of Nikkei-jin in Japan are troubling.

Perhaps most troubling for those who see the future of the Nikkei-jin in Brazil eroding as many of them become permanent residents in their ancestral homeland are the negative images that are emerging about Brazil among their young immigrant children. Again we turn to Tsuda's valuable interviews. One Japanese Brazilian woman lamented that her sister's daughter now thinks completely like a Japanese and does not want to return to Brazil because it is a backward nation, "'filled with bandits,'" and does not even have television.[62]

As the work of Tsuda, Funada-Classen, and others with the Latin American Nikkei-jin attests, it has been very difficult at times for these immigrants to face the rigid strictures of Japanese society. For example, some of the expressed attitudes of native Japanese toward the immigrants were absolutely virulent in nature. One individual interviewed by Tsuda called the Latin American Nikkei-jin "'fake Japanese'" and "'weirdos'" who were like the "'fake Ultraman you see on TV.'"[63] Other, more extreme views portrayed them as foreigners who were acting like a drug that was undermining the health and "purity" of the Japanese people.[64] These views notwithstanding, the Latin American Nikkei-jin are a fact of life in Japan, and attitudes, especially among young school children, have begun to soften somewhat. For all foreigners, even those with similar phenotypes like the Japanese Latin Americans, language difficulties will almost always breed hostility, even in nations that supposedly welcome immigrants. The Irish in the United States suffered extreme discrimination for decades, despite the familiarity of their appearance and their ability to speak English. Religion and other cultural traits were their initial undoing. But like the recent Latin American Nikkei-jin in Japan, networking and cultural solidarity are beginning to overcome the continuing hostility and coldness of the Japanese people. Moreover, the Brazilian Nikkei-jin increasingly prefer the uncomfortable social climate in Japan to the uncertainty and limited opportunities of Brazil. It can be said tentatively that this is also true of Nikkei-jin from other Latin American nations.

As the twentieth century ended, there was no sign that the vast exodus to Japan by Brazilian Nikkei was abating. Rather the reverse seemed to be true. In a poignant portrayal of the Brazilian "guest worker" phenomenon, the *New York Times* reported the story of Nobetoshi Uski, a Sansei dentist from São Paulo State who was giving up his practice to immigrate to Japan to work in an auto plant. Uski claimed he could earn double his dentist's income, or $2,500 per month, in Japan doing the dirty work his parents educated him in Brazil to avoid. The *Times* reported that immigration to Japan seems to be increasing. Keite Nakamura, fifty-two years of age and the owner of his own construction company, permitted his sons, eighteen and twenty-one, to leave Brazil for Japan rather than continue to work in the company he had built. Nakamura sadly lamented, "'I want my boys to have a taste of what Brazil can't give them, which is opportunity.'"[65]

In this new century, the central question for many of Brazil's young Nikkei-jin remains: Where does their future lie, in Brazil or their "adopted" home in Japan? For Mexico's far smaller Japanese population, this is not a crucial question, since migration to Japan is not an issue. But similar questions of ethnic identity and cultural solidarity remained pressing concerns after 1970 among Mexico's Japanese. We began this study of the Japanese Latin Americans with the story of the first Japanese colonization effort in Chiapas, Mexico, in 1897. Let us now turn to a contemporary analysis of the Nikkei-jin in this same land.

The Revolution's Demise and Mexico's Nikkei

If the 1964 Tokyo Olympic Games were a forecast of the coming Japanese economic "miracle," then the social turmoil surrounding the Mexico City Olympics of 1968 was a harbinger of the deeply rooted economic and political troubles of the next three decades in this land of many unmet promises. Mexico's relatively small Nikkei community of approximately 13,000, now centered in what was to become the most populated metropolitan area in the world by the 1990s, was forced to weather these troubled times.[66] The Japanese witnessed native Mexicans flee north to the United States by the millions, seeking work that their troubled nation was still not able to provide more than half a century after the great Mexican Revolution of 1910. Mexico modernized in the remaining decades of the twentieth century, but like so many other nations in Latin America, this modernization process often left behind the nation's poor. The caretaker of this process of modernization was the one-party political system dominated by Mexico's Partido Revolucionario Institucional, or PRI. This process maintained some degree of legitimacy with the Mexican people until the 1960s because no viable political or social alternatives emerged until then.

The year 1968 was marked by student protests throughout Europe and the United States, and Mexico was no exception. University students protesting the unresponsiveness of the ruling PRI to respond to the nation's continuing desperate poverty while hosting the costly Olympic Games prompted a brutal government response in the so-called Tlatelolco massacre. Hundreds of protesters were gunned down by Mexican security forces in central Mexico City only weeks prior to the start of the highly anticipated Olympic Games. The shock of the brutal suppression of these protests drove many, including Mexico's renowned poet Octavio Paz, to declare the Mexican revolutionary process dead.[67]

The huge federal spending and international borrowing spree of the José López Portillo presidency (1976–82) during those oil-boom years would contribute greatly to Mexico's staggering international debt of $105 billion at the end of the 1980s. Borrowing irresponsibly from overly willing international banks against the security of Mexico's large oil reserves was a mistake many Mexicans could at least understand and perhaps forgive. What disgusted so many more was the unrivaled scale of corruption of the PRI and its machine during these and subsequent years. For instance, Mexico City's police chief and childhood friend of López Portillo, Arturo "El Negro" Durazo, was later charged by the Mexican government with more than fifty murders, heavy participation in the narcotics trade, and extortion of prodigious proportions. On a legal salary of $65 per week, Durazo built a huge estate with a stable of race horses and nineteen classic automobiles, among other luxuries. When the supposedly honest and pragmatic Carlos Salinas Gortari left office in 1994, financial scandals of even greater proportions were unveiled, as were the crimes and drug dealing of the retired president's brother.

The PRI barely survived Mexico's severe economic crises of the 1970 and 1980s, including a major debt crisis, continuing massive corruption, and the Mayan Indian revolt in the state of Chiapas. As the 1990s unfolded and the promise of the North American Free Trade Agreement (NAFTA) remained largely in the future, Mexican migrants continued to expand "greater Mexico," which now encompasses not only the southwestern United States but cities such as Chicago, Detroit, and even, to a lesser degree, smaller cities of the east such as Annapolis, Maryland.[68]

✿ ✿ ✿

Mexico's far more limited economic relations with Japan have been fraught with difficulty as well. Japan's previous economic relations with Mexico were limited. A few Japanese companies, such as Nissan and Panasonic, had operations in Mexico. But Mexico's highly protectionist economic structure and troubled labor relations limited Japanese economic involvement before the petroleum boom of the mid-1970s to early 1980s. With the Arab oil embargo of 1973 raising the cost of all aspects of manufacturing and shipping, Japanese industry led the way in reforming the modes of production. Now that the emphasis was on overseas manufacturing plants and the production of component parts in cheaper labor markets, Mexico appeared more attractive. Most of all, however, Japan was desperately in need of Mexican petroleum. The year 1979 saw Japan sign a ten-year oil agreement with the Mexican petroleum monopoly PEMEX for the delivery of 100,000 barrels of crude per year. By the early 1980s, Japan was the second leading consumer of Mexican petroleum after the United States. Japanese banks were eager to assure the continued flow of oil and thus were involved in the international lending spree that was supposedly secured by the nation's vast petroleum reserves. Seizing the opportunity to force even more Japanese capital into Mexico to quickly construct the infrastructure for future increased oil exports and heavy industry, the López Portillo regime secured $650 million in loans from Japanese private banks, the nation's Export-Import Bank, and Japan's Overseas Economic Cooperation Fund. These funds were to be used to improve harbor and pipeline facilities at Salina Cruz on Mexico's west coast and to build a major steel plant at the newly created industrial city of Lázaro Cárdenas.[69] Mexico's black liquid gold erased the nation's $405 million trade deficit with Japan in 1979, so that by 1984 petroleum was primarily responsible for a five-year trade surplus of $1.4 billion. Even as the oil bubble began to burst with dramatically falling prices in the mid-1980s, Japanese investment still continued to flow into Mexico, in some measure to help secure the stability of the faltering Mexican economy in the eventual hope of maintaining a continued source for oil and of encouraging debt resolution by future Mexican governments.

By 1990, Japanese investment in Mexico was three times larger than in 1980. Some of this investment was being directed to the mushrooming network of *maquiladores,* or small component manufacturing plants, along the United States–Mexico border. In these plants, cheap Mexican labor was producing parts for Japanese companies as they were for many U.S. firms seeking to drastically cut labor costs. Still, by the early 1990s, Japan's economic foothold in Mexico was dominated by only eleven firms, with Nissan and Honda dominating the scene. Nissan made a critical decision to build a full-scale assembly plant in Aguascalientes with an eventual investment of $1.5 billion, even as Japanese banks were faltering, in part under the weight of Mexico's unpaid debt.[70] The 1990s would produce a different picture, however, as Mexico under Salinas Gortari turned away from the illusory hope of economic diversification in the Pacific Basin to the more realistic promise of NAFTA. Then again, Japan's own serious economic difficulties as the decade closed assured a far more conservative approach to relations with its once promising trade partner. As NAFTA slowly geared up in the late 1990s and Japan's own economic difficulties mounted, Mexico's trade relationship with its Asian partner once again became highly unfavorable. The year 1997 saw Mexico experience a $2.26 billion trade deficit. Japan was still exporting nearly $4 billion in products to Mexico while, with oil prices at very low levels, the former Latin American oil giant was selling only $1.6 billion worth of its products to its formerly dependent trading partner.[71]

It is not yet fully clear to what extent the Japanese community, now mainly located in Mexico City and the larger urban centers in the state of Jalisco, such as Guadalajara, was affected by the dramatic swings of the Mexican economy and increased Japanese investment in Mexico in the decades after 1970. What careful studies of the Mexico City Nikkei-jin community suggest, however, is that the Nikkei-jin in the nation's capital were able to insulate themselves quite well by keeping their businesses relatively small. They dealt with inflation by borrowing not from the damaged Mexican banks but from internal funding sources within the community as well as from family and friends. But it is significant to note that some of the key leaders of the Japanese community during the troubled days of relocation during World War II were prospering business owners by the mid-1970s. Teikichi Iwadate moved from Mexico City after the war to San Luis Potosí and opened a highly successful soybean processing plant. Teiji Sekiguchi, who was instrumental as a young man in establishing a temporary home for newly relocated Japanese from Baja California at an abandoned hacienda in Temixco, in the state of Morelos, prospered in the sale of construction equipment. Two other relocated Japanese, Tsutomu Kasuga and Manuel Nakasone, also did very well economically in the construction supply business and tire manufacturing, respectively.[72] One indirect indication that the Japanese Mexican community was not suffering the severe hardships of their counterparts in Peru and Brazil is that the younger generations did not choose to seek better economic opportunities in Japan as guest workers.[73] Perhaps some young Japanese Mexicans sought better opportunities closer to home in the United States, like so many of their native Mexican compatriots. If this was the case, their numbers were certainly not large; relatively recent studies indicate strong community and family relationships among Japanese Mexicans bound the younger generations to their roots in Mexico. We now turn our discussion to a profile of this Japanese Mexican community, its institutions, and the relationships among its members.

Mexico's Nikkei-jin and the Challenge of Cultural Adaptation

As a result of the relocation process after World War II, the majority of Mexico's Nikkei-jin by 1980 resided in the nation's core cities of Mexico City and Guadalajara. Nearly six out of every ten Nikkei-jin in the nation were living generally prosperous lives in these two cities, while the remainder were scattered, as never before, throughout Mexico. The dominance of cotton farming as the central pursuit of the Japanese Mexicans ended with World War II, and urban small business owners and professionals, particularly dentists, replaced the traditional small farmer as the typical Nikkei-jin in Mexico. We will concentrate this discussion on Mexico City's Nikkei-jin, who have been studied most intensively, particularly by Chizuko Watanabe and Takehiro Misawa, in the decades following 1970.

Very much like their counterparts in Peru and Brazil, Mexico's Nikkei-jin have created institutions and social organizations in their relatively new home in Mexico City that have enhanced cultural unity and at the same time set them apart from native Mexicans, to the point, Watanabe concludes, that they are practically "invisible" to the average Mexican. Because of their small numbers, they have not attained nor sought the political prominence of their counterparts in Peru and Brazil. Mexico's intense nationalism, its traditional distrust of foreigners since the revolution, and the prohibition of Mexican citizenship to anyone not the child of two native-born parents also explain their lack of political involvement.

At least through the early 1980s, the influx of Japanese investment and the establishment of such large firms as Nissan in Mexico have not drawn the nation's Nikkei-jin in large numbers to seek opportunities with Japanese businesses. The reasons for this are both cultural and economic. The Japanese business executives and their families in Mexico during their stay in that country have tended to view the Mexican Nikkei-jin in that nation with cultural disdain, as "the children of poor immigrants" who do not know what it means to be Japanese. And for their part, the younger Japanese in Mexico have understandably reacted to this attitude negatively by characterizing the native Japanese as "arrogant, stand-offish, ethnocentric, and intolerant." The children and grandchildren of hardworking and independent Issei, Mexico's Nisei and Sansei belittle these native Japanese as salaried workers who toil like mice. Watanabe quotes one informant at length who ventured the view, "'They may be the elite of Japanese society, but no matter how bright they may be, they are only salaried men. . . . security comes from owning your own business, since you can increase your holdings through your own effort and ingenuity. . . . those Japanese are in court service, while we are lords in our own kingdom.'"[74]

In Mexico City the Japanese population is not localized in one neighborhood but rather is scattered over the huge metropolis. As was discussed in the last chapter, what binds this community together are two institutions very similar to those that perform the same function for the Japanese in Lima, Peru. The Mexican Japanese Association constructed a Japanese-style cultural center in the Las Aguilas neighborhood of Mexico City on land donated by a prominent member of the Japanese community in Mexico.[75] The Japanese school, known as the Liceo Mexicano Japonés, is the other institution that has assumed critical importance in the education of the Mexican Nikkei-jin since its construction in 1977.[76]

What is unusual about the Liceo, and the Japanese immigrant community's intense desire to see their children imbued with their cultural heritage, is that the school was largely initiated by the Nisei generation. Established eight decades after the first Japanese immigrants arrived in Chiapas in 1897, the school's mission testifies to the wishes of the Japanese Mexicans to perpetuate their cultural heritage. Other voluntary associations such as the *kenjin-kai* (prefectural associations), which are common among Japanese immigrant communities everywhere, the Nisei-kai (Nisei Association), and the Bokuto Sogo Fuji-Kai (Association for Mutual Aid), which was formed in 1949 in the same spirit as the similar mutual aid society that helped the relocated Japanese during World War II, also reflect the collective spirit of Mexico's small immigrant community. But it is the Japanese family in Mexico, as elsewhere in Latin America, that is most indicative of traditional Japanese values and ethnic pride.

How did the Japanese immigrant family fare through the early 1990s in Mexico? We are fortunate to have a carefully researched study of this critically important social institution completed by Takehiro Misawa. Like Watanabe's work for the 1980s, Misawa placed particular emphasis upon marriage patterns, Japanese language schools, and university education as socializing forces through the generations. Primarily focused on the nation's capital, Misawa's study was principally confined to the Issei and Nisei. He concluded that the Japanese family in Mexico continued to be an institution of "cultural" security as well as the primary vehicle for the transmission of traditional Japanese social values. Specifically, this Japanese scholar argued that "the Japanese in Mexico conceptualize the family as the primary social unit maintaining issues of hierarchy, power, and authority."[77] According to Misawa, at least through the Issei and Nisei generations it is clear that traditional relationships between the Japanese father and his children were being maintained well into the 1990s. Misawa found that tremendous pressure was still placed by parents on their children to marry other Japanese. Thus, Watanabe's earlier findings on marriage patterns for the 1980s seemed to be holding firm a generation later. Still, endogamy would seem to be getting increasingly difficult, given the small size of the Japanese community in Mexico and the lack of any significant new immigration after World War II. Nonetheless, the ideal of endogamy for Japanese families seemed to be even stronger than it was before the war, when the Japanese in Mexico were widely scattered geographically and clearly less unified as an immigrant culture. For example, Misawa notes that there were still concerted efforts to maintain hierarchical relationships among the Nisei sons, based upon the order of birth.[78]

Continuing the trend of the growing solidarity of the Japanese community after its forced relocation to central Mexico during the World War II, the Japanese placed great emphasis on the education of their children in Japanese language and culture. The importance of the Liceo remained as strong as ever in this regard. As elsewhere in Latin America, particularly in Brazil, Mexico's young Nikkei-jin were encouraged to delay marriage, if necessary, to complete a university education.[79]

It would have been useful if Misawa had carried the study of the Mexican family through at least the Sansei generation. Still, it appears that the Japanese in Mexico maintained a high level of cultural solidarity into the last decade of the twentieth century. This is remarkable, given the scattered and diverse social and economic activities of Mexico's Nikkei-jin more than half a century ago. Enrique Shibayama, the former president of the Mexican Japanese Association, verified the strength and unity of Mexico's Japanese community during the World War II relocation and internment program. A successful businessman who bears a remarkable resemblance to President Alberto Fujimori of Peru, Shibayama expressed pride in the accomplishments of Mexico's Nikkei-jin since the adversity of the World War II years. Shibayama was intimately aware of the history of Mexico's Japanese community and pointed to the recent scholarship of a Mexican Nikkei on the history of the nation's Japanese as evidence of the continuing cultural awareness of the younger generations of well-educated Nikkei-jin. Shibayama was particularly impressed with María Elena Ota Mishima's study *Siete migraciones Japonesas en Mexico* (Seven Japanese Migrations in Mexico).[80]

Although it has remained small, primarily due to immigration restrictions, the Japanese community in Mexico has not only endured since the first immigrants arrived in 1897 but has actually become more unified, with stronger cultural bonds. As the twentieth-first century opened, there was as yet no evidence of a significant exodus of young Mexican Nikkei-jin to Japan as is the case with nearly every other Latin American nation with a substantial Japanese population. Why have Mexico's Japanese remained at home? For now we can only speculate on the reasons, while understanding that a future migration to Japan is always possible, depending on internal conditions in Mexico. It should be considered, when pondering this question, that Mexico's Japanese have always demonstrated the stalwart character of the many thousands of immigrants from Japan who established solid lives from very little.

We must remember that most of the original thirty-four Enomoto Imin agricultural colonists who spearheaded Japanese immigration in Latin America when they arrived in Chiapas, Mexico, in 1897 went on to build reasonably successful lives after they were abandoned by the original sponsor. They raised coffee and other crops, formed their own agricultural cooperative, and raised families with Mexican women. Within a decade of their nearly disastrous arrival, they opened a school and brought in a teacher from Japan. The Japanese pioneers in Chiapas showed very early on what mattered most to the Japanese of Mexico and the rest of Latin America. These qualities were hard work, cooperative effort, a strong commitment to family, strength in the face of adversity, and self-sacrifice for the sake of future generations.

These qualities have enabled the early Japanese of Latin America to build good lives, even while they still clung to the hope of returning to Japan. With the possible exception of Mexico, however, we now know that the Nikkei-jin of Latin America are still drawn to the sojourner tradition. Will Japan be the long-term or even permanent home of many of Latin America's Nikkei-jin as the twenty-first century unfolds? Will Japan continue to receive them in large numbers as was the case in the 1990s? Finally, there is an issue not to be forgotten: Will delayed justice be granted for those Japanese Latin Americans victimized by Washington and their own government during World War II? The Japanese of the United States and Canada have successfully sought to heal those old wounds. Now it is time for the forcefully deported Japanese of Latin America to seek justice as well. Will they ever be able to attain it? These questions will be pondered in the final section of this study.

LOOKING TO THE NEW CENTURY: CONFRONTING NEW TRENDS AND HEALING OLD WOUNDS

For the Peruvian Nikkei, as for most Peruvians, their own survival is the main concern at present. Each year more and more
Nikkei, like their grandparents, see immigration as the hope for
a better future. With the new century, they are perhaps starting a
new immigrant story.
—Amelia Morimoto, a scholar of the Japanese of Peru

The Japanese have now resided in Latin America for little more than a century. The initial thrust of immigration from Japan to Latin America, which
peaked in the 1930s, largely ended by the early 1970s. On the other hand,
Japan's expanding economy, even with the recession of the 1990s, coupled
with the decline of career opportunities in Latin America, brought about a
growing and continuing exodus of the Latin American Nikkei-jin to their
cultural homeland, Japan. As the new century began, estimates place as many
as one in every five ethnic Japanese from Latin America as residents of Japan. Will this vast exodus of the Latin American Nikkei-jin continue? What
will Japan offer them in the decades to come? How are the Japanese adapting to the consumer-dominated society of the last few decades, after the post–
World War II reconstruction years? Will the Latin American nations in which
the remaining Nikkei-jin live today be able to provide opportunities that will
stem this massive outward tide of some of their most productive and talented citizens? These are all complex questions that, of course, can only be
pondered here, because only time will provide the answers. But these issues
are now beginning to be addressed by historians seeking to find the meaning of recent trends in the immigration patterns of the Japanese Latin Americans as the third century of the Nikkei-jin in Latin American dawns.

Finally, in the new millennium, there are significant attempts to resolve past wrongs of the most violent century in human history. The Japanese government is, at last, attempting to deal with the issue of the Korean "comfort women" forced into prostitution for Japanese soldiers during World War II. In the first months of 2000, the German government approved reparations exceeding $4 billion to be paid to the surviving tens of thousands of "slave" laborers from Eastern European countries forced to work for the Nazi cause during the war. Now the U.S. government, only after a long delay following an official apology and reparations to Japanese Americans for their internment, is attempting to resolve the issue of the forced deportation and internment of the Japanese Latin Americans during World War II. This issue will be examined in more detail as this study concludes.

Japanese Society and the Question of Identity

Unquestionably, the key issue to consider when looking to future social trends in Japanese society is its very low birthrate and aging population. In Japan's population of 126.6 million (2000 estimate), the largest five-year cohort is in the forty-five to forty-nine age bracket. This is considerably older than the oldest age group in most developing nations and even advanced industrial nations. From another perspective, more than one in five, or 26 million Japanese, are sixty years of age or older. The number of Japanese over the age of sixty (28 million) nearly equals the number of those under twenty years of age. Put another way, in terms of average life span (80.7 years), Japan is one of the oldest societies in the world. And this trend will continue because Japan maintains one of the lowest birthrates in the world. As discussed in the previous chapter, this means that Japan will continue to require substantial amounts of foreign labor because fewer Japanese of productive working age will be available.[1] These demographic realities have other significant implications. Japan's military defense, never in question after World War II because of the strong but controversial treaty arrangements with the United States, is somewhat more in doubt with the demise of the Soviet Union and the increasing unpredictability of the Chinese government as it flexes its new-found economic and military muscle. At present, North Korea poses an even more immediate threat. Long a tiny military entity, the Japanese Defense Force, if ever required, will be increasingly hard-pressed to expand its manpower in such an aging society. Will Nikkei-jin from Latin America who have chosen to reside in Japan be called upon for service in defense of their new homeland? This is not as speculative a question as it may seem. Let us not forget the American Nisei who fought so bravely for the nation that interned them and their families during World War II.

Complicating the role of the Nikkei-jin in the national life of Japan is the way Japan defines citizenship. In contrast to the United States and other nations, Japan does not necessarily award citizenship for being born there. The law requires that one be the child of a Japanese citizen, which until 1984 usually meant the father. After 1984, the law was liberalized to include the mother and other very specific circumstances. What this means is the vast majority of the Nikkei-jin now living in Japan will not, under present legal standards, see their children who are born in Japan become Japanese citizens. Those children will remain legally registered citizens of the Latin American nations of their parents. Alberto Fujimori was indeed fortunate that his father, born in Japan, registered his son's birth legally in Japan. This will not be an option for most Nikkei-jin in the foreseeable future.[2]

There is also the question of whether Japan can continue to recruit sufficient numbers of Japanese Latin Americans to fulfill its labor needs. As we have seen, Japan, as much as possible, would like to confine its foreign workers to Nikkei-jin from Latin America. Still, in 2000 there were more immigrants, mostly seeking labor but others fleeing war and famine, than at any time in history. The vast majority of these 120 million immigrants worldwide were in search of more remunerative labor than they could find in their home country. Asian nations, with the exception of Japan, paid some of the lowest wages anywhere in the world. Even Hong Kong in the late 1990s was paying its average workers less than $5 per hour, while the Philippines and India paid less than $2 per hour. Chinese workers toiled for the same wages from 1980 to 1995, about $.25 per hour. Japan, on the other hand, ranked fourth in the world in labor costs per hour, behind Germany, Switzerland, and Norway. In the fifteen years following 1980, workers saw their wages increase nearly five times, to an average $23.66 per hour. The Nikkei-jin were not paid at this rate but still earned more than other workers in Asia. This is why the Latin American Nikkei-jin have arrived in droves during these years.[3] As the Japanese recession continues, the question of labor demands and the "pull" of such high wages may force Japan to make substantial concessions and changes in its immigration policy. This is certainly true in the United States today, where the federal government made significant concessions, before September 11, 2001, on the question of illegal immigrants from Latin America in the face of a substantial labor shortage in low-paying service and menial jobs.

As has been clear throughout the history of immigration, large influxes of immigrants often bring significant social tensions. The Japanese found it difficult to adjust to immigrants from Korea, the Philippines, South Asia, Iran, and even, to a lesser extent, the Nikkei-jin from Latin America. In this age of great labor mobility, will the Japanese allow a racially diverse labor pool to provide the foundation for a prosperous economy? Japanese society, so accustomed to fulfilling most of its consumer needs, may have little choice. Recent statistics bear this out. In 1999 the number of foreign residents in Japan reached an all-time record of 1.55 million. While this number represents only 1.23 percent of Japan's total population, it may signal the opening of a largely "closed" society that had characterized this nation for the vast majority of its long history. Even foreign students are getting jobs with Japanese companies to support their educational expenses. This was nearly unprecedented until the 1990s.[4] Importantly for our study, Japanese Brazilians ranked third behind the immigrants from Korea and China in the number of foreign residents. With Tokyo's efforts to limit the number of workers from the Philippines, a decline in the number of workers from Korea, and the potential growth of the Chinese economy, it is likely that the Japanese Brazilians and other Nikkei from Latin America will occupy an even more prominent role in the "foreign" community in Japan in the future, if economic conditions in Latin America do not substantially improve. This will be especially true if Japanese society continues to change in the face of the continuing fast pace of modernization and the dramatic demographic trends that we have just discussed.

Taichi Sakaiya, a prominent contemporary commentator on Japanese society, sees the onset of a possible serious social malaise in the nation, largely because of the erosion of a central feature of the country's work ethic. An important notion to consider is the concept of *shogyo soku shugyo* (all work is the pursuit of knowledge), an outlook that can be traced to the Ishida school of philosophy dating to the late seventeenth century. In other words, working with a complete commitment in any field of endeavor is a means of "training one's character."[5] If Japan returns entirely to the "economically comfortable" society of the pre-1990s recession—and there are clear signs that this is happening as this is being written—then will the concept of *shogyo soku shugyo* wane as it appeared to be doing in the final two decades of the last millennium? Then what will be the central feature of the character of Japan's young people in particular? One issue seems to be very clear: young native Japanese will continue to travel overseas, as they have done by the millions since the 1980s, but they will certainly not be immigrants in mass seeking a better life elsewhere.

In contrast to the first seven decades of Japan's history following the Meiji Restoration in 1868, in the post–World War II era the nation has experienced no warfare, no draft, and relatively limited social strife, except for the security treaty protests against the United States in the late 1960s. There are certainly some radical elements of discontent, as evidenced by the gas attacks in the Tokyo subways in the late 1990s. Still, the Nikkei-jin are beginning to feel more adjusted to living in Japan. One Peruvian Nisei, for example, told Funada-Classen in 1993 that he felt secure and satisfied with life in Japan. A key example would be the Japanese health care industry. Once off-limits to nonnative Japanese, it is beginning to drop its barriers to foreign health care workers, and Japanese Brazilian health care workers are being allowed to work in geriatric care, in particular. One of these workers, for example, was Helena Morishita, a Japanese Brazilian who had been a resident of Japan for more than five years and was likely to continue at her job even though she was in her mid-sixties.[6] She was typical of many Japanese Brazilian workers in the health care industry who are women sixty years of age and older. Clearly, these are not the young male immigrants and adventure seekers who were the first Japanese sojourners to Latin America. Instead, many of the guest workers in Japan are women close to retirement age who can find no long-term security in their native land. The sojourner tradition of the Japanese of Latin America will thus be further reinforced.

As should be quite clear, most Japanese immigrants to Latin America have survived and prospered by the philosophy of *shogyo soku shugyo*. Now many of them are able to repeat this process in their ancestral homeland, because Japan is a nation where nearly everyone considers themselves middle class and most eschew the hard factory work that built their nation into the industrial giant that it is today. Moreover, the Japanese recession of the 1990s forced some companies to abandon the practice of "life-long" employment and to lay off workers who had been with their firms for decades. This has meant psychological trauma for older male salaried workers whose careers comprised a great deal of their self-identity. Some of these men even referred to themselves as "garbage" because their self-esteem had dropped so low without the meaningful employment that was so much a part of their identity. In Japan, just like in many other advanced industrial nations, it is the immigrant more than the native worker who is now driven by an often unrelenting work ethic. But there is evidence that as the Nikkei-jin from Latin America stay for longer periods in Japan and become more financially secure, they are increasingly inclined to seek more leisure time and enjoy the benefits of their diligence. Will they continue to seek to maintain their better lifestyles as long-term immigrant residents of Japan? This will be determined in part by the future immigration policies of the Japanese government, which are changing rapidly. It will also be dependent on conditions in Latin

America. Let us now turn to take a brief look at Peru and Brazil, the largest receiver nations of Japanese immigrants, and their prospects for the future.

Peru's Nikkei: Prospects for the Future

Now that this study is nearly at an end, it is fitting to take a last look at Peru, the nation where the Japanese first settled permanently in Latin America and the only country outside of Japan to have had a Japanese as chief executive. As the new century began, Peru under the leadership of its Nisei president, Alberto Fujimori, made great strides from the dark days of violence and economic turmoil of the early 1990s. Social spending, financed by privatization of previously state-owned industries and loans from international lending agencies such as the Inter-American Development Bank, reduced poverty, particularly at what the government terms the "extreme level." As one might expect, this was largely Lima's poor. As the new century began, 43 percent of all Peruvian families were receiving some form of food assistance.[7] In addition there was Peru's effort to promote its tourism and its economy abroad. If judged on these two measures alone, Peru under Fujimori would appear to be a success story.

One vehicle for promoting Peru's progress under Fujimori was *Peru el Dorado*, one of the most professionally produced and attractive promotional magazines issued in Latin America, which has been presenting beautiful and positive images of the nation since 1995. Produced by PromPerú, a government agency, its editor proclaimed in its last issue, published in May 2000, that the magazine was printed as a "celebration of a diverse, magic . . . nation."[8] Yet interestingly, before closing its operations and leaving the promotion of Peru to the private sector, *Peru el Dorado* did not take the opportunity to even mention its Japanese population in an article entitled "A Thousand Peoples, One Nation." Private news magazines such as the highly regarded *Caretas* have consistently carried current stories about the Japanese in Peru. Thus the omission by *Peru el Dorado* is curious. But considering that so many Japanese in Peru have immigrated from their homeland, their decision to leave probably did not play well with the highly positive image of the magazine. Something else to consider is the sensitive political climate surrounding the timing of the magazine's release by PromPerú. President Fujimori's successful and controversial campaign to extend his rule well beyond a decade caused widespread political unrest. More the *caudillo* than the democrat, Fujimori's obvious efforts to manipulate the elections further added to his growing reputation as an "elected" authoritarian, or what many knowledgeable political observers are calling an "authoritarian populist."

Peruvians referred to the Nisei president's political style as "Fujimorismo," and its success gave rise to other copycat political styles, such as that practiced by former military man and president of Venezuela, Hugo Chavez.[9] Like so many political leaders before him in Peru, Fujimori refused to take the opportunity to build a pluralistic political culture and firm legal, military, and elective institutions that could help ensure the nation's future stability. Despite all his significant accomplishments since taking office in 1990, the Nisei president was forced to resign in disgrace shortly after he took office for his third term. Fleeing to exile in Japan after the exposure of massive corruption and human rights abuses during his decade in office, Fujimori's rapid downfall does not bode well for Peru's Japanese community.

Still, the high point of Fujimori's economic accomplishments was the 12 percent economic growth rate that was sustained in 1994. This figure was the highest in the world, but the impressive statistic must be couched in terms of the declining growth rates of the late 1980s and early 1990s. The growth rate declined to 1 percent by 1998. Fujimori also spent vast sums on building a new Peruvian infrastructure. The visitor to Peru in the earlier 1990s would hardly recognize Lima's internal highway system six years later. Nevertheless, Peru's continued privatization policies, despite some efforts by the government to earmark special funding for "alleviating chronic poverty," have not significantly improved the condition of the poor.

A good deal of the progress of the early 1990s was undone as the nation faced the dual problems of the financial crisis in Japan, which influenced funding for Peru's economic recovery, and the crippling floods of El Niño that devastated much of the nation's coastal infrastructure in 1998 and 1999. Significant components of this infrastructure, including roads, bridges, and hospitals, had been built or rebuilt during the recovery phase of Peru's economy during the early Fujimori years. These public works programs were a key element of Fujimori's early popularity. Now Peru must again rebuild, and the future of Peru's economy is very uncertain. This has undoubtedly encouraged many Nikkei-jin in Peru to seek either a short-term or possibly permanent solution to this uncertainty in Japan. Still popular with many in Peru for what he accomplished, Fujimori and his tactics hurt the image of the Japanese community in Peru and led some to "grow tired" of a president they once admired. Now Peru's Nikkei-jin must adjust to the political and economic instabilities that have developed in the aftermath of Fujimori's fall from power.

Ironically, when I interviewed leaders of the Japanese community in 1990 regarding Fujimori's candidacy, these individuals expressed reluctance to support a candidate of their own people lest he fail or bring violent reaction against his government, which would spill over again into the Nikkei community in Peru. More than a decade later, this was not a remote possibility by any means. Once again, the Nikkei-jin of Peru confront the possibility of a potentially hostile citizenry who identify them with the broken image of a fallen president.

Peru's more than 50,000 ethnic Japanese, most of whom reside in Lima's Nikkei community, may be as politically insecure as they were before Fujimori first became president. This may be an important consideration in the decision of many Japanese Peruvians in Japan whether to return to their cultural homeland in the twenty-first century. Yet there is a strong core of strength and stability that still remains in Peru. The nation's Nikkei-jin, it will be recalled, primarily made their living as shopkeepers in Lima after fleeing the sugar plantations. In Peru's teeming capital of 6.2 million residents, there still exist the small shops run by Japanese Peruvians, as they have since the early 1900s. Many of these shops have moved to Lima's middle-class suburbs, such as Miraflores, where conditions are more secure and business is more regular. In 1997 I visited one of these small grocery stores in Miraflores run by a Nisei woman who appeared to be in her late fifties. She employed four non-Japanese helpers and ran the establishment with confidence and efficiency. This is but one small example of continuity and stability in the Nikkei community of Peru, which is in such a state of transition because of the exodus of many members of the younger generations to Japan.

Continuing Unity: The Panamerican Nikkei Movement

Also indicative of the continuing strength and pride of Japanese ethnic identity in Peru and elsewhere in Latin America is the aforementioned example of the Eighth Convention of Panamerican Nikkei, held in Lima in 1995. This convention was attended by representatives of the Japanese of nearly every nation in the Americas. As previously mentioned, meetings have been held every two years since 1981 throughout the Americas. During the plenary session of the 1995 convention in Lima, the Japanese ambassador to Peru, Morhisha Aoki, made remarks that seemed timely, if not very delicately phrased. The ambassador urged the delegates to "leave the traditional Japanese culture to the third and fourth generations which are the Nikkei generations in the world. I would like to ask all the participants' cooperation, so that the third and fourth generations can move from being simple Nikkei and become Nikkei of international transcendence."[10] Clearly implied in the ambassador's remarks was recognition of the emergence of the Sansei and

Yonsei generations in leadership roles in Peru and elsewhere in Latin America. But reflecting the long-held belief of the Japanese that the Nikkei-jin of Latin America were "simple" people, his call for their rise to "international transcendence" was both an appeal to them for closer cultural ties with their homeland and perhaps further encouragement to come to Japan as guest workers. Thus as early as 1995, in the midst of this event of cultural unity among the Japanese Latin Americans, the main issues facing the Nikkei-jin of Peru and most of Latin America were already being foretold.

In contrast, another key speaker, Les Hamasaki, a prominent businessman from Los Angeles, struck a far different and more militant tone. Hamasaki declared to the conference, "Today the Pacific River led by the Japanese is flowing into the economic mainstream of the Americas creating crosscurrents and turbulence. We must decide to take the high profile road or the low road to help rebuild our respective countries. I believe we must take the high road."[11] Toward this end, Hamasaki proposed the creation of a "Pacific Century Entrepreneurial Institute" to develop local business connections with Japanese-based companies. This has never happened, to any substantial degree, in the more than a century of Japanese presence in Latin America, and Hamasaki pointed out that the educated talent was there. He noted that 30 percent of the high technology workers in California's "Silicon Valley" were Asians. Much the way the Republic of Ireland has built its modern economy on a well-educated workforce in a newly transformed high-tech business sector, Hamasaki envisioned the Latin American Nikkei-jin following the example of high-tech business leaders in their own nations. A closely related recommendation was the establishment of a "Nikkei Cultural Center Network in the Americas," to enhance cooperation among the Nikkei-jin communities, but most of all, to ensure the retention of the Japanese cultural heritage in the hemisphere.[12] These proposals by a successful Japanese American businessman manifested the growing links between all the Japanese in the Americas and the ethnic pride of these descendants of immigrants. At the same time, Hamasaki was not in touch with the economic realities of the Latin American nations he was primarily addressing.

Over the next five years, no Latin American nation would even begin to emulate the Irish high-tech model, and many Latin American Nikkei-jin lost faith that it would ever occur in their native lands. Thus the flight of many Peruvian Nikkei-jin to Japan continued. This prompted Japanese Peruvian scholars, such as the late Mary Fukumoto, both to make a strong plea for a renewal of cultural pride in being Japanese and at the same time to implore the younger Peruvian Nikkei-jin to embrace that heritage in their native land of Peru. Fukumoto recognized clearly what Japanese Peruvian immigrants soon discovered upon their arrival in Japan. They always knew that they were not Peruvians in Peru but were Japanese. In Japan, they were not Japanese either but an ethnic group set apart. These Nikkei-jin were called *gajin,* a term they often used to refer to the native peoples of Latin America. This was less true for what Fukumoto refers to as the *"nikkei puros,"* or those with an exclusively Japanese heritage. Yet even these Nikkei would always be between two worlds. And in that sense, Fukumoto saw their future being more in Peru, where they have established a greater cultural identity, than in Japan.[13] This is the primary dilemma that Peru's Japanese and those of all of Latin America confront. Can they maintain a Nikkei identity that has undergone significant challenges from intermarriage, generational transitions, and migration to Japan?

The Ongoing Redress Movement by World War II Internees

One important element of restoring a sense of completeness and healing for those Japanese Latin Americans arrested, exiled, and interned during World War II is the ongoing campaign for redress by Japanese Americans that mirrors the one that was successfully pursued during the Reagan administration. The survivors of this group and their descendants are now residing in Latin America and Japan as well as in the United States. They are seeking to right a wrong now more than a half-century old. For many it will help resolve some of the intense feelings still remaining from the most traumatic experience of their lives. Their numbers are much smaller now, but one of the bonds that continues to hold them together is the internment experience and their strong feelings that justice must come for them as it did for the Japanese American internees.

A significant number of the surviving internees of the Crystal City camp in Texas have been meeting on a regular basis since July 1984, when the first discussion of redress from the U.S. government was undertaken. Crystal City was the last camp to close when it ceased operations in February 1948, more than two and one-half years after the end of the war. It will be remembered that many of its former internees, left without a home or gainful employment, were brought to Seabrook, New Jersey, where they labored under very difficult conditions with other former Japanese American internees in the vegetable packing plant there. Subsequent Crystal City reunions have kindled a sense of friendship and purpose among the former internees that has not substantially lessened since their years in the camps. Remembrance of the internment experience and coordination of the demand for a satisfactory redress response from the U.S. government have been headed on both coasts by the Japanese-Peruvian Oral History Project in San Francisco, primarily directed by Grace Shimizu. In the east, the Seabrook Educational and Cultural Center has taken the lead in educating the public about Japanese internment in both the United States and Latin America through impressive displays, videos, and a highly useful library of videotaped interviews of the former internees and their families. Both of the projects have kept very much alive a sense of unity among the former internees. This unity is especially true in Seabrook, where internees from both the United States and Latin America who remained in the area have developed long-term friendships. It was through the Seabrook Center's help that I was able to interview Ginzo Murono and his wife Hisako, an aging couple who had been deported from Peru during World War II and decided to raise their children in the Seabrook Community, where they became highly educated and successful. One of their sons, for example, became a star athlete in the community, later went on to become a prominent international banker, and now lives in San Francisco. The aging Muronos, who once owned a small shop in Lima, were living in a comfortable ranch house in southern New Jersey, near Seabrook. Above all else, they expressed great pride in the accomplishments of their children and grandchildren, whose pictures were everywhere in the household.[14] The Muronos reflect the attitude of many Latin American Issei after the war who chose to live their lives for their children as the possibility of their own future in their Japanese homeland faded away. Clearly, the Japanese attitude of *kodomo no tame ni* (for the sake of the children) is shared by many aging Issei, such as the Muronos and another group of former internees I interviewed on Chicago's North Side, in a retirement apartment complex largely inhabited by people of Japanese descent. Many of these Chicago-based Japanese still have vivid memories of the internment experience and have the same feelings as the Muronos about their children and grandchildren. It is now up to their children to try to resolve the issue of equity and justice that is the goal of the redress movement.

What must be remembered is that the last internment camp housing the Japanese Latin Americans did not close until long after the war with Japan was concluded. Moreover, the U.S. Congress did not suspend until 1953 the deportation orders against the remaining Japanese from Latin America who were residing in the United States. The former Issei internees were thus growing older and were far less inclined to challenge a government that had deported them from their adopted lands and sent most of them to Japan during and immediately after the war. Thus the younger Latin American Nisei in the United States have inherited the responsibility of carrying on the campaign for redress. That campaign began as early as 1974, when the Japanese American Citizens League proposed a legislative redress plan in Seattle that would have compensated all who were interned during World War II, including the Japanese from Latin America and the Aleuts from Alaska. Over the course of the next fifteen years, this ambitious plan, amid much discussion and some anguish by leaders of the Japanese community in the United States, was modified to place nearly exclusive emphasis on redress for the Issei and Nisei from the West Coast of the United States. When the Civil Liberties Act of 1988 granted an official apology and $20,000 in compensation to the estimated 60,000 Japanese interned in the United States who were still living, the legislation did not specifically exclude the Japanese Latin Americans.

Nevertheless, within one year the Department of Justice adopted rules to deny compensation to the internees from Latin America on the grounds that they were "illegal aliens." However, the Alaskan Aleuts were to be compensated for personal property destroyed during the military occupation of the Aleutian Islands during the war. The apology contained in the 1988 act was strong, claiming that the action taken by the U.S. government represented a "failure of political leadership" and was taken because of "racial prejudice" and "wartime hysteria."[15] These words certainly characterized the deportation of the Japanese Latin Americans yet were not applied in their special case. In characterizing them as illegal aliens, the Department of Justice continued to maintain the wrong that was first perpetrated on them when their passports were confiscated by INS officials during the deportation and internment process almost half a century before. In a most curious case, mentioned before, one of these former internees, Arturo Shibayama, was even drafted into the army during the Korean War but upon returning to civilian status was still denied citizenship as an illegal alien![16]

Frustrated by a lack of response by the U.S. government, the leaders of the campaign for redress brought the issue to the United Nations Commission for Human Rights in 1994. The "Campaign for Justice," a coalition of the American Civil Liberties Union of Southern California, the Japanese-Peruvian Oral History Project, and the National Coalition for Redress Reparations, was formed in 1996 and began placing consistent political pressure on Congress and the president. Finally, in June 1998 the Clinton administration offered the Japanese internees from Latin America an apology and a $5,000 reparation sum under what was called the "Mochizuke settlement." But this offer was flawed because the government claimed it did not have "sufficient funds" to compensate all the surviving internees. The leaders of the campaign for redress were seeking an apology and compensation for all the former internees, not just for those residing in the United States but in Japan and Latin America as well. Further complicating the initial offer of redress was the unwillingness of many Japanese Latin Americans to accept an offer that was not commensurate with that granted to the Japanese Americans a decade earlier.

Responding to continuing pressure from the Japanese Latin American community in the United States to resolve this issue, the Clinton administration, with the urging of Congress, particularly the delegations from California and Hawaii, appropriated $4.3 million for compensation but inexplicably gave the potential recipients only six weeks to apply. By May 1999, only 730 of the more than 2,000 Japanese Latin Americans had applied. The reparation sum remained the same at $5,000, and many potential recipients were either never informed of the new awards or applied too late. Eventually, the U.S. House of Representatives extended the deadline for applications for compensation to September 1999, but still many eligible Japanese Latin Americans from the great triangle of deportation—Latin America, the United States, and Japan—were not able to meet these terms. Caught up in the web of violence, suspicion, and racial animosity during World War II, Japanese Latin Americans were now caught up in partisan politics, forgotten governmental responsibilities, and a growing legal maze surrounding reparations. There is even now a pending lawsuit against the Japanese government by the remaining few Japanese who survived the largely failed experiment to settle Japanese immigrants on marginal farmland in the Dominican Republic. The suit charges that the land was never suitable for farming and the immigrants were knowingly misled. As we have seen, the reparations issue could apply to many thousands of Japanese immigrants to Latin America over the past century. One significant example should illustrate the complexity of the issue. California State Assemblyman Mike Honda of San José has advocated legislation for a nonbinding resolution urging Japan to make a "clear and unambiguous apology" for war misdeeds and offer reparations to its victims. Honda, who was interned during World War II by the U.S. government, argues that Asia's war victims should receive the same $20,000 in compensation and an apology as did the Japanese American internees.[17] His efforts have caused tensions in the Japanese community in southern California and added to the flurry of campaigns, resolutions, and lawsuits seeking some form of moral absolution to rectify the terrible wrongs committed during the past century. The campaign continues as of this writing, and a new bill, HR 779, is before Congress, introduced by Representative Xavier Becerra of California to resolve this issue.

Arturo Shibayama, Teresa Masatani, Grace Shimizu, and Libby Maoki-Yamamoto are articulate veterans of the internment experience and should have their voices heard expressing their feelings about this matter as we bring our discussion of this lingering question to a close. Shibayama admits that he feels "'some bitterness'" about what he has gone through but says that the "'United States is the best country to live in.'" Nevertheless, he insists that "'people make mistakes, big mistakes.'" Shibayama has refused the $5,000 compensation offer because he regarded it as a "'slap in the face.'" He explained, "'The offer said nothing about how we were brought here . . . and when I tell people what happened, they don't believe it. . . . we did that to you [they say], yes you did,'" Shibayama assures them.[18]

Teresa (Terri) Masatani is an open and vibrant woman who is busy with the Seabrook Center and a very active family life, now as a grandmother. In 1943, when she was only three years old and living an "idyllic life in Lima," her father, Koshiro Mukoyama, a graduate of law school and a successful businessman in Lima, was deported along with the rest of the family to Crystal City's internment camp. Her father worked in the camp for 10 cents per hour, and the family's four children spent their formative years at Crystal City. After the internment experience, Mukoyama struggled to support his children in difficult circumstances in Seabrook, New Jersey, and subsequently in Venezuela. Both Masatani's parents passed away in 1961, and now Teresa feels that "my only regret in life is that my parents did not hear President Clinton's apology to the Japanese Peruvians. I know it would have meant more [to them] than the reparation." Yet she is still content in her adopted home. Married to a Japanese American, she emphatically states, "I am an American, not by birth but by choice."[19]

Grace Shimizu has been instrumental in having the stories of the former internees told through the Japanese-Peruvian Oral History Project, which she directs. Invaluable for historians, these records and tapes have been essential in providing much of the documentation needed for the redress movement's campaign. Her parents, who were deported from Peru during the war, rebounded to lead successful lives before settling in El Cerrito, California, for their retirement. Shimizu, perhaps more than any other individual, has persevered during the redress campaign, through many years of frustration and disappointment. She clearly represents the strength of the Japanese Peruvian Nisei in seeking not only redress but closure to an episode that badly needs resolution.

Libby Maoki-Yamamoto, a reserved, elegant woman now living in San Francisco, was also interned in Crystal City. Her father, before being deported from Peru, managed a store on a hacienda in Chiclayo. Her account is particularly poignant because the family was separated after the war and her older sister was deported to Japan, where she later died of malnutrition.

Bitterness or anger were not apparent as Maoki-Yamamoto accounted this tragic episode. Rather, she explained that her parents approached their internment experience with the fundamental Japanese attitude, *shikata ganai* (it can't be helped). Maoki-Yamamoto seemed to share some of this thinking: "This was war, they had to do what they had to do." A highly aware individual, she clearly saw the Japanese Peruvian experience as only a part of the enormous tragedy of World War II, involving millions upon millions of individual and collective brutal acts and injustices. Still, she understood that what happened to her family and other internees should not be forgotten or left unresolved. Maoki-Yamamoto is proud of her heritage: "I am a person of three cultures, Japanese, Spanish [Peruvian], and English [United States]."[20] Unquestionably, this forced sojourner's inner strength had allowed her to embrace all three of these very diverse cultures.

Crossings of Cultures: Japan and Latin America

For most of the last century, the diverse cultures of Japan and Latin America were drawn together as the Asian nation's immigrants settled and built new lives in the distant lands of Mexico, the Caribbean, and South America. The cultural thread binding these cultures, however, was thin at best. Sons and daughters of the wealthiest Japanese were sent for schooling in Japan, but they were relatively few in number, and this practice largely ended with World War II. The return rate for the Issei was also one of the lowest among all the immigrant groups that settled in Latin America. Japanese trade was never as substantial as many Latin American and Japanese leaders hoped it would become. The influence of Japan upon the literature, music, drama, and other forms of artistic expression in Latin American culture never remotely approached that of Europe or the United States on the region. This is understandable when one considers that Japan was still largely an insular society until well after World War II. Moreover, Japan's immigrants and their children remained largely within Japanese cultural traditions. Now these strict limitations on cultural interchange are no longer the case. The cultural impact of hundreds of thousands of Japanese Latin Americans who are now residing in Japan are not being ignored. Their language, food, music, and forms of expression are slowly beginning to have some influence on Japanese culture. One of Japan's foremost novelists, Murakami Haruki, has adopted the primarily Latin American literary form of "magical realism." Much like the countercultural statements of Latin America's "magical realists," such as Gabriel García Marquez, Haruki's work has sought to achieve a "highly individualized, personal sense of identity" in his characters.[21] For a Latin American example, one can look to the Japanese Brazilian abstract artist Tomie Ohtake, who gained fame for her work drawing upon the themes of her two cultures to achieve, in the words of one Brazilian critic, "pure vibration."[22]

These are just some examples of where these diverse cultures have meshed. This trend can be expected to continue when it is considered that more people of Japanese descent live in Latin America than in any other region of the world beyond the home islands. Nevertheless, the questions of the future of the many Latin American Nikkei, their choice of a permanent homeland, and thus their cultural identity still remain open. Much will depend upon what Latin America can offer them in the future. What is still certain in the midst of all these questions is that after more than a century, the Japanese in Latin America continue to strive for better lives for themselves and their children through individual hard work and collective support. This they are doing as both citizens of their adopted Latin American lands and sojourners like their forebears.

AFTERWORD

What can be learned from the Japanese experience in Latin America? It would seem that for many Japanese immigrants who settled there, the decision to do so was made by default. Judging by the patterns of early immigration to the West, the Japanese clearly preferred to settle in North America and particularly the United States, with its rapidly growing industrial base and commensurate economic opportunities. Despite efforts on the part of a number of Latin American governments to establish the diplomatic framework to facilitate trade and immigration with Japan, the first Issei did not arrive in Latin America for more than a generation after their counterparts in the United States and Canada. Only with the highly restrictive immigration measures adopted by the United States and Canada beginning in 1908 was Japanese immigration redirected to Latin America.

Notably, Brazil would attract far more immigrants than the rest of Latin America combined, because in some ways it mirrored the opportunities available to the Issei pioneers in the United States before the turn of the century. Brazil was a large country offering immigrants the opportunity to own land and open businesses as their financial status improved. There, even more than in the United States, the Japanese were able to establish isolated colonies on remote tracts of land, where they were free to re-create, as much as possible, the cultural milieu they left behind in Japan. Early Japanese immigrants were rarely fully aware of the difficulties they would confront when they arrived in their new homes in Latin America. This situation improved as immigrant communities were established and accurate information became available. Immigration to the "lesser" receiver nations in Latin America often came about because of already established family networks, clearly available economic opportunities, or poor estimations about the degree of hardship and anti-Japanese sentiment they would confront upon their arrival. Outside of

Brazil, the Japanese immigrant populations in Latin America grew slowly. Relatively limited immigration and low birthrates explain this. Uncertainty about their futures expressed in the hope, if not the firm belief, that they would someday return with their families to Japan kept many Issei from making a full social and psychological commitment to their adopted Latin American homelands. More so than other immigrant groups in Latin America, the Japanese before World War II strove to maintain both ethnic and cultural conformity to their Japanese heritage. A central component of this was a staunch loyalty to their Japanese homeland. Sometimes this loyalty became intense, as in the case of Shindo Renmei in Brazil.

But more often this loyalty to the homeland was reflected in a lack of involvement in the social and political mainstream of their adopted Latin American nations. For example, the number of first-generation Japanese immigrants who became citizens of those nations was very small. Fewer still ran for public office or entered the armed forces of those nations. A review of the graduation lists for Peru's Naval Academy from the turn of the twentieth century until the 1980s reveals a mere handful of graduates of Japanese heritage. Part of the reason for this is that Japanese Peruvians were actually barred from admission before the 1960s. Indeed, the Japanese were a people that were a part of, but fundamentally apart from, the Latin American nations where they made their new homes.

How much psychological and social integration has occurred in the decades since World War II certainly varies from one Latin American nation to another. As their censuses indicate, the Japanese in Brazil and Peru have been able to maintain a level of ethnic and cultural autonomy that is very likely unmatched in the rest of Latin America. This has been beneficial for the Nikkei-jin in providing the secure social environment that many craved. A case in point is Seiichi Higashide, the Japanese Peruvian who was deported to the United States during World War II, after creating a successful life for himself and his family. Higashide recalled upon his arrival in Peru as a young man that "I was deeply impressed with the strong bond that linked the immigrants—they interacted with a closeness and intimacy that was even stronger than between brothers and sisters in Japan."[1] Such unity fostered close cooperation and self-help programs for most Japanese communities in Latin America and was one of the keys to their general success. But as demonstrated throughout this study, cultural "isolation" proved to have significant costs for the immigrants.

Contributing to the generally consistent and sometimes violent anti-Japanese sentiment that plagued the immigrants almost from the beginning was their late arrival in Latin America. Only by the 1930s were there significant numbers of Japanese in Brazil and Peru. Bolivia and Paraguay witnessed their first arrivals in the 1930s, but it was not until after 1950 that the greatest numbers of Japanese arrived. This meant that, unlike earlier immigrants groups, particularly the Italians, the Japanese settled in Latin America when the modernization process was in full swing. Thus economic tensions made more volatile by emerging class conflict often proved to be key components of the resentment the Japanese confronted. Middle- and working-class parties in Peru like the APRA, for example, tried to use their anti-Japanese programs as a fulcrum for attaining political power during the World War II years. Similarly, nationalist movements, like that of Brazilian president Getulio Vargas's Estado Nôvo, found it politically expedient to close Japanese schools and disband the Japanese associations in the late 1930s to facilitate their own program of cultural conformity, while exploiting the proclaimed threat of Japanese militarism. The same was true of the Prado regime in Peru during World War II. The ironic dilemma of the Japanese Latin Americans was that the very insularity and strong community bonding that helped them build successful lives in their new lands also fed the intense anti-Japanese feeling that prevailed for most of their first six decades in Latin America. As noted earlier, as late as 1990, Japanese in Peru expressed reluctance to support Alberto Fujimori for president for fear that his presidency might expose the community to confrontation, criticism, and violence. His sudden fall from power in disgrace produced the very reaction that was initially feared by the Japanese Peruvian community.

A hallmark of the strength of the Japanese immigrants' character is that they have prevailed against anti-Japanese feelings for much of their presence in Latin America and have overcome it. This is one of the central lessons of this study. It also seems clear that the Japanese immigrants in Latin America, more often than not, sought to be masters of their own economic destiny. The first Japanese took jobs as miners and agricultural laborers in Mexico, but many soon took up independent cotton farming in Baja California Norte. Many of the Japanese workers who were contracted to cut sugarcane on the coastal haciendas in Peru quickly fled to Lima, where they became small shopkeepers. Those families brought to Brazil to pick coffee beans often sought from the very beginning of their tenure as laborers to acquire their own land. Significantly, nearly all of the Japanese immigrant settlement in Brazil after 1930 was on independent colonies far from the main population centers along the São Paulo railroad. When post–World War II settlement was carried out in Paraguay and Bolivia, it was also in self-contained colonies deep in the interior of these nations. In these enclaves the Japanese farmed their own land, produced the crops of their choice, and remained true to the cultural concept of *ikigai,* or giving life a meaning. For the Japanese immigrants, independent work of their own choice was supremely important, as it was to workers in their homeland. It was an integral part of their personal identity, and as immigrants they often found greater opportunities to be their own masters than if they had remained in Japan. During the first decades of their presence in Latin America, Japanese tried to create immigrant worlds very much under their own control. Whether in colonies where only the Japanese language was spoken or in urban neighborhoods that contained their schools, community organizations, hospitals, and recreational facilities, they largely succeeded. But in the course of the last few decades, these carefully created Japanese "nations within nations" were being steadily eroded by the exodus of the younger generations to Japan.

One only need look at the Japanese Brazilians to see how significant this continuing exodus is. Brazil's Japanese community of 1.3 million must now cope with the fact that a quarter of a million members of their community were residing in Japan at the end of 2001. Many of the Japanese Brazilians were preparing for long-term or permanent residence in Japan. Forty-one private Brazilian schools served the immigrant children. Significantly, the sum of money sent home by the immigrants to Brazil fell more than 60 percent from 1997 to 2001, suggesting that the immigrants were intending to stay and build lives in Japan.[2] There are indications that the Japanese Brazilians would like to slowly integrate themselves into Japanese society. It may be a difficult process. Merry White, in her study of Japanese workers and travelers overseas, noted that even native Japanese who travel abroad for extended periods face a difficult transition to Japanese society upon their return. White argues, "The person who has lived and worked or studied outside Japan may indeed have acquired some 'dysfunctional' foreign ways or forgotten Japanese habits and knowledge crucial to his or her integration into a group that demands a very precise and exacting socialization."[3] If such difficult social standards are applied to native Japanese sojourners, then the Japanese of Brazil and other Latin American nations will undoubtedly confront significant obstacles. Jeffrey Lesser makes the important distinction between *assimilation* and *acculturation* with regard to the Japanese and other ethnic groups in Brazil. He notes that the modification, but not the extinction, of one culture as it came in contact with another was common. This held true for those immigrant groups like the Japanese who remained in closed community settings.[4] Thus the Japanese adopted some aspects of Brazilian culture but retained fundamental qualities of their Japanese ethnicity. Clearly, the possibility of full transition to Japanese cultural standards awaits the first generation of Japanese Brazilians born in Japan. Then the circle of migration begun in 1908 by the first Japanese to Brazil will have been completed, and one of the most remarkable sagas in the history of modern immigration will have been realized.

Looking at the Japanese experience in Latin America from the broadest perspective, it must be said that the Japanese and their descendants faced constant challenges from within and without their own communities. Despite their strong collective spirit, there were significant divisions with the immigrant community. Okinawans frequently dealt with discrimination from mainland Japanese, especially during the early days of the Japanese presence. There was less but still significant tension between the prefectural associations that were often formed by the immigrants as a way of ensuring even closer bonds after their arrival in Latin America. Most of all, intense nationalism, especially during the pre–World War II years, often divided the older immigrants, who mostly resigned themselves to permanent settlement in Latin America, from the younger, primarily male, newer arrivals, who often were ready to return to Japan to aid the military campaign or to immigrate to newly captured lands in Asia or the Pacific. This intense division flared into violence in Brazil and, to a lesser extent, Peru after the war. Now the primary issue that divides the Japanese in Latin America is fundamental. Namely, who is prepared to stay in their adopted lands, and who wants to leave for perhaps a permanent new life in Japan? With the historically low repatriation rates from Japanese Latin American communities, such a question has never been as important as it is today.

What I hope readers will remember most from this study is the individual experiences of the Japanese immigrants and their families. Unquestionably, the immigrants benefited from the collective assistance of the Japanese communities in which they settled. But fundamentally, the immigrant pioneers succeeded because of their own personal strength, hard work, and loyalty to their families. The Mexican Issei pioneer Antonio Kisaburo Yamani, for example, labored fifty-four years, growing and selling chrysanthemums during one of the most tumultuous periods in that nation's history, to build a future for his wife and family. In the end, he only desired to return to Japan to settle in the village where he was born. Readers will also recall the experience of the deeply impoverished Okinawan immigrant Kicho Sukagawa, who initially migrated to Brazil as a contracted coffee laborer but soon fled to Argentina because of the wretched conditions on the coffee *fazendas*. Sukagawa, penniless when he began his life in Argentina as a blacksmith's assistant, eventually built a highly profitable truck gardening enterprise on the outskirts of Buenos Aires, where he raised his family in a fine six-room house. Then, too, there are the stories of the courage of those immigrants whose lives were disrupted by World War II. The courage of the Higashide, Mukoyama, and Shibayama families in facing hostility, deportation, internment, and forced relocation is compelling. What should be remembered about them and the vast majority of the Japanese who came to call Latin America their home is that they did not return to Japan dressed in "golden brocade," as the earliest Issei naively dreamed. Instead they lived quiet lives of dignity, while confronting hardship and hostility. At the same time, they contributed to the well-being of their communities. This, of course, does not distinguish them from other immigrant groups, who often displayed the same qualities. But the Japanese made their lives and built their communities with so little fanfare that few outside the Latin American nations were even aware of their presence until the election of Alberto Fujimori in 1990. My hope is that this book will make these "unknown immigrants" more familiar and better understood.

GLOSSARY

Dekasegi: temporary migration: "go and gain"; originally means "seasonal worker"

Gosei: fifth-generation immigrant

Ie: household

Imin: immigration or immigrant

Issei: first-generation immigrant

Kaigai: overseas

Kachigumi: group that believes Japan was victorious in World War II

Makegumi: group that believes Japan was defeated in World War II

Naichi-jin: mainland, or home-island, Japanese

Nikkei: ethnic category of the people of Japanese origin in the country where they settled. In this book, it is used mainly to refer to Japanese immigrants who decided to stay in Latin America after World War II.

Nikkei-jin: a variation of *Nikkei,* applied in this book to the second-generation Japanese (Nisei) and succeeding generations who reside in Latin America

Nisei: second-generation immigrant

Sansei: third-generation immigrant

Yobiyose: calling immigrants from the homeland; one who is called

Yonsei: fourth-generation immigrant

CHRONOLOGY

1868   Meiji government in Japan begins the modernization process and soon encourages emigration.

1873   Japan enacts a military draft that is widely resented by the rural population, who refer to it as the "blood tax." Young rural males begin to emigrate from Japan to avoid the draft.

1870s   Japanese contract workers travel to Hawaii in large numbers to work in the sugarcane fields. Many use Hawaii as a base to transmigrate to Canada and the United States.

1882   The United States passes the Chinese Exclusion Act, which establishes the precedent for the later restriction of Japanese immigration in the early twentieth century.

1880s   A series of commercial treaties between Japan and Latin American nations creates diplomatic channels that will later facilitate Japanese immigration to the region.

1897   The first attempt to create a Japanese immigrant colony in Latin America is made in Chiapas, Mexico. The effort fails because of poor planning, but some of the original colonists remain in Mexico.

1899   Peru becomes the first Latin American nation with significant Japanese settlement when a group of 790 male laborers arrives to work in the coastal sugar plantations.

1900–1907   Japanese contract labor to northern Mexico and Peru expands significantly. Many Japanese laborers in Mexico flee illegally to the United States in search of better wages and working conditions. Rural laborers in Peru take flight from the plantations to seek work in Lima for the same reason.

1907–8   The Gentlemen's Agreement negotiated between Japan and the United States substantially limits Japanese immigration to the United States. A similar measure in Canada brings the same results. Japanese immigration to North America from Hawaii is also terminated. These measures begin to shift Japanese immigration away from North America to Latin America.

1908   Almost 800 Japanese immigrants, mostly in family groups, arrive in Brazil destined for the coffee fields of São Paulo State. Brazil quickly becomes the largest receiver nation of Japanese immigrants in the Western Hemisphere.

1910–20   The violence of the Mexican Revolution prevents any further Japanese immigration to this nation for a decade. Some Japanese Mexicans serve in the armies of the revolution when they become caught up in the nationwide struggle.

1910–18   Rice shortages in Japan cause widespread rural unrest, convincing many young Japanese farmers to leave their homeland for better prospects in Latin America.

1920s   Japanese contract immigration ebbs and is primarily replaced in Brazil by joint subsidized colonization between the two nations. "Free immigration" becomes common elsewhere in Latin America.

1923   The great Kanto earthquake in Japan causes massive destruction and loss of life, further stimulating immigration, mainly to Brazil.

1931   The Japanese army's occupation of Manchuria begins to redirect the nation's immigrants away from Latin America to the Asian mainland.

1934–39   The nationalist government of Getulio Vargas in Brazil permits the enactment of restrictive immigration quotas for the Japanese over the objections of the nation's coffee growers. After Vargas establishes an authoritarian regime in 1937, most Japanese schools are closed and the activities of the Japanese in their remote colonies are restricted.

1936   The small isolated colony of La Colmena is established by Japanese immigrants southeast of Asunción, Paraguay. It is the first agricultural colony established by the Japanese outside of Brazil.

1940   Highly destructive anti-Japanese riots occur in Lima, Peru. Fear of continued harassment prompts large numbers of Japanese families to return to Japan.

1941   The Japanese attack on Pearl Harbor prompts most Latin American governments to restrict Japanese activities. The government of Panama initiates these restrictions even before 7 December.

1942–44   More than 2,000 Japanese are deported from Latin America, the majority of them from Peru, in a cooperative effort between the governments of the United States and the Latin American nations. The deportees are interned in camps in the southwestern United States, where some remain until 1947. Most are deported again to war-devastated Japan beginning in 1944.

1945   With the end of World War II, the Issei generation in Latin America begin relegating their leadership of the immigrant communities to their children.

1944–47   Shindo Renmei, an intensely pro-Japan secret society in Brazil, terrorizes Japanese who openly accept Japan's wartime defeat. It is broken up by the Brazilian police only after the Japanese community is badly traumatized.

1952–56   Large numbers of immigrants from Okinawa begin arriving in Bolivia and Paraguay. Because of the difficult conditions on the war-torn island, the U.S. administrators of the island promote immigration to Latin America as a way of relieving pressure on the Okinawan population.

1952–65   Brazil once again becomes the leading receiver nation for Japanese immigrants in Latin America but in numbers that are far below those of the pre–World War II years.

1970s   The economic recovery in Japan effectively ends almost eight decades of immigration to Latin America.

1981   The First Convention of Panamerican Nikkei is held in Mexico City. Conferences will be held throughout the Americas every two years thereafter.

1988–2002 The Japanese government revises its immigration laws to give priority to the "ethnic Japanese" of Latin America. A vast exodus of Japanese Latin Americans to Japan in search of better economic opportunities, primarily in blue-collar jobs, begins.

1990–2000 Alberto Fujimori, a Peruvian Nisei, is the first Japanese Latin American to be elected to high political office. He accomplishes much during his decade in office, but his tenure is marked by scandal and corruption.

NOTES

Preface

1. Jeffrey Lesser, *Negotiating National Identity: Immigrants, Minorities, and the Struggle for Ethnicity in Brazil* (Durham, N.C.: Duke University Press, 1999), 141.

2. Panamerican Nikkei Association USA East, "XI COPANI Final Report" (New York, 25–28 July 2001). Online. <http://www.pnausaeast.org>.

3. Seiichi Higashide, *Adios to Tears: The Memoirs of a Japanese-Peruvian Internee in U.S. Concentration Camps* (Seattle: University of Washington Press, 2000), 44–88.

Chapter 1: Before Latin America

1. *Christian Science Monitor,* 15 Dec. 2000.

2. Walter Nugent, *Crossings: The Great Transatlantic Migrations, 1870–1914* (Bloomington: Indiana University Press, 1992); John Bodnar, *The Transplanted: A History of Immigrants in Urban America* (Bloomington: Indiana University Press, 1985).

3. Nugent, *Crossings,* 35.

4. Bodnar, *Transplanted,* 55–56.

5. Thomas C. Smith, *The Agrarian Origins of Modern Japan* (Stanford, Calif.: Stanford University Press, 1965), 204–9.

6. Ibid., 212.

7. Eiko Ikegami, *The Taming of the Samurai: Honorific Individualism and the Making of Modern Japan* (Cambridge, Mass.: Harvard University Press, 1995), 366.

8. Ibid.

9. Qtd. in ibid., 101.

10. Ibid., 102–3.

11. Christopher Reichl, "Stages in the Historical Process of Ethnicity: The Japanese in Brazil, 1908–1988," *Ethno-History* 42:1 (Winter 1995): 31–62.

12. Mikisio Hane, *Modern Japan: A Historical Survey* (Boulder, Colo.: Westview Press, 1986), 94.

13. James Stanlaw, "Japanese Emigration: From Meiji to Modern Times" (paper delivered at American Anthropological Association annual meeting, New Orleans, 21 Nov. 2002), 8.

14. Yukichi Fukuzawa, *The Autobiography of Yukichi Fukuzawa,* trans. Eichi Kiyooka (New York: Columbia University Press, 1960), ix.

15. Qtd. in Tetsuji Kada, *Meiji shoki shakai keizai shiso shi,* qtd. in Thomas C. Smith, *Political Change and Industrial Development in Japan: Government Enterprise, 1868–1880* (Stanford, Calif.: Stanford University Press, 1955), 84.

16. The standard book on Japanese immigration to Hawaii is Hilary Conroy, *The Japanese Frontier in Hawaii, 1868–1898* (Berkeley: University of California Press, 1953). Two recent and valuable studies are Eileen H. Tamura, *Americanization, Acculturation, and Ethnic Identity: The Nisei Generation in Hawaii* (Urbana: University of Illinois Press, 1994); and Gary Okihiro, *Cane Fires: The Anti-Japanese Movement in Hawaii, 1865–1945* (Philadelphia: Temple University Press, 1991).

17. Tamura, *Americanization, Acculturation, and Ethnic Identity,* 2.

18. Ibid.

19. Roger Daniels, *Asian America: Chinese and Japanese in the United States since 1850* (Seattle: University of Washington Press, 1988), 100–101.

20. Lauren Kessler, *Stubborn Twig: Three Generations in the Life of a Japanese American Family* (New York: Random House, 1993).

21. Two recent studies on the topic of the Japanese in the Americas that should be consulted are *The Encyclopedia of Japanese Descendents in the Americas: An Illustrated History of the Nikkei,* ed. Akemi Kikumura-Yano (Walnut Creek, Calif.: Altimira Press, 2002); and Lane Hirabayashi, ed., *New World/New Lives: Globalization and People of Japanese Descent in the Americas and from Latin America to Japan* (Stanford: Stanford University Press, 2002).

Chapter 2: The Latin American Pioneers

1. Gaimusho Ryoji Iiju-bu, *Waga kokumin no kaigai hatten: Iiju hyakunen no ayumi* (Tokyo: Ministry of Foreign Affairs, 1971), 137–47. Japanese immigration figures were based on the number of passports issued. Prospective emigrants not leaving Japan within six months after the passport was issued were compelled to return their document. After emigrating, the Dekasegi (those who migrate temporarily) were obliged to re-register with the local Japanese consulate every ten years. This system was generally accurate in recording those leaving and returning to Japan, but since re-registration in foreign countries, particularly those without a Japanese consulate, was not always regular, the determination of actual immigrant populations at any given time was not always precise. What also must be taken into account is the infrequency and relative lack of specificity of the censuses conducted in the Latin American nations. These caveats must be taken into account when im-

migration figures are cited in this study. For Japanese regulations on passport issuances, see Naikaku Kiroku-Kyoko, *Genko horei shuran* (Tokyo: Yuhikuku, 1907), 43-47. A very useful source for recent statistical data on immigration to the Southern Cone nations is Hernan Asdrubal Silva et al., eds., *Inmigración y estadisticas en el cono sur de America* (Mexico City: Organization of American States, 1990). Not all Japanese immigrants traveled on passports, and thus the number who went to Latin America is likely higher than official estimates.

2. Hane, *Modern Japan*, 161.

3. *Encomienda* and *repartimiento* were the foundation of Spain's early colonial economic system. Debt peonage assumed a variety of forms throughout Latin America but must be understood as a labor system that bound the peasantry to the hacienda by means of accumulated and inherited debt. Debt peonage continued to exist well into the 1960s in many areas of Latin America. The primary labor system in Brazil and the sugar producing islands of the Caribbean was, of course, African slavery.

4. Anita Bradley, *Trans-Pacific Relations of Latin America: An Introductory Essay and Bibliography* (New York: Institute of Pacific Relations, 1942), 68.

5. Ibid., 1-23; Zelia Nuttal, "The Earliest Historical Relations between Mexico and Japan," *American Archaeology and Ethnology* 4:1 (1906-7): 1-48.

6. Nuttal, "Earliest Historical Relations," 11, 43-46; Chizuko Watanabe, "The Japanese Immigrant Community in Mexico: Its History and Present" (M.A. thesis, California State University at Los Angeles, 1983), 2.

7. C. Harvey Gardiner, *The Japanese and Peru, 1873-1973* (Albuquerque: University of New Mexico Press, 1973), 1-22. Gardiner's study is the standard work in English on Japanese-Peruvian relations.

8. Toraji Irie, "History of Japanese Migration to Peru" (translation of *Hojin kaigai hattenshi*, pt. 1, by William Himel), *Hispanic American Historical Review* 31:1 (Feb. 1951): 438.

9. Iyo Iimura Kunimoto, "Japan and Mexico, 1888-1917" (Ph.D. diss., University of Texas at Austin, 1975), 24.

10. Ibid., 33.

11. Ibid., 39-46.

12. *El Tiempo*, 4 July 1889, p. 2, qtd. in Kunimoto, "Japan and Mexico," 52.

13. Alan T. Moriyama, *Imingaisha: Japanese Emigration Companies and Hawaii, 1894-1908* (Honolulu: University of Hawaii Press, 1985), 50-51.

14. Ibid., 50; James L. Tigner, "The Okinawans in Latin America" (Ph.D. diss., Stanford University, 1956), 7-8. Tigner's comprehensive study of both homeland Japanese and Okinawan immigration in Latin America through the early 1950s remains the best survey in English.

15. Moriyama, *Imingaisha*, 37.

16. Michael C. Meyer and William L. Sherman, *The Course of Mexican History*, 5th ed. (New York: Oxford University Press, 1995), 418-20.

17. Moises Gonzalez Navarro, *La Colonización en Mexico* (Mexico City: N.p., 1960), 37-44.

18. Ibid., 64–65.

19. Evelyn Hu-DeHart, "Coolies, Shopkeepers, and Pioneers: The Chinese of Mexico and Peru, 1849–1930," *Amerasia* 15:2 (1989): 91–99; Evelyn Hu-DeHart, "Racism and Anti-Chinese Persecution in Northern Mexico," *Amerasia* 9:2 (1982): 1–28; Charles C. Cumberland, "The Sonora Chinese and the Mexican Revolution," *Hispanic American Historical Review* 40 (1960): 191–211.

20. Hu-DeHart, "Coolies, Shopkeepers, and Pioneers," 98.

21. Ibid., 91–95.

22. Martin S. Stabb, "Indigenism and Racism in Mexican Thought, 1857–1911," *Journal of Inter-American Studies* 1 (1959): 418–20.

23. William D. Raat, "Ideas and Society in Don Porfirio's Mexico," *Americas* 30:1 (July 1973): 53.

24. María Elena Ota Mishima, *Siete migraciones Japonesas en Mexico, 1890–1978* (Mexico City: El Colegio de Mexico, 1982), 30.

25. Kunimoto, "Japan and Mexico," 56.

26. Ibid., 58.

27. Ibid., 56–58.

28. The most detailed study of nineteenth-century Peru is Jorge Basadre's *Historia de la Republica del Perú, 1822–1933*, 7th ed., 8 vols. (Lima: Editorial Universitaria, 1983).

29. Peter Blanchard, *Slavery and Abolition in Early Republican Peru* (Wilmington, Del.: Scholarly Resources Press, 1992), 151–88.

30. See the letter from José Gregorio Paz-Soldan to the Prefect of Lima, 11 Jan. 1860, claiming that the Agricultural Society voted unanimously to request the government's assistance in bringing African colonists to Peru. The letter is reprinted in Ministerio de Relaciones Exteriores del Perú, *Inmigración en la Republica* (Lima: Imprenta del Estado, 1892), 18.

31. Ministerio de Relaciones Exteriores del Perú, *Inmigración,* 139–40; Michael J. Gonzalez, "Chinese Plantation Workers and Social Conflict in Peru in the Late Nineteenth Century," *Journal of Latin American Studies* 21:3 (Oct. 1989): 389–90.

32. The standard study of the Chinese contract labor system in Peru is Watt Stewart, *Chinese Bondage in Peru: A History of the Chinese Coolie in Peru, 1849–1974* (Westport, Conn.: Greenwood Press, 1951). Michael J. Gonzalez offers a valuable study of the Peruvian Chinese in the aftermath of the coolie trade in *Plantation Agriculture and Social Control in Northern Peru, 1875–1933* (Austin: University of Texas Press, 1985).

33. Qtd. in W. Stewart, *Chinese Bondage,* 96.

34. Ibid.; Hu-DeHart, "Collies, Shopkeepers, and Pioneers," 91–116.

35. Gonzalez, "Chinese Plantation Workers," 390–424.

36. See Nils Jacobsen, *Mirages of Transition: The Peruvian Altiplano, 1780–1930* (Berkeley: University of California Press, 1993).

37. Janet Worral, "Growth and Assimilation of the Italian Colony in Peru, 1860–1914," *Estratto dalla Rivista Studi Emigrazione* 41 (Mar. 1976): 42–46. See also

Worral, "Italian Immigrants in the Peruvian Economy," *Italian Americana* 2:1 (Autumn 1975): 50–63.

38. Basadre, *Historia de la Republica del Perú*, 7:179.

39. Rosemary Thorp and Geoffrey Bertram, *Peru, 1890–1977: Growth and Policy in an Open Economy* (New York: Columbia University Press, 1978), 54.

40. Katia M. de Queiros Mattoso, *To Be a Slave in Brazil, 1550–1888* (New Brunswick, N.J.: Rutgers University Press, 1986), 12. The historical literature on African slavery in Brazil is vast and beyond the scope of this study to review. The select bibliography in the De Queiros Mattoso study offers an excellent overview of the best scholarship.

41. George Reid Andrews, *Blacks and Whites in São Paulo Brazil, 1888–1988* (Madison: University of Wisconsin Press, 1991), 32.

42. Robert W. Slenes, "The Demography and Economics of Brazilian Slavery, 1850–1888" (Ph.D. diss., Stanford University, 1976), 36, 262, cited in Nugent, *Crossings,* 191.

43. Andrews, *Blacks and Whites in São Paulo,* 37.

44. Ibid., 48.

45. For the concept of "whitening" in the context of Brazilian racial thought, see Thomas Skidmore, *Black into White: Race and Nationality in Brazilian Thought,* 2d ed. (Durham, N.C.: Duke University Press, 1993).

46. Nugent, *Crossings,* 122–24.

47. Ibid., 124.

48. Emilio Willems, "Immigrants and Their Assimilation in Brazil," in *World Migrations in Modern Times,* ed. Franklin D. Scott (Englewood Cliffs, N.J.: Prentice-Hall, 1968), 66; Willems, "Recreacão e assimilacão: Entre imigrantes alemaes e japoneses e seus descendentes," *Sociologia* (São Paulo) 3:4 (Oct. 1941): 302–10.

49. Robert F. Foerster, *The Italian Immigration of Our Times* (New York: Arno Press, 1969), 290.

50. Ibid., 287; Nugent, *Crossings,* 124.

51. Thomas Holloway, *Immigrants on the Land: Coffee and Society in São Paulo, 1886–1934* (Chapel Hill: University of North Carolina Press, 1980), 163.

52. Ibid., 179. For a breakdown of Italian repatriation to individual provinces in Italy, see Silva et al., *Inmigración y estadisticas en el cono sur de America,* 158.

53. Foerster, *Italian Immigration of Our Times,* 299.

54. Warren Dean, *Rio Claro: A Brazilian Plantation System, 1820–1920* (Stanford, Calif.: Stanford University Press, 1976), 158.

55. *Waga kokumin no kaigai hatten,* 141.

56. Watanabe, "Japanese Immigrant Community," 15.

57. Kunimoto, "Japan and Mexico," 59.

58. Ota Mishima, *Siete migraciones,* 42–46.

59. Watanabe, "Japanese Immigrant Community," 18–19; Kunimoto, "Japan and Mexico," 61.

60. Marvin Bernstein, *The Mexican Mining Industry, 1890–1950* (Albany: State University of New York Press, 1965), 27.

61. Ibid., 77.

62. Ibid., 35–51.

63. Watanabe, "Japanese Immigrant Community," 21.

64. Ibid.

65. Ota Mishima, *Siete migraciones*, 53–55; Watanabe, "Japanese Immigrant Community," 22.

66. Watanabe, "Japanese Immigrant Community," 22–23.

67. Ibid., 24–25.

68. Ibid., 24.

69. Ota Mishima, *Siete migraciones*, 58–59.

70. The Okinawan Club of America, *History of the Okinawans in North America*, trans. Ben Kobashigawa (Los Angeles: UCLA Asian American Studies Center, 1988), 22.

71. Kunimoto, "Japan and Mexico," 58–59.

72. Meyer and Sherman, *Course of Mexican History*, 461.

73. Qtd. in Watanabe, "Japanese Immigrant Community," 26–27.

74. Qtd. in ibid., 27–28.

75. For the distribution of Japanese immigrants by state in Mexico, see Ota Mishima, *Siete migraciones*, table 30, pts. 1 and 2.

76. Kunimoto, "Japan and Mexico," 73.

77. Ibid., 75.

78. Qtd. in Ota Mishima, *Siete migraciones*, 57–58.

79. Thorp and Bertram, *Peru*, 41.

80. Ibid., 48.

81. Irie, "History of Japanese Migration to Peru," pt. 1, 443.

82. Amelia Morimoto, *Fuerza de trabajo inmigrante Japonesa y su desarrollo en el Peru* (Lima: Universidad Nacional de Agraria, 1979), 6–11; Gardiner, *Japanese and Peru*, 24.

83. Elena Kishimoto de Inamine, *Tradiciones y costumbres de los inmigrantes Japoneses en el Peru* (Lima: Centro de Investigaciones Histórico Sociales, 1979), 15.

84. Irie, "History of Japanese Migration to Peru," pt. 1, 443; Gardiner, *Japanese and Peru*, 25.

85. Malaria had taken a great toll on earlier Chinese immigrant laborers in Peru.

86. Qtd. in Irie, "History of Japanese Migration to Peru," pt. 1, 447.

87. Ibid., 451.

88. Qtd. in Toraji Irie, "History of Japanese Migration to Peru" (translation of *Hojin kaigai hattenshi*, pt. 2, by William Himel), *Hispanic American Historical Review* 31:3 (Aug. 1951), 648–49.

89. Irie, "History of Japanese Migration to Peru," pt. 1, 447.

90. Anti-Japanese sentiment in Peru would peak with the 1940 Lima riots that drove many Japanese immigrants to abandon Peru for their Japanese homeland.

91. Qtd. in Irie, "History of Japanese Migration to Peru," pt. 2, 650.

92. Ibid.

93. Kishimoto de Inamine, *Tradiciones y costumbres,* 18; Gardiner, *Japanese and Peru,* 27.

94. Tigner, "Okinawans in Latin America," 590.

95. Irie, "History of Japanese Migration to Peru," pt. 2, 653.

96. Ibid.

97. Ibid., 655–58.

98. Qtd. in ibid., 656.

99. James Tigner, "The Ryukyuans in Peru, 1906–1952," *Americas* 35:1 (July 1978): 20–44.

100. Morimoto, *Fuerza de trabajo,* 29.

101. Tigner, "Okinawans in Latin America," 591.

102. Guillermo Thorndike, ed. *Los imperios del sol: Una historia de los Japoneses en el Perú* (Lima: Editorial Brasa, 1996), 38–39.

103. Higashide, *Adios to Tears,* 39, 47.

104. José Matos Mar, "Las haciendas del valle Chancay," in *La hacienda en el Peru,* ed. Henri Favre et al. (Lima: Instituto de Estudios Peruanos, 1967), 348–53; Thorndike, *Los imperios del sol,* 36.

105. Qtd. in Toraji Irie, *Hojin kaigai hattenshi,* vol. 2 (Tokyo: Hara Shobo, 1981), 11.

106. Holloway, *Immigrants on the Land,* 177.

107. Irie, *Hojin kaigai hattenshi,* 2:23–27.

108. Nabuya Tsuchida, "The Japanese in Brazil, 1908–1941" (Ph.D. diss., University of California at Los Angeles, 1978), 119–23.

109. Ibid., 110.

110. Nugent, *Crossings,* 122–36.

111. Tsuchida, "Japanese in Brazil," 123–24.

112. Katsuo Uchiyama, *Kaigai Nikkeijin* (Tokyo: Kaigai Nikkeijin Kyokai, 1980), 20.

113. Tigner, "Okinawans in Latin America," 66.

114. Ibid.

115. Tsuchida, "Japanese in Brazil," 145, 152.

116. Ibid., 153.

117. Qtd. in ibid., 146n.36.

118. Qtd. in ibid., 151n.46.

119. Irie, "History of Japanese Migration to Peru," pt. 1, 449.

120. Iyo Kunimoto, *Boribia no Nihonjinmura* (Tokyo: Chuo University, 1989), 58–63.

121. Qtd. in Valerie Fifer, "Bolivian Rubber Boom," *Journal of Latin American Studies* 2:2 (Nov. 1970): 113–46.

122. Tigner, "Okinawans in Latin America," 473.

123. Ibid., 472–73.

124. Ariel Takeda, "Japanese Immigrants and Nikkei Chileans," in *Encyclopedia of Japanese Descendents in the Americas*, ed. Kikumura-Yano, 182.

125. Tigner, "Okinawans in Latin America," 643; *Waga kokumin no kaigai hatten*, 139.

126. Brian Loveman, *Chile: The Legacy of Hispanic Capitalism*, 2d ed. (New York: Oxford University Press, 1988), 150.

127. Carl Solberg, *Immigration and Nationalism: Argentina and Chile, 1890–1914* (Austin: University of Texas Press, 1970), 46.

128. Qtd. in ibid., 68.

129. *El Pueblo Obrero*, 13 June 1907, qtd. in Solberg, *Immigration and Nationalism*, 70.

Chapter 3: Issei and Nisei in Mexico, Peru, and Brazil, 1908–37

1. The figure of 960 yen is drawn from the autobiography of Seiichi Higashide, *Adios to Tears*. The original immigrants to Peru who signed four-year contracts calculated that by earning a monthly salary of 25 yen and spending 5 yen per month for food costs, they could save 960 yen over four years. The return passage to Japan cost 100 yen. Thus the hopeful immigrants dreamed of returning with the princely sum of 860 yen to begin new, prosperous lives in Japan. See Higashide, *Adios to Tears*, 54.

2. *Waga kokumin no kaigai hatten*, 138–39.

3. Brazil-Japan Cultural Association, *Brazil nihon imin 80 nenshi* (São Paulo: Toppan Press, 1991), 103–4.

4. These comparative statistics are listed in Teiiti Suzuki, *The Japanese Immigrant in Brazil: Narrative Part* (Tokyo: University of Tokyo Press, 1969), 14.

5. During peak periods of immigration from these countries, the average annual migration per 100,000 inhabitants of the nation always exceeded 1,000. See Nugent, *Crossings*, 43.

6. Kakuzo Okakura, *The Awakening of Japan* (New York: Appleton, 1905), 189–92.

7. E. H. Norman, *Japan's Emergence as a Modern State* (New York: Institute of Pacific Relations, 1940), 8, qtd. in Hane, *Modern Japan*, 186.

8. Hane, *Modern Japan*, 97.

9. Ibid., 212.

10. Stephen S. Large, "The Patterns of *Taisho* Democracy," in *Japan Examined: Perspectives on Modern Japanese History*, ed. Harry Wray and Hilary Conroy (Honolulu: University of Hawaii Press, 1983), 177.

11. Naikaku Tokeikyoku, *Nihon teikoku tokei nenkan, 1932* (Tokyo: Naikaku Tokeikyoku, 1932), 238.

12. Ibid., 234.

13. Harry D. Smith II, "The Non-Liberal Roots of *Taisho* Democracy," in *Japan Examined*, ed. Wray and Conroy, 191.

14. Junichiro Kisaka, "The 1930s: A Logical Outcome of *Meiji* Policy," in *Japan Examined,* ed. Wray and Conroy, 242–43.

15. Richard J. Smethurst, *A Social Basis for Prewar Japanese Militarism: The Army and the Rural Community* (Berkeley: University of California Press, 1974). Smethurst's study was based on research primarily in the Aichi and Yamanashi prefectures.

16. Qtd. in Elsie F. Wiel, "Training Japanese for Emigration: South America Is on Trial as a Field for Colonization," *Asia* 17 (Nov. 1917): 722.

17. Qtd. in Watanabe, "Japanese Immigrant Community," 209.

18. Ibid., 209–10.

19. Higashide, *Adios to Tears,* 35.

20. Ibid., 38.

21. Ibid., 39.

22. Accounts of two hundred successful Japanese immigrants in Mexico were published in Yasutaro Taki, *Sekai muhi no shin-nichi koku—dihoko mekishiko* (Mexico City: Chuo Koron-sha, 1927). These minibiographies were often reprinted in popular magazines in Japan.

23. Qtd. in Wiel, "Training Japanese for Emigration," 721.

24. Qtd. in ibid., 724.

25. Qtd. in ibid., 727.

26. For information on emigration from Wakayama Prefecture, see *Wakayama-ken Iminishi* (E/000/234/W) in the Japan International Cooperation Agency Library, Tokyo.

27. Watanabe, "Japanese Immigrant Community," 32–33.

28. Ibid., 36.

29. Ibid., 37–38.

30. Ibid., 39–40, 57.

31. Ota Mishima, *Siete migraciones,* 28.

32. Watanabe, "Japanese Immigrant Community," 52–53.

33. Ibid., 53.

34. Ota Mishima, *Siete migraciones,* 87.

35. Yasutaro Taki, *Mekishiko kokujo taikan* (Mexico City: Mehiki Shimpo, 1968), 75, qtd. in Watanabe, "Japanese Immigrant Community," 56.

36. Watanabe, "Japanese Immigrant Community," 56.

37. Masafumi Ayoma survey, qtd. in Taki, *Mekishiko kokujo taikan,* 72.

38. Watanabe, "Japanese Immigrant Community," 46; Ota Mishima, *Siete migraciones,* appendix 3.

39. William Beezley and Colin MacLachlan, *El Gran Pueblo: A History of Greater Mexico, 1911 to the Present,* vol. 2 (Englewood Cliffs, N.J.: Prentice-Hall, 1994), 300.

40. Tigner, "Okinawans in Latin America," 609.

41. *Waga kokumin no kaigai hatten,* 138.

42. Thorp and Bertram, *Peru,* 134.

43. Matos Mar, "Las Haciendas del valle Chancay," 350–52.

44. Ibid., 352.

45. Ibid., 348, 350.

46. Qtd. in Gardiner, *Japanese and Peru*, 70.

47. Qtd. in ibid.

48. Thorp and Bertram, *Peru*, 148–49.

49. Tigner, "Okinawans in Latin America," 611–13.

50. Qtd. in ibid., 613.

51. Ibid., 585–86.

52. Gardiner, *Japanese and Peru*, 76; Tigner, "Okinawans in Latin America," 615; Higashide, *Adios to Tears*, 68–69.

53. Higashide, *Adios to Tears*, 69.

54. Ibid., 70.

55. Gardiner, *Japanese and Peru*, 75.

56. Ibid.; Tigner, "Okinawans in Latin America," 616.

57. *Peru Jiho*, 27 May 1939, pp. 2–3.

58. See Gardiner, *Japanese and Peru*; and Higashide, *Adios to Tears*.

59. Victor J. Guevara, *Las grandes cuestiones nacionales: El petróleo, los ferrocarriles, la inmigración japonesa y el problema rural* (Cuzco: H. G. Rozas, 1939), 136, qtd. in Tigner, "Okinawans in Latin America," 624.

60. Qtd. in Higashide, *Adios to Tears*, 72.

61. Ibid., 76.

62. Ibid., 69.

63. Tigner, "Okinawans in Latin America," 587–88, 591.

64. Kurusu was given the fateful task by Tokyo of submitting its ultimatum to the Roosevelt administration on 7 Dec. 1941.

65. Gardiner, *Japanese and Peru*, 49.

66. Ibid., 44.

67. Qtd. in ibid., 47.

68. Ibid., 49.

69. Ibid., 38.

70. Ibid., 37.

71. Ibid., 38.

72. *Waga kokumin no kaigai hatten*, 137–45.

73. Thomas H. Holloway, "Immigration in the Rural South," in *Modern Brazil: Elites and Masses in Historical Perspective*, ed. Michael L. Conniff and Frank D. McCann (Lincoln: University of Nebraska Press, 1989), 148. Holloway cites statistics from the 1872 and 1920 census figures.

74. E. Bradford Burns, *A History of Brazil* (New York: Colombia University Press, 1970), 259.

75. Tsuchida, "Japanese in Brazil," 166.

76. Qtd. in ibid., 193.

77. Ibid., 180–81.

78. Ibid., 180–84.

79. *Masuji kiyotani, iwanami kikuji* (São Paulo: Centro de Estudos Nipo-Brasileiro, 1993), 13.

80. Nugent, *Crossings,* 130–31.

81. Tsuchida, "Japanese in Brazil," 173–74.

82. These preparatory schools were almost exclusively for Japanese female immigrants who were thought to face the most difficulty in adjusting to the immigrant experience.

83. Tsuchida, "Japanese in Brazil," 188.

84. Ibid., 196.

85. Ibid.

86. Ibid., 230–31.

87. Kunhiro Haraguchi, "1924 nen no Imin Mondai," in *Nichibei kiki no kigen to hainichi imino,* ed. Kimitada Miwa (Tokyo: Ronso-sha, 1997), 9.

88. Reichl, "Stages in the Historical Process of Ethnicity," 41.

89. Takashi Maeyama, "Ancestor, Emperor, and Immigrant: Religion and Group Identification of the Japanese in Rural Brazil, 1908–1950," *Journal of Inter-American Studies and World Affairs* 14:2 (1972): 151–82.

90. Reichl, "Stages in the Historical Process of Ethnicity," 42.

91. *Waga kokumin no kaigai hatten,* 140.

92. Suzuki, *Japanese Immigrant in Brazil,* 188. This statistic is drawn from the comprehensive 1958 Japanese Brazilian self-census detailed in this publication.

93. Tsuchida, "Japanese in Brazil," 249–72.

94. Ibid., 249–52.

95. Ibid., 251–52.

96. Ibid., 256–57.

97. Qtd. in ibid., 256–59. The hyperbole in accounts such as these was often later criticized by immigrants once they arrived in Brazil and faced a much more harsh reality than they originally imagined.

98. *Waga kokumin no kaigai hatten,* 141.

Chapter 4: The Smaller Japanese Communities, 1908–38

1. Francesca Arena de Tejedor, Manuel Domecq García, Patricia Falconi, Carlos J. Fraguío, *Argentina y Japón: Se conocieron en el violento amanecer del mundo moderno* (Buenos Aires: Instituto de Publicaciones Navales, 1992), 57; Tigner, "Okinawans in Latin America," 533.

2. Toshio Yanaguida and Dolores Rodríguez del Alisal, *Japoneses en América* (Madrid: Editorial MAPFRE, 1992), 261.

3. Tigner, "Okinawans in Latin America," 533.

4. Tejedor et al., *Argentina y Japón,* 57.

5. Ibid., 56.

6. Tigner, "Okinawans in Latin America," 534.

7. Yanaguida and Rodríguez del Alisal, *Japoneses en América*, 265.

8. Tigner, "Okinawans in Latin America," 535.

9. Yanaguida and Rodríguez del Alisal, *Japoneses en América*, 266.

10. Ibid., 269–70.

11. Tejedor et al., *Argentina y Japón*, 57–58.

12. Tigner, "Okinawans in Latin America," 539–40.

13. Ibid., 539.

14. Ibid., 540.

15. Ibid., 544; Yanaguida and Rodríguez del Alisal, *Japoneses en América*, 267. The survey was conducted by the Japanese Residents Association of Argentina and was originally cited in *Nihon chiri takei*, ed. Sansei Yamano (Tokyo: Kaizosha, 1932), 79.

16. Tigner, "Okinawans in Latin America," 556–57.

17. Ibid., 559–78.

18. *Waga kokumin no kaigai hatten*, 143.

19. Ibid., 145.

20. Ibid., 149–210.

21. James L. Tigner, "The Ryukyuans in Bolivia," *Hispanic American Historical Review* 43:2 (May 1963): 207–8.

22. Ibid., 211.

23. Ibid., 212.

24. Alcides Parejas Moreno, "Historia de la Inmigración Japonesa a Bolivia," in *La inmigración japonesa en Bolivia: Estudios históricos y socio-económicos*, ed. Yasuo Wakatsuki and Iyo Kunimoto (Tokyo: Chuo University, 1985), 14.

25. Interview with Thomas Fujiike, president of the Japanese Association of La Paz, Bolivia, 1952, in Tigner, "Ryukyuans in Bolivia," 212.

26. Parejas Moreno, "Historia de la Inmigración Japonesa a Bolivia," 28.

27. Yanaguida and Rodríguez del Alisal, *Japoneses en América*, 243.

28. Parejas Moreno, "Historia de la Inmigración Japonesa a Bolivia," 37. See also *Boribia nihonjin shunenshi hensan Iinkei, Boribia niikiru: Nihonjin iju shunenshi* (Santa Cruz, Bolivia: N.p., 2000). This is a publication commemorating the 100th anniversary of the Japanese in Bolivia.

29. Parejas Moreno, "Historia de la Inmigración Japonesa a Bolivia," 38–39.

30. Ibid., 31.

31. Tigner, "Okinawans in Latin America," 481.

32. Ibid., 490. An additional and useful source for the pre–World War II Japanese settlement in Bolivia is Wakatsuki and Kunimoto, *La inmigración japonesa en Bolivia*.

33. Tigner, "Okinawans in Latin America," 489.

34. Ibid., 49–492.

35. Virginia Garrard-Burnett, "Mennonites," in *Encyclopedia of Latin American History and Culture*, ed. Barbara A. Tennenbaum et al., vol. 3 (New York: Charles Scribner's Sons, 1996), 584–85.

36. Harris Gaylord Warren, *Paraguay: An Informal History* (Norman: University of Oklahoma Press, 1949), 269.

37. Norman R. Stewart, *Japanese Colonization in Eastern Paraguay* (Washington, D.C.: National Academy of Sciences, 1967), 79. A geographer, Stewart's work is the seminal study on Japanese immigration and colonization in Paraguay. See also Yanaguida and Rodríguez del Alisal, *Japoneses en América,* 272–75; and Wallace E. Keiderling, "The Japanese Immigration in Paraguay" (M.A. thesis, University of Florida, 1962).

38. N. Stewart, *Japanese Colonization in Eastern Paraguay,* 85–86.

39. Ibid., 86–88.

40. Ibid., 88.

41. Ibid.

42. Ibid., 89.

43. Qtd. in ibid.

44. Ibid., 89–90.

45. Ibid., 137–38.

46. Loveman, *Chile,* 199.

47. Qtd. in ibid.

48. *Waga kokumin no kaigai hatten,* 139.

49. Loveman, *Chile,* 210.

50. Tigner, "Okinawans in Latin America," 643.

51. *Waga kokumin no kaigai hatten,* 139.

52. Tigner, "Okinawans in Latin America," 645.

53. Ibid.

54. Interviews with Okinawan residents of Santiago, Valparaíso, and San Antonio, summarized in Tigner, "Okinawans in Latin America," 645.

55. Ibid., 646.

56. For an excellent overview of this era in Colombia, see David Bushnell, *Colombia: A Nation in Spite of Itself* (Berkeley: University of California Press, 1993), 155–201. Peasant landholding patterns are carefully discussed in Nola Reinhardt, *Our Daily Bread: The Peasant Question and Family Farming in the Colombian Andes* (Berkeley: University of California Press, 1988).

57. Reinhardt, *Our Daily Bread,* 77–131.

58. Imin Kenkyu-kai, *Nihon no imin kenkyu* (Tokyo: Nichigai Associates, 1994), 121; *Waga kokumin no kaigai hatten,* 139.

59. Robert C. Eidt, "A Note on Japanese Farmers in the Cauca Valley, Colombia," *Revista geográfica de Instituto Panamericano* 18 (1956): 43–44.

60. Ibid., 44.

61. Ibid., 45–46.

62. Corombia Nikkeijin Kyokai Iju Gojunen Shi Hensan Iinkai, *Corombia iju-shi* (Nara: Tenri-Jiho, 1981), 22–27.

63. C. Harvey Gardiner, "The Japanese and Central America," *Journal of Inter-American Studies and World Affairs* 14:1 (Winter 1972): 20.

64. Ibid.

65. *Waga kokumin no kaigai hatten,* 140.

66. Louis A. Pérez Jr., *Cuba: Between Revolution and Reform* (New York: Oxford University Press, 1988), 115.

67. Ibid., 116–18.

68. Yanaguida and Rodríguez del Alisal, *Japoneses en América,* 277.

69. Ibid., 279.

70. Ibid., 278–79.

71. *Waga kokumin no kaigai hatten,* 140.

72. Yanaguida and Rodríguez del Alisal, *Japoneses en América,* 282.

73. Imin Kenkyu-kai, *Nihon no imin kenkyu,* 115; Yanaguida and Rodríguez del Alisal, *Japoneses en América,* 283.

Chapter 5: The Impact of the Asian War, 1938–52

1. For details of the 1940 Tokyo conference, see *Kigen Nisenryoppay ku-nen hoshuku Zaigai doho daihyosha kaigai gijiroku* (Tokyo: Nihon Takushoku Kyokai, 1940), 240–44.

2. Cordell Hull, *The Memoirs of Cordell Hull,* vol. 1 (New York: Macmillan, 1948), 602.

3. María Emilia Paz, *Strategy, Security, and Spies: Mexico and the U.S. as Allies in World War II* (University Park: Pennsylvania State University Press, 1997), 21.

4. Memorandum, Admiral Stark to Secretary of the Navy, 12 Nov. 1940, WPD, 4175-15, Record Group (hereafter RG) 165, National Archives, qtd. in Paz, *Strategy, Security, and Spies,* 23.

5. For useful discussion of Japanese wartime policy and intelligence gathering in Mexico, see Paz, *Strategy, Security, and Spies;* and Steven Niblo, *War, Diplomacy, and Development: The United States and Mexico, 1938–1954* (Wilmington, Del.: Scholarly Resources Press, 1995).

6. Niblo, *War, Diplomacy, and Development,* 67–70.

7. U.S. Department of Defense (hereafter DOD), *The Magic Background of Pearl Harbor,* 5 vols. (Washington, D.C.: Government Printing Office, 1946), 1:A-81, document summary 129. The MAGIC intercepts are provided in summary form rather than complete translations of the decoded transmissions.

8. Ibid., 2:98–100, document summaries 110 and 113. See also Paz, *Strategy, Security, and Spies,* 175–77.

9. DOD, *Magic Background of Pearl Harbor,* 2:100, document summary 113.

10. Paz, *Strategy, Security, and Spies,* 128.

11. These reports are available in the Franklin D. Roosevelt Presidential Library in Hyde Park, New York (hereafter cited as FDR-LB), in FDR's office file and that of his principal adviser, Harry L. Hopkins. See, for example, "Totalitarian Activities: Chile Today," Mar. 1943, box 143, Harry L. Hopkins Papers, FDR-LB. These

reports were generally filed monthly until late 1943, when the Axis threat in Latin America was perceived to have substantially diminished.

12. Paz, *Strategy, Security, and Spies,* 185–202.

13. C. Harvey Gardiner, "The Panamanian Japanese and World War II," *Ibero Amerika kenkyu* 4:1 (Jan. 1982): 25–26.

14. DOD, *Magic Background of Pearl Harbor,* 3:126–27, documents 141 and 142.

15. Gardiner, "Panamanian Japanese and World War II," 27.

16. See Yuriko Nagata, "Japanese Internees at Loveday," *Journal of the Royal South Australian History Society* 15 (1987): 65–81.

17. For an excellent overview of the North American internment programs through the redress issue, see Roger Daniels, "From Relocation to Redress: Japanese Americans and Canadians, 1941–1988," in *Minorities in Wartime: National and Racial Groupings in Europe, North America, and Australia during the Two World Wars,* ed. Panikos Panayi (Oxford: Berg, 1993), 216–39. Daniels reviews the primary studies in a most useful manner. For the United States, see Daniels, *Asian America;* Ronald Takaki, *Strangers from a Distant Shore: A History of Asian Americans* (Boston: Little, Brown, 1989). For Canada, see Ann G. Sunahara, *The Politics of Racism: The Uprooting of Japanese-Canadians during the Second World War* (Toronto: Lorimer, 1981); and Ken Adachi, *The Enemy That Never Was: A History of Japanese Canadians* (Toronto: McClelland and Stewart, 1991). John Armor and Peter Wright's *Manzanar* (New York: Time Books, 1988) contains the stunning photographs of Ansel Adams and the commentary of John Hersey. The best-selling novel by David Guterson entitled *Snow Falling on Cedars* (New York: Vintage Press, 1998) is a beautifully written fictional account of Japanese and American relations in the Northwest before, during, and after World War II.

18. P. Scott Corbett, *Quiet Passages: The Exchange of Civilians between the United States and Japan during World War II* (Kent, Ohio: Kent State University Press, 1987), 33.

19. Qtd. in Daniels, "From Relocation to Redress," 218–20.

20. The best study on the exchange issue is Corbett, *Quiet Passages.*

21. Franklin D. Roosevelt to Secretary of State Cordell Hull, 24 Apr. 1941, Department of State Records, 740.0011 5, 1939/1024_, RG 59, National Archives, qtd. in Thomas Connell, *America's Japanese Hostages: The World War II Plan for a Japanese Free Latin America* (Westport, Conn.: Praeger, 2002), 5.

22. Daniels, "From Relocation to Redress," 222.

23. Corbett, *Quiet Passages,* 161.

24. Qtd. in Paz, *Strategy, Security, and Spies,* 107. This OSS report was filed after a comprehensive aerial photography survey of Mexico's coastline.

25. On German spying in Mexico, see Leslie B. Rout Jr. and John F. Bratzel, *The Shadow War: German Espionage and United States Counterespionage in Latin America during World War II* (Washington, D.C.: University Publications of America, 1986), 53–106.

26. Office of Naval Intelligence, document 17016, 30 Mar. 1942, National Archives, Washington, D.C.

27. Paz, *Strategy, Security, and Spies,* 133.

28. The story of this unfortunate youth who spent nearly the entire war in Perote is discussed in the U.S. Intelligence Documents, FBI report 13923, Hoover to Donovan, 24 Mar. 1942. This story was confirmed personally by the former president of the Mexican Japanese Association, Enrique Shibayama, in an interview with Masterson in San José, California, May 1998.

29. The relationship of Cardenas to the U.S. government is discussed in the *History of the Western Defense Command,* vol. 2, United States Army War College Archive, Carlisle, Pennsylvania.

30. Paz discusses these failed efforts to establish a joint defense operation in Mexico. See particularly the chapter entitled "An Impasse on Defense Cooperation," *Strategy, Security, and Spies,* 209–26.

31. Rout and Bratzel, *Shadow War,* 89.

32. "Totalitarian Activities: Mexico Today" (1942), box 43, Hopkins Papers, FDR-LB.

33. Minoru Izawa, *Nipponjin Mekishiko Iju-shi* (Tokyo: Nihonjin Mekishiko Iju-shi Hensan Iinkai, 1971), 345.

34. Watanabe, "Japanese Immigrant Community," 64.

35. See, for example, Ministerio de Relaciones Exteriores de Mexico, "Quinta Columa en Mexico," 28 Apr. 1943, document III-908-2. The U.S. embassy reported in this case that a certain Japanese was suspected of carrying on "improper activities." No evidence of these activities was provided by the embassy.

36. Izawa, *Nipponjin Mekishiko Iju-shi,* 262.

37. See Hoover to General Watson, 17 Feb. 1942, Franklin D. Roosevelt's Official File, box 18, FDR-LB.

38. Watanabe, "Japanese Immigrant Community," 65.

39. Ibid., 65–68.

40. Archivo Histórico, "Genero Estrada de la Secretaria de Relaciones Exteriores de Mexico. Ciudadanos del Eje Concentrados en Mexico, Japoneses, Informe," document 111-917-6. Thanks to Professor Joseph Stout for calling attention to this document.

41. Izawa, *Nipponjin Mekishiko Iju-shi,* 286–87; Watanabe, "Japanese Immigrant Community," 70; Izawa, *Nipponjin Mekishiko Iju-shi,* 346.

42. Watanabe, "Japanese Immigrant Community," 72. Watanabe draws on the work of Izawa and Sunshi Yoshida for information on this farm cooperative. See also Ota Mishima, *Siete migraciones,* 95–99.

43. Watanabe, "Japanese Immigrant Community," 72–73.

44. Ibid., 79.

45. Izawa, *Nipponjin Mekishiko Iju-shi,* 287, 345.

46. Watanabe, "Japanese Immigrant Community," 77–79.

47. Ibid., 88.

48. Ibid., 89.

49. Ibid.; Ota Mishima, *Siete migraciones,* 99–105.

50. Nawoshi Ikari in Mogi das Cruzes and Takenobu Yano in Bastos, São Paulo State, interviewed by Funada-Classen, Jan. 1994.

51. Qtd. in Joseph Page, *The Brazilians* (New York: Addison Wesley, 1995), 104.

52. Yano interview; Patrick Makoto Fukunaga, "The Brazilian Experience: The Japanese Immigrants during the Period of the Vargas Regime and Its Immediate Afermath, 1930–1946" (Ph.D. diss., University of California at Santa Barbara, 1983), 131–33.

53. Tomoo Handa, *Burajiru nihon imim/Nikkei shakai shi nenpyo (Katei zohoban)* (São Paulo: Toppan Press, 1996), 622.

54. Rokuro Koyama, *Koyama Rokuru kaisoroku: Burajiru daiikkai imin no kiroku* (São Paulo: San Pauro Jinmon Kagaku Kenkujo, 1976), 144.

55. See, particularly, the work of the Japanese Brazilian historian Handa *(Burajiru nihon imim/Nikkei shaikai)* on the issue of reported police brutality.

56. Interviews conducted by Sayaka Funada-Classen with Issei who experienced considerable trouble from Brazilian authorities are one source that confirms this.

57. James L. Tigner, "*Shindo Renmei*: Japanese Nationalism in Brazil," *Hispanic American Historical Review* 41:4 (Nov. 1961): 516.

58. Maeyama, "Ancestor, Emperor, and Immigrant," 131–32.

59. Karen Tei Yamashita, *Brazil-maru* (Minneapolis: Coffee House Press, 1992), 91.

60. For a review of Brazil's changing position before the war, see Stanley Hilton, *Brazil and the Great Powers, 1930–1939* (Austin: University of Texas Press, 1985). For the FEB and the evolution of close Brazilian-U.S. relations, the best source is Frank D. McCann Jr., *The Brazilian-American Alliance* (Princeton, N.J.: Princeton University Press, 1973). For the influence of U.S. propaganda and culture during the war, see Thomas E. Skidmore, *Brazil: Five Centuries of Change* (New York: Oxford University Press, 1999), 122.

61. The involvement of Japanese Brazilians in the FEB is discussed in *Imin hachijurnen shi hensan iinkai, Burajiru imin hachijurnen shi* (São Paulo: Toppan Press, 1991), 226.

62. Carlos de Souza de Moraes, *A Ofensiva Japonesa do Brasil* (Porto Alegre: Livaria do Globo, 1943).

63. J. Edgar Hoover to General Edwin M. Watson, 10 June 1943, box 17, Hopkins Papers, FDR-LB.

64. "Field Notes on the Japanese in Latin America," OSS memorandum 791, 26 Mar. 1943. A review of this highly detailed and generally accurate document seems to indicate that while the OSS was not given primary responsibility for counterespionage in Latin America, its information was easily as good or better than that of the FBI.

65. Tigner's conclusions on this issue proved remarkably accurate over the long run.

66. Tigner, "*Shindo Renmei,*" 517–18.
67. Ibid., 518–19.
68. Ibid.
69. Anonymous interview by Funada-Classen in Bastos, São Paulo state, Apr. 1993.
70. Tigner, "*Shindo Renmei,*" 525.
71. Chiyoko Mita, "Kokumin Kokka'kara Tajinshu Kokk'ke—Burajiru Nikkeijin no Tadotta Michi," in *Nihon to Raten America no Kankei* (Tokyo: Ibero American Institute, Sofia University, 1990), 51–69; Takashi Maeyama, "Burajiru Nikkeijin niokero Aidenty no Hensen—Tokuni Sutoratejii tono Karen niote," in *Raten America Kenkyu,* no. 4, 1982, 180–219; and Toomo Handa, *Imin no Seikatsu no Rekishi* (São Paulo: Centro de Estudos Nipo-Brasileiro, 1970).
72. Maeyama, "Ancestor, Emperor, and Immigrant," 177.
73. Qtd. in ibid., 178.
74. Rout and Bratzel, *Shadow War,* focuses primarily on German espionage in Argentina and Chile. Specific mention of the Japanese envoy's threats is offered in OSS document 24520, discussed in John F. Bratzel, "The Battle of Chile: Allies vs. Allies in World War II," working paper, Michigan State University, 1993, p. 7.
75. C. Harvey Gardiner, *Pawns in a Triangle of Hate: The Peruvian Japanese and the United States* (Seattle: University of Washington Press, 1981), 134. Gardiner's book has become a classic on the internment of Japanese Latin Americans during World War II. It is extremely well researched and written with great sensitivity.
76. Gardiner, "Japanese and Central America," 22–24; Thomas Leonard, "Central America, the United States, and World War II," working paper, University of North Florida, 2003.
77. For a careful evaluation of the acculturation and adaption of the Japanese Cubans, see Dennison Nash and Louis C. Schaw, "Achievement and Acculturation: A Japanese Example," in *Context and Meaning: A Cultural Example* (New York: Free Press, 1965), 206–25.
78. N. Stewart, *Japanese Colonization in Eastern Paraguay,* 138.
79. Ibid., 138–45.
80. For a useful overview of Bolivian economic conditions during this era, see Herbert S. Klein, *Bolivia: The Evolution of a Multi-Ethnic Society,* 2d. ed. (New York: Oxford University Press, 1992), 149–227.
81. See the letter dated 4 Mar. 1946, to Edward J. Ennis, Director of the Alien Control Unit of the Department of Justice, signed by Tetsuyo Michimata, Mitsuto Shirakawa, Nobuo Shimoida, Ichizo Tono, and Takaki Sunahase, Records of the Special War Problems Division of the Department of State, RG 59, National Archives. This record group is especially rich in material on alien internees during World War II.
82. See Gardiner, *Pawns in a Triangle of Hate,* 23; and Tigner, "Okinawans in Latin America," 478. The usually careful research found in OSS memorandum 791 cited earlier is not present regarding Bolivia. Only one page is devoted to the review.

83. See, in particular, "Totalitarian Activities in Chile Today," FBI summary for President Roosevelt, Mar. 1943, box 141, Hopkins Papers, FDR-LB.

84. Loveman, *Chile*, 255.

85. OSS document 24520, p. 10, qtd. in Bratzel, "Battle of Chile," 7.

86. See Rout and Bratzel, *Shadow War*, 234–300, for a highly detailed discussion of Axis espionage efforts in Chile during World War II. The Japanese position is summarized in Bratzel, "Battle of Chile," 6–8.

87. MAGIC Intercepts (summaries) reel 3, frame 0279, 8 Nov. 1942, qtd. in Bratzel, "Battle of Chile," 12.

88. Rout and Bratzel, *Shadow War*, 337–449.

Chapter 6: Exiles and Survivors

1. Gardiner, *Pawns in a Triangle of Hate*, 8.

2. Orazio Ciccarelli, "Peru's Anti-Japanese Campaign in the 1930s: Economic Dependency and Abortive Nationalism," *Canadian Review of Studies in Nationalism* 9:1 (Spring 1982): 116.

3. Ibid., 119–20.

4. Gardiner, *Pawns in a Triangle of Hate*, 8.

5. Law 8526, 20 Apr. 1937, *Compilacíon de legislacíon Peruano*, III, pp. 1092–93; "Resolution of the Peruvian Ministry of Foreign Relations and Culture," *El Peruano*, 29 Nov. 1940, p. 1086.

6. *Waga kokumin no kaigai hatten*, 138.

7. Gardiner, *Japanese and Peru*, 81–90; Ciccarelli, "Peru's Anti-Japanese Campaign," 125–26.

8. Ciccarelli, "Peru's Anti-Japanese Campaign," 125–26.

9. Higashide, *Adios to Tears*, 104.

10. J. Edgar Hoover to Adolf A. Berle Jr., 6 Aug. 1941, 862.2023/181, RG 59, National Archives. This APRA memorandum is discussed in Gardiner, *Pawns in a Triangle of Hate*, 10.

11. *La Tribuna*, Dec. 1940. A copy of this issue was enclosed in the memorandum of Peru's Ministry of Government and Police. See Ministerio del Interior, folder 402, memorandum 388, 6 Dec. 1940, Peru, Archivo General de la Nación.

12. Mary Fukumoto, *Hacia un nuevo sol: Japoneses y sus descendientes en el Perú* (Lima: Asociación Peruano-Japonesa del Perú, 1997), 243–44.

13. R. Henry Norweb, interviewed by Masterson, Cleveland, Ohio, 9 Sept. 1980.

14. OSS memo, 12294, 20 Dec. 1941, RG 226, National Archives.

15. Secretary of State Cordell Hull to Norweb, 31 July 1943, and Hull to Robert F. Corrigan, 21 Aug. 1943, box 2506, RG 59, National Archives, qtd. in Corbett, *Quiet Passages*, 159; Yuriko Mishima Suetomi, interviewed by Masterson, Lima, Peru, 8 Apr. 1991. Mishima Suetomi's parents owned three stores in Lima that were lost during the war.

16. Hoover to Donovan, OSS memo 10422, 22 Jan. 1942, RG 226, National Archives; "Peru," box 117, Henry Wallace Papers, FDR-LB.

17. John K. Emmerson, *The Japanese Thread: A Life in the U.S. Foreign Service* (New York: Holt, Rinehart and Winston, 1978), 127–28.

18. Crystal City internee questionnaire response, Mar. 1993.

19. For careful discussions of the May 1940 anti-Japanese riots, see Gardiner, *Japanese and Peru,* 52–54; Fukumoto, *Hacia un nuevo sol,* 243–47; and Higashide, *Adios to Tears,* 105–11.

20. Qtd. in Gardiner, *Japanese and Peru,* 54.

21. FBI Report, "Totalitarian Activities in Peru Today," May 1942, box 143, Hopkins Papers, FDR-LB.

22. Higashide, *Adios to Tears,* 111.

23. Gardiner, *Japanese and Peru,* 82–83.

24. Ministerio de Guerra del Perú, *Escalafón General del Ejercito de Perú, 1938–52* (Lima: Centro de Estudios Histórico-Militares del Perú, n.d.). Graduate lists for the Escuela Militar de Chorrillos (Military Academy) and the Escuela Naval (Naval Academy) from the early 1900s through the 1980s reveal only 5 officers with Japanese surnames. Typical graduating classes for the period of World War II and the following decade ranged from 40 to 80 cadets for each class.

25. Gardiner, *Pawns in a Triangle of Hate,* 12.

26. For more on the exchange program, see Corbett, *Quiet Passages.* Building upon Gardiner's account of the Japanese Peruvians during World War II is Connell, *America's Japanese Hostages.* Connell primarily relies upon U.S. public documentation to expand upon and update Gardiner's *Pawns in a Triangle of Hate.*

27. Gardiner, *Pawns in a Triangle of Hate,* 16.

28. Norweb interview; Gardiner, *Pawns in a Triangle of Hate,* 13.

29. James C. Carey, *Peru and the United States, 1900–1962* (Notre Dame, Ind.: University of Notre Dame Press, 1964), 107.

30. Gardiner, *Pawns in a Triangle of Hate,* 14–18; Fukumoto, *Hacia un nuevo sol,* 247–55.

31. Phillip Bonsal to Lawerence Duggan, 13 Oct. 1942, box 2500, Records of the Department of State Relating to Peru, RG 59, National Archives, qtd. in Corbett, *Quiet Passages,* 150.

32. Qtd. in Gardiner, *Pawns in a Triangle of Hate,* 21.

33. Ibid., 27–28.

34. Tom Blake to Grace Tully, 23 Aug. 1944, Official File 287, FDR-LB; "Agenda for the Conference," 29 Aug. 1944, box 2076, RG 59, National Archives, qtd. in Corbett, *Quiet Passages,* 163; Gardiner, *Pawns in a Triangle of Hate,* 106.

35. Speech by Arturo Shibayama at the "Topaz Reunion" of Japanese American internees, San José, Calif., 20 May 1998.

36. Gardiner, *Pawns in a Triangle of Hate,* 56.

37. Marshall to Caribbean Defense Command, 11 Dec. 1942, Army file AG

014.311, National Archives, qtd. in Edward N. Barnhart, "Japanese Internees from Peru," *Pacific Historical Review* 31 (May 1962): 171.

38. "Totalitarian Activities in Latin America" (1942), Wallace Papers, FDR-LB, qtd. in Corbett, *Quiet Passages,* 146–47.

39. Barnhart, "Japanese Internees from Peru," 173.

40. Emmerson, *Japanese Thread,* 126–29; "Exposicíon General del Plan," 22 Jan. 1942, Perú, Ministerio de Gobierno y Policía, folder 421, Archivo General de la Nación.

41. Emmerson, *Japanese Thread,* 140.

42. Former Japanese Peruvian internees of the Crystal City, Texas, camp, interviewed by Masterson, San José, Calif., 30 May 1998.

43. Emmerson, *Japanese Thread,* 143.

44. Qtd. in Gardiner, *Pawns in a Triangle of Hate,* 26–29.

45. Ibid., 77–78.

46. Emmerson, *Japanese Thread,* 145.

47. Gardiner, *Pawns in a Triangle of Hate,* 104–5.

48. Qtd. in Fukumoto, *Hacia un nuevo sol,* 248.

49. Higashide, *Adios to Tears,* 115.

50. Gardiner, *Pawns in a Triangle of Hate,* 106–7.

51. Crystal City Internees questionnaire response, Mar. 1993. The respondent to this questionnaire was an infant at the time of time of internment but recalled vividly the struggles of the family in the aftermath of World War II.

52. The excerpt is from a poem by a Japanese named Tochio, qtd. in Gardiner, *Pawns in a Triangle of Hate,* 77.

53. Special War Problems Division Records, box 19, RG 59, National Archives. The Special War Problems Division records are rich in detail about the Japanese Peruvian internment experience. The list of meals was prepared for an inspection by Spanish diplomatic officials, who regularly reviewed the camps where the Japanese Latin Americans were interned. The menus reflected an attempt on the part of the camp administrators to provide what they may have assumed the Japanese Peruvians desired, such as "fried fish Peru style." More likely the Japanese would have preferred *ceviche,* or raw fish prepared in lemon sauce.

54. Qtd. in Emmerson, *Japanese Thread,* 145.

55. Higashide, *Adios to Tears,* 158.

56. Ibid., 159–60.

57. INS policy statement, qtd. in Karen L. Riley, "Schools behind Barbed Wire: A History of Schooling in the United States Department of Justice Internment Camp at Crystal City, Texas, during World War II" (Ph.D. diss., University of Texas at Austin, 1996), 15.

58. Higashide, *Adios to Tears,* 164–65.

59. Two former Crystal City internees interviewed by Masterson, Lima, Peru, 31 May 1990.

60. "Circular to all Officers and Employees," U.S. Department of Justice, Immigration and Naturalization Service, 28 Apr. 1943, Alien Interment Camp, Crystal City, Texas, box 1, RG 85, National Archives, qtd. in Riley, "Schools behind Barbed Wire," 88.

61. Libby Maoki-Yamamoto, interviewed by Masterson, 19 May 1998, San Francisco, Calif. She was interned in Crystal City when she was seven years old.

62. Crystal City Internee questionnaire response, Mar. 1993.

63. Higashide, *Adios to Tears,* 166–70.

64. Presentation by Evelyn Suzuki on the internment of Japanese Australians during World War II, "Topaz Reunion" conference, San José, Calif., 30 May 1998.

65. Higashide, *Adios to Tears,* 173.

66. Ibid.

67. Ibid., 174.

68. Qtd. in Gardiner, *Pawns in a Triangle of Hate,* 126–27.

69. "Policy on Enemy Aliens from Latin America," Dec. 15, 1945, 711.62115 AR/12-1245, RG 59, National Archives.

70. Qtd. in Barnhart, "Japanese Internees from Peru," 173.

71. Qtd. in ibid., 174.

72. Transcript response of Rikio Kubo, 13 May 1995, Japanese Peruvian Oral History Project, San Francisco, Calif.

73. Transcript response of Kimiko Saeki Matsubyashi, 8 May 1995, Japanese Peruvian Oral History Project, San Francisco, Calif.

74. Sumi Utsushigawa Shimatsu, "A *Shibai* in Uraga," *Crystal City 50th Anniversary Reunion Album* (Monterey, Calif.: Crystal City Group, 1993), 76.

75. Higashide, *Adios to Tears,* 178.

76. Pawley to Secretary of State, qtd. in Gardiner, *Pawns in a Triangle of Hate,* 135.

77. Fukumoto, *Hacia un nuevo sol,* 253.

78. Special War Problems Division Files, box 123, Oct. 10, 1945, RG 59, National Archives.

79. Ginzo Murono, interviewed by Masterson, Bridgeton, N.J., 6 Sept. 1996; transcript of an interview with Seiki Murono, Seabrook Educational and Cultural Center, Seabrook, N.J.

80. Teresa M. Mukoyama Masatani, interviewed by Masterson, Bridgeton, N.J., 6 Sept. 1996.

81. Arturo "Art" Shibayama, interviewed by Masterson, San José, Calif., May 30, 1998.

82. Fukumoto, *Hacia un nuevo sol,* 247–55.

83. Ibid., 248; Higashide, *Adios to Tears,* 130–35.

84. Gardiner, *Japanese and Peru,* 89.

85. Tigner, "Ryukyuans in Peru," 42–43.

86. Thorndike, *Los imperios del sol,* 129–30.

87. *Mundo Grafico,* 8 Jan. 1944, p. 6.

88. *Mundo Grafico*, 1 Dec. 1945, p. 1.

89. Tigner, "Okinawans in Latin America," 617-19; Gardiner, *Pawns in a Triangle of Hate*, 151.

90. Tigner, "Okinawans in Latin America," 617.

91. Gardiner, *Pawns in a Triangle of Hate*, 151.

92. Fukumoto, *Hacia un nuevo sol*, 269.

93. Tigner, "Okinawans in Latin America," 624.

Chapter 7: New *Colonias* and the Older Nikkei Communities, 1952-70

1. Michael Schaller, *The American Occupation of Japan: The Origins of the Cold War in Asia* (New York: Oxford University Press, 1985), 110.

2. Ibid., 348.

3. Ibid., 366-68.

4. Robert C. Eidt, "Japanese Agricultural Colonization: A New Attempt at Land Opening in Argentina," *Economic Geography* 44:1 (Jan. 1968): 2.

5. Mitsugu Sakihara, "History of Okinawa," in *Uchinanchu: A History of the Okinawans in Hawaii* (Honolulu: University of Hawaii Press, 1981), 13. For a valuable collection of essays on the Okinawan immigrant experience, see Ronald Y. Nakasone, ed., *The Okinawan Diaspora* (Honolulu: University of Hawaii Press, 2002).

6. Sakihara, "History of Okinawa," 15.

7. Ibid.

8. Daniel, Mann, Johnson, and Mendenhall, *Economic Development Study: Ryukyu Islands* (Tokyo: Japan Economic and Engineering Consultants, 1968), 29; Tigner, "Ryukyuans in Bolivia," 219.

9. For an excellent study of rural Okinawa, see Clarence J. Glacken, *The Great Loochoo: A Study of Okinawan Village Life* (Rutland, Vt.: Charles E. Tuttle and Sons, 1955).

10. Daniel et al., *Economic Development Study*, 12.

11. Iyo Kunimoto, "Japanese Bolivians," in *Encyclopedia of Japanese Descendents in the Americas*, ed. Kikumura-Yano, 96-104.

12. See Tigner, "Ryukyuans in Bolivia," 219-20; and Tigner, "Okinawans in Latin America."

13. Tigner, "Ryukyuans in Bolivia," 219.

14. *Brazil: Censo Demografico*, vol. 1 (Rio de Janeiro: Conselho Nacional de Estadistica, 1956), 16, 30, 69, qtd. in Yukio Fujii and T. Lynn Smith, *The Acculturation of the Japanese Immigrants of Brazil* (Gainesville: University of Florida Press, 1959), 19-23.

15. Lesser, *Negotiating National Identity*, 141.

16. Qtd. in Maeyama, "Ancestor, Emperor, and Immigrant," 161-62. This study offers valuable insights on the issue of Japanese acculturation in Brazil.

17. Lesser, *Negotiating National Identity*, 146.

18. Maeyama, "Ancestor, Emperor, and Immigrant," 177.

19. Sociedade Brasileira de Cultural Japonesa, *Uma epopéia moderna: 80 anos da imigração japonesa no Brasil* (São Paulo: Editora Hucitec, 1992), 381.

20. Ibid., 386.

21. Ibid., 393.

22. Ibid., 387.

23. Ibid., 387–88.

24. Maeyama, "Ancestor, Emperor, and Immigrant," 177.

25. Sociedade Brasileira, *Uma epopéia moderna,* 399.

26. Ibid., 217–18.

27. Mario Hiraoka, "Pioneer Settlement in Eastern Bolivia" (Ph.D. diss., University of Wisconsin at Milwaukee, 1974), 14.

28. Klein, *Bolivia,* 238.

29. Amemiya, "Bolivian Connection," 1–12.

30. Tigner, "Ryukyuans in Bolivia," 220–23.

31. Ibid., 220.

32. Ibid., 221.

33. Ibid., 223.

34. Ibid., 224.

35. Amemiya, "Bolivian Connection," 6–7.

36. Ibid., 7–8.

37. Hiraoka, "Pioneer Settlement in Eastern Bolivia," 309–10.

38. Ibid.; Tigner, "Ryukyuans in Bolivia," 226–27.

39. Tigner, "Okinawans in Latin America," 227.

40. For informative analyses of the San Juan de Yapacaní community, see Hiraoka, "Pioneer Settlement in Eastern Bolivia"; Alcides Parejas Moreno, *Colonias Japonesas en Bolivia* (La Paz: Grafico, 1981); Iyo Kunimoto, *Un pueblo Japonés en la Bolivia Tropical: Colonia San Juan de Yapacaní en el Departmento de Santa Cruz* (Santa Cruz: Editorial Casa de Cultura, 1989); Kunimoto, *Boribia no Nihonjinmura;* Yasuo Wakatsuki and Iyo Kunimoto, *La inmigración Japonesa en Bolivia: Estudios Históricos y Socio-Económicos* (Tokyo: Universidad de Chuo, 1985); Stephen I. Thompson, "San Juan de Yapacaní: A Japanese Pioneer Colony in Eastern Bolivia" (Ph.D. diss., University of Illinois at Urbana-Champaign, 1970); and Amemiya, "Bolivian Connection."

41. Thompson, "San Juan de Yapacaní," 204; Kunimoto, *Un pueblo Japonés en Bolivia,* 50–51.

42. Thompson, "San Juan de Yapacaní," 33–34; Kunimoto, *Un pueblo Japonés en Bolivia,* 52–54; Parejas Moreno, *Colonias Japonesas,* 103.

43. Parejas Moreno, *Colonias Japonesas,* 103.

44. Thompson, "San Juan de Yapacaní," 35.

45. Ibid., 43.

46. Ibid., 48.

47. Ibid., 52; Amemiya, "Bolivian Connection," 6.

48. Thompson, "San Juan de Yapacaní," 131–32.

49. Ibid., 134.

50. Ibid., 164–65.

51. Ibid., 180–81.

52. A small number of German Jews fleeing Nazi Germany sought to settle in Bolivia in the late 1930s. While Bolivia gave these refugees a temporary home, many chose to move on after the war. For a moving account of this episode, see Leo Spitzer, *Hotel Bolivia: The Culture of Memory in a Refuge from Nazism* (New York: Hill and Wang, 1998).

53. For a detailed discussion of conditions in San Juan de Yapacaní through the 1980s, see Kunimoto, *Un pueblo Japonés en Bolivia.*

54. *Waga kokumin no kaigai hatten,* 32–33.

55. N. Stewart, *Japanese Colonization in Eastern Paraguay,* 94–159.

56. Ibid., 115–37.

57. Ibid., 142–43.

58. Ibid., 137–39.

59. Ibid., 115–17.

60. Ibid., 144–49.

61. For analyses of the colonies in the Encarnación region, see N. Stewart, *Japanese Colonization in Eastern Paraguay;* Keiderling, "Japanese Immigration in Paraguay"; Daijiro Nishikawa, "A espansão dos nucleos colonais japoneses no Paraguai apos a segunda guerra mundial," *Sociologia* (São Paulo) 26:1 (1964): 33–81; and Kazuei Kido, "Paraguai no nikkei noka," *Iju Kenkyu* (Tokyo) 9 (Mar. 1973): 14–46. For a useful overview of Japanese colonization in South America that places Paraguayan colonization in historical contexts, see Eidt, "Japanese Agricultural Colonization," 1–6. The details of the negotiations involving the sales of the river gunboats can be found in the *Hispanic American Report* 12:9 (Oct. 1959): 517.

62. Eidt, "Japanese Agricultural Colonization," 4; Keiderling, "Japanese Immigration in Paraguay," 43–45.

63. Keiderling, "Japanese Immigration in Paraguay," 67–68.

64. Ibid., 70–71.

65. Keiderling noted the sharp difference between the La Colmena Japanese and the later arriving Issei in the Encarnación colonies regarding the care of infants, patterns of deference to visitors, and group social activities.

66. The Japanese government continued to promote Japanese economic investment in Paraguay well past 1970. See, for example, *Gyomu Gaiyou* (Tokyo: Kokusai Kyoryoku Jigo dan, 1979), 16–39.

67. Sandra Dibble, "Paraguay: Plotting a New Course," *National Geographic* 182:2 (Aug. 1992): 88–113.

68. Keiderling, "Japanese Immigration in Paraguay," 90–91.

69. Yoshiro Moriya de Freundorfer, "Identidad Nikkei en el Paraguay" (paper delivered at the Eighth Convention of Panamerican Nikkei, Lima, Peru, 7 July 1995).

70. Perón continued to maintain very good relations with the Japanese community in Argentina throughout his years in power.

71. James L. Tigner, "The Ryukyuans in Argentina," *Hispanic American Historical Review* 47:2 (May 1967): 220.

72. Okinawa, G.R.I., Bureau of Social Affairs, *Kosei Hakusho,* cited in Tigner, "Ryukyuans in Argentina," 221.

73. *Waga kokumin no kaigai hatten,* 32–33.

74. Asociación Universitaria Nikkei, *La otra inmigración* (Buenos Aires: Asociación Universitaria Nikkei, 1990), 117–21; Tigner, "Ryukyuans in Argentina," 214–15.

75. Tigner, "Ryukyuans in Argentina," 209–22.

76. Ibid., 208–10.

77. Eidt, "Japanese Agricultural Colonization," 5.

78. Ibid.

79. Ibid., 8.

80. Ibid., 10–20.

81. See Bushnell, *Colombia,* 170–201; Eidt, "Note on Japanese Farmers," 41–44; and a useful Web site entitled Fukuoka Latina, <http://www.fukuokalatina.com>.

82. G. Pope Atkins and Larman C. Wilson, *The Dominican Republic and the United States* (Athens: University of Georgia Press, 1998), 78–79.

83. *Karibukai no takujin tachi: Dominika iju niju-go shunen kinen-shi* (Tokyo: Kodan-sha Shuppan Service Center, 1981), 24–34.

84. Taki, *Mekishiko kokujo taikan,* 78, 83; Watanabe, "Japanese Immigrant Community," 89–90.

85. Daniels, "From Relocation to Redress," 231.

86. *Waga kokumin no kaigai hatten,* 32–33.

87. Beezley and MacLachlan, *El Gran Pueblo,* 2: 347–82.

88. Ota Mishima, *Siete migraciones,* appendix for chaps. 1–5.

89. Taki, *Mekishiko kokujo taikan,* 83; Watanabe, "Japanese Immigrant Community," 92–93.

90. The administration of President Fernando Belaúnde Terry (1963–68) quietly offered the money to the Japanese community of Peru when better relations with Tokyo were being cultivated. See Watanabe, "Japanese Immigrant Community," 148–49.

91. Ibid., 152–57.

92. Ota Mishima, *Siete migraciones,* 113–15; Watanabe, "Japanese Immigrant Community," 152–57.

93. Watanabe, "Japanese Immigrant Community," 178–83.

94. Takeshi Ishida, *Mehiko to nipponjin—Daisan sekai de kangaeru* (Tokyo: Tokyo University, 1973), 199; Watanabe, "Japanese Immigrant Community," 178.

95. Watanabe, "Japanese Immigrant Community," 180–81.

96. Toshiro Katagiri, interviewed by Chizuko Watanabe, 30 Oct. 1981, summarized in Watanabe, "Japanese Immigrant Community," 209–16.

97. Gardiner, *Japanese and Peru,* 101.

98. Fukumoto, *Hacia un nuevo sol,* 269–70.

99. Qtd. in Gardiner, *Japanese and Peru,* 96.

100. Ibid., 97.

101. Fukumoto, *Hacia un nuevo sol,* 270-71.

102. Ibid., 274-75.

103. Ibid., 280.

104. Gardiner, *Japanese and Peru,* 106.

105. Kaigai Nikkeijin Kyokai, *Dai kyokai kaigai nikkeijin taikai* (Tokyo: Kaigai Nikkeijin Kyokai, 1968), 16, cited in Gardiner, *Japanese and Peru,* 106.

106. Zai Peru nikkeijin shakai jittai chosa iinkai, *Peru koku ni okeru nikkeijin shakai* (Tokyo: Japanese Ministry of Foreign Affairs, 1969), 69-70.

107. Luis Rocca Torres, *Japoneses bajo el sol de Lambayeque* (Lambayeque: Universidad Nacional Pedro Ruiz Gallo, 1997).

108. Ibid., 225-30.

109. Ibid., 227-31.

110. Ibid., 240.

111. Response of Robert Kato to Crystal City internees questionnaire, Sept. 1993.

112. Higashide, *Adios to Tears,* 200-215. On the Chicago Japanese, see Masaro K. Osako, "Japanese Americans: Melting into the All-America Pot," in *Ethnic Chicago,* 4th ed., ed. Peter Jones and Melvin G. Holli (Grand Rapids, Mich.: Erdmans, 1995), 409-37.

113. Higashide, *Adios to Tears,* 213-28.

Chapter 8: Nikkei Communities in Transition

1. See Daniels, *Asian America,* 317-44; and Daniels, "From Relocation to Redress," 232-38.

2. See Congressional Research Service Report by James Sayler, "Redress for Japanese Americans under the Civil Liberties Act of 1988: Questions and Answers," 28 Sept. 1990.

3. For a useful biography of Fujimori, see Luis Jochmamowitz, *Ciudadano Fujimori* (Lima: Piesa, 1993). Information on Fujimori's parents was obtained by 1989 census records submitted by Alberto Fujimori for his family.

4. Four Japanese communities leaders, interviewed by Masterson, at Jinnai Center in Lima, Peru, Apr. 1990.

5. Recent estimates of 80,000 for Peru's Japanese community have appeared, but these figures seem high if placed in the framework of the 1989 self-census and its long-term projections.

6. For a careful analysis of Japanese trade with Peru in the modern era, see Pablo de la Flor Belaúnde, *Japón en la escena internacional sus relaciones con America Latina y Perú* (Lima: CEPI, 1991).

7. Fukumoto, *Hacia un nuevo sol,* 276-77.

8. The best review of the military government's reforms is Abraham Lowenthal, *The Peruvian Experiment: Continuity and Change Under Military Rule* (Princeton,

N.J.: Princeton University Press, 1975). On the motivations and ideology of this unusual military government, see Daniel Masterson, *Militarism and Politics in Latin America: Peru from Sánchez Cerro to Sendero Luminoso* (New York: Greenwood Press, 1990).

9. De la Flor Belaúnde, *Japón en la escena internacional*, 115.

10. See Amelia Morimoto, ed., *Población de origen Japones en Perú: Perfil actual* (Lima: Commission Celebrating the 90th Anniversary of the Japanese in Peru, 1991).

11. The raw data for both surveys are housed in the research room of the Japanese Cultural Center in Lima. Masterson was able to review these data on two occasions in the mid-1990s. The 1966 census data are summarized in Fukumoto, *Hacia un nuevo sol*, 299–303. Morimoto, *Población de origen Japones*, offers these statistics as well.

12. Isabelle Lausent-Herrera, *Pasada y presente de la comunidad Japones en el Perú* (Lima: Instituto de Estudios Peruanos, 1991), 64–65.

13. Ibid., 65.

14. Torres, *Japoneses bajo el sol.*

15. Ibid., 261–74.

16. Speech of President Alberto Fujimori to the Eighth Convention of Panamerican Nikkei, Lima, Peru, 5 July 1995, in *Revista Oficial VIII COPANI Peru*, 4.

17. *Revista Oficial VIII COPANI*, 20.

18. Morimoto, *Población de origen Japones*, 31–45; Fukumoto, *Hacia un nuevo sol*, 363–72.

19. Morimoto, *Población de origen Japones*, 115.

20. Ibid., 134–47.

21. Ibid., 176; Masterson reviewed the 1989 census questionnaire in May 1996.

22. Fukumoto, *Hacia un nuevo sol*, 406–22.

23. Morimoto, *Población de origen Japones*, 212. The Japanese Foreign Ministry figures are drawn from a study by the World Bank on the "International *Nikkei*," cited in *New York Times*, 16 Oct. 1999, p. B-1.

24. These interviews were conducted by the Kaigai Nikkeijin Kyokai and published as *Nikkeijin honpo juro jittai chosa hokoku-sho* (Tokyo: Japan International Cooperation Agency, 1992).

25. Ibid.

26. Fukumoto, *Hacia un nuevo sol*, 355.

27. See "Once Lucrative Job Market Now Bleak for Japanese Brazilians," *Japan Times*, 23 Oct. 1998, p. 3.

28. Merry White, *The Japanese Overseas: Can They Go Home Again?* (Princeton, N.J.: Princeton University Press, 1988), 1, 27, 110.

29. The two highly valuable works by Takeyuki Tsuda are: "The Stigma of Ethnic Difference: The Structure of Prejudice and 'Discrimination' toward Japan's New Immigrant Minority," *Journal of Japanese Studies* 24:2 (Summer 1998): 317–61; and "The Permanence of 'Temporary Migration': The 'Structural Embeddedness' of Japanese-Brazilian Immigrant Workers in Japan," *Journal of Asia Studies* 58:3 (Aug.

1999): 687–723. Tsuda's research took place over eighteen months in both Japan and Brazil and involved more than 100 interviews of Japanese Brazilians both in Japan and Brazil. Tsuda went to great lengths to validate his research, even to the point of working for four months alongside Japanese Brazilians in a Japanese auto plant.

30. Fukumoto, *Hacia un nuevo sol,* 357.

31. Qtd. in ibid., 359.

32. Qtd. in ibid., 361.

33. For excellent studies of this era, see Thomas Skidmore, *The Politics of Military Rule in Brazil* (New York: Oxford University Press, 1988); and Skidmore, *Brazil.*

34. Skidmore, *Brazil,* 260. For a revealing portrait of life in these *favelas,* see the autobiographical account by Carolina Maria de Jesus, *Child of the Dark: The Diary of Carolina Maria de Jesus, My Life in the Slums of São Paulo* (New York: Penguin, 2003). This published diary is now considered one of the most important statements about poverty and its consequences in urban Latin America.

35. Riorden Roett, "Brazil and Japan: Potential versus Reality," in *Japan and Latin America,* ed. Susan K. Purcell and Robert Immerman (Boulder: Lynne Reinner, 1992), 106–8.

36. Ibid., 112.

37. Ibid., 105.

38. *Burajiru niokero Nikkei jinko chosa hokoku-sho* (São Paulo: Centro de Estudos Nipo-Brasileiro, 1989), 3.

39. Ibid., 30, 35–36.

40. Ibid.

41. Ibid., 102.

42. Ibid., 104–8.

43. Ibid., 117–18.

44. Ibid., 45–49.

45. Anonymous interviews by Funada-Classen in Bastos, Mogi das Cruzes, and Cambara, Brazil, during the months of January and February 1994.

46. Christopher Reichl, "Japanese Newcomers in Brazil: A Social Mode of Migration" (Ph.D. diss., University of Iowa, 1988), 63–65.

47. For the influence of Nikkei religions on Brazilian societies, see San Pauro Jimmon Kagaku Kenkyujo, *Burajiru no Nikkei shinshukyo* (São Paulo: Toppan Press, 1985).

48. Reichl, "Japanese Newcomers in Brazil," 128–29.

49. Sociedade Brasileira, *Uma epopéia moderna,* 434–58.

50. Ibid., 434.

51. Page, *Brazilians,* 107–8.

52. Qtd. in ibid., 106–7.

53. Ibid., 109–10.

54. Qtd. in Tsuda, "Permanence of 'Temporary Migration,'" 688.

55. Ibid., 688–89.

56. Japan's Ministry of Justice, Immigration Bureau Statistics, qtd. in Tsuda, "Permanence of 'Temporary Migration,'" 690–91.

57. Interviews in Yokohama, Japan, by Masterson, Oct. 1998.

58. Qtd. in *Asian Migration News,* 16–30 Nov. 2001.

59. Tsuda, "Permanence of 'Temporary Migration,'" 695–97.

60. Qtd. in ibid., 705.

61. Ibid., 709.

62. Qtd. in ibid., 710.

63. Qtd. in Tsuda, "Stigma of Ethnic Difference," 318.

64. Ibid., 389.

65. Qtd. in *New York Times,* 16 Oct. 1999, pp. 1, 4.

66. The Japanese embassy's own census of 1980 lists 12,545 Japanese residing in Mexico. Watanabe, in "Japanese Immigrant Community," concedes that "it is very difficult to assess the number of [ethnic Japanese] offspring that have been culturally absorbed into Mexican society. But their number is thought to be much greater than those who were included in this tabulation" (91).

67. See Octavio Paz's scathing attack on the PRI and its policies in his book of poetry entitled *The Other Mexico: Critique of the Pyramid* (New York: Grove Press, 1972). Paz resigned his post as ambassador to India in protest of the massacre.

68. For a very useful overview of Mexican national affairs during these years, see Meyer and Sherman, *Course of Mexican History,* 663–704.

69. This discussion of Japanese-Mexican economic relations draws heavily upon the excellent article by Luis Rubio, "Japan in Mexico: A Changing Pattern," in *Japan and Latin America,* ed. Purcell and Immerman, 69–100.

70. Ibid., 83, 89.

71. *Directions of Trade Statistics Quarterly* (Washington, D.C.: International Monetary Fund, June 1999), p. 158.

72. Ota Mishima, *Siete migraciones,* appendix to chap. 4. Ota Mishima provides useful photographs of these business owners and their plants in this appendix.

73. The *New York Times* (16 Oct. 1999, p. 1) carried a story of Japanese Latin American guest workers in Japan and provided statistics compiled by the Japanese Foreign Ministry on the total number of guest workers from each Latin American nation with a sizable Japanese community. No Japanese from Mexico were listed in the statistics.

74. Qtd. in Watanabe, "Japanese Immigrant Community," 142–43.

75. Ibid.; Ota Mishima, *Siete migraciones,* appendix.

76. For discussion of the Liceo, see Watanabe, "Japanese Immigrant Community," 147–55.

77. Takehiro Misawa, "Familia como Institución de Seguridad Transgeneracional: Reprodución Social y Cultural de los Descendientes Japonesas en Mexico" (thesis, El Colegio de Mexico, Centro de Estudios Demográficos, 1996), 6.

78. Ibid.

79. Ibid., 303–19.

80. Enrique Shibayama, interviewed by Masterson, San José, Calif., 30 May 1998. Shibayama was attending a symposium on World War II relocation and internment sponsored by the former internees of the Topaz camp in the United States. Japanese internees from Australia, Canada, and Mexico besides the Topaz group were in attendance.

Chapter 9: Looking to the New Century

1. U.N. Department of Social and Economic Affairs, *Demographic Yearbook* (New York: United Nations, 1998), 198–99.

2. Stanlaw, "Japanese Emigration," 2–3.

3. "Migrant Workers Make More Passages of Hope," *Washington Post,* Mar. 7, 2000, p. E-1.

4. These statistics are from the Japanese Bureau of Immigration and were used through the courtesy of Professor Roger Daniels.

5. Taichi Sakaiya, *What Is Japan? Contradictions and Transformations* (Tokyo: Kodansha International, 1993), 222–25.

6. Correspondence with Roger Daniels, Apr. 20, 2000.

7. Coletta A. Youngers, *Deconstructing Democracy: Peru under Alberto Fujimori* (Washington, D.C.: Office on Latin America, Feb. 2000), 1.

8. Cover letter from Beatriz Boza D., Chairwoman of the Board, PromPerú.

9. See Youngers, *Deconstructing Democracy,* for an insightful discussion of this phenomenon.

10. *Revista Oficial VIII COPANI,* 7.

11. Les Hamasaki, "Pacific Century Megatrends" (paper delivered at the Eighth Convention of Panamerican Nikkei, Lima, Peru, 6 July 1995), p. 6.

12. Ibid., 10.

13. Fukumoto, *Hacia un nuevo sol,* 560–64.

14. Ginzo and Hisako Murono, interviewed by Masterson, 15 July 1996, Upper Deerfield, N.J.

15. See Public Law 100-183, 100 Cong., 2d sess. (10 Aug. 1988), pp. 1–2.

16. Arturo "Art" Shibayama, interviewed by Masterson, San José, Calif., 28 May 1998.

17. *Los Angeles Times,* 16 Aug. 1999, Home News Section, pp. 1–2.

18. Qtd. in Brendan Riley, "JLA Reparations Plan," *Asian Week,* 27 Apr. 2000, p. 1. The Shibayama interview concluded this short article on the reparations issue.

19. Correspondence with Teresa Masatani, 22 June 2000. Other interviews were conducted with Masatani at her home and at the Seabrook Center in New Jersey from 1996 to 1998.

20. Maoki-Yamamoto interview.

21. Matthew C. Strecher, "Magical Realism and the Search for Identity in the

Fiction of Murakami Haruki," *Journal of Japanese Studies* 25:2 (Summer 1999): 263–98.

22. Page, *Brazilians,* 107.

Afterword

1. Higashide, *Adios to Tears,* 51.
2. *New York Times,* 27 Nov. 2001, p. 4A.
3. White, *Japanese Overseas,* 13.
4. Lesser, *Negotiating National Identity,* 4–5.

INDEX

Frederick C. Johnson (ship), 164–66
Freyre, Gilberto, 24
Fujiike, Tomás, 143
Fujimori, Alberto: addresses Panamerican Nikkei conference in Lima, 234; on economic and social policy, 230; as elected dictator, 227–28; and progress in Peru, 274–75, 287, 290; status as Japanese citizen, 271
Fukoku kyohei (enrichment of nation-state), 12
Fukumoto, Mary, 233–34; on Japanese Peruvians in Japan, 239; on cultural pride, 277
Fukuzawa, Yakichi, 8
Funada-Classen, Sayaka: interviews in Osaka prefecture, 257, 259–60; on police brutality toward Japanese Brazilians, 249

Gajin (foreigner), 77
Gambari group. *See* Kachigumi (victory) group
García, Alan, 224, 228
Gardiner, C. Harvey, 64, 72, 149, 158–60
Gentlemen's Agreement of 1907–8, 9, 33, 53, 58–59
Giichi, Tanaka, 58
Golindrinas (seasonal immigrants), 91
Gonzales, Michael, 20
Goto, Shojiro, 8
Guahapé colony (western Argentina), 208–9
Guano industry, 20
Guaraní, 100
Guevara, Víctor, 68
Gripsholm (ship), 164, 171
Gurpo Sansei (Sansei Group), in Mexico, 215
Guzman Reynoso, Abimael, 230

Hamanka, Capt., 124
Hamasaki, Les, 277
Handa, Toomo, 139
Haruki, Murakami, 283–84
Haya de la Torre, Víctor Raul, 153–54
Higashide, Seiichi: on anti-Japanese feeling in Peru, 153–57; on bonds of Japanese in Peru, 51; early immigrant experiences of, 56–57, 67–70; on INS release interview, 173; as internee in the U.S., 168–70; on life in the U.S. after WWII, 223–24
Holloway, Thomas, 26
Hoover, J. Edgar: on espionage in Mexico, 125; as head of the FBI, 117; on Japanese Brazilian threat, 136–37; on Japanese Peruvian community, 155–61
Hopkins, Harry, 117
Hull, Cordell: on Axis danger in the Western Hemisphere, 114; on interning all Japanese Latin Americans, 161
Hussa, Norman, 117–18

Ibañez, Carlos, 145
Ickes, Raymond, 155, 161
Iguape colony (Brazil), 78
Ikegami, Eiko, 7
Imin Hogoho (Immigrant Protection Ordinance in Japan, 1894), 16
Immigration Act of 1924 (Peru), 71–72
Immigration Act of 1934 (Brazil), 75
Immigration Act of 1936 (Peru), 72–73
Immigration and Naturalization Service (INS), 117; and internment camps, 166; and family care in internment camps, 168–69; on legal status of Japanese Latin American internees, 164
Imperial Congress for the Economy (Tokyo, 1924), 79–80
Inca Rubber Company, 39–40
Indigenismo (Indian identity), 19
INS. *See* Immigration and Naturalization Service
Internment camps. *See* Crystal City, Tex., internment camp; Kenedy, Tex., internment camp; Seagoville, Tex., interment camp
Ishii, Monzaburo, 37
Italian immigrants: in Brazil, 25–26; in Mexico, 17–18; in Peru, 22
Izawa, Minoru, 126

Japanese Barbers Association (Lima), 39
Japanese Benevolent Association (Juarez), 33

Maeyama, Takashi: on ancestor worship in Brazil, 40; on ethnicity of Japanese Brazilians, 80–81; on reaction to Shindo Renmei, 139; on separate identities of Japanese Brazilians, 187–88; on transplanting Japanese values to Brazil, 186; on war relief movement and Japanese "wayfarers," 185
MAGIC (counterintelligence operation), 115
Makegumi (defeat) group, among Japanese Brazilians, 134, 170
Makino, Kinzo, 88
Makudo, Mario, 4
Manchuria: Japanese militarism in, 81; as priority for Japanese immigration, 113
Manila-Acapulco galleon trade, 13–14
Maoki-Yamamoto, Libby, 169, 280–82
Marshall, George, 161
Masatani, Teresa, 174–78, 280–81
Masters and Servants Act of 1850 (Hawaii), 9
Matsubayashi, Saeki, 172
Matsumoto, Sanshiro, 128, 213
Matsuoka, Yasuki, 116
Meiggs, Henry, 120
Meiji era, nation building and immigration policy in, 13–19
Meiji Shokumin-Gaisha (Meiji Colonization Company), 16
Mekishiko Ija Kumei (Mexican Immigration Cooperative), 28
Mennonite colonies in Paraguay, 101
Mexico City Conference on the Problems of War and Peace (1945), 171
Meyer, Michael, 32
Misawa, Takehiro, 266–67
Mita, Chiyo, 139
Mitsuyu, Ricardo, 236
Miura, Yoshiaki: on efforts to coordinate espionage for Japan, 116–17; expulsion from Mexico, 123
Mochizuke settlement, 280
Morales Bermúdez, Francisco, 229
Morashita, Helena, 272
Mori, Kochi, 251
Morimoto, Amelia, 239: as director of Japanese Peruvian census of 1989, 231–33; on race mixture, 236

Morioka Imin Gaisha (Morioka Immigration Company), 16, 37, 38, 47, 93
Morita, Paulo, 138
Mundo Grafico (newspaper), in Peru, 176
Murono, Ginzo, 174–75

NAFTA. *See* North American Free Trade Agreement
Nakane, Chie, 7
National Geographic, 203
Nichia Takushoku Gaisha (Colonial Society of the Japanese Argentines), 90
Nichiboka Kyokai (Mexican Japanese Association), 214
Nihon Sensai Doho Kyuen-kai (Committee for the Relief of the War Victims in Japan), 140
El Nisei (periodical), in Peru, 233
Nisei-kai (Nisei Association), in Mexico, 215
Nishi, Yoshiaki, 116
Noda, Ryoji, 37–38
Nokyo-kumiai (Agricultural Cooperative Union), in Paraguay, 142
North American Free Trade Agreement (NAFTA), 262, 264
Norweb, R. Henry, 154
Núcleos (immigrant colonies), in southern Brazil, 77
Nugent, Walter, 5–6

Obregón Alvaro, 60
Odría, Manuel, 178, 218
Office of Naval Intelligence (ONI), 117
Office of Strategic Services (OSS), 123, 137
Ogawa, Teizo, 146
Ohiro, Kietaro, 109
Ohtake, Tomie, 254, 284
Okada, Ikumatsu: blacklisting and deportation of, 160; as cotton farmer in Peru, 41, 65
Okinawa, in the aftermath of WWI, 179–83
Okinawans: in Argentina, 89; in Bolivia, 189–92; in Chile and Peru before 1938, 67; as a component of the Japanese Peruvian census of 1989, 235

DANIEL M. MASTERSON, a professor of history at the United States Naval Academy, is the author of *Militarism and Politics in Latin America: Peru from Sánchez Cerro to Sendero Luminoso* (1991) and the updated and revised Spanish edition *Fuerza armada y sociedad en el Perú moderno, 1930–2000* (2000). He is the author of numerous articles on civil-military relations and Japanese immigration in Latin America. His most recent article, coauthored with Sayaka Funada-Classen, is "The Japanese in Peru and Brazil: A Comparative Perspective," in *Mass Migration to Modern Latin America* (2003).

SAYAKA FUNADA-CLASSEN is a researcher at the Institute of International and Cultural Studies, Tsuda College, Tokyo. She is presently doing field research on African development issues in Mozambique.

The Asian American Experience

The University of Illinois Press
is a founding member of the
Association of American University Presses.

University of Illinois Press
1325 South Oak Street
Champaign, IL 61820-6903
www.press.uillinois.edu